YANKEES MAGAZINE
1986 Yankees Information Guide

Official Publication of Yankees Magazine and the New York Yankees

David S. Szen
Publisher

Lou D'Ermilio
Major League Editor

Pete Jameson
Minor League Editor

Contributors: Dave Fleming and Charles Alfaro

TABLE OF CONTENTS

NEW YORK YANKEES
YANKEE STADIUM, BRONX, NY 10451, (212) 293-4300

Principal Owner .... George M. Steinbrenner
Limited Partners .... Harold M. Bowman, Lester Crown, Michael Friedman,
Marvin Goldklang, Barry Halper, Harvey Leighton,
Daniel McCarthy, Harry Nederlander, James Nederlander,
Robert Nederlander, William Rose, Sr., Edward Rosenthal,
Jack Satter, Joan Z. Steinbrenner, Charlotte Witkind, Richard Witkind
President .... Eugene J. McHale
Administrative Vice President and Treasurer .... M. David Weidler
Vice President and General Manager.. Clyde King
Vice President, Baseball Administration .... Woody Woodward
Vice President, General Counsel............................... William F. Dowling
Vice President, Stadium Operations .... Patrick Kelly
Vice President, Customer Services............................. James H. Naples
Vice President, Marketing .... Richard Kraft
Vice President, Publications .... David S. Szen
Vice President .... Ed Weaver

Baseball Administration
Director of Player Development .... Bobby Hofman
Assistant Scouting Director................................... Roy Krasik
Assistant Player Development Director.................... Peter Jameson
Computer Statistics Director............................ Mark J. Batchko
Video Coordinator Director .... Mike Barnett

Ticket Operations
Executive Director of Ticket Operations .... Frank Swaine
Ticket Director.. Mike Rendine
Assistant Ticket Director .... Jim Hodge
Director of Group Sales .... Debbie Tymon

Media Relations
Director of Media Relations.............................. Harvey Greene
Assistant Media Relations Director .... Lou D'Ermilio

Marketing
Director, Television & Radio Relations....................... Kim Gallas
Director, Scoreboard Operations .... Betsy Leesman
Director, Speakers Bureau .... Bob Pelegrino
Public Relations Assistant................................ Keith Wiarda

Publications
Editor/Yankees Magazine .... Tom Bannon
Business Manager/Yankees Magazine...................... Dave Fleming
Sales Manager/Yankees Magazine......................... Robert Zeig
Account Executives/Yankees Magazine .... Michele Ernst, Jay Sharin,
Jim Tessmer

Administration
Traveling Secretary.. Bill Kane
Director of Accounting .... Warren Atkinson
Assistant Director of Accounting .... Tony West
Director, Alumni Association .... Jim Ogle
Spring Training Coordinator .... Marsh Samuels

• • • • •

Stadium Superintendent .... Jimmy Esposito
Team Physician .... Dr. John J. Bonamo
Public Address Announcer .... Bob Sheppard
Organist .... Eddie Layton

CHAMPIONSHIP YANKEE CLUBS
33 American League Pennant Winners—
22 World Championship Teams

Year	Won	Lost	Pct.	Games Won By	Manager	World Series Opp	Games Record W	L
1921	98	55	.641	4½	Miller Huggins	Giants	3	5
1922	94	60	.610	1	Miller Huggins	Giants	**0	4
*1923	98	54	.645	16	Miller Huggins	Giants	4	2
1926	91	63	.591	3	Miller Huggins	Cardinals	3	4
*1927	110	44	.714	19	Miller Huggins	Pirates	4	0
*1928	101	53	.656	2½	Miller Huggins	Cardinals	4	0
*1932	107	47	.695	13	Joe McCarthy	Cubs	4	0
*1936	102	51	.667	19½	Joe McCarthy	Giants	4	2
*1937	102	52	.662	13	Joe McCarthy	Giants	4	1
*1938	99	53	.651	9½	Joe McCarthy	Cubs	4	0
*1939	106	45	.702	17	Joe McCarthy	Reds	4	0
*1941	101	53	.656	17	Joe McCarthy	Dodgers	4	1
1942	103	51	.689	9	Joe McCarthy	Cardinals	1	4
*1943	98	56	.636	13½	Joe McCarthy	Cardinals	4	1
*1947	97	57	.630	12	Bucky Harris	Dodgers	4	3
1949	97	57	.630	1	Casey Stengel	Dodgers	4	1
*1950	98	56	.636	3	Casey Stengel	Phillies	4	0
*1951	98	56	.636	5	Casey Stengel	Giants	4	2
*1952	95	59	.617	2	Casey Stengel	Dodgers	4	3
*1953	99	52	.656	8½	Casey Stengel	Dodgers	4	2
1955	96	58	.623	3	Casey Stengel	Dodgers	3	4
*1956	97	57	.630	9	Casey Stengel	Dodgers	4	3
1957	98	56	.636	8	Casey Stengel	Braves	3	4
1958	92	62	.597	10	Casey Stengel	Braves	4	3
1960	97	57	.630	8	Casey Stengel	Pirates	3	4
*1961	109	53	.673	8	Ralph Houk	Reds	4	1
*1962	96	66	.593	5	Ralph Houk	Giants	4	3
1963	104	57	.646	10½	Ralph Houk	Dodgers	0	4
1964	99	63	.611	1	Yogi Berra	Cardinals	3	4
1976	97	62	.610	10½	Billy Martin	Reds	0	4
*1977	100	62	.617	2½	Billy Martin	Dodgers	4	2
*1978	100	63	.613	1	Martin-Lemon	Dodgers	4	2
†1981	34	22	.607	2	Gene Michael			
	25	26	.490	−5	Michael-Lemon	Dodgers	2	4
						W.S. Totals	109	77

*World Champions
†1st Half Winner

**Tie game in 1922

2

NEW YORK YANKEES—Year-by-Year

Year	Position	Won	Lost	Pct.	Manager	Attendance
1903	Fourth	72	62	.537	Clark Griffith	211,808
1904	Second	92	59	.609	Clark Griffith	438,919
1905	Sixth	71	78	.477	Clark Griffith	309,100
1906	Second	90	61	.596	Clark Griffith	434,700
1907	Fifth	70	78	.473	Clark Griffith	350,020
1908	Eighth	51	103	.331	Griffith-N. Elberfeld	305,500
1909	Fifth	74	77	.490	George T. Stallings	501,000
1910	Second	88	63	.583	Stallings-Hal Chase	355,857
1911	Sixth	76	76	.500	Hal Chase	302,444
1912	Eighth	50	102	.329	Harry Wolverton	242,194
1913	Seventh	57	94	.377	Frank Chance	357,551
1914	†Sixth	70	84	.455	Chance-R. Peckinpaugh	359,477
1915	Fifth	69	83	.454	William E. Donovan	256,035
1916	Fourth	80	74	.519	William E. Donovan	469,211
1917	Sixth	71	82	.464	William E. Donovan	330,294
1918	Fourth	60	63	.488	Miller J. Huggins	282,047
1919	Third	80	59	.576	Miller J. Huggins	619,164
1920	Third	95	59	.617	Miller J. Huggins	1,289,422
1921	First	98	55	.641	Miller J. Huggins	1,230,696
1922	First	94	60	.610	Miller J. Huggins	1,026,134
1923	‡First	98	54	.645	Miller J. Huggins	1,007,066
1924	Second	89	63	.586	Miller J. Huggins	1,053,533
1925	Seventh	69	85	.448	Miller J. Huggins	697,267
1926	First	91	63	.591	Miller J. Huggins	1,027,095
1927	‡First	110	44	.714	Miller J. Huggins	1,164,015
1928	‡First	101	53	.656	Miller J. Huggins	1,072,132
1929	Second	88	66	.571	Huggins-Fletcher	960,148
1930	Third	86	68	.558	Robert Shawkey	1,169,230
1931	Second	94	59	.614	Joe McCarthy	912,437
1932	‡First	107	47	.695	Joe McCarthy	962,320
1933	Second	91	59	.607	Joe McCarthy	728,014
1934	Second	94	60	.610	Joe McCarthy	854,682
1935	Second	89	60	.597	Joe McCarthy	657,508
1936	‡First	102	51	.667	Joe McCarthy	976,913
1937	‡First	102	52	.662	Joe McCarthy	998,148
1938	‡First	99	53	.651	Joe McCarthy	970,916
1939	‡First	106	45	.702	Joe McCarthy	859,785
1940	Third	88	66	.571	Joe McCarthy	988,975
1941	‡First	101	53	.656	Joe McCarthy	964,731
1942	First	103	51	.669	Joe McCarthy	988,251
1943	‡First	98	56	.636	Joe McCarthy	645,006
1944	Third	83	71	.539	Joe McCarthy	822,864
1945	Fourth	81	71	.533	Joe McCarthy	881,846
1946	Third	87	67	.565	McCarthy-W. Dickey-Neun	2,265,512
1947	‡First	97	57	.630	Bucky Harris	2,178,937
1948	Third	94	60	.610	Bucky Harris	2,373,901
1949	‡First	97	57	.630	Casey Stengel	2,281,676
1950	‡First	98	56	.636	Casey Stengel	2,081,380
1951	‡First	98	56	.636	Casey Stengel	1,950,107
1952	‡First	95	59	.617	Casey Stengel	1,629,665
1953	‡First	99	52	.656	Casey Stengel	1,537,811
1954	Second	103	51	.669	Casey Stengel	1,475,171
1955	First	96	58	.623	Casey Stengel	1,490,138
1956	‡First	97	57	.680	Casey Stengel	1,491,784
1957	First	98	56	.636	Casey Stengel	1,497,134
1958	‡First	92	62	.597	Casey Stengel	1,428,428
1959	Third	79	75	.513	Casey Stengel	1,552,030
1960	First	97	57	.630	Casey Stengel	1,627,349
1961	‡First	109	53	.673	Ralph Houk	1,747,736
1962	‡First	96	66	.593	Ralph Houk	1,493,574
1963	First	104	57	.646	Ralph Houk	1,308,920
1964	First	99	63	.611	Yogi Berra	1,305,638
1965	Sixth	77	85	.475	Johnny Keane	1,213,552
1966	Tenth	70	89	.440	Keane-Houk	1,124,648
1967	Ninth	72	90	.444	Ralph Houk	1,141,714
1968	Fifth	83	79	.512	Ralph Houk	1,125,124
1969	Fifth	80	81	.497	Ralph Houk	1,067,996
1970	Second	93	69	.574	Ralph Houk	1,136,879
1971	Fourth	82	80	.506	Ralph Houk	1,070,771
1972	Fourth	79	76	.510	Ralph Houk	966,328
1973	Fourth	80	82	.494	Ralph Houk	1,262,077
1974	Second	89	73	.549	Bill Virdon	1,273,075
1975	Third	83	77	.519	Virdon-Martin	1,288,048
1976	First	97	62	.610	Billy Martin	2,012,434
1977	‡First	100	62	.617	Billy Martin	2,103,092
1978	‡First	100	63	.613	Martin-Lemon	2,335,871
1979	Fourth	89	71	.556	Lemon-Martin	2,537,765
1980	*First	103	59	.636	Dick Howser	2,627,417
1981	First	34	22	.607	Gene Michael	
	Sixth	25	26	.490	Michael-Lemon	1,614,533
1982	Fifth	79	83	.488	Lemon-Michael-King	2,041,219
1983	Third	91	71	.562	Billy Martin	2,257,976
1984	Third	87	71	.537	Yogi Berra	1,821,815
1985	Second	97	64	.602	Berra-Martin	2,214,587
Totals		**7303**	**5480**	**.571**		

†Tied with Chicago.
‡World Championship.
*Lost to K.C. in ALCS.

World Champions—22; American League Champions—33
Finished First—34; Second—13; Third—11; Fourth—8; Fifth—6;
Sixth—6; Seventh—2; Eighth—2; Ninth—1; Tenth—1.
Highest Percentage—.714 in 1927; Lowest—.329 in 1912.

DID YOU KNOW ... that the 1927 Yankees were in first place the whole season and that they went through the entire year using just 25 players and made no roster moves?

IMPORTANT DATES IN YANKEE HISTORY

March 12, 1903—New York Highlanders officially approved as members of American League.

April 22, 1903—Highlanders lose opener at Washington 3-1 under manager Clark Griffith.

April 30, 1903—Highlanders win home opener at Hilltop Park 6-2 over Washington.

April, 1913—Highlanders change name to Yankees.

April 22, 1915—Pinstripes first appear on Yankee uniforms.

January 3, 1920—Ed Barrow is appointed General Manager of the Yankees.

September, 1921—Yankees clinch first American League pennant.

April 18, 1923—Yankee Stadium opens.

October 15, 1923—Yankees win first World Championship, defeating Giants.

June 1, 1925—Lou Gehrig replaces Wally Pipp at first base.

September 30, 1927—Ruth's record 60th home run caps off season for "Murderer's Row" Yankees.

April 16, 1929—Yankees appear with numbers on uniforms, first team to do so on a permanent basis.

September 29, 1929—Manager Miller Huggins dies.

April 12, 1931—Joe McCarthy debuts as Yankee manager.

November 21, 1934—Yankees buy Joe DiMaggio from San Francisco (Pacific Coast League).

May 2, 1939—Lou Gehrig's playing streak of 2,130 consecutive games ends.

July 4, 1939—Gehrig's uniform is the first to be retired as capacity crowd attends Lou Gehrig Day.

June 2, 1941—Lou Gehrig dies at age 37.

July 17, 1941—DiMaggio's 56-game hitting streak is ended in Cleveland.

April 27, 1947—Babe Ruth Day is celebrated in Yankee Stadium.

June 13, 1948—Ruth's uniform retired in farewell Stadium appearance.

August 16, 1948—Babe Ruth dies at age 53.

October 12, 1948—George Weiss brings Casey Stengel to New York as new manager.

April 17, 1951—Mickey Mantle makes Yankee debut.

December 12, 1951—Joe DiMaggio announces his retirement.

April 17, 1953—Mantle hits 565 foot home run in Washington.

October 5, 1953—Yankees win record fifth consecutive World Championship.

October 8, 1956—Don Larsen hurls only perfect game in World Series history.

October 1, 1961—Roger Maris' 61st home run establishes new record.

June 24, 1962—Jack Reed's 22nd inning homer wins longest Yankee game in history.

June 8, 1969—Mickey Mantle Day at Yankee Stadium, uniform retired.

December 31, 1974—Catfish Hunter signs record five-year contract.

November 18, 1976—Don Gullett becomes the first free agent signed by the Yankees in the 1976 re-entry draft.

November 29, 1976—Yankees sign free agent Reggie Jackson to five-year contract.

October 2, 1978—Yankees clinch comeback that saw them come from 14 games out, by defeating Boston, 5-4, in only the 2nd playoff game in American League history.

October 17, 1978—Yankees take Dodgers, 4 games to 2, winning their 22nd World Championship.

August 2, 1979—Thurman Munson dies in plane crash at age 32.

December 15, 1980—Free agent Dave Winfield signs record long term contract with Yankees.

October 15, 1981—Yankees win 33rd American League pennant, sweeping three-game series from Oakland.

July 4, 1983—Dave Righetti pitches no-hit win over Red Sox at Yankee Stadium.

August 4, 1985—On Phil Rizzuto Day at Yankee Stadium uniform #10 is retired.

December 14, 1985—Roger Maris dies at age 51.

GREAT GAMES ...Myrl Hoag had six singles in a game, June 6, 1934, Johnny Lindell (8/17/44) and Jim Mason (7/8/74) had four doubles in a game. Hal Chase (8/30/06), Earle Combs (9/22/27) and Joe DiMaggio (8/27/38) had three triples in a game. Lou Gehrig had 16 total bases on June 3, 1932. Tony Lazzeri drove in 11 runs on 5/24/36; ten Yankees have had eight RBI in a game, most recently Elston Howard (8/19/62). Nine Yankees have had five walks in a game, most recently Maris (5/22/62). Eleven Yankees have scored five runs in a game, most recently Bobby Murcer (6/3/72).

HISTORY OF THE MVP AWARD

The Baseball Writers Association of America officially balloted and named the Most Valuable Player in each major league since 1931. The earlier awards were known as the Chalmers (an automobile) Award (1911-14) and then the league made the award from 1922 through 1928. Under league rules, no player could repeat as winner. A complete list of A.L. winners follows.

NEW YORK YANKEES MOST VALUABLE PLAYERS

YEAR	PLAYER	AGE	POS	G	AB	R	H	2B	3B	HR	RBI	BA	E
1923	Babe Ruth	28	OF-1B	152	522	151*	205	45	13	41*	130°	.393	11
1927	Lou Gehrig	24	1B	155*	584	149	218	52*	18	47	175*	.373	15
1936	Lou Gehrig	33	1B	155°	579	167	205	37	7	49*	152	.354	9
1939	Joe DiMaggio	25	OF	120	462	108	176	32	6	30	126	.381*	5
1941	Joe DiMaggio	27	OF	139	541	122	193	43	11	30	125*	.357	9
1942	Joe Gordon	27	2B	147	538	88	173	29	4	18	103	.322	28*

YEAR	PLAYER	AGE	POS	G	IP	W	L	PCT.	H	R	ER	BB	SO	ERA
1943	Spud Chandler	36	RHP	30	253	20*	4	.833*	197	62	46	134	54	1.64*

YEAR	PLAYER	AGE	POS	G	AB	R	H	2B	3B	HR	RBI	BA	E
1947	Joe DiMaggio	33	OF	141	534	97	168	31	10	20	97	.315	1
1950	Phil Rizzuto	32	SS	155	617	125	200	36	7	7	66	.324	14
1951	Yogi Berra	26	C	141	547	92	161	19	4	27	88	.294	13°
1954	Yogi Berra	29	C-3B	151	584	88	179	28	6	22	125	.307	8
1955	Yogi Berra	30	C	147	541	84	147	20	3	27	108	.272	13*
1956	Mickey Mantle	25	OF	150	533	132*	188	22	5	52*	130*	.353*	4
1957	Mickey Mantle	26	OF	144	474	121*	173	28	6	34	94	.365	7
1960	Roger Maris	26	OF	136	499	98	141	18	7	39	112*	.283	4
1961	Roger Maris	27	OF	161	590	132*	159	16	4	61*	142*	.269	9
1962	Mickey Mantle	31	OF	123	377	96	121	15	1	30	89	.321	5
1963	Elston Howard	34	C	135	487	75	140	21	6	28	85	.287	5
1976	Thurman Munson	29	C-OF-DH	152	616	79	186	27	1	17	105	.302	14
1985	Don Mattingly	24	1B	159	652	107	211	48*	3	35	145*	.324	7

*LEAGUE LEADER °TIED FOR LEAGUE LEAD

AMERICAN LEAGUE MOST VALUABLE PLAYERS

1985-DON MATTINGLY, NY
1984-W. Hernandez, DET
1983-Cal Ripken, BAL
1982-Robin Yount, MIL
1981-R. Fingers, MIL
1980-George Brett, KC
1979-Don Baylor, CAL
1978-Jim Rice, BOS
1977-Rod Carew, MIN
1976-T. MUNSON, NY
1975-Fred Lynn, BOS
1974-J. Burroughs, TEX
1973-R. Jackson, OAK
1972-Dick Allen, CHI
1971-Vida Blue, OAK
1970-Boog Powell, BAL
1969-H. Killebrew, MIN

1968- Denny McLain, DET
1967-C. Yastrzemski, BOS
1966-F. Robinson, BAL
1965-Z. Versalles, MIN
1964-B. Robinson, BAL
1963-ELLIE HOWARD, NY
1962-MICKEY MANTLE, NY
1961-ROGER MARIS, NY
1960-ROGER MARIS, NY
1959-Nelson Fox, CHI
1958-Jackie Jensen, BOS
1957-MICKEY MANTLE, NY
1956-MICKEY MANTLE, NY
1955-YOGI BERRA, NY
1954-YOGI BERRA, NY
1953-Al Rosen, CLE
1952-Bobby Shantz, PHI

1951-YOGI BERRA, NY
1950-PHIL RIZZUTO, NY
1949-Ted Williams, BOS
1948-L. Boudreau, CLE
1947-JOE DiMAGGIO, NY
1946-Ted Williams, BOS
1945-Hal Newhouser, DET
1944-Hal Newhouser, DET
1943-SPUD CHANDLER, NY
1942-JOE GORDON, NY
1941-JOE DiMAGGIO, NY
1940-H. Greenberg, DET
1939-JOE DiMAGGIO, NY
1938-Jimmy Foxx, BOS
1937-C. Gehringer, DET
1936-LOU GEHRIG, NY
1935-H. Greenberg, DET

1934-M. Cochrane, DET
1933-Jimmy Foxx, PHI
1932-Jimmy Foxx, PHI
1931-Lefty Grove, PHI
1928-M. Cochrane, PHI
1927-LOU GEHRIG, NY
1926-George Burns, CLE
1925-R. Peckinpaugh, WAS
1924-W. Johnson, WAS
1924-W. Johnson, WAS
1923-BABE RUTH, NY
1922-George Sisler, St. L
1914-Eddie Collins, PHI
1913-W. Johnson, WAS
1912-Tris Speaker, BOS
1911-Ty Cobb, DET

DID YOU KNOW that with a Yankee having been named A.L. MVP 19 times in the past, NY out-does the next best team better than 2-1P ... The Detroit Tigers own the next highest number of A.L. MVP winners with 9, followed by Boston, with 8

Yankees Most Valuable Player Voting At a Glance

1923
1. Babe Ruth (.393, 41 HR, 130 RBI) 64 points
2. Eddie Collins, White Sox (.360, 89 runs, 47 s.b.) 37 points
   Note: Ruth, who led AL in homers, RBI, runs, slugging and total bases was a unanimous choice, garnering all eight first-place votes. Collins, the Chisox' veteran shortstop, led the league in stolen bases and was fourth in batting on a seventh-place team.

1927:
1. Lou Gehrig (.373, 47 HR, 175 RBI) 56 points
2. Harry Heilmann, Tigers (.393, 14 HR, 120 RBI) 35 points
   Note: Gehrig received seven of eight first-place votes (Yankee teammate Tony Lazzeri got the other) and led league in RBI, doubles and total bases. Heilmann was AL batting champion and tied for third in RBI. Babe Ruth, despite his record 60 homers, was ineligible for MVP award due to peculiar rule that prohibited it from being won more than once. That rule was finally waived by baseball writers in 1931.

1936:
1. Lou Gehrig (.354, 49 HR, 152 RBI) 73 points
2. Luke Appling, White Sox (.388, 6 HR, 128 RBI) 65 points
   Note: First-place vote breakdown is unavailable. Gehrig led league in homers, runs, walks and slugging, was second in RBI and fifth in batting. Appling, playing for third-place Chisox, led league in batting and was sixth in RBI.

1939:
1. Joe DiMaggio (.381, 30 HR, 126 RBI) 280 points
2. Jimmie Foxx, Red Sox (.360, 35 HR, 105 RBI) 170 points
   Note: DiMaggio, who received 15 of the 24 first-place votes, led league in batting, was second in RBI and fourth in homers. Foxx was second in batting and total bases and led league in homers and slugging for second-place Red Sox.

1941:
1. Joe Dimaggio (.357, 30 HR, 125 RBI) 291 points
2. Ted Williams, Red Sox (.406, 37 HR, 120 RBI) 249 points
   Note: DiMaggio, off his 56-game hitting streak and his team's first-place finish was able to impress the voters over Williams' .406. DiMag led league in RBI, was third in batting and fourth in homers. Williams led in batting, runs, homers and slugging for second-place Bosox.

1942:
1. Joe Gordon (.322, 18 HR, 103 RBI) 270 points
2. Ted Williams, Red Sox (.356, 37 HR, 137 RBI) 249 points
   Note: Even though Williams won the triple crown with the second-place Red Sox, Gordon, the batting leader for the first-place Yankees won the MVP. Oddly, Gordon also led the league in errors at second base as well as grounding into the most double plays. Gordon ranked fourth in the AL in batting and RBI. Williams blamed this bitter defeat on his draft difficulties as he had been granted a deferment until after the '42 season for being the sole support of his mother.

1943:
1. Spud Chandler (20-4, 1.64 ERA) 246 points
2. Luke Appling, White Sox (.328, 3 HR, 80 RBI) 215
   Note: Chandler was clearly the outstanding pitcher in a year in which the war began taking its toll on major league talent. The Yank righthander led the league in wins, winning percentage, complete games, shutouts and ERA and was third in strikeouts. Appling, second again, won the batting title for the fourth-place Chisox and was fourth in stolen bases.

1947:
1. Joe DiMaggio (.315, 20 HR, 97 RBI) 202 points
2. Ted Williams, Red Sox (.343, 32 HR, 114 RBI) 201 points
   Note: In the closest election in the history of the MVP voting, DiMaggio edged out Williams, who again won the triple crown only to lose out to a Yankee. This time, Williams could point to Boston writer Melville Webb who, it was reported, left him entirely off the 10-place ballot. DiMaggio was third in RBI, second in total bases.

1950:
1. Phil Rizzuto (.324, 125 runs, 66 RBI) 284 points
2. Billy Goodman, Red Sox (.354, 91 runs, 68 RBI) 180 points
   Note: Rizzuto, the clear cut MVP in '50, ranked sixth in batting, second in runs, tied for second in stolen bases (12) and led all AL shortstops in putouts and fielding pct. Goodman, a utility player for the third-place Red Sox, won the batting title.

1951:
1. Yogi Berra (.294, 27 HR, 88 RBI) 184 points
2. Ned Garver, Browns (20-12, 3.73 ERA) 157
   Note: Berra, who received six first-place votes and was named on 22 of 24 ballots cast, led first-place Yanks in homers and RBI and topped AL catchers in putouts and assists. Garver, who also got six first-place votes had 20 of the last-place Browns' 52 victories.

1954:
1. Yogi Berra (.307, 22 HR, 125 RBI) 230 points
2. Larry Doby, Indians (.272, 32 HR, 126 RBI) 210 points
   Note: In what must be considered a major upset, Berra won MVP despite the fact that Doby led the league in homers and RBI for a first-place team that set an all-time record for victories. Doby was hurt by impressive season by his teammate, batting champ Bobby Avila, who pulled five first place votes. Doby also had five first while Berra polled seven.

1955:
1. Yogi Berra (.272, 27 HR, 108 RBI) 218 points
2. Al Kaline, Tigers (.340, 27 HR, 102 RBI) 201 points
   Note: Berra, who polled seven of possible 24 first-place votes, was third in AL in RBI. Kaline, named on four first-place ballots, was youngest ever batting champion (20) and ranked 5th in RBI for fifth-place Tigers. Yanks' Gil McDougald got two first-place votes.

1956:
1. Mickey Mantle (.353, 52 HR, 130 RBI) 336 points
2. Yogi Berra (.298, 30 HR, 105 RBI) 186
   Note: Mantle was unanimous choice, being named first on all 24 ballots, and

rightfully so as he won triple crown and led Yanks to their seventh AL pennant in eight years.

1957:
1. Mickey Mantle (.365, 34 HR, 94 RBI) 239 points
2. Ted Williams, Red Sox (.388, 38 HR, 87 RBI) 209 points
   Note: Another heartbreak for Red Sox' slugger Williams who protested loudly that writers had again done him wrong. Williams won his 5th batting title (for a team that finished third) and was second in homers, while Mantle missed 10 games due to injuries. Still Mick led Yanks in RBI and was second in AL in batting and third in homers.

1960:
1. Roger Maris (.283, 39 HR, 112 RBI) 225 points
2. Mickey Mantle (.275, 40 HR, 94 RBI) 222 points
   Note: In second-closest MVP voting in history (excluding ties), Maris, who had been acquired by Yankees over the winter from Kansas City, edged teammate Mantle. Maris led AL in RBI, Mantle led in homers, runs and total bases. Maris had eight first-place votes, five seconds, three thirds, four fourths, one fifth and two for sixth. Mantle had 10 first place votes, four seconds, but ony two each for third and fourth, one for fifth and two for sixth.

1961:
1. Roger Maris (.269, 61 HR, 142 RBI) 202 points
2. Mickey Mantle (.317, 54 HR, 128 RBI) 198 points
   Note: In another close race between the Yankees M&M Boys, Maris received seven first-place votes, six seconds, and three each for third and fourth. Mantle had six firsts, seven seconds, just two thirds and five fourths. Yankee relief ace Luis Arroyo got one first-place vote that year.

1962:
1. Mickey Mantle (.321, 30 HR, 89 RBI) 234 points
2. Bobby Richardson (.302, 99 runs, 59 RBI) 152 points
   Note: After two straight narrow losses to Maris, Mantle finally got his due, easily beating out teammate Richardson, who led AL in hits (209) and was fourth in doubles (38). Maris, despite leading Yanks in homers (33) and RBI (100), did not even get a vote.

1963:
1. Elston Howard (.287, 28 HR, 85 RBI) 248 points
2. Al Kaline, Tigers (.312, 27 HR, 101 RBI) 148 points
   Note: Howard, the acknowledged catalyst to Yanks' fourth straight flag, had little competition. RBI leader that year was Boston's "no glove" Dick Stuart. Kaline was second in AL in batting and RBI.

1976:
1. Thurman Munson (.302, 17 HR, 105 RBI) 304 points
2. George Brett, Royals (.333, 7HR, 67 RBI) 217
   Note: Though they both led their clubs to division titles and Brett won the batting title, Munson received the heavy support for his RBI (2nd in AL) and his importance to club as a catcher.

1985 A.L. MVP VOTING

Player	1	2	3	4	5	6	7	8	9	10	Pts.
Mattingly, Don	23	5	—	—	—	—	—	—	—	—	367
Brett, George	5	20	3	—	—	—	—	—	—	—	274
Henderson, Rickey	—	1	8	10	—	3	3	—	2	—	174
Boggs, Wade	—	2	5	3	8	3	1	3	2	—	159
Murray, Eddie	—	—	1	5	4	6	5	2	3	1	130
Moore, Donnie	—	—	5	2	2	4	1	1	—	3	96
Barfield, Jesse	—	—	1	4	3	2	2	2	4	2	88
Bell, Jorge	—	—	3	2	3	2	3	1	1	1	84
Baines, Harold	—	—	—	—	2	1	2	3	4	7	49
Saberhagen, Bret	—	—	1	1	2	1	1	1	3	—	45
Quisenberry, Dan	—	—	—	—	1	1	2	6	—	2	39
Winfield, Dave	—	—	—	1	1	1	2	2	1	1	35
Fisk, Carlton	—	—	1	—	1	1	2	—	—	2	29
Evans, Dwight	—	—	—	—	—	2	2	—	—	3	17
Guidry, Ron	—	—	—	—	—	1	1	2	—	—	15
Bradley, Phil	—	—	—	—	—	—	1	1	4	1	12
Ripken, Cal Jr.	—	—	—	—	—	—	1	—	2	1	9
Gibson, Kirk	—	—	—	—	—	1	—	—	—	2	7
Balboni, Steve	—	—	—	—	1	—	—	—	—	—	6
Henke, Tom	—	—	—	—	—	1	—	—	—	—	5
Lamp, Dennis	—	—	—	—	—	—	—	1	—	—	3
Puckett, Kirby	—	—	—	—	—	—	—	1	—	—	3
Alexander, Doyle	—	—	—	—	—	—	—	—	1	1	3
Garcia, Damaso	—	—	—	—	—	—	—	—	1	—	2
Gedman, Rich	—	—	—	—	—	—	—	—	—	1	1

GEORGE M. STEINBRENNER III

Every young man searching for his own place in today's world would be well advised to heed the advice and example of sportsman, business executive and civic leader, George M. Steinbrenner.

Steinbrenner, a national figure before he was 40, offers a succinct basic formula for success. "Work as hard as you ask others to. Strive for what you believe is right, no matter the odds. Learn that mistakes can be the best teacher of all." Certainly the meteoric career of this energetic son of a distinguished Great Lakes shipping family bears out the practical results of these simple beliefs.

In 1963, he entered the business world in earnest. In a way, it was a difficult adjustment for a man who had already been an assistant football coach at two Big Ten universities, Northwestern and Purdue, and put together national championship teams in both the National Industrial and American Basketball Leagues.

In the business world, Steinbrenner is Chairman of The American Shipbuilding Company which he and associates took over and revitalized in 1967. Under his early leadership American Ship tripled its annual revenues and since has climbed to the $200 million mark in annual sales.

In 1973, Steinbrenner put together the group which purchased the New York Yankees from CBS. As the Principal Owner, it took only five years for his keen foresight and aggressive leadership to turn the Yankees, once again, into World Champions.

Apart from corporate business and civic involvements, he devotes a great deal of time to his extensive interest in thoroughbred breeding and racing which includes his 800 acre stud farm in Florida, The Florida Breeders Sales Company and Florida Horse Magazine. In 1983 he was honored as the Industrialist of the Year in Florida. In partnership with James Nederlander of the famous theatrical family, he produced long-running, Tony Award winning musical, "Applause" and another musical hit, "See-Saw." They also put together highly successful national tours of "Funny Girl," "George M." and "On a Clear Day."

NEW YORK YANKEE OWNERSHIP CHRONOLOGY

January 9, 1903—Frank Ferrell and Bill Devery purchase Baltimore franchise of American League and move team to New York City. Cost is $18,000.

January 11, 1915—Col. Jacob Ruppert and Col. Tillinghast L'Hommedieu Huston purchase Yankees for $460,000.

May 21, 1922—Ruppert buys out Huston for $1,500,000.

January 13, 1939—Col. Ruppert dies.

January 25, 1945—Dan Topping, Del Webb and Larry McPhail purchase Yankees for $2,800,000.

November 2, 1964—CBS purchases 80% of Yankees for $11,200,000, later buys remaining 20%.

January 3, 1973—Group headed by George M. Steinbrenner purchases Yankees from CBS.

NEW YORK YANKEE PRESIDENTS

(Chief Executive Officers)

Joseph W. Gordon	1903-06	Daniel R. Topping	1964-66
Frank J. Farrell	1907-14	Michael Burke	1966-73
Jacob Ruppert	1915-39	Gabriel Paul	1973-77
Edward G. Barrow	1939-45	Albert Rosen	1978-79
Leland S. MacPhail	1945-47	George M. Steinbrenner	1979-80
Daniel R. Topping	1947-53	Lou Saban	1981-82
Daniel R. Topping &		Eugene J. McHale	1983-
Del E. Webb	1954-64		

GENE McHALE

In naming Gene McHale as President of the New York Yankees on January 5, 1983, Principal Owner George M. Steinbrenner said, "In filling this key position, there was no need to look anywhere else but within the Yankee organization. Gene has a solid and proven administrative, business and financial background and has been a longtime employee of the Yankees.

"Much of the progress the Yankees have made in the areas of television, radio, publications, merchandising and ticketing is due to the efforts of him. The Yankees are proud to have employees of the caliber of Gene McHale and to promote from within the organization to fill this position."

Eugene J. "Gene" McHale, 47, has been with the Yankees since December, 1972. As an employee of CBS, who then owned the Yankees, he was assigned to supervise the Yankee accounting department. When George Steinbrenner and associates purchased the Yankees from CBS in January, 1973, McHale remained with the team as controller. He was named administrative vice president in 1977. Before coming to the Yankees, he worked for seven years with CBS with responsibilities in financial and business affairs in their radio division.

A native of the Washington Heights section of Manhattan, McHale graduated from Cardinal Hayes High School several blocks away from Yankee Stadium in the Bronx. He is a graduate of Fordham University and also served three years in the U.S. Navy. Gene is a resident of Locust Valley, NY.

CLYDE KING

On April 9, 1984 Clyde King was named Vice President and General Manager of the New York Yankees. In making the announcement, Yankees' Principal Owner George Steinbrenner said, "Clyde is a great company man, and is highly respected in the baseball community, both on and off the field. He is a man who has served the Yankees for nine years as a manager, coach, and scout. He has been a total friend and confidant, and I think that he will be an outstanding general manager."

King, 60, has been a member of the Yankee organization since 1975 in a variety of roles. He originally joined the Yankees as a special assignment scout, and his duties have included working and traveling with the team in 1978 and 1980. He served as interim Yankee manager from August 3, 1982 until the end of that season, compiling a 29-33 record. He began the 1982 season as an advance scout, before being named pitching coach on June 11. He served in that capacity until being shifted to the front office on special assignments on July 19.

He managed the San Francisco Giants in 1969 and 1970, and the Atlanta Braves in 1974 and 1975. He also served as coach for five years with the Reds, Cardinals and Pirates.

As a player, Clyde pitched in the majors for a total of seven years with the Brooklyn Dodgers and Cincinnati Reds. His best season was 1951 when he was 14-7 for the Dodgers. Clyde is a graduate of the University of North Carolina where he played basketball and baseball. In 1983 he was named to the North Carolina Sports Hall of Fame.

WOODY WOODWARD

Woody Woodward was named the Yankees' Vice President of Baseball Administration on October 22, 1984.

Woody came to the Yankees from the Cincinnati Reds where he was the assistant general manager. While with the Reds he handled player contract negotiations and was involved in all areas of player personnel work. He assumed his former position in November, 1980 after 2½ years as the Reds' minor league field coordinator.

A former coach and All-American player at Florida State University, Woodward earned his Bachelor's and Master's degree in Education. He coached his alma mater from 1975 to 1978, recording the second best winning percentage in Seminole history (170-57, .749 W-L Pct.).

As a professional player Woodward spent 8½ seasons in the major leagues as an infielder with the Milwaukee and Atlanta Braves and the Cincinnati Reds.

GENE McHALE　　　**CLYDE KING**　　　**WOODY WOODWARD**

YANKEE STADIUM HISTORY

May 5, 1922—Construction begins on Yankee Stadium.

April 18, 1923—Yankee Stadium opens, Babe Ruth hits first home run.

April, 1928—Season opens with left field stands in Stadium enlarged.

April, 1937—Season opens with right field stands in Stadium enlarged.

May 30, 1938—Record 81,841 attend doubleheader vs Boston.

May 28, 1946—First night game played in Yankee Stadium.

April, 1953—Stadium sold to Earl and Arnold Johnson of Kansas City.

January 29, 1955—John Williams Cox buys Yankee Stadium, sells grounds to Knights of Columbus, later leaves structure to Rice University (1962).

April, 1959—First message scoreboard unveiled at Yankee Stadium.

Winter, 1966-67—Stadium painted blue and white in face lift.

August 8, 1972—Yankees sign 30 year lease to play in remodeled Yankee Stadium beginning in 1976.

September 30, 1973—Yankees complete 50th anniversary season at Yankee Stadium.

1974-75—Yankees play at Shea Stadium, while Yankee Stadium is remodeled.

April 15, 1976—Fully remodeled Yankee Stadium reopens.

The Largest crowd in the "New" Yankee Stadium (opened in April, 1976) was **56,821** for the final game of the 1976 ALCS vs. Kansas City, October 14, 1976.

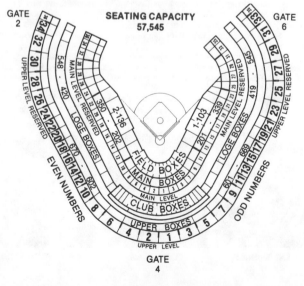

NEW YORK YANKEE HOME BALL PARKS

1903-1912 Hilltop Park, 168th St. & Broadway, Manhattan
1913-1922 Polo Grounds, 155th St. & 8th Ave., Manhattan
1923-1973 Yankee Stadium, 161st St. & River Ave., Bronx
1974-1975 Shea Stadium, 126th St. & Roosevelt Ave., Flushing
1976-   Yankee Stadium, 161st St. & River Ave., Bronx

YANKEE STADIUM GROUND RULES

Foul poles are outside the playing field. Any batted ball hitting foul pole above fence line is a home run. Bat racks are within the dugouts.

Any thrown ball hitting dugout railing or foundation and rebounding on field is in play. Ball going into dugout or hitting other parts of dugout—out of play.

YANKEE STADIUM DIMENSIONS

Left field foul pole	312 ft.	Right center field	385 ft.
Left field	379 ft.	Right field	353 ft.
Left center field	411 ft.	Right field foul pole	310 ft.
Centerfield	410 ft.		

Yankee Stadium's playing field covers approximately 3.5 acres . . . the entire stadium area is on 11.6 acres. A combination of some 800 multi-vapor and incandescent lamps illuminate the field, with powers of up to 1500 watts.

MEMORIAL PARK SECTION

Monuments (l-r) Lou Gehrig, Miller Huggins, Babe Ruth. Plaques—Ed Barrow, Jacob Ruppert, Joe DiMaggio, Mickey Mantle, Casey Stengel, Joe McCarthy, Thurman Munson, Elston Howard, Roger Maris, Phil Rizzuto, Pope Paul VI for his 1965 Stadium Mass for Peace, and Pope John Paul II for his 1979 Stadium Mass.

DID YOU KNOW . . . that Yankee Stadium is built almost in the spot where baseball originated in the Bronx? The Unions of Morrisania, who called themselves the champions of the world around 1866, played near the spot where the old Melrose station of the Harlem Railroad was located.

TICKET INFORMATION—1986
(212) 293-6000

YANKEE STADIUM GAME TIMES

*Weekend Day Games . . . . 1:30 P.M.
*Midweek Day Games . . . . 1:00 P.M.
*Night Games . . . . 7:30 P.M.

*Except where designated.

TICKET PRICES

Box Seats. $9.75
Reserved $8.25
*General Admission $4.50
*Bleachers $3.00
*Senior Citizens $1.00
(Including all City and State Taxes)
*Sold only at Stadium on day or night of game.

*Except where designated.

HOW TO BUY TICKETS IN ADVANCE

Tickets to Yankee home games are on sale throughout the season at the Yankee Stadium Advance Ticket Windows, from 9-5, Monday-Sunday and through the conclusion of all night games. Tickets are also available at the more than 50 Ticket Master ticket centers throughout the metropolitan area, including Record World and Toys and Sports Warehouse locations.

Credit card phone reservations can be made for Yankee tickets by calling (212) 307-7171 or (914) 965-2700.

BY MAIL . . . Make check or money order payable to NEW YORK YANKEES (add $1.25 to cover postage and handling). Mail to Mail Order Department, New York Yankees, Yankee Stadium, Bronx, N.Y. 10451.

For information on Group Sales, Season Sales, Combination Plans or Luxury Suites, contact the Group Sales Department at (212) 293-6013.

YANKEE ATTENDANCE RECORDS
(New Yankee Stadium)

Largest Night Game Attendance (vs. Boston, Tuesday, September 13, 1977)	55,269
Largest Single Day Game Attendance (vs. Detroit, Saturday, June 15, 1985)	55,623
Largest Doubleheader Attendance (vs. Detroit, Saturday, October 4, 1980)	55,410
Largest Twi-Night Doubleheader Attendance (vs. Baltimore, Saturday, September 10, 1983)	55,605
Largest Weekday, Day Game Attendance (vs. California, July 26, 1977)	43,136
Largest Home Series Attendance (4 game series) (Yankees vs. Toronto, September 12, 13, 14, 15, 1985)	214,510
Largest Home Series Attendance (3 games) (Yankees vs. Boston September 15-17, 1978)	165,080

TOP 20 CROWDS AT NEW YANKEE STADIUM

1. 56,821 (vs KC, 5th game of 1976 ALCS)
2. 56,808 (vs KC, 3rd game of 1976 ALCS)
3. 56,700 (vs Cincinnati, 4th game of 1976 W.S.)
4. 56,891 (vs LA, 2nd game of 1977 W.S.)
5. 56,683 (All Star Game, July 19, 1977)
6. 56,668 (vs LA, 1st game of 1977 W.S.)
7. 56,667 (vs Cincinnati, 3rd game of 1976 W.S.)
8. 56,588 (vs KC, 3rd game of 1980 ALCS)
9. 56,513 (vs LA, 6th game of 1981 W.S.)
10. 56,505 (vs LA, 2nd game of 1981 W.S.)
11. 55,470 (vs LA, 1st game of 1981 W.S.)
12. 56,448 (vs LA, 5th game of the 1978 W.S.)
13. 56,447 (vs LA, 3rd game of 1978 W.S.)
14. 56,445 (vs LA, 4th game of 1978 W.S.)
15. 56,411 (vs Milwaukee, 3rd game of 1981 D.S.)
16. 56,407 (vs LA, 6th game of 1977 W.S.)
17. 56,356 (vs KC, 4th game of 1978 ALCS)
18. 56,355 (vs KC, 4th game of 1976 ALCS)
19. 56,230 (vs KC, 2nd game of 1977 ALCS)
20. 55,740 (vs Oakland, 1st game of 1981 ALCS)

TOP 20 REGULAR SEASON CROWDS AT NEW YANKEE STADIUM

1. 55,623 (vs Detroit, June 15, 1985)
2. 55,605 (vs Baltimore, September 10, 1983, TN-DH)
3. 55,593 (vs Seattle, June 5, 1983)
4. 55,579 (vs Detroit, April 12, 1983, Opening Day)
5. 55,521 (vs Cleveland, June 27, 1982)
6. 55,410 (vs Detroit, October 4, 1980, DH)
7. 55,367 (vs Toronto, May 27, 1978)
8. 55,218 (vs Boston, September 15, 1977)
9. 55,132 (vs Boston, June 27, 1978)
10. 55,123 (vs Texas, April 9, 1981 Opening Day)
11. 55,091 (vs Boston, September 16, 1978)
12. 55,090 (vs California, June 18, 1978)
13. 55,088 (vs Boston, September 17, 1978)
14. 55,083 (vs Milwaukee, September 7, 1981)
15. 55,073 (vs Chicago, June 3, 1979)
16. 55,049 (vs Cleveland, June 24, 1979)
17. 55,039 (vs Boston, June 26, 1977)
18. 55,007 (vs Cleveland, September 30, 1978)
19. 54,940 (vs Boston, June 24, 1977)
20. 54,901 (vs Boston, September 15, 1978)

1985 ATTENDANCE RECORDS

HOME

Largest Night Game Attendance (vs. Toronto, Saturday, September 14)	54,367
Largest Day Game Attendance (vs. Detroit, Saturday, June 15)	55,623
Largest Doubleheader Attendance (vs. Minnesota, Sunday, July 7)	31,549

ROAD

Largest Night Game Attendance (at California, Friday, May 17)	61,066
Largest Day Game Attendance (at Cleveland, Saturday, April 13)	61,978
Largest Doubleheader Attendance (at Cleveland, Tuesday, July 30)	18,271
Yankee 1985 Home Attendance (80 games, 77 dates)	2,214,587
Yankee 1985 Road Attendance (81 games, 80 dates)	2,366,626
Yankee 1985 Total Attendance (161 games, 157 dates)	4,581,213

Total Attendances—

Hilltop Park (1903-12)	3,451,542
Polo Grounds (1913-22)	6,220,031
Yankee Stadium (1923-73)	64,188,862
Shea Stadium (1974-75)	2,561,123
Yankee Stadium (1976-)	21,566,709
	97,988,267

Note: The Yankees need 2,011,733 in home attendance to reach 100 million in home attendance since the franchise located in New York in 1903.

YANKEE ATTENDANCE RECORDS

Largest Season Home Attendance (1980)	2,627,417
Largest Single Game Home Attendance (vs. Boston, May 16, 1947—Night)	74,747
Largest Single Game Home Attendance—Day (vs. Boston, Sept. 26, 1948)	69,755
Largest Doubleheader Home Attendance (vs. Boston, May 30, 1938)	81,841
Largest Twi-Night Home Doubleheader Attendance—(vs. Baltimore, September 10, 1983)	55,605
Largest Opening Day Home Attendance (vs. Detroit, April 12, 1983)	55,579
Largest Home Series Attendance (vs. Toronto, Sept. 12, 13, 14, 15, 1985)	214,510
Largest Crowd in Baseball History (Yankees at Los Angeles—Exhibition Game, May 7, 1959)	93,103
Largest Yankee Old Timers' Day Attendance (vs. Boston, Aug. 9, 1958)	67,916
Largest Season Road Attendance (1980)	2,461,240*

*Major League Record

1985—OFFICIAL A.L. STATISTICS

STANDINGS

AMERICAN LEAGUE EAST

	Won	Lost	Pct.	Games Behind
Toronto	99	62	.615	
New York	97	64	.602	2
Detroit	84	77	.522	15
Baltimore	83	78	.516	16
Boston	81	81	.500	18½
Milwaukee	71	90	.441	28
Cleveland	60	102	.370	39½

AMERICAN LEAGUE WEST

	Won	Lost	Pct.	Games Behind
Kansas City	91	71	.562	
California	90	72	.556	1
Chicago	85	77	.525	6
Minnesota	77	85	.475	14
Oakland	77	85	.475	14
Seattle	74	88	.457	17
Texas	62	99	.385	28½

CLUB BATTING

CLUB	AVG	G	AB	R	H	2B	3B	HR	RBI	GW RBI	SH	SF	TBB	SO	SB	CS	GI DP	LOB	SHO
Boston	.282	163	5720	800	1615	292	31	162	760	80	50	57	562	816	66	27	164	1241	8
Toronto	.269	161	5508	759	1482	281	53	158	714	90	21	44	503	807	143	77	121	1067	5
New York	.267	161	5458	839	1458	272	31	176	793	87	48	60	620	771	155	53	119	1125	6
Cleveland	.265	162	5527	729	1465	254	31	116	689	58	38	48	492	817	132	72	139	1068	12
Oakland	.264	162	5558	757	1475	230	34	155	690	71	63	47	508	861	116	58	129	1073	5
Minnesota	.264	162	5509	705	1453	282	41	141	678	74	39	47	502	779	68	44	117	1144	12
Milwaukee	.263	161	5568	690	1467	250	44	101	636	64	54	55	462	746	69	34	145	1130	10
Baltimore	.263	161	5517	818	1451	234	22	214	773	80	31	40	604	908	69	43	132	1124	7
Seattle	.255	162	5521	719	1410	277	38	171	686	69	28	41	564	942	94	35	147	1143	8
Texas	.253	161	5361	617	1359	213	41	129	578	56	34	45	530	819	130	76	136	1100	9
Chicago	.253	163	5470	736	1386	247	37	146	695	78	59	45	471	843	108	56	119	1009	7
Kansas City	.252	162	5500	687	1384	261	49	154	657	87	44	41	473	840	128	48	125	1057	4
California	.251	162	5442	732	1364	215	31	153	685	80	99	35	648	902	106	51	139	1165	10
TOTALS	.261	1132	77257	10317	20182	3562	528	2178	9737	1055	648	658	7465	11777	1459	715	1813	15588	109

CLUB PITCHING

CLUB	W	L	ERA	G	CG	SHO	SV	IP	H	R	ER	HR	HB	TBB	SO	WP	BK
Toronto	99	62	3.31	161	18	9	47	1448.0	1312	588	532	147	26	484	823	36	5
Kansas City	91	71	3.49	162	27	11	41	1461.0	1433	639	566	103	28	463	846	43	9
New York	97	64	3.69	161	25	9	49	1440.1	1373	660	590	157	13	518	907	34	5
Detroit	84	77	3.78	161	31	11	40	1456.0	1313	688	612	141	23	556	943	62	6
California	90	72	3.91	162	22	8	41	1457.1	1453	703	633	171	27	514	767	45	4
Boston	81	81	4.06	163	35	8	29	1461.1	1487	720	659	130	35	540	913	34	13
Chicago	85	77	4.07	163	20	8	39	1451.2	1411	720	656	161	36	569	1023	54	5
Baltimore	83	78	4.38	161	32	6	33	1427.1	1480	764	694	160	23	568	793	32	7
Milwaukee	71	90	4.39	161	34	6	37	1437.0	1510	802	701	175	33	499	777	51	4
Oakland	77	85	4.41	162	10	6	41	1453.0	1451	787	712	172	25	607	785	48	5
Minnesota	77	85	4.48	162	41	7	34	1426.1	1468	782	710	164	30	462	767	51	11
Texas	62	99	4.56	161	18	5	33	1411.2	1479	785	715	173	36	501	863	43	7
Seattle	74	88	4.68	162	23	8	30	1432.0	1456	818	744	154	41	637	868	61	18
Cleveland	60	102	4.91	162	24	7	28	1421.0	1556	861	776	170	43	547	702	46	7
TOTALS	1131	1131	4.15	1132	360	109	522	20184.0	20182	10317	9300	2178	419	7465	11777	640	106

CLUB FIELDING

CLUB	AVG	G	PO	A	E	TC	DP	TP	PB
California	.982	162	4372	1841	112	6325	202	0	8
Chicago	.982	163	4355	1677	111	6143	152	0	11
Seattle	.980	162	4296	1836	122	6254	156	0	22
Minnesota	.980	162	4279	1732	120	6131	139	0	13
Kansas City	.980	162	4383	1907	127	6417	160	1	10
Texas	.980	161	4235	1703	120	6058	145	0	23
Toronto	.980	161	4344	1729	125	6198	164	0	3
New York	.979	161	4321	1563	126	6010	172	0	18
Baltimore	.979	161	4282	1714	129	6125	168	0	4
Boston	.977	163	4384	1846	145	6375	161	0	14
Oakland	.977	162	4359	1566	140	6065	136	0	19
Cleveland	.977	162	4263	1703	141	6107	161	0	13
Milwaukee	.977	161	4311	1686	142	6139	153	0	12
Detroit	.977	161	4368	1671	143	6182	152	0	10
TOTALS	.979	1132	60552	24174	1803	86529	2221	1	180

YANKEES DAY-BY-DAY—1985

Date	Game No.	Opponent	W-L	Score	Rec'd	Pos	G A/B	League Leader & Lead	Winning-Losing Pitchers	Paid Attend.
4/8	1	@ Bos	L	2-9	0-1	5 (T)	−1	Bal-Bos-Det (+½)	Boyd-Niekro	34,282
4/10	2	@ Bos	L	5-14	0-2	6 (T)	−2	Bal-Bos-Det (+1)	Hurst-Whitson	19,615
4/11	3	@ Bos	L	4-6	0-3	6 (T)	−3	Bos-Det (+½)	Clemens-Rasmussen	19,060
4/12	EXH.	Columbus	L	5-14		4 (T)	−3	Bos-Det-Bal (+1)	Williams-Fisher	8,750
4/13	4	@ Cle	W	6-3	1-3	6	−3	Bal-Bos-Det (+1)	Guidry-Blyleven	61,978
4/14	5	@ Cle	W	2-1	2-3	6	−3	Det (+1)	Niekro-Waddell	12,085
4/15		OFF DAY				6	−3	Det (+1)		
4/16	6	CHI	W	5-4	3-3	4 (T)	−2½	Det (+1)	Righetti-Spillner	53,019
4/17		OFF DAY				4 (T)	−2½	Det (+1)		
4/18	7	CHI	W	3-2	4-3	4	−2	Det (+1)	Bordi-**Bannister**	15,126
4/19	8	CLE	L	1-2	4-4	4 (T)	−2	Det (+1)	Heaton-Guidry	21,229
4/20	9	CLE	W	5-2	5-4	3 (T)	−2	Det (+1)	Niekro-Ramon	20,188
4/21	10	CLE	L	0-3	5-5	4 (T)	−2	Det (+1)	Von Ohlen-Whitson	34,443
4/22		OFF DAY				4 (T)	−1½	Det (+1)		
4/23	11	BOS	L	4-5	5-6	6	−2½	Det (+1½)	Ojeda-Righetti	25,207
4/24	12	BOS	L	6-7	5-7	7	−2½	Det (+1½)	Crawford-**Guidry**	23,229
4/25	13	BOS	W	5-1	6-7	6	−2	Bal (+½)	Niekro-Hurst	22,179
4/26	14	@ Chi	L	2-4	6-8	6	−3	Bal (+½)	Seaver-Whitson	19,174
4/27	15	@ Chi	L	4-5	6-9	7	−3½	Det (+½)	Nelson-Shirley	22,788
4/28	16	@ Chi	L	3-4	6-10	7	−4½	Det (+½)	Burns-**Cowley**	27,367
4/29	17	@ Tex	L	5-7	6-11	7	−5	Det (+.032)	Schmidt-Guidry	10,066
4/30	18	@ Tex	L	4-8	6-12	7	−6	Tor (+½)	Noles-Niekro	15,416
5/1	19	@ Tex	W	5-1	7-12	7	−6	Tor (+½)	Whitson-Hough	15,528
5/2		OFF DAY				7	−5½	Bal (+.014)		
5/3	20	KC	W	7-1	8-12	7	−5½	Bal (+.015)	**Rasmussen**-Jackson	20,603
5/4	21	KC	W	5-2	9-12	7	−4½	Bal (+.011)	**Guidry**-Liebrandt	22,532
5/5	22	KC	W	6-2	10-12	5	−4½	Bal (+1)	Niekro-Black	50,209
5/6		OFF DAY				5	−4½	Bal (+1)		
5/7	23	@ Min	L	6-10	10-13	6	−5½	Bal (+1)	Viola-Whitson	21,704
5/8	24	@ Min	L	6-8	10-14	5	−5½	Bal (+½)	Smithson-Cowley	22,832
5/9		OFF DAY				5	−5½	Bal (+½)		
5/10	25	@ KC	W	6-4	11-14	5	−5½	Bal (+½)	Guidry-Leibrandt	34,000
5/11	26	@ KC	W	11-3	12-14	5	−5½	Bal (+1)	Rasmussen-Black	38,011
5/12	27	@ KC	L	5-6	12-15	5	−5½	Bal (+.010)	Quisenberry-Righetti	31,009
5/13	28	MIN	W	9-8	13-15	5	−5	Tor (+½)	Cowley-Davis	15,136
5/14	29	MIN	W	10-7	14-15	5	−5	Tor (+1)	Fisher-Wardle	18,319
5/15	30	TEX	W	6-5	15-15	4	−4	Tor (+1)	Righetti-Schmidt	17,232
5/16	31	TEX	W	6-5	16-15	4	−3½	Tor (+1)	Righetti-Stewart	21,020
5/17	32	@ Cal	W	6-0	17-15	4	−2½	Bal-Tor (+½)	Niekro-Witt	61,066
5/18	33	@ Cal	W	6-1	18-15	4	−2½	Tor (+½)	Cowley-John	32,936
5/19	34	@ Cal	L	1-4	18-16	4	−2½	Bal-Tor (+½)	Slaton-Whitson	39,724
5/20		OFF DAY				4	−3	Tor (+½)		
5/21	35	@ Sea	W	11-1	19-16	4	−3	Tor (+1½)	Guidry-Langston	16,054
5/22	36	@ Sea	L	1-4	19-17	4	−4	Tor (+1½)	**Young**-**Rasmussen**	13,363
5/23	37	@ Sea	L	4-6	19-18	4	−5	Tor (+2½)	Beattie-**Niekro**	15,790
5/24	38	@ Oak	W	10-3	20-18	4	−5	Tor (+2½)	Cowley-Codiroli	22,919
5/25	39	@ Oak	L	7-8	20-19	4	−6	Tor (+3)	Howell-Righetti	30,273
5/26	40	@ Oak	W	13-1	21-19	4	−6	Tor (+3)	Guidry-Krueger	36,966
5/27	41	@ Oak	L	1-2	21-20	4	−6½	Tor (+3½)	Howell-Righetti	31,294
5/28		OFF DAY				4	−7	Tor (+4)		
5/29	42	CAL	W	7-2	22-20	4	−6	Tor (+4)	Niekro-Slaton	25,049
5/30	43	CAL	W	3-1	23-20	4	−5½	Tor (+3½)	Cowley-**Romanick**	17,226
5/31	44	SEA	W	8-3	24-20	4	−5½	Tor (+3½)	Fisher-Langston	20,309
6/1	45	SEA	W	8-2	25-20	3 (T)	−5½	Tor (+5)	**Guidry**-Young	25,109
6/2	46	SEA	L	6-7	25-21	4	−6	Tor (+4½)	Nunez-Rasmussen	50,150
6/3	47	OAK	W	5-2	26-21	3 (T)	−5½	Tor (+4)	Niekro-Codiroli	15,228
6/4	48	OAK	L	0-2	26-22	3 (T)	−6½	Tor (+5)	Birtsas-Cowley	20,242
6/5		PPD-RAIN				4	−7	Tor (+5)		
6/6	49	@ Mil	L	1-5	26-23	4	−8	Tor (+5½)	**Darwin**-Whitson	15,452
6/7	50	@ Mil	W	9-10	26-24	4	−9	Tor (+6½)	Searge-Righetti	24,463
6/8	51	@ Mil	W	2-1	27-24	4	−8	Tor (+6½)	Righetti-Gibson	40,913
6/9	52	@ Mil	L	4-9	27-25	5	−8	Tor (+6½)	Vuckovich-Niekro	44,621
6/10	53	TOR	W	4-2	28-25	5	−7	Tor (+5½)	Shirley-Alexander	20,329
6/11	54	TOR	L	1-4	28-26	5	−8	Tor (+6)	Lamp-Fisher	22,620
6/12	55	TOR	L	2-3	28-27	5	−9	Tor (+6)	Acker-Bordi	25,129
6/13		OFF DAY				5	−8½	Tor (+5½)		
6/14	56	DET	L	0-4	28-28	5	−8½	Tor (+5½)	Terrell-Rasmussen	35,224
6/15	57	DET	L	8-10	28-29	5	−8½	Tor (+3½)	Morris-Niekro	55,623*
6/16	58	DET	W	2-1	29-29	5	−7½	Tor (+3½)	**Shirley**-O'Neal	36,036
6/17	59	@ Bal	W	10-0	30-29	5	−6½	Tor (+2½)	**Guidry**-McGregor	34,844
6/18	60	@ Bal	W	6-4	31-29	5	−5½	Tor (+2½)	Cowley-Davis	33,794
6/19	61	@ Bal	W	10-0	32-29	5	−5½	Tor (+2½)	**Whitson**-Martinez	37,470
6/20	62	@ Det	L	9-10	32-30	5	−6½	Tor (+2½)	Bair-Righetti	36,565
6/21	63	@ Det	L	4-6	32-31	5	−7½	Tor (+2½)	O'Neal-Niekro	47,499
6/22	64	@ Det	W	4-0	33-31	5	−6½	Tor (+2½)	**Guidry**-Petry	41,774
6/23	65	@ Det	L	1-3	33-32	5	−7½	Tor (+2½)	Tanana-Shirley	40,929
6/24	66	BAL	W	5-4	34-32	5	−7	Tor (+3)	Cowley-Martinez	25,201
6/25	67	BAL	W	7-4	35-32	4 (T)	−7	Tor (+3)	Whitson-Boddicker	30,650
6/26	68	BAL	W	4-3	36-32	3 (T)	−6	Tor (+2)	Righetti-McGregor	30,929
6/27		OFF DAY				3 (T)	−6½	Tor (+2½)		
6/28	69	MIL	W	5-2	37-32	3 (T)	−6½	Tor (+2½)	Guidry-**Darwin**	21,649
6/29	70	MIL	L	0-6	37-33	3 (T)	−6½	Tor (+2½)	**Haas**-Niekro	25,369
6/30	71	MIL	L	5-7	37-34	3 (T)	−7½	Tor (+2½)	McClure-Fisher	51,459
7/1	72	@ Tor	W	4-1	38-34	3	−6½	Tor (+2½)	Cowley-Alexander	41,476
7/2	73	@ Tor	W	5-3	39-34	3	−5½	Tor (+2½)	Whitson-Key	35,202
7/3	74	@ Tor	L	2-3	39-35	3	−6½	Tor (+2½)	Acker-Bordi	40,376
7/4	75	MIN	W	3-2	40-35	3	−5½	Tor (+2½)	**Guidry**-Butcher	35,110
7/5	76	MIN	W	6-3	41-35	3	−5½	Tor (+3)	Rasmussen-Schrom	26,046
7/6		PPD-RAIN				3	−5	Tor (+2½)		
7/7(1)	77	MIN	W	3-2	42-35				Righetti-Wardle	
7/7(2)	78	MIN	W	14-2	43-35	3	−4½	Tor (+2½)	Bordi-Lysander	31,549
7/8	79	KC	L	2-5	43-36	3	−5½	Tor (+3½)	**Saberhagen**-**Niekro**	17,193
7/9	80	KC	W	6-4	44-36	3	−5½	Tor (+3½)	Guidry-Black	24,528

14

Date	Game No.	Opponent	W-L	Score	Rec'd	Pos	G A/B	League Leader & Lead	Winning-Losing Pitchers	Paid Attend.
7/10	81	KC	W	6-5	45-36	3	-5½	Tor (+3½)	Righetti-Quisenberry	35,274
7/11	82	TEX	W	11-7	46-36	3	-5½	Tor (+4½)	Shirley-Cook	21,863
7/12	83	TEX	W	6-0	47-36	2 (T)	-4½	Tor (+4½)	**Whitson**-Sebra	21,832
7/13	84	TEX	W	3-1	48-36	2	-3½	Tor (+3½)	Niekro-Mason	45,274
7/14	85	TEX	W	7-1	49-36	2	-2½	Tor (+2½)	**Guidry**-Hooton	28,168
7/16		ALL-STAR GAME: NL-6, AL-1								
7/18	86	@ Min	L	4-8	49-37	2	-2½	Tor (+2½)	Eufemia-Bordi	43,018
7/19	87	@ Min	W	6-4	50-37	2	-2½	Tor (+2½)	Cowley-Butcher	37,687
7/20	88	@ Min	W	8-3	51-37	2	-1½	Tor (+1½)	**Guidry**-Schrom	37,919
7/21	89	@ Min	W	5-2	52-37	2	-1½	Tor (+1½)	**Niekro**-Viola	30,387
7/22	90	@ KC	L	4-5	52-38	2	-2½	Tor (+2½)	Jones-Rasmussen	40,938
7/23	91	@ KC	L	2-5	52-39	2	-3½	Tor (+3½)	Saberhagen-Whitson	32,450
7/24	92	@ KC	L	3-5	52-40	2	-4½	Tor (+4½)	Liebrandt-Cowley	31,580
7/25		OFF DAY				2	-5	Tor (+5)		
7/26	93	@ Tex	L	8-9	52-41	2	-6	Tor (+6)	Noles-Righetti	30,069
7/27	94	@ Tex	W	14-2	53-41	2	-6	Tor (+6)	Niekro-Cook	40,084
7/28	95	@ Tex	L	2-8	53-42	2	-7	Tor (+7)	Welsh-Bystrom	22,523
7/29	96	@ Cle	W	8-2	54-42	2	-7	Tor (+7)	Whitson-Blyleven	15,042
7/30(1)	97	@ Cle	W	8-5	55-42	2			Cowley-Thompson	
7/30(2)	98	@ Cle	L	2-3	55-43	2	-6½	Tor (+6½)	Romero-Shirley	18,271
7/31	99	@ Cle	L	5-6	55-44	2	-7½	Tor (+7½)	Waddell-Guidry	7,593
8/1	100	@ Cle	L	1-9	55-45	2	-8½	Tor (+8½)	**Smith**-Niekro	8,294
8/2	101	CHI	L	5-6	55-46	2	-9½	Tor (+9½)	Agosto-Bordi	27,118
8/3	102	CHI	W	8-4	56-46	2	-9½	Tor (+9½)	Whitson-Long	37,226
8/4	103	CHI	L	1-4	56-47	2 (T)	-9½	Tor (+9½)	Seaver-Cowley	54,032
8/5	104	CHI	W	7-3	57-47	2 (T)	-9	Tor (+9)	**Guidry**-Bannister	28,320
		STRIKE								
8/8(1)	105	CLE	W	8-1	58-47	2			Bystrom-Wardle	
8/8(2)	106	CLE	W	7-6	59-47	2	-9	Tor (+9)	Fisher-Reed	25,692
8/9	107	@ Bos	W	10-6	60-47	2	-8	Tor (+8)	Bordi-Hurst	33,767
8/10	108	@ Bos	W	7-3	61-47	2	-7	Tor (+7)	Cowley-Boyd	33,009
8/11	109	@ Bos	W	5-3	62-47	2	-7	Tor (+7)	Guidry-Clemens	33,685
8/12	110	@ Chi	W	10-4	63-47	2	-6	Tor (+6)	**Niekro**-Nelson	28,801
8/13	111	@ Chi	L	3-4	63-48	2	-7	Tor (+7)	Burns-Fisher	18,294
8/14	112	@ Chi	W	10-7	64-48	2	-7	Tor (+7)	Fisher-James	21,184
8/15		OFF DAY				2	-7	Tor (+7)		
8/16	113	BOS	W	5-4	65-48	2	-6	Tor (+6)	Righetti-Crawford	42,787
8/17	114	BOS	W	3-1	66-48	2	-5	Tor (+5)	Guidry-Nipper	40,179
8/18	115	BOS	W	4-2	67-48	2	-5	Tor (+5)	Righetti-Lollar	44,170
8/19	116	BOS	W	6-5	68-48	2	-4	Tor (+4)	Bystrom-Clear	38,164
8/20	117	@ Cal	W	8-5	69-48	2	-4	Tor (+4)	Bordi-Slaton	38,791
8/21	118	@ Cal	W	13-10	70-48	2	-3	Tor (+3)	Righetti-Moore	40,363
8/22	119	@ Cal	L	2-3	70-49	2	-3½	Tor (+3½)	**Witt**-Bordi	44,796
8/23	120	@ Sea	W	3-1	71-49	2	-4	Tor (+4)	Niekro-Swift	18,821
8/24	121	@ Sea	W	4-3	72-49	2	-4	Tor (+4)	Bystrom-Langston	21,489
8/25	122	@ Sea	W	8-5	73-49	2	-3	Tor (+3)	Whitson-Moore	26,678
8/26	123	@ Oak	L	2-3	73-50	2	-4	Tor (+4)	Langford-Shirley	42,118
8/27	124	@ Oak	L	0-3		2	-5	Tor (+5)	John-**Guidry**	24,555
8/28		OFF DAY			73-51	4	-4½	Tor (+4½)		
8/29	125	CAL	W	4-0	74-51	2	-4	Tor (+4)	Niekro-**McCaskill**	32,169
8/30	126	CAL	L	1-4	74-52	2	-5	Tor (+5)	Candelaria-Bystrom	22,256
8/31	127	CAL	W	10-4	75-52	2	-5	Tor (+5)	Righetti-Corbett	26,991
9/1	128	CAL	W	5-3	76-52	2	-4	Tor (+4)	Shirley-Holland	33,080
9/2	129	SEA	W	8-7	77-52	2	-4	Tor (+4)	Guidry-Wills	26,427
9/3	130	SEA	W	6-3	78-52	2	-3½	Tor (+3½)	Niekro-Swift	17,255
9/4	131	SEA	W	4-3	79-52	2	-2½	Tor (+2½)	Bordi-Langston	21,605
9/5	132	OAK	W	7-3	80-52	2	-2½	Tor (+2½)	Whitson-Birtsas	20,594
9/6	133	OAK	W	8-4	81-52	2	-2½	Tor (+2½)	Shirley-Codiroli	22,519
9/7	134	OAK	W	3-2	82-52	2	-1½	Tor (+1½)	Guidry-John	25,539
9/8	135	OAK	W	9-6	83-52	2	-1½	Tor (+1½)	Niekro-Rijo	26,809
9/9	136	@ Milw	W	9-4	84-52	2	-1½	Tor (+1½)	Righetti-Searage	7,176
9/10	137	@ Milw	W	13-10	85-52	2	-1½	Tor (+1½)	Whitson-Burris	7,971
9/11	138	@ Milw	L	3-4	85-53	2	-2½	Tor (+2½)	**Higuera**-Bordi	8,540
9/12	139	TOR	W	7-5	86-53	2	-1½	Tor (+1½)	Guidry-Lavelle	52,141
9/13	140	TOR	L	2-3	86-54	2	-2½	Tor (+2½)	Lavelle-**Niekro**	53,303
9/14	141	TOR	l	4-7	86-55	2	-3½	Tor (+3½)	**Key**-Bordi	54,367
9/15	142	TOR	L	5-8	86-56	2	-4½	Tor (+4½)	Alexander-Whitson	54,699
9/16	143	CLEV	L	5-9	86-57	2	-5	Tor (+5)	Reed-Fisher	15,320
9/17	144	@ Det	L	1-9	86-58	2	-5	Tor (+5)	Petry-Guidry	20,213
9/18	145	@ Det	L	2-5	86-59	2	-5	Tor (+5)	Mahler-**Niekro**	20,318
9/19	146	@ Det	L	3-10	86-60	2	-5½	Tor (+5½)	Tanana-J. Niekro	19,588
9/20	147	@ Balt	L	2-4	86-61	2	-6½	Tor (+6½)	Flanagan-Bordi	33,957
9/21	148	@ Balt	W	5-2	87-61	2	-6½	Tor (+6½)	Cowley-Davis	33,873
9/22	149	@ Balt	W	5-4	88-61	2	-5½	Tor (+5½)	Guidry-Dixon	33,045
9/23		OFF DAY				2	-6	Tor (+6)		
9/24	150	DET	L	1-9	88-62	2	-7	Tor (+7)	Tanana-Niekro	16,702
9/25	151	DET	W	10-2	89-62	2	-6	Tor (+6)	J. Niekro-Morris	17,010
9/26		PPD-RAIN				2	-5½	Tor (+5½)		
9/26		PPD-HURRICANE GLORIA				2	-6	Tor (+6)		
9/28	152	BALT	W	6-5	90-62	2	-6	Tor (+6)	**Guidry**-Stewart	30,486
9/29(1)	153	BALT	W	4-0	91-62	2			Cowley-McGregor	
9/29(2)	154	BALT	W	9-2	92-62	2	-5½	Tor (+5½)	Bordi-Havens	30,291
9/30	155	BALT	W	5-4	93-62	2	-5	Tor (+5)	Allen-Ase	15,041
10/1	156	MILW	W	6-1	94-62	2	-4	Tor (+4)	J. Niekro-Cocanower	15,101
10/2	157	MILW	L	0-1	94-63	2	-4	Tor (+4)	**Higuera**-Shirley	11,879
10/3	158	MILW	W	3-0	95-63	2	-3	Tor (+3)	Guidry-Leary	15,226
10/4	159	@ Tor	W	4-3	96-63	2	-2	Tor (+2)	Scurry-Henke	47,686
10/5	160	@ Tor	L	1-5	96-64	2	-3	Tor (+3)	**Alexander**-Cowley	44,608
10/6	161	@ Tor	W	8-0	97-64	2	-2	Tor (+2)	**Niekro**-Cerutti	44,422

BOLD FACE denotes complete game.
Niekro Denotes Phil Niekro
J. Niekro Denotes Joe Niekro

DID YOU KNOW ... that the 1941 Yankees clinched the pennant with 18 games remaining on the schedule and that September 4th is still the major league record for earliest clinching date?

15

YANKEE FINAL OFFICIAL STATISTICS—1985

Batter	AVG	G	AB	R	H	2B	3B	HR	RBI	GW RBI	SH	SF	HB	BB	SO	SB	CS	E
Baylor	.231	142	477	70	110	24	1	23	91	10	1	10	24	52	90	0	4	0
Berra	.229	48	109	8	25	5	1	1	8	1	2	0	0	7	20	1	1	9
Bonilla	.125	8	16	0	2	1	0	1	2	0	0	0	0	0	3	0	0	1
Bradley	.163	19	49	4	8	2	1	0	1	0	0	0	1	1	5	0	0	1
Cotto	.304	34	56	4	17	1	0	1	6	0	1	0	0	3	12	1	1	1
Espino	.364	9	11	0	4	0	0	0	0	0	0	0	0	0	0	0	0	0
Griffey	.274	127	438	68	120	28	4	10	69	6	0	8	0	41	51	7	7	7
Hassey	.296	92	267	31	79	16	1	13	42	6	0	0	3	28	21	0	0	6
Henderson	.314	143	547	146	172	28	5	24	72	6	0	5	3	99	65	80	10	9
Hudler	.157	20	51	4	8	0	1	0	1	0	5	0	0	1	9	0	1	2
Mata	.143	6	7	1	1	0	0	0	0	0	0	0	0	0	0	0	0	0
Mattingly	.324	159	652	107	211	48	3	35	145	21	2	15	2	56	41	2	2	7
Meacham L	.228		302	49	69	10	2	1	33	0	14	3	2	34	61	17	5	11
Meacham R	.201		179	21	36	6	0	0	14	3	9	0	3	20	41	8	2	13
Meacham T	.218	156	481	70	105	16	2	1	47	3	23	3	5	54	102	25	7	24
Moreno	.197	34	66	12	13	4	1	1	4	0	1	0	0	1	16	1	1	0
Pagliarulo	.239	138	380	55	91	16	2	19	62	5	3	3	4	45	86	0	0	13
Pasqua	.209	60	148	17	31	3	1	9	25	1	0	1	1	16	38	0	0	0
Randolph	.276	143	497	75	137	21	2	5	40	6	5	6	4	85	39	16	9	11
Robertson	.328	50	125	16	41	5	0	2	17	0	2	2	1	6	24	1	2	10
Sample	.288	59	139	18	40	5	0	1	15	0	2	2	2	9	10	2	1	1
Smith L	.000		0	1	0	0	0	0	0	0	0	0	0	0	0	0	0	0
Smith T	.000	4	0	1	0	0	0	0	0	0	0	0	0	0	0	0	0	0
Winfield	.275	155	633	105	174	34	6	26	114	19	0	4	0	52	96	19	7	3
Wynegar L	.233		172	13	40	7	0	3	21	2	0	0	0	33	19	0	0	1
Wynegar R	.212		137	14	29	8	0	2	11	1	1	1	0	31	24	0	0	5
Wynegar T	.223	102	309	27	69	15	0	5	32	3	1	1	0	64	43	0	0	6
DH Hitters	.232		596	88	138	28	2	28	111	12	1	10	26	59	110	0	4	0
PH Hitters	.223		130	15	29	1	1	4	15	1	0	3	1	16	22	0	0	0
Pitchers	.000		0	0	0	0	0	0	0	0	0	0	0	0	0	0	0	14
TOTALS	**.267**		**5458**	**839**	**1458**	**272**	**31**	**176**	**793**	**87**	**48**	**60**	**50**	**620**	**771**	**155**	**53**	**125**

Pitcher		W L	ERA	G	GS	CG	SHO	SV	IP	H	R	ER	HR	HB	BB	SO	WP
Allen	R	1- 0	2.76	17	0	0	0	1	29.1	26	9	9	1	0	13	16	2
Armstrong	R	0- 0	3.07	9	0	0	0	0	14.2	9	5	5	4	0	2	11	1
Bordi	R	6- 8	3.21	51	3	0	0	2	98.0	95	41	35	5	1	29	64	1
Bystrom	R	3- 2	5.71	8	8	0	0	0	41.0	44	29	26	8	1	19	14	1
Cooper	R	0- 0	5.40	7	0	0	0	0	10.0	12	6	6	2	0	4	3	1
Cowley	R	12- 6	3.95	30	26	1	0	0	159.2	132	75	70	29	6	85	97	5
Fisher	R	4- 4	2.38	55	0	0	0	14	98.1	77	32	26	4	0	29	85	3
Guidry	R	22- 6	3.27	34	33	11	2	0	259.0	243	104	94	28	0	42	143	3
Montefusco	R	0- 0	10.29	3	1	0	0	0	7.0	12	8	8	3	0	2	2	0
Murray	R	0- 0	13.50	3	0	0	0	0	2.0	4	3	3	0	0	0	0	1
Niekro, J	R	2- 1	5.84	3	3	0	0	0	12.1	14	8	8	3	0	8	4	0
Niekro, P	R	16-12	4.09	33	33	7	1	0	220.0	203	110	100	29	2	120	149	5
Rasmussen	L	3- 5	3.98	22	16	2	0	0	101.2	97	56	45	10	1	42	63	3
Righetti	L	12- 7	2.78	74	0	0	0	29	107.0	96	36	33	5	0	45	92	7
Scurry	L	1- 0	2.84	5	0	0	0	1	12.2	5	4	4	2	0	10	17	0
Shirley	L	5- 5	2.64	48	8	2	0	2	109.0	103	34	32	5	0	26	55	1
Whitson	R	10- 8	4.88	30	30	2	2	0	158.2	201	100	86	19	2	43	89	1
TOTALS		**97-64**	**3.69**	**432**	**161**	**25**	**9**	**49**	**1440.1**	**1373**	**660**	**590**	**157**	**13**	**518**	**907**	**34**

DESIGNATED HITTERS—1985

Batter	AVG	G	AB	R	H	2B	3B	HR	RBI	GW RBI	SH	SF	HB	BB	SO	SB	CS
Baylor	.232	140	475	70	110	24	1	23	91	10	1	10	24	6	89	0	4
Bradley	.226	9	31	3	7	2	0	0	1	0	0	0	1	1	4	0	0
Griffey	.250	7	28	5	7	0	0	0	5	1	0	0	0	1	3	0	0
Hassey	1.000	2	6	1	6	1	0	0	4	0	0	0	0	0	0	0	0
Henderson	.000	1	4	0	0	0	0	0	0	0	0	0	0	0	2	0	0
Moreno	.000	1	0	1	0	0	0	0	0	0	0	0	0	0	0	0	0
Pasqua	.114	14	44	6	5	0	1	3	7	0	0	0	1	4	12	0	0
Winfield	.375	2	8	2	3	1	0	2	3	1	0	0	0	1	2	0	0
TOTALS	**.232**	**161**	**596**	**88**	**138**	**28**	**2**	**28**	**111**	**12**	**1**	**10**	**26**	**59**	**110**	**0**	**4**

YANKEES HOME AND AWAY—1985

Vs. A.L. East	Home W-L	Road W-L	Total W-L	Vs. A.L. West	Home W-L	Road W-L	Total W-L
Baltimore	7-0	5-1	12-1	California	5-1	4-2	9-3
Boston	5-2	3-3	8-5	Chicago	4-2	2-4	6-6
Cleveland	3-3	4-3	7-6	Kansas City	5-1	2-4	7-5
Detroit	2-3	1-6	3-9	Minnesota	6-0	3-3	9-3
Milwaukee	3-3	3-4	6-7	Oakland	5-1	2-4	7-5
Toronto	2-5	4-2	6-7	Seattle	5-1	4-2	9-3
				Texas	6-0	2-4	8-4
Totals vs. East	**22-16**	**20-19**	**42-35**	**Total vs. West**	**36-6**	**19-23**	**55-29**
				Grand Totals	**58-22**	**39-42**	**97-64**

DID YOU KNOW ... that the 1932 Yankees were never shutout?

DID YOU KNOW ... that Solly Hofman, who played 6 games for the Yankees in 1916, is the uncle of Bobby Hofman, who is the Yankees' Director of Player Development? Bobby Hofman was a major leaguer himself playing for the New York Giants in 1949, and 1952-57.

16

RELIEF PITCHING—1985

Pitcher	GR	W-L	SV	Pitcher	GR	W-L	SV
Allen	17	1-0	1	Montefusco	2	0-0	0
Armstrong	9	0-0	0	Murray	3	0-0	0
Bordi	48	4-7	2	Rasmussen	6	0-0	0
Cooper	7	0-0	0	Righetti	74	12-7	29
Cowley	4	1-0	0	Scurry	5	1-0	1
Fisher	55	4-4	14	Shirley	40	3-2	2
Guidry	1	0-0	0				
				Totals	**271**	**26-20**	**49**

GR: Games Relieved

PINCH HITTERS—1985

Batter	AVG	G	AB	R	H	2B	3B	HR	RBI	GW RBI	SH	SF	HB	BB	SO	SB	CS
Baylor	.385	16	13	3	5	1	0	2	6	1	0	0	1	2	1	0	0
Berra	.286	7	7	0	2	0	0	0	1	0	0	0	0	0	1	0	0
Bonilla	.000	2	2	0	0	0	0	0	0	0	0	0	0	0	1	0	0
Bradley	.143	7	7	1	1	0	1	0	0	0	0	0	0	0	1	0	0
Cotto	.250	4	4	0	1	0	0	0	0	0	0	0	0	0	1	0	0
Griffey	.111	24	18	2	2	0	0	1	2	0	0	1	0	5	1	0	0
Hassey	.250	23	20	0	5	0	0	0	0	0	0	0	0	2	2	0	0
Henderson	.000	1	1	0	0	0	0	0	0	0	0	0	0	0	0	0	0
Mata	.000	2	2	0	0	0	0	0	0	0	0	0	0	0	0	0	0
Moreno	.000	7	7	0	0	0	0	0	0	0	0	0	0	0	2	0	0
Pagliarulo	.278	22	18	4	5	0	0	0	1	0	0	1	0	3	4	0	0
Pasqua	.133	19	15	1	2	0	0	0	1	0	0	1	0	3	6	0	0
Robertson	.000	2	2	0	0	0	0	0	0	0	0	0	0	0	1	0	0
Sample	.400	5	5	1	2	0	0	0	2	0	0	0	0	0	0	0	0
Winfield	1.000	1	1	0	1	0	0	0	0	0	0	0	0	0	0	0	0
Wynegar	.375	9	8	3	3	0	0	1	2	0	0	0	0	1	1	0	0
TOTALS	**.223**	**157**	**130**	**15**	**29**	**1**	**1**	**4**	**15**	**1**	**0**	**3**	**1**	**16**	**22**	**0**	**0**

YANKEES MISCELLANEOUS FIGURES—1985

Home Games	Won 58, Lost 22
Road Games	Won 39, Lost 42
Night Games	Won 60, Lost 44
Day Games	Won 37, Lost 20
Doubleheaders	Won 3, Lost 0, Split 1
Extra Inning Games	Won 6, Lost 10
One Run Games	Won 24, Lost 23
Two Run Games	Won 13, Lost 14
Winning Streak	11 Games, 8/31—9/10
Losing Streak	8 Games, 9/13—9/20
Shutouts	Won 9, Lost 6
Most Runs, Game	14, July 7 (2nd G) @ Minn, July 27 @ Tex
Most Hits, Game	19, May 26 @ Oak, Aug 9 @ Bos
Most Home Runs, Game	5, July 27 @ Tex, Aug 20 @ Cal
Most Runs, Inning	9, May 11 @ KC, 4th inning
Most Hits, Inning	7, Aug 12 @ Chgo, 7th inning
Most Home Runs, Inning	3, July 7 (2nd G) vs Minn, 3rd inning
Longest Hitting Streak	20, Don Mattingly
Double Plays	Yankees 172, Opponents 158
Errors	Yankees 125, Opponents 134
Vs Righthanders (Decisions)	Won 65, Lost 37
Vs Lefthanders (Decisions)	Won 32, Lost 27
Vs Righthanders (Starters)	Won 57, Lost 39
Vs Lefthanders (Starters)	Won 40, Lost 25
Complete Games	Yankees 25, Opponents 17
Left on Base	Yankees 1125, Opponents 1084
Home Runs (Home-Road-Total)	Yankees 92-84-176, Opponents 67-90-157
Stolen Bases-Caught Stealing	Yankees 155-53, Opponents 106-45
Longest Game (Innings)	15, Aug 26 @ Oak
Longest Game Time (9 innings)	3:38, Aug 14 @ Cal
Longest Game Time (extra innings)	5:02, Aug 26 @ Oak
Shortest Game Time	2:02, July 12 vs Tex
Most Home Runs, Game	2, 16 Times
Most RBI, Game	6, Griffey, Winfield
Most Hits, Game	5, Henderson, June 17 @ Balt
Low Hit Game by Yankees	3, 6 times
Low Hit Game by Opponents	1, vs Milw, June 29, Haas
Largest Victory Margin	12, 3 times
Largest Loss Margin	9, April 10 @ Bos
Managerial Records	Yogi Berra (through Apr 28), 6-10
	Billy Martin, 91-54

MONTH BY MONTH—1985

Month	W-L
April	6-12
May	18-8
June	13-14
July	18-10
August	20-8
September	18-10
October	4-2

1985 FIELDING STATISTICS

Catchers	PCT.	G	PO	A	E	TC	DP
Bradley	.923	3	12	0	1	13	0
Espino	1.000	9	16	4	0	20	0
Hassey	.984	69	402	20	7	429	2
Wynegar	.990	96	547	34	6	587	7

PASSED BALLS: Hassey (15); Wynegar (3).

1st Basemen	PCT.	G	PO	A	E	TC	DP
Griffey	1.000	1	5	0	0	5	0
Hassey	1.000	2	18	0	0	18	2
Hudler	1.000	1	6	0	0	6	2
Mattingly	.995	159	1318	87	7	1412	154

2nd Basemen	PCT.	G	PO	A	E	TC	DP
Bonilla	.955	7	7	14	1	22	3
Hudler	.977	16	36	50	2	88	12
Randolph	.985	143	303	425	11	739	104
Robertson	1.000	2	5	4	0	9	2

3rd Basemen	PCT.	G	PO	A	E	TC	DP
Berra	.917	41	20	68	8	96	9
Pagliarulo	.951	134	67	187	13	267	15
Robertson	.867	33	11	41	8	60	6

Shortstops	PCT.	G	PO	A	E	TC	DP
Berra	.889	6	2	6	1	9	0
Hudler	1.000	1	0	1	0	1	0
Meacham	.963	155	236	390	24	650	103
Robertson	.950	14	16	22	2	40	8
Smith	1.000	3	0	1	0	1	0

Outfielders	PCT.	G	PO	A	E	TC	DP
Cotto	.977	30	41	2	1	44	0
Griffey	.970	110	222	8	7	237	3
Henderson	.980	141	439	7	9	455	3
Mata	1.000	3	1	0	0	1	0
Moreno	1.000	26	56	2	0	58	0
Pasqua	1.000	37	72	2	0	74	0
Sample	.989	55	89	1	1	91	0
Winfield	.991	152	316	13	3	332	3

Pitchers	PCT.	G	PO	A	E	TC	DP
Allen	1.000	17	3	3	0	6	0
Armstrong	1.000	9	1	1	0	2	0
Bordi	.933	51	2	12	1	15	1
Bystrom	.909	8	1	9	1	11	0
Cooper	.000	7	0	0	0	0	0
Cowley	.903	30	6	22	3	31	1
Fisher	.944	55	4	13	1	18	1
Guidry	.976	34	6	34	1	41	3
Montefusco	1.000	3	1	1	0	2	0
Murray	.000	3	0	0	0	0	0
Niekro, J	1.000	3	3	2	0	5	0
Niedro, P	1.000	33	11	20	0	31	5
Rasmussen	1.000	22	7	13	0	20	2
Righetti	.929	74	1	12	1	14	2
Scurry	1.000	5	0	1	0	1	0
Shirley	.864	48	4	15	3	22	1
Whitson	.889	30	8	16	3	27	3

YANKEES WHO LED LEAGUE IN FIELDING

1B—Ganzel (1903), Pipp (1915, 1924), Skowron (1958), Pepitone (1965-66, 1969), Chambliss (1978), Mattingly (1984-85)

2B—Ward (1923), Stirnweiss (1944, 1948), Coleman (1949), McDougald (1955), Clarke (1967), Alomar (1975)

SS—Scott (1922-23). Crosetti (1939), Rizzuto (1949-50), Dent (1980)

3B—Dugan (1923), Rolfe (1935-36)

OF—Cree (1913), Witt (1923), Byrd (1934), Selkirk (1939), DiMaggio (1947), Woodling (1952-53), Mantle (1959), Tresh (1964), White (1971)

C—Sweeney (1912), Dickey (1931, 1935, 1937, 1939, 1941), Berra (1957, 1959), Howard (1962, 1964), Munson (1971)

P—Howell (1903), Griffith (1906), Pennock (1924), Chandler (1938), Terry (1961), Ford (1965), Stottlemyre (1968)

YANKEES' HIGHEST FIELDING PERCENTAGE

(by position)

1b—Joe Pepitone	.997	(1965)		**c**—Elston Howard	.998	(1964)
Chris Chambliss	.997	(1978)		Thurman Munson	.998	(1971)
2b—Geo. Stirnweiss	.993	(1948)		**p**—George Mogridge	1.000	(1917)
3b—Graig Nettles	.975	(1978)		Leslie Bush	1.000	(1922)
ss—Fred Stanley	.983	(1976)		**(77 chances)**		
of—Roy White	1.000	(1971)				
(314 chances)						

YANKEE GOLD GLOVE WINNERS

1957	Bobby Shantz, p		1969	Joe Pepitone, 1b
1958	Bobby Shantz, p		1972	Bobby Murcer, of
	Norm Siebern, of		1973	Thurman Munson, c
1959	Bobby Shantz, p		1974	Thurman Munson, c
1960	Bobby Shantz, p		1975	Thurman Munson, c
	Roger Maris, of		1977	Graig Nettles, 3b
1961	Bobby Richardson, 2b		1978	Chris Chambliss, 1b
1962	Bobby Richardson, 2b			Graig Nettles, 3b
	Mickey Mantle, of		1982	Ron Guidry, p
1963	Elston Howard, c			Dave Winfield, of
	Bobby Richardson, 2b		1983	Ron Guidry, p
1964	Elston Howard, c			Dave Winfield, of
	Bobby Richardson, 2b		1984	Ron Guidry, p
1965	Joe Pepitone, 1b			Dave Winfield, of
	Bobby Richardson, 2b		1985	Ron Guidry, p
	Tom Tresh, of			Don Mattingly, 1b
1966	Joe Pepitone, 1b			Dave Winfield, of

RECENT YANKEE STATISTICS

	Runs	Hits	HR	SB	AVG.	ERA	W-L	CG	SO
1976	730	1496	120	163	.269	3.19	97-62	62	674
1977	831	1576	184	93	.281	3.61	100-62	52	758
1978	735	1489	125	98	.267	3.18	100-63	39	817
1979	734	1443	150	63	.266	3.83	89-71	43	731
1980	820	1484	189	86	.267	3.59	103-59	29	845
1981	421	889	100	46	.252	2.90	59-48	16	606
1982	709	1417	161	69	.256	3.99	79-83	24	939
1983	770	1535	153	84	.273	3.86	91-71	47	892
1984	758	1560	130	62	.276	3.78	87-75	15	673
1985	839	1458	176	155	.267	3.69	94-67	25	907

RECENT YEARLY SERIES RESULTS VS. AMERICAN LEAGUE OPPONENTS

Year	Bal	Bos	Cle	Det	Mil	Tor	Cal	Chi	KC	Min	Oak	Sea	Tex
1976	5-13	11-7	12-4	8-9	13-5	—	7-5	11-1	5-7	10-2	6-6	—	9-3
1977	7-8	7-8	12-3	9-6	7-8	9-6	7-4	7-3	5-5	8-2	9-2	6-4	7-3
1978	9-6	9-7	9-6	11-4	5-10	11-4	5-5	9-1	5-6	7-3	8-2	6-5	6-4
1979	6-5	8-5	8-5	6-7	4-9	9-4	5-7	8-4	7-5	5-7	9-3	6-6	8-4
1980	6-7	10-3	8-5	8-5	8-5	10-3	10-2	7-5	4-8	8-4	8-4	9-3	7-5
1981	6-7	3-3	5-7	7-3	3-3	2-3	2-2	7-5	10-2	3-3	4-3	2-3	5-4
1982	2-11	6-7	9-4	5-8	5-8	6-7	5-7	4-8	7-5	10-2	7-5	6-6	7-5
1983	7-6	6-7	7-6	8-5	9-4	7-6	7-5	4-8	6-6	8-4	8-4	7-5	7-5
1984	8-5	6-7	11-2	6-7	7-6	8-5	4-8	5-7	7-5	4-8	8-4	7-5	6-6
1985	12-1	8-5	7-6	3-9	6-7	6-7	9-3	6-6	7-5	9-3	7-5	9-3	8-4

YANKEE ATTENDANCE MARKS

HOME ATTENDANCE: 1985 was the 48th year the Yankees have drawn more than one million.

ROAD ATTENDANCE: The Yankees have drawn over one million on the road for 40 consecutive years, including a Major League record 2,461,240 in 1980.

1985 YANKEES ...

... extended major league record for most years, 100 or more home runs, club, 60 ... extended American League record for most games won, club—7,303.

YANKEES ON THE AIR

Yankee baseball will be broadcast for the 48th consecutive year in 1986. WPIX-TV, 11 Alive, will be the New York City television station for the 36th straight season. WABC, Talkradio 77 AM, is leading the Yankee radio network as the flagship station for the sixth straight season. A network covering 12 states also participates in the Yankees TV and radio coverage. SportsChannel is the Yankee pay cable television carrier for the eighth consecutive season in the tri-state area. And Yankee games will be broadcast in Latin America by Vene International Productions for the 17th straight season.

PHIL RIZZUTO, the greatest shortstop in Yankee history, is in his 30th season as a Yankee broadcaster. The 1950 American League MVP moved to the broadcast booth immediately following his playing career (1941-1956) in 1957. BILL WHITE, former star first baseman with the Giants, Cardinals and Phillies (1956-69), who played in 6 All-Star Games and won 7 Gold Gloves, is now in his 16th season with the Yankees.

Joining Phil and Bill in the WPIX booth this year will be newcomer JIM KAAT. Kaat, former big leaguer who pitched in four decades, 1959-1983, has recent broadcast experience with NBC, ESPN and Home Team Sports in Washington, DC. BILLY MARTIN, former Yankee player and manager, will also work some of the WPIX telecasts, handling pre and post-game chores.

In the radio booth for WABC, Rizzuto and White will be joined by BOBBY MURCER and SPENCER ROSS. Bobby Murcer, former Yankee star outfielder, returns to the booth for his second season of broadcasting following a year in the Yankee front office as Assistant Vice President. Veteran Spencer Ross moves to the radio booth this season after joining the Yankee broadcast team in the TV booth last year. JOHN GORDON, the Yankees Director of Television and Radio Relations, is in his 5th year with the Yankees and will handle the pre and post game shows for WABC.

On SportsChannel, the "Voice of the Yankees," MEL ALLEN is back for his 8th season on cable and is joined for a second year by Yankee great, MICKEY MANTLE. Allen and Mantle give SportsChannel a Hall of Fame broadcast crew. Mel, who broadcast Yankee games from 1939 to 1964, was inducted into the Baseball Hall of Fame in 1978 and Mickey, who won three MVP awards and hit 536 homers, was inducted into the Hall in 1974.

DID YOU KNOW ... that Lefty Gomez was 6-0 is World Series competition?

OPPOSING PITCHERS VS YANKEES
1985 AND LIFETIME
EASTERN DIVISION

BALTIMORE	1985	Lifetime vs NYY	M.L. Career
Aase	0-2	2-3	45-27
Bell	0-0	0-0	0-0
Boddicker	0-1	5-3	49-37
Bordi	0-0	0-0	11-14
Davis	0-2	1-5	45-28
Dixon	0-1	0-1	8-5
Flanagan	1-0	12-7	129-92
Habyan	0-0	0-0	1-0
Havens	0-1	1-5	18-29
Huffman	0-0	0-0	0-0
D. Martinez	0-2	2-9	108-93
T. Martinez	0-0	9-6	55-40
McGregor	0-2	6-11	125-83
Snell	0-0	1-0	4-3
Swaggerty	0-0	0-1	4-3

BOSTON	1985	Lifetime vs NYY	M.L. Career
Boyd	1-1	2-2	31-34
Brown	0-0	1-0	8-14
Clemens	1-1	1-1	16-9
Crawford	1-1	3-1	14-10
Dorsey	0-0	0-0	0-1
Gardner	0-0	0-0	1-3
Hurst	1-2	6-6	42-46
Kison	0-0	0-1	115-88
Lollar	0-1	0-1	45-52
McCarthy	0-0	0-0	0-0
Nipper	0-1	2-1	21-19
Schiraldi	0-0	0-0	2-3
Sellers	0-0	0-0	2-0
Stanley	0-0	5-3	94-70
Stewart	0-1	2-4	51-45
Trujillo	0-0	0-0	4-4
Woodward	0-0	0-0	1-0

CLEVELAND	1985	Lifetime vs NYY	M.L. Career
Barkley	0-0	0-0	0-3
Behenna	0-0	0-1	3-10
Camacho	0-0	0-1	5-12
Clark	0-0	3-2	18-23
Creel	0-0	0-0	2-5
Easterly	0-0	1-2	22-30
Heaton	1-0	3-2	32-41
Oelkers	0-0	0-0	0-5
Reed	1-1	2-1	4-5
Roman	0-1	0-1	0-6
Ruhle	0-0	4-2	66-85
Schultze	0-0	0-1	7-16
Schrom	0-2	1-2	31-31
Thompson	0-1	0-1	3-8
Von Ohlen	1-0	1-0	7-4
Waddell	1-1	1-2	15-10
Yett	0-0	0-0	0-0

DETROIT	1985	Lifetime vs NYY	M.L. Career
Cary	0-0	0-0	0-1
Hernandez	0-0	1-1	51-45
LaPoint	0-0	0-0	42-39
Lopez	0-0	4-2	57-32
Morris	1-1	8-6	123-86
O'Neal	1-1	1-2	7-6
Petry	1-1	6-4	93-64
Scherrer	0-0	0-0	7-7
Stoddard	0-0	0-1	16-24
Tanana	3-0	10-13	147-144
Terrell	1-0	1-0	34-33
Wilcox	0-0	4-12	119-105

MILWAUKEE	1985	Lifetime vs NYY	M.L. Career
Burris	0-1	1-2	102-127
Clear	0-1	5-3	57-39
Cocanower	0-1	0-2	16-24
Darwin	1-1	3-4	61-68
Fingers	0-0	6-2	114-117
Gibson	0-1	0-2	11-16
Haas	1-0	6-5	91-78
Higuera	2-0	2-0	15-8
Kern	0-0	2-3	51-56
Ladd	0-0	2-2	9-17
Leary	0-1	0-1	5-8
McClure	1-0	7-4	44-42
Porter	0-0	2-2	13-13
Searage	1-1	0-0	4-5
Vuckovich	1-0	2-2	91-65
Waits	0-0	9-12	79-92
Wegman	0-0	0-0	2-0

TORONTO	1985	Lifetime vs NYY	M.L. Career
Acker	2-0	2-1	15-8
Alexander	2-2	5-10	149-125
Caudill	0-0	3-3	33-48
Cerutti	0-1	0-1	0-2
Clancy	0-0	6-9	88-102
Clarke	0-0	0-0	1-1
Davis	0-0	0-0	2-1
Filer	0-0	0-0	8-2
Henke	0-1	0-1	6-4
Key	1-1	1-1	18-11
Lamp	1-0	3-2	72-70
Lavelle	1-1	1-1	78-74
Leal	0-0	4-4	51-58
Musselman	0-0	0-0	4-2
Stieb	0-0	5-8	95-80

TOP CAREER WINNING PERCENTAGE VS YANKEES
(Based on Ten Victories)

	W-L	PCT.		W-L	PCT.
Kerr, Chi	14-4	.778	**Flanagan, Balt**	**12-7**	**.632**
Ruth, Bos	17-5	.773	Hall, KC, Balt	12-7	.632
Bannister, Sea, Chi	**10-4**	**.714**	Hiller, Det	12-7	.632
Lee, Bos	12-5	.706	Rowe, Det	20-12	.625
Boland, Det, StL	16-7	.696	McLain, Det, Was.	15-9	.625
Lary, Det	28-13	.683	Cuellar, Balt	18-11	.621
Palmer, Balt	30-15	.659	**Caldwell, Milw**	**13-8**	**.619**
Marberry, Was, Det	22-11	.667	Kinder, StL, Bos	14-9	.609
Boswell, Min	10-5	.667	Barber, Balt	17-11	.607
Gura, KC	**11-6**	**.647**	Chance, Cal, Min	15-10	.600
Blue, Oak, KC	16-9	.640	Tiant, Cle, Min, Bos	22-15	.595

Boldface denotes active pitcher.

THIRTY CAREER WINS VS YANKEES

Johnson	60	S. Coveleski	32
Grove	35	Feller	30
Cicotte	35	Bender	30
Wynn	33	Mullin	30
Newhouser	33	Dauss	30
Faber	32	Palmer	30

OPPOSING PITCHERS VS YANKEES
1985 AND LIFETIME
WESTERN DIVISION

CALIFORNIA	1985	Lifetime vs NYY	M.L. Career
Candelaria	1-0	1-0	129-83
Clements	0-0	0-0	5-0
Cliburn	0-0	0-0	9-3
Corbett	0-1	2-1	20-26
Fowlkes	0-0	0-0	4-2
Holland	0-1	0-1	32-26
Lucas	0-0	0-0	24-38
Lugo	0-0	0-0	3-4
Mack	0-0	0-0	0-1
McCaskill	0-1	0-1	12-12
Moore	0-1	0-1	32-31
Romanick	0-1	1-3	26-21
Slaton	1-2	10-15	147-152
Smith	0-0	0-0	0-0
Sutton	0-0	2-1	295-228
Witt	1-1	2-3	53-49
Zahn	0-0	11-11	111-109

MINNESOTA	1985	Lifetime vs NYY	M.L. Career
Blyleven	0-2	10-13	212-183
Brown	0-0	0-1	1-2
Burtt	0-0	0-0	2-2
Butcher	0-2	0-5	35-41
Davis	0-1	1-4	44-44
Eufemia	1-0	1-0	4-2
Filson	0-0	2-0	14-23
Howe	0-0	0-0	25-27
Klawitter	0-0	0-0	0-0
Latham	0-0	0-0	0-0
Lysander	0-1	0-2	9-17
Mitchell	0-0	0-0	0-0
Portugal	0-0	0-0	1-3
Romero	1-0	1-0	2-3
Smith	1-0	1-1	6-9
Smithson	1-0	3-2	43-45
Viola	1-1	3-5	47-51
Wardle	0-3	0-3	8-9
Whitehouse	0-0	2-0	9-4

CHICAGO	1985	Lifetime vs NYY	M.L. Career
Agosto	1-0	1-0	8-6
Bannister	0-2	10-4	91-103
Cowley	0-0	0-0	22-10
Davis	0-0	0-0	3-3
Dotson	0-0	4-3	73-59
Fallon	0-0	0-0	0-0
Fireovid	0-0	0-0	0-1
Gleaton	0-0	0-3	6-10
James	0-1	0-2	15-16
Jones	0-0	0-0	2-1
Long	0-1	0-1	0-1
Nelson	1-1	1-4	22-28
Schmidt	1-1	1-2	20-22
Seaver	2-0	2-1	304-192
Spillner	0-1	1-6	75-89
Stanton	0-0	0-2	13-22
Tanner	0-0	0-0	1-2
Wehrmeister	0-0	0-0	4-9

OAKLAND	1985	Lifetime vs NYY	M.L. Career
Andujar	0-0	0-0	110-101
Atherton	0-1	1-1	13-18
Birtjas	1-0	1-0	10-6
Codiroli	0-3	1-4	33-32
Howell	2-0	2-0	23-20
John	1-2	10-16	259-207
Kaiser	0-0	0-0	0-0
Krueger	0-1	1-2	26-26
Langford	1-0	4-10	72-95
McCatty	0-0	1-7	63-63
Mura	0-0	0-0	1-1
Ontiveros	0-0	0-0	1-3
Rijo	0-1	0-1	8-12
Tellman	0-0	1-1	18-7
Warren	0-0	1-0	9-13
Young	0-0	0-0	9-9

SEATTLE	1985	Lifetime vs NYY	M.L. Career
Barojas	0-0	3-1	18-21
Beattie	1-0	3-9	52-81
Best	0-0	0-0	3-3
Geisel	0-0	0-0	5-5
Langston	0-4	1-6	24-24
Lazorko	0-0	0-0	0-1
Lewis	0-0	0-0	0-1
Long	0-0	0-0	0-0
Mirabella	0-0	0-2	11-24
Moore	0-1	0-2	37-49
Morgan	0-0	0-2	10-28
Nunez	1-0	1-0	10-11
Snyder	0-0	0-0	1-2
Stanton	0-0	0-2	13-22
Swift	0-2	0-2	6-10
Thomas	0-0	1-0	19-11
Tobik	0-0	3-1	14-23
Wilkinson	0-0	0-0	0-2
Wills	0-1	0-1	9-15
Young	1-1	4-2	29-42

KANSAS CITY	1985	Lifetime vs NYY	M.L. Career
Beckwith	0-0	0-0	18-19
Black	0-3	2-6	41-40
Farr	0-0	1-1	5-12
Ferreira	0-0	0-0	0-0
Gubicza	0-0	1-1	24-24
Gura	0-0	11-6	126-94
Huismann	0-0	0-0	6-4
Jackson	0-1	0-1	17-19
Jones	1-0	2-0	11-10
LaCoss	0-0	0-0	51-54
Leibrandt	1-2	2-3	44-33
Leonard	0-0	6-8	136-93
Quisenberry	1-1	4-2	44-35
Saberhagen	2-0	2-1	30-17

TEXAS	1985	Lifetime vs NYY	M.L. Career
Boggs	0-0	0-1	20-44
Cook	0-2	0-2	2-3
Correa	0-0	0-0	1-0
Guzman	0-0	0-0	3-2
Harris	0-0	0-0	5-4
Henry	0-0	0-0	2-2
Hooton	0-1	0-1	151-136
Hough	0-1	6-2	114-105
Mahler	1-0	1-0	31-28
Mason	0-1	1-2	18-32
Noles	2-0	3-0	27-44
Rozema	0-0	1-3	60-53
Russell	0-0	0-0	13-29
Surhoff	0-0	0-0	0-1
Tanana	0-0	10-13	147-144
Welsh	1-0	1-0	16-22
Williams	0-0	1-1	3-2
Wright	0-0	0-0	2-3

OPPONENTS VS YANKEES, 1985

TEAM	AVG (Min. 20 AB)	HR	RBI
Balt.	.317 Lacy (13-41)	2 by 3 Players	6 Murray
Bost.	.308 Evans (16-52)	5 Rice	12 Evans
	.308 Gedman (12-39)		
Calif.	.324 Carew (11-34)	3 by Downing, Jones	7 Jackson
Chgo.	.410 Guillen (16-39)	4 Fisk	10 Fisk
Clev.	.471 Bernazard (16-34)	3 by Bernazard, Thornton	9 by Franco, Thornton
Det.	.500 EVANS (17-34)	7 EVANS	11 Evans
K.C.	.314 McRae (11-35)	4 White	11 White
Milw.	.453 Molitor (24-53)	2 by Cooper, Householder	8 Cooper
Minn.	.364 Hatcher (8-22)	3 Hrbek	13 HRBEK
Oak.	.407 Henderson (11-27)	4 Kingman	7 Murphy
Sea.	.333 Bradley (17-51)	2 by Bradley, Henderson	8 Henderson
Tex.	.353 Tolleson (12-34)	3 by McDowell, Parrish	9 Bell
Tor.	.345 Iorg (10-29)	2 Whitt	6 Johnson

THE BEST

.500 Evans (17-34), Detroit
.471 Bernazard (16-34), Cleveland
.453 Molitor (24-53), Milwaukee
.435 Ready (10-23), Milwaukee
.410 Guillen (16-39), Chicago
.407 Henderson (11-27), Oakland
.404 Franco (19-47), Cleveland
.385 Baines (20-52), Chicago
.385 Phillips (10-26), Oakland
.364 Hatcher (8-22), Minnesota
.357 Smalley (10-28), Minnesota
.353 Tolleson (12-34), Texas
.351 Teufel (13-37), Minnesota
.346 Bush (9-26), Minnesota
.345 Iorg (10-29), Toronto

THE WORST

.057 Baker (2-35), Oakland
.121 Schofield (4-33), California
.130 Hill (3-23), Oakland
.130 Wilfong (3-23), California
.136 Concepcion (3-22), Kansas City
.136 Romero (3-22), Milwaukee
.140 Wilson (7-50), Kansas City
.143 Vukovich (5-35), Cleveland
.150 Jones (3-20), Kansas City
.154 Dwyer (4-26), Baltimore
.156 Sundberg (5-32), Kansas City
.156 Whitaker (7-45), Detroit
.159 Brunansky (7-44), Minnesota
.162 Jackson (6-37), California
.167 Bell (8-48), Toronto

YANKEES WHO ALSO PLAYED FOR METS (33)

	N.Y.Y. Years	N.Y.M. Years
Neil Allen	1985	1979-83
Jack Aker	1969-72	1974
Sandy Alomar	1974-76	1967
Tucker Ashford	1981	1983
Yogi Berra	1946-63	1965
Ray Burris	1979	1979-80
Duke Carmel	1965	1963
Billy Cowan	1969	1965
Dock Ellis	1976-77	1979
Tim Foli	1984	1978-79
Bob Friend	1966	1966
Rob Gardner	1970-72	1965-66
Jesse Gonder	1960-61	1963-65
Dave Kingman	1977	1975-77, 1981-83
Phil Linz	1962-65	1967-68
Elliott Maddox	1974-76	1978-80
Lee Mazzilli	1982	1976-81
Doc Medich	1972-75	1977
Dale Murray	1983-84	1978-79
John Pacella	1982	1977, 1979-80
Lenny Randle	1979	1977-78
Hal Reniff	1961-67	1967
Bill Short	1960	1968
Charley Smith	1967-68	1964-65
Roy Staiger	1979	1975-77
Tom Sturdivant	1955-59	1964
Bill Sudakis	1974	1972
Ron Swoboda	1971-73	1965-70
Ralph Terry	1956-57, 1959-64	1966-67
Marv Throneberry	1955-59	1962-63
Dick Tidrow	1974-79	1984
Mike Torrez	1977	1983-84
Gene Woodling	1949-54	1962

DID YOU KNOW ... that Babe Ruth twice hit grand slam home runs on consecutive days?

YANKEES' MOST RECENT TRADE
WITH EACH MAJOR LEAGUE TEAM

AMERICAN LEAGUE EAST

BALTIMORE ORIOLES—December 11, 1985—Orioles traded outfielder Gary Roenicke and a player to be named later to Yankees for pitcher Rich Bordi and infielder Rex Hudler.

BOSTON RED SOX—March 22, 1972—Yankees traded first baseman-outfielder Danny Cater to Red Sox for pitcher Al (Sparky) Lyle.

CLEVELAND INDIANS—December 11, 1985—Indians traded infielder Mike Fischlin to Yankees for a player to be named later.

DETROIT TIGERS—March 19, 1974—In deal involving three clubs, Tigers sent pitcher Jim Perry to Indians and pitcher Ed Farmer to Syracuse, Yankees' affiliate; Indians sent pitcher Rick Sawyer and outfielder Walt Williams to Yankees and Yankees assigned catcher Gerry Moses to Tigers.

MILWAUKEE BREWERS—May 13, 1974—Brewers purchased first baseman Mike Hegan from Yankees.

TORONTO BLUE JAYS—April 5, 1983—Yankees purchased infielder Tucker Ashford from Blue Jays.

AMERICAN LEAGUE WEST

CALIFORNIA ANGELS—December 19, 1983—Yankees traded pitcher Mike Browning, on Columbus roster, to Angels for pitcher Curt Brown, who was assigned to Columbus.

CHICAGO WHITE SOX—December 12, 1985—White Sox traded pitcher Britt Burns, infielder Mike Soper, outfielder Glen Braxton and two players to be named later to Yankees for pitcher Joe Cowley and catcher Ron Hassey.

KANSAS CITY ROYALS—December 8, 1983—Yankees traded first baseman Steve Balboni and pitcher Roger Erickson to Royals for pitcher Mike Armstrong and catcher Duane Dewey.

MINNESOTA TWINS—May 12, 1982—Twins traded catcher Butch Wynegar and pitcher Roger Erickson to Yankees for infielder Larry Milbourne and pitchers John Pacella and Pete Filson. Pacella and Filson were on the Columbus, O. roster.

OAKLAND ATHLETICS—December 8, 1984—Yankees traded pitchers Jay Howell, Jose Rijo, Eric Plunk and Tim Birtsas and outfielder Stan Javier to Athletics for outfielder Rickey Henderson and pitcher Bert Bradley.

SEATTLE MARINERS—April 1, 1982—Yankees traded pitchers Gene Nelson, Bill Caudill, cash and a player to be named later to Mariners for pitcher Shane Rawley; Mariners acquired outfielder Bobby Brown and assigned him to Salt Lake City to complete deal, April 6.

TEXAS RANGERS—February 28, 1985—Rangers traded outfielder Billy Sample and a player to be named later to Yankees for infielder Toby Harrah. Pitcher Eric Dersin assigned to Yankees, July 14, 1985, to complete deal.

NATIONAL LEAGUE

ATLANTA BRAVES—December 6, 1985—Braves traded infielder Miguel Sosa to Yankees for outfielder Billy Sample.

CHICAGO CUBS—December 4, 1984—Yankees traded outfielder Brian Dayett and pitcher Ray Fontenot to Cubs for outfielder Henry Cotto, catcher Ron Hassey and pitchers Rich Bordi and Porfi Altamirano. Cotto and Altamirano were assigned to Columbus.

CINCINNATI REDS—November 4, 1981—Reds traded outfielder Ken Griffey to Yankees for pitcher Brian Ryder, on Columbus roster, and a player to be named; pitcher Freddie Toliver was assigned to Indianapolis to complete deal, December 9.

HOUSTON ASTROS—September 15, 1985—Astros traded pitcher Joe Niekro and a player to be named later to Yankees for pitcher Jim Deshaies and a player to be named later. Infielder Neder Horta assigned to Yankees, September 24, 1985, and pitcher Dody Rather assigned to Astros, January 11, 1986, to complete deal.

LOS ANGELES DODGERS—February 15, 1979—Yankees traded outfielder Gary Thomasson to Dodgers for catcher Brad Gulden.

MONTREAL EXPOS—November 3, 1982—Expos purchased catcher Bobby Ramos from Yankees.

NEW YORK METS—August 2, 1979—Mets purchased pitcher Ray Burris from Yankees.

PHILADELPHIA PHILLIES—June 30, 1984—Yankees acquired pitcher Marty Bystrom and minor league outfielder Keith Hughes from Phillies for pitcher Shane Rawley.

PITTSBURGH PIRATES—September 14, 1985—Pitcher Rod Scurry sold to Yankees.

ST. LOUIS CARDINALS—July 17, 1985—Traded pitcher Neil Allen and other considerations to Yankees for a player to be named later.

SAN DIEGO PADRES—March 30, 1984—Yankees traded infielder Graig Nettles to Padres for pitcher Dennis Rasmussen and a player to be named later. Yankees acquired pitcher Darin Cloninger to complete deal, April 26.

SAN FRANCISCO GIANTS—March 30, 1982—Giants traded pitcher Doyle Alexander to Yankees for pitcher Andy McGaffigan and outfielder Ted Wilborn; McGaffigan and Wilborn were assigned to Phoenix.

The Yankees and Mets have played 72 times, with the Yanks winning 40, losing 31 and one ending in a tie ... in the spring they hold a 31-23 edge, and were 9-8-1 in Mayor's Trophy games.

ALL TIME YANKEE ROSTER

(through 1984 1016 players have appeared in at least one game for the Yankees)

A (25)

Harry Ables 1911
Spencer Adams 1926
Doc Adkins 1903
Jack Aker 1969-72
Doyle Alexander 1976, 1982-83
Walt Alexander 1915-17
Bernie Allen 1972-73
Johnny Allen 1932-35
Neil Allen 1985
Sandy Alomar 1974-76
Felipe Alou 1971-73
Matty Alou 1973
Dell Alston 1977-78
Ruben Amaro 1966-68
John Anderson 1904-05
Rick Anderson 1979
Ivy Andrews 1931-32, 1937-38
Pete Appleton 1933
Angel Aragon 1914, 1916-17
Rugger Ardizola 1947
Mike Armstrong 1984-85
Luis Arroyo 1960-63
Tucker Ashford 1981
Jimmy Austin 1909-10
Martin Autry 1924

B (102)

Loren Babe 1952-53
Stan Bahnsen 1966, 1968-71
Bill Bailey 1911
Frank Baker 1916-19, 1921-22
Frank Baker 1970-71
Steve Balboni 1981-83
Neal Ball 1907-09
Steve Barber 1967-68
Cy Barger 1906-07
Ray Barker 1965-67
Frank Barnes 1930
Honey Barnes 1926
Ed Barney 1915
George Batten 1912
Hank Bauer 1948-59
Paddy Baumann 1915-17
Don Baylor 1983-85
Walter Beall 1924-27
Jim Beattie 1978-79
Rick Beck 1965
Zinn Beck 1918
Fred Beene 1972-74
Joe Beggs 1938
Rudy Bell 1907
Zeke Bella 1957
Benny Bengough 1923-30
Juan Beniquez 1979
Lou Berberet 1954-55
Dave Bergman 1975, 1977
Juan Bernhardt 1976
Walter Bernhardt 1918
Dale Berra 1985
Yogi Berra 1946-63
Bill Bevens 1944-47
Monte Beville 1903-04
Harry Billiard 1908
Doug Bird 1980-81
Ewell Blackwell 1952-53
Rick Bladt 1975
Paul Blair 1977-80
Walter Blair 1907-11
Johnny Blanchard 1955, 1959-65
Gil Blanco 1965
Wade Blasingame 1972
Steve Blateric 1972
Gary Blaylock 1959
Curt Blefary 1970-71
Elmer Bliss 1903-04
Ron Blomberg 1969, 1971-77
Eddie Bockman 1946
Ping Bodie 1918-21
Len Boehmer 1969, 1971
Don Bollweg 1953
Bobby Bonds 1975

Ernie Bonham 1940-46
Juan Bonilla 1985
Luke Boone 1913-16
Frenchy Bordagaray 1941
Rich Bordi 1985
Hank Borowy 1942-45
Babe Borton 1913
Jim Bouton 1962-68
Clete Boyer 1959-66
Scott Bradley 1984-85
Neal Brady 1915
Ralph Branca 1954
Norm Branch 1941-42
Marshall Brant 1980
Garland Braxton 1925-26
Don Brennan 1933
Jim Brenneman 1965
Ken Brett 1976
Marv Breuer 1939-43
Fritzie Brickell 1958-59
Jim Brideweser 1951-53
Marshall Bridges 1962-63
Harry Bright 1963-64
Ed Brinkman 1975
Johnny Broaca 1934-37
Lew Brockett 1907, 1909
Jim Bronstad 1959
Boardwalk Brown 1914-15
Bobby Brown 1946-52, 1954
Bobby Brown 1979-81
Curt Brown 1984
Hal Brown 1962
Jumbo Brown 1932-33, 1935-36
Billy Bryan 1966-67
Jess Buckles 1916
Bill Burbach 1969-71
Lew Burdette 1950
George Burns 1928-29
Alex Burr 1914
Ray Burris 1979
Joe Bush 1922-24
Tom Buskey 1973-74
Ralph Buxton 1949
Joe Buzas 1945
Harry Byrd 1954
Sammy Byrd 1929-34
Tommy Byrne 1943, 1946-51, 1954-57
Marty Bystrom 1984-85

C (85)

Charlie Caldwell 1925
Ray Caldwell 1910-18
Johnny Callison 1972-73
Howie Camp 1917
Bert Campaneris 1983
Archie Campbell 1928
Mike Cantwell 1916
Andy Carey 1952-60
Roy Carlyle 1926
Duke Carmel 1965
Dick Carroll 1909
Ownie Carroll 1930
Tommy Carroll 1955-56
Hugh Casey 1949
Roy Castleton 1907
Bill Castro 1981
Danny Cater 1970-71
Rick Cerone 1980-84
Bob Cerv 1951-56, 1960-62
Chris Chambliss 1974-79
Frank Chance 1913-14
Spud Chandler 1937-47
Les Channell 1910
Ben Chapman 1930-36
Mike Chartak 1940
Hal Chase 1905-13
Jack Chesbro 1903-09
Clay Christiansen 1984
Al Cicotte 1957
Allie Clark 1947
George Clark 1913
Horace Clarke 1965-74

24

Walter Clarkson 1904-07
Ken Clay 1977-79
Tex Clevenger 1961-62
Lou Clinton 1966-67
Al Closter 1971-72
Andy Coakley 1911
Jim Coates 1956, 1959-62
Jim Cockman 1905
Rich Coggins 1975-76
Rocky Colavito 1968
King Cole 1914-15
Curt Coleman 1912
Jerry Coleman 1949-57
Rip Coleman 1955-56
Bob Collins 1944
Dave Collins 1982
Joe Collins 1948-57
Orth Collins 1904
Pat Collins 1926-28
Rip Collins 1920-21
Frank Colman 1946-47
Lloyd Colson 1970
Earle Combs 1924-35
Tom Connelly 1920-21
Joe Connor 1905
Wid Conroy 1903-08
Doc Cook 1913-16
Dusty Cooke 1930-32
Johnny Cooney 1944
Phil Cooney 1905
Don Cooper 1985
Guv Cooper 1914
Dan Costello 1913
Henry Cotto 1985
Ensign Cottrell 1915
Clint Courtney 1951
Ernie Courtney 1903
Stan Coveleski 1928
Billy Cowan 1969
Joe Cowley 1984-85
Bobby Cox 1968-69
Casey Cox 1972-73
Birdie Cree 1908-15
Lou Criger 1910
Herb Crompton 1945
Frankie Crosetti 1932-48
Jack Cullen 1962, 1965-66
Roy Cullenbine 1942
Nick Cullop 1916-17
Nick Cullop 1926
John Cumberland 1968-70
Jim Curry 1911
Fred Curtis 1905

D (47)
Babe Dahlgren 1937-40
Buddy Daley 1961-64
Tom Daley 1914-15
Bert Daniels 1910-13
George Davis 1912
Kiddo Davis 1926
Lefty Davis 1903
Ron Davis 1978-81
Brian Dayett 1983-84
John Deering 1903
John Deidel 1974
Frank Delahanty 1905-06, 1908
Bobby Del Greco 1957-58
Jim Delsing 1949-50
Joe DeMaestri 1960-61
Ray Demmitt 1909
Rick Dempsey 1973-76
Bucky Dent 1977-82
Claud Derrick 1913
Russ Derry 1944-45
Jim Deshaies 1984
Jimmie DeShong 1934-35
Charlie Devens 1932-34
Al DeVormer 1921-22
Bill Dickey 1928-43, 1946
Murry Dickson 1958
Joe DiMaggio 1936-42, 1946-51
Kerry Dineen 1975-76
Art Ditmar 1957-61
Sonny Dixon 1956
Pat Dobson 1973-75

Cozy Dolan 1911-12
Atley Donald 1938-45
Mike Donovan 1908
Wild Bill Donovan 1915-16
Patsy Dougherty 1904-06
Al Downing 1961-69
Brian Doyle 1978-80
Jack Doyle 1905
Slow Joe Doyle 1906-10
Bill Drescher 1944-46
Karl Drews 1946-48
Monk Dubiel 1944-45
Joe Dugan 1922-28
Ryne Duren 1958-61
Leo Durocher 1925, 1928-29
Cedric Durst 1927-30

E (14)
Rawly Eastwick 1978
Doc Edwards 1965
Foster Edwards 1930
Kid Elberfeld 1903-09
Gene Elliott 1911
Dock Ellis 1976-77
John Ellis 1969-72
Red Embree 1948
Clyde Engle 1909-10
John Enright 1917
Roger Erickson 1982-83
Juan Espino 1982-83, 1985
Nick Etten 1943-46
Barry Evans 1982

F (30)
Charles Fallon 1905
Doc Farrell 1932-33
Alex Ferguson 1918, 1921, 1925
Frank Fernandez 1967-69
Mike Ferraro 1966, 1968
Wes Ferrell 1938-39
Tom Ferrick 1950-51
Chick Fewster 1917-22
Ed Figueroa 1976-80
Happy Finneran 1918
Brian Fisher 1985
Gus Fisher 1912
Ray Fisher 1910-17
Mike Fitzgerald 1911
Tim Foli 1984
Ray Fontenot 1983-84
Barry Foote 1981-82
Russ Ford 1909-13
Whitey Ford 1950, 1953-67
Eddie Foster 1910
Jack Fournier 1918
Ray Francis 1925
George Frazier 1981-83
Mark Freeman 1959
Ray French 1920
Lonny Frey 1947-48
Bob Friend 1966
John Frill 1910
Dave Fultz 1903-05
Liz Funk 1929

G (50)
John Gabler 1959-60
Joe Gallagher 1939
Oscar Gamble 1976, 1979-84
John Ganzel 1903-04
Mike Garbark 1944-45
Damaso Garcia 1978-79
Billy Gardner 1961-62
Earl Gardner 1908-12
Rob Gardner 1970-72
Ned Garvin 1904
Milt Gaston 1924
Mike Gazella 1923, 1926-28
Joe Gedeon 1916-17
Lou Gehrig 1923-39
Al Gettel 1945-46
Joe Giard 1927
Jake Gibbs 1962-71
Sam Gibson 1930
Frank Gilhooley 1913-18

Fred Glade 1908
Frank Gleich 1919-20
Joe Glenn 1932-33, 1935-38
Lefty Gomez 1930-42
Jesse Gonder 1960-61
Fernando Gonzalez 1974
Pedro Gonzalez 1963-65
Wilbur Good 1905
Art Goodwin 1905
Joe Gordon 1938-43, 1946
Tom Gorman 1952-54
Rich Gossage 1978-83
Dick Gossett 1913-14
Larry Gowell 1972
Johnny Grabowski 1927-29
Wayne Granger 1973
Ted Gray 1955
Eli Grba 1959-60
Willie Greene 1903
Ken Griffey 1982-85
Mike Griffin 1979-81
Clark Griffith 1903-07
Bob Grim 1954-58
Burleigh Grimes 1934
Oscar Grimes 1943-46
Lee Grissom 1940
Ron Guidry 1975-85
Brad Gulden 1979-80
Don Gullett 1977-80
Randy Gumpert 1946-48
Larry Gura 1974-76

H (79)

Bump Hadley 1936-40
Kent Hadley 1960
Ed Hahn 1905-06
Noodles Hahn 1906
Hinkey Haines 1923
George Halas 1919
Bob Hale 1961
Jimmie Hall 1969
Roger Hambright 1971
Steve Hamilton 1963-70
Mike Handiboe 1911
Jim Hanley 1913
Truck Hannah 1918-20
Ron Hansen 1970-71
Joe Hanson 1913
Jim Hardin 1971
Bubbles Hargrave 1930
Harry Harper 1921
Toby Harrah 1984
Joe Harris 1914
Jim Hart 1973-74
Roy Hartzell 1911-16
Buddy Hassett 1942
Ron Hassey 1985
Chicken Hawks 1921
Fran Healy 1976-78
Mike Heath 1978
Don Heffner 1934-37
Mike Hegan 1964, 1966-67, 1973-74
Fred Heimach 1928-29
Woodie Held 1954
Charlie Hemphill 1908-11
Rollie Hemsley 1942-44
Bill Henderson 1930
Rickey Henderson 1985
Harvey Hendrick 1923-24
Elrod Hendricks 1976-77
Tim Hendryx 1915-17
Tommy Henrich 1937-42, 1946-50
Bill Henry 1966
Ed Herrmann 1975
Hugh High 1915-18
Oral Hildebrand 1939-40
Jesse Hill 1935
Frank Hiller 1946, 1948-49
Mack Hillis 1924
Rich Hinton 1972
Myril Hoag 1931-32, 1934-38
Butch Hobson 1982
Red Hoff 1911-13
Danny Hoffman 1906-07
Solly Hofman 1916
Fred Hofmann 1919-25

Bill Hogg 1905-08
Bobby Hogue 1951-52
Ken Holcombe 1945
Bill Holden 1913-14
Ken Holloway 1930
Fred Holmes 1903
Roger Holt 1980
Ken Holtzman 1976-78
Don Hood 1979
Wally Hood 1949
Johnny Hopp 1950-52
Shags Horan 1924
Ralph Houk 1947-54
Elston Howard 1955-67
Harry Howell 1903
Jay Howell 1982-84
Dick Howser 1967-68
Waite Hoyt 1921-30
Rex Hudler 1984-85
Long Tom Hughes 1904
Tom Hughes 1906-07, 1909-10
John Hummel 1918
Ken Hunt 1959-60
Billy Hunter 1955-56
Catfish Hunter 1975-79
Ham Hyatt 1918

J (28)

Fred Jacklitsch 1905
Grant Jackson 1976
Reggie Jackson 1977-81
Johnny James 1958, 1960-61
Stan Javier 1984
Jackie Jensen 1950-52
Elvio Jimenez 1964
Tommy John 1979-82
Alex Johnson 1974-75
Billy Johnson 1943, 1946-51
Cliff Johnson 1977-79
Darrell Johnson 1957-58
Deron Johnson 1960-61
Don Johnson 1947
Ernie Johnson 1923-25
Hank Johnson 1925-26, 1928-32
Johnny Johnson 1944
Ken Johnson 1969
Otis Johnson 1911
Roy Johnson 1936-37
Jay Johnstone 1978-79
Gary Jones 1970-71
Darryl Jones 1979
Ruppert Jones 1980
Sad Sam Jones 1922-26
Tim Jordan 1903
Art Jorgens 1929-39
Mike Jurewicz 1965

K (40)

Jim Kaat 1979-80
Bob Kammeyer 1978-79
Frank Kane 1919
Bill Karlon 1930
Herb Karpel 1946
Benny Kauff 1912
Curt Kaufman 1982-83
Eddie Kearse 1942
Ray Keating 1912-16, 1918
Bob Keefe 1907
Willie Keeler 1903-09
Mike Kekich 1969-73
Charlie Keller 1939-43, 1945-49, 1952
Steve Kemp 1983-84
John Kennedy 1967
Jerry Kenney 1967, 1969-72
Matt Keough 1983
Dave Kingman 1977
Harry Kingman 1914
Fred Kipp 1960
Frank Kitson 1907
Ted Kleinhans 1936
Red Kleinow 1904-10
Ed Klepfer 1911
Ron Klimkowski 1969-70, 1972
Steve Kline 1970-74
Mickey Klutts 1976-78

Bill Knickerbocker 1938-40
John Knight 1909-11, 1913
Mark Koenig 1925-30
Jim Konstanty 1954-56
Andy Kosco 1968
Steve Kraly 1953
Jack Kramer 1951
Ernie Krueger 1915
Dick Kryhoski 1949
Tony Kubek 1957-65
Johnny Kucks 1955-59
Bill Kunkel 1963
Bob Kuzava 1951-54

L (40)
Joe Lake 1908-09
Bill Lamar 1917-19
Hal Lanier 1972-73
Frank LaPorte 1905-10
Dave LaRoche 1981-83
Don Larsen 1955-59
Lyn Lary 1929-34
Gene Layden 1915
Tony Lazzeri 1926-37
Joe Lefebvre 1980
Frank Leja 1954-55
Jack Lelivelt 1912-13
Eddie Leon 1975
Louis LeRoy 1905-06
Ed Levy 1942, 44
Duffy Lewis 1919-20
Jim Lewis 1982
Terry Ley 1971
Paul Lindblad 1978
Johnny Lindell 1941-50
Phil Linz 1962-65
Jack Little 1912
Clem Llewellyn 1922
Gene Locklear 1976-77
Sherm Lollar 1947-48
Tim Lollar 1980
Dale Long 1960, 1962-63
Herman Long 1903
Ed Lopat 1948-55
Art Lopez 1965
Hector Lopez 1959-66
Baldy Louden 1907
Slim Love 1916-18
Johnny Lucadello 1947
Joe Lucey 1920
Ray Luebbe 1925
Jerry Lumpe 1956-59
Sparky Lyle 1972-78
Al Lyons 1944, 1946-47
Jim Lyttle 1969-71

M (114)
Duke Maas 1958-61
Danny MacFayden 1932-34
Ray Mack 1947
Bunny Madden 1910
Elliott Maddox 1974-76
Dave Madison 1950
Lee Magee 1916-17
Sal Maglie 1957-58
Stubby Magner 1911
Jim Magnuson 1973
Fritz Maisel 1913-17
Hank Majeski 1946
Frank Makosky 1937
Pat Malone 1935-37
Pat Maloney 1912
Al Mamaux 1924
Rube Manning 1907-10
Mickey Mantle 1951-68
Cliff Mapes 1948-51
Roger Maris 1960-66
Cliff Markle 1915-16, 1924
Jim Marquis 1925
Armando Marsans 1917-18
Cuddles Marshall 1946, 1948-49
Billy Martin 1950-53, 1955-57
Hersh Martin 1944-45
Jack Martin 1912
Tippy Martinez 1974-76
Jim Mason 1974-76

Vic Mata 1984-85
Don Mattingly 1982-85
Carlos May 1976-77
Rudy May 1974-76, 1980-83
John Mayberry 1982
Carl Mays 1919-23
Lee Mazzilli 1982
Larry McCall 1977-78
Joe McCarthy 1905
Pat McCauley 1903
Larry McClure 1910
George McConnell 1909, 1912-13
Mike McCormick 1970
Lindy McDaniel 1968-73
Mickey McDermott 1956
Danny McDevitt 1961
Dave McDonald 1969
Jim McDonald 1952-54
Gil McDougald 1951-60
Sam McDowell 1973-74
Lou McEvoy 1930-31
Herm McFarland 1903
Andy McGaffigan 1981
Lynn McGlothen 1982
Bob McGraw 1917-20
Deacon McGuire 1904-07
Marty McHale 1913-15
Irish McIlveen 1908-09
Bill McKechnie 1913
Rich McKinney 1972
Frank McManus 1904
Norm McMillan 1922
Tommy McMillan 1912
Mike McNally 1921-24
Herb McQuaid 1926
George McQuinn 1947-48
Bobby Meacham 1983-85
Charlie Meara 1914
George Medich 1972-75
Fred Merkle 1925-26
Andy Messersmith 1978
Tom Metcalf 1963
Bud Metheny 1943-46
Bob Meusel 1920-29
Bob Meyer 1964
Gene Michael 1968-74
Ezra Midkiff 1912-13
Pete Mikkelsen 1964-65
Larry Milbourne 1981-82, 1983
Bill Miller 1952-54
Elmer Miller 1915-18, 1921-22
John Miller 1966
Buster Mills 1940
Mike Milosevich 1944-45
Paul Mirabella 1979
Willie Miranda 1953-54
Bobby Mitchell 1970
Fred Mitchell 1910
Johnny Mitchell 1921-22
Johnny Mize 1949-53
George Mogridge 1915-20
Fenton Mole 1949
Bill Monbouquette 1967-68
Ed Monroe 1917-18
Zack Monroe 1958-59
John Montefusco 1983-85
Archie Moore 1964-65
Earl Moore 1907
Wilcy Moore 1927-29, 1932-33
Ray Morehart 1927
Omar Moreno 1983-85
Mike Morgan 1982
Tom Morgan 1951-52, 1954-56
George Moriarty 1906-08
Ross Moschitto 1965, 1967
Gerry Moses 1973
Charlie Mullen 1914-16
Jerry Mumphrey 1981-83
Bob Muncrief 1951
Thurman Munson 1969-79
Bobby Murcer 1965-66, 1969-74, 1979-83
Johnny Murphy 1932, 1934'43, 1946
Dale Murray 1983-85
George Murray 1922
Larry Murray 1974-76

27

N (18)

Jerry Narron 1979
Bots Nekola 1929
Gene Nelson 1981
Luke Nelson 1919
Graig Nettles 1973-83
Tacks Neuer 1907
Ernie Nevel 1950-51
Floyd Newkirk 1934
Bobo Newsom 1947
Doc Newton 1905-09
Gus Niarhos 1946, 1948-50
Joe Niekro 1985
Phil Niekro 1984-85
Harry Niles 1908
Otis Nixon 1983
Irv Noren 1952-56
Don Nottebart 1969
Les Nunamaker 1914-17

O (19)

Johnny Oates 1980-81
Mike O'Berry 1984
Andy O'Connor 1908
Jack O'Connor 1903
Paddy O'Connor 1918
Heinle Odom 1925
Lefty O'Doul 1919-20, 1922
John O'Dowd 1912
Rowland Office 1983
Rube Oldring 1905, 1916
Bob Oliver 1975
Nate Oliver 1969
Steve O'Neill 1925
Queenie O'Rourke 1908
Al Orth 1904-09
Champ Osteen 1904
Joe Ostrowski 1950-52
Bill Otis 1912
Stubby Overmire 1951

P (36)

John Pacella 1982
Del Paddock 1912
Dave Pagan 1973-76
Joe Page 1944-50
Mike Pagliarulo 1984-85
Ben Paschal 1924-29
Dan Pasqua 1985
Gil Patterson 1977
Mike Patterson 1981-82
Monte Pearson 1936-40
Roger Peckinpaugh 1913-21
Steve Peek 1941
Herb Pennock 1923-33
Joe Pepitone 1962-69
Marty Perez 1977
Cecil Perkins 1967
Cy Perkins 1931
Gaylord Perry 1980
Fritz Peterson 1966-74
Eddie Phillips 1932
Jack Phillips 1947-49
Cy Pieh 1913-15
Bill Piercy 1917
Duane Pillette 1949-50
Lou Piniella 1974-84
George Pipgras 1923-24, 1927-33
Wally Pipp 1915-25
Jim Pisoni 1959-60
Bob Porterfield 1948-51
Jack Powell 1904-05
Jake Powell 1936-40
Mike Powers 1905
Del Pratt 1918-20
Jerry Priddy 1941-42
Johnnie Priest 1911-12
Ambrose Puttman 1903-05

Q (3)

Mel Queen 1942, 1944, 1946-47
Ed Quick 1903
Jack Quinn 1909-12, 1919-21

R (57)

Dave Rajsich 1978
Bobby Ramos 1982
Domingo Ramos 1978
Pedro Ramos 1964-66
Lenny Randle 1979
Willie Randolph 1976-85
Vic Raschi 1946-53
Dennis Rasmussen 1984-85
Shane Rawley 1982-84
Jack Reed 1961-63
Jimmy Reese 1930-31
Hal Reniff 1961-67
Bill Renna 1953
Tony Rensa 1933
Roger Repoz 1964-66
Rick Reuschel 1981-82
Dave Revering 1981-83
Allie Reynolds 1947-54
Bill Reynolds 1913-14
Gordon Rhodes 1929-32
Harry Rice 1930
Bobby Richardson 1955-66
Nolan Richardson 1935
Branch Rickey 1907
Dave Righetti 1979, 1981-85
Jose Rijo 1984
Mickey Rivers 1976-79
Phil Rizzuto 1941-42, 1946-56
Roy Roach 1910-11
Dale Roberts 1967
Andre Robertson 1981-85
Gene Robertson 1928-29
Aaron Robinson 1943, 1945-47
Bill Robinson 1967-69
Bruce Robinson 1979-80
Eddie Robinson 1954-56
Hank Robinson 1918
Aurelio Rodriguez 1980-81
Edwin Rodriguez 1982
Ellie Rodriguez 1968
Oscar Roettger 1923-24
Jay Rogers 1914
Tom Rogers 1921
Jim Roland 1972
Red Rolfe 1931, 1934-42
Buddy Rosar 1939-42
Larry Rosenthal 1944
Steve Roser 1944-46
Braggo Roth 1921
Muddy Ruel 1917-20
Dutch Ruether 1926-27
Red Ruffing 1930-42, 1945-46
Allan Russell 1915-19
Marius Russo 1939-43, 1946
Babe Ruth 1920-34
Blondy Ryan 1935
Rosy Ryan 1928

S (104)

Johnny Sain 1951-55
Jack Saltzgaver 1932, 1934-37
Billy Sample 1985
Celerino Sanchez 1972-73
Roy Sanders 1918
Charlie Sands 1967
Fred Sanford 1949-51
Don Savage 1944-45
Rick Sawyer 1974-75
Ray Scarborough 1952-53
Germany Schaefer 1916
Harry Schaeffer 1952
Ray Schalk 1932
Art Schallock 1951-55
Wally Schang 1921-25
Bob Schmidt 1965
Butch Schmidt 1909
Johnny Schmitz 1952-53
Pete Schneider 1919
Dick Schofield 1966
Paul Schreiber 1945
Art Schult 1953
Al Schulz 1912-14
Bill Schwartz 1914
Pius Schwert 1914-15
Everett Scott 1922-25

George Scott 1979
Rodney Scott 1982
Rod Scurry 1985
Ken Sears 1943
Bob Seeds 1936
Kal Segrist 1952
George Seikirk 1934-42
Ted Sepkowski 1947
Hank Severeid 1926
Joe Sewell 1931-33
Howard Shanks 1925
Billy Shantz 1960
Bobby Shantz 1957-60
Bob Shawkey 1915-27
Spec Shea 1947-49, 1951
Al Shealy 1928
George Shears 1912
Tom Sheehan 1921
Rollie Sheldon 1961-62, 1964-65
Skeeter Shelton 1915
Roy Sherid 1929-31
Dennis Sherrill 1978, 1980
Ben Shields 1924-25
Bob Shirley 1983-85
Urban Shocker 1916-17, 1925-28
Tom Shopay 1967, 1969
Ernie Shore 1919-20
Bill Short 1960
Norm Siebern 1956, 1958-59
Charlie Silvera 1948-56
Ken Silvestri 1941, 1946-47
Hack Simmons 1912
Dick Simpson 1969
Harry Simpson 1957-58
Duke Sims 1973-74
Bill Skiff 1926
Camp Skinner 1922
Lou Skizas 1956
Bill Skowron 1954-62
Roger Slagle 1979
Enos Slaughter 1954-59
Roy Smalley 1982-84
Walt Smallwood 1917
Charley Smith 1967-68
Elmer Smith 1922-23
Joe Smith 1913
Keith Smith 1984-85
Klondike Smith 1912
Harry Smythe 1934
Eric Soderholm 1980
Tony Solaita 1968
Steve Souchock 1945
Jim Spencer 1978-81
Charlie Spikes 1972
Bill Stafford 1960-65
Jake Stahl 1908
Roy Staiger 1979
Tuck Stainback 1942-45
Gerry Staley 1955-56
Charley Stanceu 1941
Fred Stanley 1973-80
Dick Starr 1947-48
Dave Stegman 1982
Dutch Sterrett 1912-13
Bud Stewart 1948
Lee Stine 1938
Snuffy Stirnweiss 1943-50
Mel Stottlemyre 1964-74
Hal Stowe 1960
Gabby Street 1912
Martin Stuart 1954
Bill Stumpf 1912-13
Tom Sturdivant 1955-59
Johnny Sturm 1941
Bill Sudakis 1974
Steve Sundra 1936, 1938-40
Ed Sweeney 1908-15
Ron Swoboda 1971-73

T (35)
Fred Talbot 1966-69
Vito Tamulis 1934-35
Jesse Tannehill 1903
Zack Taylor 1934
Frank Tepedino 1967, 1969-72
Ralph Terry 1956-57, 1959-64

Dick Tettelbach 1955
Ira Thomas 1906-07
Lee Thomas 1961
Myles Thomas 1926-29
Stan Thomas 1977
Gary Thomasson 1978
Homer Thompson 1912
Tommy Thompson 1912
Jack Thoney 1904
Hank Thormahlen 1917-20
Marv Throneberry 1955, 1958-59
Luis Tiant 1979-80
Dick Tidrow 1974-79
Bobby Tiefenauer 1965
Eddie Tiemeyer 1909
Ray Tift 1907
Bob Tillman 1967
Thad Tillotson 1967-68
Dan Tipple 1915
Earl Torgeson 1961
Rusty Torres 1971-72
Mike Torrez 1977
Cesar Tovar 1976
Tom Tresh 1961-69
Gus Triandos 1953-54
Virgil Trucks 1958
Frank Truesdale 1914
Bob Turley 1955-62
Jim Turner 1942-45

U (4)
George Uhle 1933-34
Tom Underwood 1980-81
Bob Unglaub 1904
Cecil Upshaw 1974

V (11)
Elmer Valo 1960
Russ Van Alta 1933-35
Dazzy Vance 1915, 1918
Joe Vance 1937-38
Bobby Vaughn 1909
Hippo Vaughn 1908, 1910-12
Bobby Veach 1925
Otto Velez 1973-76
Joe Verbanic 1967-68, 1970
Frank Verdi 1953
Sammy Vick 1917-20

W (66)
Jake Wade 1946
Dick Wakefield 1950
Curt Walker 1919
Dixie Walker 1931, 1933-36
Mike Wallace 1974-75
Jimmy Walsh 1914
Joe Walsh 1910-11
Roxy Walters 1915-18
Danny Walton 1971
Paul Waner 1944-45
Jack Wanner 1909
Pee Wee Wanninger 1925
Aaron Ward 1917-26
Joe Ward 1909
Pete Ward 1970
Jack Warhop 1908-15
George Wasburn 1941
Gary Waslewski 1970-71
Bob Watson 1980-82
Roy Weatherly 1943, 1946
Jim Weaver 1931
Dave Wehrmeister 1981
Lefty Weinert 1931
Ed Wells 1929-32
Butch Wensloff 1943, 1947
Julie Wera 1927
Bill Werber 1930
Dennis Werth 1979-81
Stefan Wever 1982
Steve Whitaker 1966-68
Roy White 1965-79
George Whiteman 1913
Terry Whitfield 1974-76
Ed Whitson 1985
Kemp Wicker 1936-38

Al Wickland 1919
Bob Wiester 1951, 1954-55
Bill Wight 1946-47
Ted Wilborn 1980
Ed Wilkinson 1911
Bob Williams 1911-14
Harry Williams 1913
Jimmy Williams 1903-07
Stan Williams 1963-64
Walt Williams 1974-75
Archie Wilson 1951-52
George Wilson 1956
Pete Wilson 1908-09
Snake Wiltse 1903
Gordie Windhorn 1959
Dave Winfield 1981-85
Mickey Witek 1949
Whitey Witt 1922-25
Bill Wolfe 1903-04
Harry Wolter 1910-13
Harry Wolverton 1912
Dooley Womack 1966-68
Gene Woodling 1949-54

Ron Woods 1969-71
Dick Woodson 1974
Hank Workman 1950
Ken Wright 1974
Yats Wuestling 1930
John Wyatt 1968
Butch Wynegar 1982-85
Jimmy Wynn 1977

Y (3)
Joe Yeager 1905-06
Jim York 1976
Ralph Young 1913

Z (6)
Tom Zachary 1928-30
Jack Zalusky 1903
George Zeber 1977-78
Rollie Zelder 1913
Guy Zinn 1911-12
Bill Zuber 1943-46

DID YOU KNOW ... That when Jim Deshaies took the mound for the Yankees on 8/7/84 vs. the White Sox, he became the 1000th player to appear in a game as a Yankee?

YANKEES IN THE HALL OF FAME

Babe Ruth 1936	Home Run Baker 1955	Geo. M. Weiss 1970
Lou Gehrig 1939	Joe DiMaggio 1955	Yogi Berra 1971
Willie Keeler 1939	Joe McCarthy 1957	Lefty Gomez 1972
Clark C. Griffith. 1945	Burleigh Grimes 1964	Mickey Mantle. 1974
Frank Chance 1946	Miller Huggins 1964	Whitey Ford 1974
Jack Chesbro 1946	Casey Stengel 1966	Bucky Harris 1975
Herb Pennock. 1948	Branch Rickey. 1967	Joe Sewell 1977
Paul Waner 1952	Red Ruffing 1967	Larry Mac Phail 1978
Edw. G. Barrow 1953	Waite Hoyt. 1969	Johnny Mize 1981
Bill Dickey 1954	Earle Combs. 1970	Enos Slaughter 1985

YANKEE ALUMNI ASSOCIATION, started by George Steinbrenner in 1974, is the only one of its kind in professional baseball. Former Yankee players with two years on the club are eligible, and over 400 are members. They each receive a pin, and a quarterly newsletter. Jim Ogle directs the association out of Ft. Lauderdale Stadium.

YANKEE CAPTAINS

1914-1921	Roger Peckinpaugh
5/20-5/25/22	Babe Ruth
1922-1925	Everett Scott
4/21/35-6/2/41	Lou Gehrig
4/17/76-8/2/79	Thurman Munson
1/29/82-3/30/84	Graig Nettles

YANKEE PITCHERS AT BAT ... Since the inception of the Designated Hitter rule in 1973, only 4 Yankee pitchers have come to bat in regular season play ... Lindy McDaniel was 0-2 in 1973 ... Sparky Lyle was 0-1 in 1974 ... and Catfish Hunter was 0-1 in 1976 ... Ron Davis, the last pitcher to hit, struckout against Mark Clear in Anaheim on July 14, 1979, and struckout against Bill Castro of Milwaukee on April 20, 1980.

DID YOU KNOW ... that the 1941 Yankees homered in 25 straight games, a major league record ... they hit 40 home runs in that stretch?

DID YOU KNOW ... The Yankees have won doubleheaders via shutouts in both games 13 times, most recently on September 25, 1977 when Guidry and a combined Figueroa, Lyle shutout stopped the Blue Jays in Toronto. It's happened to the Yankees only four times, most recently on July 27, 1975 when Lee and Moret of Boston did the damage at Shea Stadium.

PINCH-HIT, GRAND SLAM HOMERS AND TRIPLE PLAYS ... The Yankees had four pinch-hit homers in 1985 ... Ken Griffey vs Kansas City & Joe Beckwith on May 5th, Butch Wynegar at Milwaukee vs Rollie Fingers on June 7th, Don Baylor had a pinch-hit grand slam vs Texas and Chris Welsh on July 11th and Baylor had a second pinch-hit homer vs California & Al Holland on September 1st ... The Yankees had three grand slams in 1985 ... Don Baylor's pinch-hit grand slam on July 11th and another on May 11th vs Bud Black giving Don a career total of 10, tying him for 23rd place on the all-time grand slam list ... Ken Griffey hit his 3rd career grand slam in 1985, connecting on May 14 vs Minnesota and Curt Wardle ... the opponents hit three grand slams vs the Yankees in 1985 ... Gary Gaetti vs Joe Cowley at Minnesota on May 8, Ken Phelps vs Phil Niekro at Seattle on May 23, and Fran White vs Dennis Rasmussen on July 10 ... The Yankees have performed 21 triple plays in their history, the last one occurred on May 29, 1968 (Womack-Cox-Mantle) ... the last one against the Yankees occurred on May 3, 1985 vs Kansas City when Rickey Henderson hit a liner to Frank White who doubled Bobby Meacham off first with a throw to Steve Balboni who then tripled Billy Sample off second with a throw to Onix Concepcion.

CAREER GRAND SLAMS

	OPP.	DATE	PITCHER
Don Baylor (10)–	at Oak.	July 27, 1977	Paul Mitchell
	at Chi.	May 18, 1978	Ron Schueler
	vs. K.C.	Sept. 10, 1978	Paul Splittorff
	vs. Oak.	April 21, 1979	Bob Lacey
	at Tor.	August 25, 1979	Balor Moore
	at Min.	August 11, 1982	Ron Davis
	at Cle.	June 16, 1983	Bert Blyleven
	at Chi.	July 31, 1983	Dennis Lamp
	at K.C.	May 11, 1985	Bud Black
	vs. Tex.	July 11, 1985	Chris Welsh
Dave Winfield (5)–	at L.A.	April 13, 1976	Stan Wall
	vs. Cin.	May 21, 1976	Gary Nolan
	at S.F.	July 4, 1978	John Montefusco
	at Bal.	Sept. 13, 1982	Dennis Martinez
	vs. Tex.	July 16, 1984	Dickie Noles
Gary Roenicke (5)–	at Cle.	September 18, 1978	David Clyde
	at Oak.	May 10, 1982	Steve McCatty
	at Bos.	September 13, 1983	John H. Johnson
	at N.Y.	June 17, 1984	D. Rasmussen
	vs. Chi.	July 13, 1985	Britt Burns
Ken Griffey (3)–	at Chi.(N)	May 9, 1976	Oscar Zamora
	vs. Tor.	August 8, 1983(2)	Matt Williams
	vs. Min.	May 14, 1985	Curt Wardle
Dale Berra (2)–	vs. N.Y.(N)	June 1, 1980	Mark Bomback
	at St.L.	August 8, 1984	Jeff Lahti
Mike Fischlin (1)–	vs. Mil.	September 20, 1983	Mike Caldwell
Mike Pagliarulo (1)–	vs. Bal.	September 18, 1984	Dennis Martinez
Willie Randolph (1)–	vs. Oak.	July 21, 1979	Craig Minetto
Butch Wynegar (1)–	vs. Oak.	July 30, 1976	Dick Bosman

INSIDE THE PARK HOMERS ... The Yankees had none in 1985 ... Don Baylor was the last Yankee to hit one, dating back to June 4, 1984 vs Boston ... Mickey Mantle's 6 are the most by a Yankee ... Pat Sheridan at Kansas City on May 12th was the only opponent last year to hit an inside the park homer.

Yankee players have hit for the cycle (single, double, triple and homer in the same game) 13 times, tops in the American League. The last one to do it was Bobby Murcer on August 29, 1972. Other Yankees were Bert Daniels, Bob Meusel (3 times), Tony Lazzeri, Lou Gehrig (twice), Joe DiMaggio (twice), Buddy Rosar, Joe Gordon, and Mickey Mantle.

*Led League

Year	Batting Avg		Runs		Hits	
1903	Keeler	.318	Keeler	98	Keeler	164
1904	Keeler	.343	Dougherty*	80	Keeler	185
1905	Keeler	.302	Keeler	81	Keeler	169
1906	Chase	.323	Keeler	96	Chase	193
1907	Chase	.287	Hoffman	81	Chase	143
1908	Hemphill	.297	Hemphill	62	Hemphill	150
1909	LaPorte	.298	Demmitt	68	Engle	137
1910	Knight	.312	Daniels	68	Cree	134
1911	Cree	.348	Cree	90	Cree	181
1912	Paddock	.288	Daniels	72	Chase	143
1913	Cree	.272	Hartzell	60	Cree	145
1914	Cook	.283	Maisel	78	Cook	133
1915	Maisel	.281	Maisel	77	Maisel	149
1916	Pipp	.262	Pipp	70	Pipp	143
1917	Baker	.282	Pipp	82	Baker	156
1918	Baker	.306	Baker, Pratt	65	Baker	154
1919	Peckinpaugh	.305	Peckinpaugh	89	Baker	166
1920	Ruth	.376	Ruth*	158	Pratt	180
1921	Ruth	.378	Ruth*	177	Ruth	204
1922	Pipp	.329	Witt	98	Pipp	190
1923	Ruth	.393	Ruth*	151	Ruth	205
1924	Ruth*	.378	Ruth*	143	Ruth	200
1925	Combs	.343	Combs	117	Combs	203
1926	Ruth	.372	Ruth*	139	Ruth	184
1927	Gehrig	.373	Ruth*	158	Combs*	231
1928	Gehrig	.374	Ruth*	163	Gehrig	210
1929	Lazzeri	.354	Gehrig	127	Combs	202
1930	Gehrig	.379	Ruth	150	Gehrig	220
1931	Ruth	.373	Gehrig*	163	Gehrig*	211
1932	Gehrig	.349	Combs	142	Gehrig	208
1933	Gehrig	.334	Gehrig*	138	Gehrig	198
1934	Gehrig*	.363	Gehrig*	128	Gehrig	210
1935	Gehrig	.329	Gehrig	125	Rolfe	192
1936	Dickey	.362	Gehrig*	167	DiMaggio	206
1937	Gehrig	.351	DiMaggio*	151	DiMaggio	215
1938	DiMaggio	.324	Rolfe*	132	DiMaggio	194
1939	DiMaggio*	.381	Rolfe*	139	Rolfe*	213
1940	DiMaggio*	.352	Gordon	112	DiMaggio	179
1941	DiMaggio	.357	DiMaggio	122	DiMaggio	193
1942	Gordon	.322	DiMaggio	123	DiMaggio	186
1943	Johnson	.280	Keller	97	Johnson	166
1944	Stirnweiss	.319	Stirnweiss*	125	Stirnweiss*	205
1945	Stirnweiss*	.309	Stirnweiss*	107	Stirnweiss*	195
1946	DiMaggio	.290	Keller	98	Keller	148
1947	DiMaggio	.315	Henrich	109	DiMaggio	168
1948	DiMaggio	.320	Henrich*	138	DiMaggio	190
1949	Henrich	.287	Rizzuto	110	Rizzuto	169
1950	Rizzuto	.324	Rizzuto	125	Rizzuto	200
1951	McDougald	.306	Berra	92	Berra	161
1952	Mantle	.311	Berra	97	Mantle	171
1953	Bauer	.304	Mantle	105	McDougald	154
1954	Noren	.319	Mantle*	129	Berra	179
1955	Mantle	.306	Mantle	121	Mantle	158
1956	Mantle*	.353	Mantle*	132	Mantle	188
1957	Mantle	.365	Mantle*	121	Mantle	173
1958	Mantle	.304	Mantle*	127	Mantle	158
1959	Richardson	.301	Mantle*	104	Mantle	154
1960	Skowron	.309	Mantle*	119	Skowron	166
1961	Howard	.348	Mantle, Maris*	132	Richardson	173
1962	Mantle	.321	Richardson	99	Richardson*	209
1963	Howard	.287	Tresh	91	Richardson	167
1964	Howard	.318	Mantle	92	Richardson	181
1965	Tresh	.279	Tresh	94	Tresh	168
1966	Mantle	.288	Pepitone	85	Richardson	153
1967	Clarke	.272	Clarke	74	Clarke	160
1968	White	.267	White	89	White	154
1969	White	.290	Clarke, Murcer	82	Clarke	183
1970	Munson	.302	White	109	White	180
1971	Murcer	.331	Murcer	94	Mucer	175
1972	Murcer	.292	Murcer*	102	Murcer	171
1973	Murcer	.304	White	88	Murcer	187
1974	Piniella	.305	Maddox	75	Murcer	166
1975	Munson	.318	Bonds	93	Munson	190
1976	Rivers	.312	White*	104	Chambliss	188
1977	Rivers	.326	Nettles	99	Rivers	184
1978	Piniella	.314	Randolph	87	Munson	183
1979	Piniella, Jackson	.297	Randolph	98	Randolph, Chambliss	155
1980	Watson	.307	Randolph	99	Jackson	154
1981	Mumphrey	.307	Randolph	59	Winfield	114
1982	Mumphrey	.300	Randolph	85	Randolph	155
1983	Baylor	.303	Winfield	99	Winfield	169
1984	Mattingly*	.343	Winfield	106	Mattingly*	207
1985	Mattingly	.324	Henderson*	146	Mattingly	211

Year	Doubles		Triples		Home Runs	
1903	Williams	30	Williams, Conroy	12	McFarland	5
1904	Williams	31	Anderson, Conroy	12	Ganzel	6
1905	Williams	20	Williams	8	Williams	6
1906	Williams	25	Chase, Conroy	10	Conroy	4
1907	Chase	23	Conroy, LaPorte, Williams	11	Hoffman	5
1908	Conroy	22	Hemphill	9	Niles	4
1909	Engle	20	Demmitt	12	Chase, Demmitt	4
1910	Knight	25	Cree	16	Wolter, Cree	4
1911	Chase	32	Cree	22	Wolter, Cree	4
1912	Daniels	25	Hartzell, Daniels	11	Zinn	6
1913	Cree	25	Peckinpaugh	7	Wolter, Sweeney	2
1914	Maisel	23	Maisel Hartzell	9	Peckinpaugh	3
1915	Pipp	20	Pipp	13	Peckinpaugh	5
1916	Baker	23	Pipp	14	Pipp	12
1917	Pipp	29	Pipp	12	Pipp*	9
1918	Baker	24	Pipp	2	Baker	6
1919	Pratt, Bodie	27	Pipp	10	Baker	10
1920	Meusel	40	Peckinpaugh	14	Ruth*	54
1921	Ruth	44	Ruth	16	Ruth	59
1922	Pipp	32	Meusel	11	Ruth	35
1923	Ruth	45	Ruth	13	Ruth*	41
1924	Meusel	40	Pipp*	19	Ruth*	46
1925	Combs	36	Combs	13	Meusel*	33
1926	Gehrig	47	Gehrig*	20	Ruth*	47
1927	Gehrig*	52	Combs*	23	Ruth*	60
1928	Gehrig*	47	Combs*	21	Ruth*	54
1929	Lazzeri	37	Combs	15	Ruth*	46
1930	Gehrig	42	Combs*	22	Ruth*	49
1931	Lary	35	Gehrig	17	Ruth*, Gehrig*	46
1932	Gehrig	42	Chapman	15	Ruth	41
1933	Gehrig	41	Combs	15	Ruth	34
1934	Gehrig	40	Chapman*	13	Gehrig*	49
1935	Chapman	38	Selkirk	12	Gehrig	30
1936	DiMaggio	44	DiMaggio*, Rolfe*	15	Gehrig*	49
1937	Gehrig	37	DiMaggio	15	DiMaggio*	46
1938	Rolfe*	36	DiMaggio	13	DiMaggio	32
1939	Rolfe*	46	Rolfe	10	DiMaggio	30
1940	Gordon	32	Keller	15	DiMaggio	31
1941	DiMaggio	43	DiMaggio	11	Keller	33
1942	Henrich	30	DiMaggio	13	Keller	26
1943	Etten	35	Lindell*	12	Keller	31
1944	Stirnweiss	35	Stirnweiss*, Lindell*	16	Etten*	22
1945	Stirnweiss	32	Stirnweiss*	22	Etten	18
1946	Keller	29	Keller	10	Keller	30
1947	Henrich	35	Henrich*	13	DiMaggio	20
1948	Henrich	42	Henrich*	14	DiMaggio*	39
1949	Rizzuto	22	Rizzuto, Woodling	7	Henrich	24
1950	Rizzuto	36	Bauer, DiMaggio	10	DiMaggio	32
1951	McDougald	23	Woodling	8	Berra	27
1952	Mantle	37	Rizzuto	10	Berra	30
1953	McDougald	27	McDougald	7	Berra	27
1954	Berra	28	Mantle	12	Mantle	27
1955	Mantle	25	Mantle*, Carey*	10	Mantle*	37
1956	Berra	29	Bauer	7	Mantle*	52
1957	Mantle	28	Bauer*, Simpson*, McDougald*	9	Mantle	34
1958	Bauer, Skowron	22	Bauer	6	Mantle*	42
1959	Lopez	27	McDougald	8	Mantle	31
1960	Skowron	34	Maris	7	Mantle*	40
1961	Kubek	38	Mantle, Kubek	6	Maris*	61
1962	Richardson	38	Skowron	6	Maris	33
1963	Tresh	28	Howard, Richardson	6	Howard	28
1964	Howard	27	Tresh, Boyer	5	Mantle	35
1965	Tresh	29	Tresh, Boyer	6	Tresh	26
1966	Boyer	22	Boyer, Clarke, Tresh, Pepitone	4	Pepitone	31
1967	Tresh	23	Pepitone, Smith, Tresh, Whitaker	3	Mantle	22
1968	White	20	White, Robinson	7	Mantle	18
1969	White	30	Clarke	7	Pepitone	27
1970	White	31	Kenney	7	Murcer	23
1971	Murcer	25	Clarke, White	7	Murcer	25
1972	Murcer	30	Murcer	7	Murcer	33
1973	Murcer, Munson	29	Munson	4	Murcer, Nettles	22
1974	Maddox, Piniella	26	White	8	Nettles	22
1975	Chambliss	38	White	5	Bonds	32
1976	Chambliss	32	Rivers	8	Nettles*	32
1977	Jackson	39	Randolph	11	Nettles	37
1978	Piniella	34	Rivers	8	Jackson, Nettles	27
1979	Chambliss	27	Randolph	13	Jackson	29
1980	Cerone	30	Randolph	7	Jackson*	41
1981	Winfield	25	Mumphrey	5	Jackson, Nettles	15
1982	Mumphrey, Winfield	24	Mumphrey	10	Winfield	37
1983	Baylor	33	Winfield	8	Winfield	32
1984	Mattingly*	44	Moreno	6	Baylor	27
1985	Mattingly*	48	Winfield	6	Mattingly	35

NEW YORK YANKEE LEADERS   1903–1985

Year	RBIS	Stolen Bases	Strikeouts (Pitchers)
1903	Williams 82	Conroy 33	Chesbro 147
1904	Anderson 82	Conroy 30	Chesbro 239
1905	Williams 60	Fultz 44	Chesbro 156
1906	Williams 77	Hoffman 33	Chesbro 152
1907	Chase 68	Conroy 41	Doyle 94
1908	Hemphill 44	Hemphill 42	Chesbro 124
1909	Engle 71	Austin 30	Lake 117
1910	Chase 73	Daniels 41	Ford 209
1911	Hartzell 91	Cree 48	Ford 158
1912	Chase 58	Daniels 37	Ford 112
1913	Cree 63	Daniels 27	Fisher 92
1914	Peckinpaugh 51	Maisel* 74	Keating 109
1915	Pipp 58	Maisel 51	Caldwell 130
1916	Pipp* 99	Magee 29	Shawkey 122
1917	Pipp 72	Maisel 29	Caldwell 102
1918	Baker 68	Bodie 16	Love 95
1919	Baker 78	Pratt 22	Shawkey 122
1920	Ruth* 137	Ruth 14	Shawkey 126
1921	Ruth* 170	Meusel, Pipp, Ruth ... 17	Shawkey 126
1922	Ruth 96	Meusel 13	Shawkey 130
1923	Ruth* 130	Ruth 17	Bush, Shawkey 125
1924	Ruth 121	Meusel 26	Shawkey 114
1925	Meusel* 138	Paschal 14	Jones 92
1926	Ruth* 155	Meusel 16	Hoyt 79
1927	Gehrig* 175	Meusel 24	Hoyt 86
1928	Gehrig*, Ruth* 142	Lazzeri 15	Pipgras 139
1929	Ruth 154	Combs, Lazzeri 11	Pipgras 125
1930	Gehrig* 174	Combs 16	Ruffing 117
1931	Gehrig* 184	Chapman* 61	Gomez 150
1932	Gehrig 151	Chapman* 38	Ruffing* 190
1933	Gehrig 139	Chapman* 27	Gomez* 163
1934	Gehrig* 165	Chapman 26	Gomez* 158
1935	Gehrig 119	Chapman 17	Gomez 138
1936	Gehrig 152	Crosetti 18	Pearson 118
1937	DiMaggio 167	Crosetti 13	Gomez* 194
1938	DiMaggio 140	Crosetti* 27	Gomez 129
1939	DiMaggio 126	Selkirk 12	Gomez 102
1940	DiMaggio 133	Gordon 18	Ruffing 97
1941	DiMaggio* 125	Rizzuto 14	Russo 105
1942	DiMaggio 114	Rizzuto 22	Borowy 85
1943	Etten 107	Stirnweiss 11	Chandler 134
1944	Lindell 103	Stirnweiss* 55	Borowy 107
1945	Etten* 111	Stirnweiss* 33	Bevens 76
1946	Keller 101	Stirnweiss 18	Chandler 138
1947	Henrich 98	Rizzuto 11	Reynolds 129
1948	DiMaggio* 155	Rizzuto 6	Raschi 124
1949	Berra 91	Rizzuto 18	Byrne 129
1950	Berra 124	Rizzuto 12	Reynolds 160
1951	Berra 88	Rizzuto 18	Raschi* 164
1952	Berra 98	Rizzuto 17	Reynolds* 160
1953	Berra 108	Mantle 8	Ford 110
1954	Berra 125	Mantle, Carey 5	Ford 125
1955	Berra 108	Hunter 9	Turley 210
1956	Mantle* 130	Mantle 10	Ford 141
1957	Mantle 94	Mantle 16	Turley 152
1958	Mantle 97	Mantle 18	Turley 168
1959	Lopez 93	Mantle 21	Ford 114
1960	Maris* 112	Mantle 14	Terry 92
1961	Maris* 142	Mantle 12	Ford 209
1962	Maris 100	Richardson 11	Terry 176
1963	Pepitone 89	Richardson 15	Ford 189
1964	Mantle 111	Tresh 13	Downing* 217
1965	Tresh 74	Richardson 7	Downing 179
1966	Pepitone 83	White 14	Downing 152
1967	Pepitone 64	Clarke 21	Downing 171
1968	White 62	Clarke, White 20	Bahnsen 162
1969	Murcer 62	Clarke 33	Peterson 150
1970	White 94	White 24	Peterson 127
1971	Murcer 94	Clarke 17	Peterson 139
1972	Murcer 96	White 23	Stottlemyre 110
1973	Murcer 95	White 16	Medich 145
1974	Murcer 88	White 15	Dobson 157
1975	Munson 102	Bonds 30	Hunter 177
1976	Munson 105	Rivers 43	Hunter 173
1977	Jackson 110	Rivers 22	Guidry 176
1978	Jackson 97	Randolph 36	Guidry 248
1979	Jackson 89	Randolph 32	Guidry 201
1980	Jackson 111	Randolph 30	Guidry 166
1981	Winfield 68	Randolph 14	Guidry 104
1982	Winfield 106	Randolph 16	Righetti 163
1983	Winfield 116	Baylor 17	Righetti 169
1984	Mattingly 110	Moreno 20	Niekro 136
1985	Mattingly* 145	Henderson* 80	Niekro 149

Year	Innings	Wins	ERA
1903	Chesbro 325	Chesbro 21-15	Griffith 2.70
1904	Chesbro* 455	Chesbro* 41-12	Chesbro 1.82
1905	Orth 305	Chesbro 20-15	Chesbro 2.20
1906	Orth* 339	Orth 27-17	Clarkson 2.32
1907	Orth 249	Orth 14-21	Chesbro 2.53
1908	Chesbro 289	Chesbro 14-20	Chesbro 2.93
1909	Warhop 243	Lake 14-11	Lake 1.88
1910	Ford 300	Ford 26-6	Ford 1.65
1911	Ford 281	Ford 22-11	Ford 2.28
1912	Ford 292	Ford 13-21	McConnell 2.75
1913	Fisher 246	Fisher 11-17, Ford 11-18	Caldwell 2.43
1914	Warhop 217	Caldwell 17-9	Caldwell 1.94
1915	Caldwell 305	Caldwell 19-16	Fisher 2.11
1916	Shawkey 277	Shawkey 23-14	Cullop 2.05
1917	Shawkey 236	Shawkey 13-15	Fisher 2.19
1918	Mogridge 230	Mogridge 16-13	Mogridge 2.27
1919	Quinn 264	Shawkey 20-11	Magridge 2.50
1920	Mays 312	Mays 26-11	Shawkey* 2.45
1921	Mays* 337	Mays* 27-9	Mays 3.04
1922	Shawkey 300	Bush 26-7	Shawkey 2.91
1923	Bush 276	Jones 21-8	Hoyt 3.01
1924	Pennock 286	Pennock 21-9	Pennock 2.83
1925	Pennock* 277	Pennock 16-17	Pennock 2.96
1926	Pennock 266	Pennock 23-11	Shocker 3.38
1927	Hoyt 256	Hoyt* 22-7	W. Moore* 2.28
1928	Pipgras 301	Pipgras* 24-13	Pennock 2.56
1929	Pipgras 225	Pipgras 18-12	Zachary 2.47
1930	Ruffing 222	Pipgras 15-15, Ruffing 15-8	Pipgras 4.11
1931	Gomez 243	Gomez 21-9	Gomez 2.63
1932	Gomez 265	Gomez 24-7	Ruffing 3.09
1933	Gomez, Ruffing 235	Gomez 16-10	Gomez 3.18
1934	Gomez* 282	Gomez* 26-5	Gomez* 2.33
1935	Gomez 246	Ruffing 16-11	Ruffing 3.12
1936	Ruffing 271	Ruffing 20-12	Pearson 3.71
1937	Gomez 278	Gomez* 21-11	Gomez* 2.33
1938	Ruffing 247	Ruffing* 21-7	Ruffing 3.32
1939	Ruffing 233	Ruffing 21-7	Ruffing 2.94
1940	Ruffing 226	Ruffing 15-12	Russo 3.29
1941	Russo 210	Ruffing 15-6, Gomez 15-5	Russo 3.09
1942	Chandler 201	Bonham 21-5	Bonham 2.27
1943	Chandler 253	Chandler* 20-4	Chandler* 1.64
1944	Borowy 253	Borowy 17-12	Borowy 2.63
1945	Bevens 184	Bevens 13-9	Bonham 3.28
1946	Chandler 257	Chandler 20-8	Chandler 2.10
1947	Reynolds 242	Reynolds 19-8	Chandler* 2.46
1948	Reynolds 236	Raschi 19-8	Shea 3.41
1949	Raschi 275	Raschi 21-10	Lopat 3.27
1950	Raschi 257	Raschi 21-8	Lopat 3.47
1951	Raschi 258	Raschi 21-10, Lopat 21-9	Lopat 2.91
1952	Reynolds 244	Reynolds 20-8	Reynolds* 2.07
1953	Ford 207	Ford 18-6	Lopat* 2.43
1954	Ford 211	Grim 20-6	Ford 2.82
1955	Ford 254	Ford 18-7	Ford 2.62
1956	Ford 226	Ford 19-6	Ford* 2.47
1957	Sturdivant 202	Sturdivant 16-6	Shantz* 2.45
1958	Turley 245	Turley* 21-7	Ford* 2.01
1959	Ford 204	Ford 16-10	Ditmar 2.90
1960	Ditmar 200	Ditmar 15-9	Ditmar 3.06
1961	Ford* 283	Ford* 25-4	Stafford 2.68
1962	Terry* 299	Terry* 23-12	Ford 2.90
1963	Ford 269	Ford 24-7	Bouton 2.53
1964	Bouton 271	Bouton 18-13	Ford 2.13
1965	Stottlemyre 291	Stottlemyre 20-9	Stottlemyre 2.63
1966	Stottlemyre 251	Stottlemyre 12-20, Peterson 12-11	Peterson 3.31
1967	Stottlemyre 255	Stottlemyre 15-15	Downing 2.63
1968	Stottlemyre 279	Stottlemyre 21-12	Bahnsen 2.06
1969	Stottlemyre 303	Stottlemyre 20-14	Peterson 2.55
1970	Stottlemyre 271	Peterson 20-11	Peterson 91
1971	Peterson 274	Stottlemyre 16-12	Stottlemyre 2.87
1972	Stottlemyre 200	Peterson 17-15	Kline 2.40
1973	Stottlemyre 273	Stottlemyre 16-16	Medich 2.95
1974	Dobson 281	Dobson 19-15, Medich 19-15	Dobson 3.07
1975	Hunter 328	Hunter 23-14	Hunter 2.58
1976	Hunter 299	Figueroa 19-10	Figueroa 3.01
1977	Figueroa 239	Guidry 16-7, Figueroa 16-11	Guidry 2.82
1978	Guidry 274	Guidry* 25-3	Guidry* 1.74
1979	John 276	John 21-9	Guidry* 2.78
1980	John 265	John 22-9	May* 2.47
1981	May 148	Guidry 11-5	John 2.64
1982	Guidry 220	Guidry 14-8	John 3.66
1983	Guidry 250	Guidry 21-9	Guidry 3.42
1984	Niekro 216	Niekro 16-8	Niekro 3.09
1985	Guidry 259	Guidry* 22-6	Guidry 3.27

YANKEES POSITION LEADERS
(By Games)

Year	Catcher	1st Base	2nd Base
1903	Beville 75	Ganzel 129	Williams 104
1904	McGuire 97	Ganzel 118	Williams 146
1905	Kleinow 83	Chase 122	Williams 129
1906	Kleinow 95	Chase 150	Williams 139
1907	Kleinow 86	Chase 121	Williams 139
1908	Kleinow 89	Chase 98	Niles 85
1909	Kleinow 77	Chase 118	LaPorte 83
1910	Sweeney 78	Chase 130	LaPorte 79
1911	Blair 84	Chase 124	Gardner 101
1912	Sweeney 108	Chase 121	Simmons 88
1913	Sweeney 112	Knight 50	Hartzell 81
1914	Sweeney 78	Mullen 93	Boone 90
1915	Nunamaker 77	Pipp 134	Boone 134
1916	Nunamaker 79	Pipp 148	Gedeon 122
1917	Nunamaker 91	Pipp 155	Maisel 100
1918	Hannah 88	Pipp 91	Pratt 126
1919	Ruel 81	Pipp 140	Pratt 140
1920	Ruel 80	Pipp 153	Pratt 154
1921	Schang 132	Pipp 153	Ward 123
1922	Schang 119	Pipp 152	Ward 152
1923	Schang 81	Pipp 144	Ward 152
1924	Schang 106	Pipp 153	Ward 120
1925	Bengough 94	Gehrig 114	Ward 113
1926	Collins 100	Gehrig 155	Lazzeri 149
1927	Collins 89	Gehrig 155	Lazzeri 113
1928	Grabowski 75	Gehrig 154	Lazzeri 110
1929	Dickey 127	Gehrig 154	Lazzeri 147
1930	Dickey 101	Gehrig 153	Lazzeri 77
1931	Dickey 125	Gehrig 154	Lazzeri 90
1932	Dickey 108	Gehrig 155	Lazzeri 133
1933	Dickey 127	Gehrig 152	Lazzeri 138
1934	Dickey 104	Gehrig 153	Lazzeri 92
1935	Dickey 118	Gehrig 149	Lazzeri 118
1936	Dickey 107	Gehrig 155	Lazzeri 148
1937	Dickey 137	Gehrig 157	Lazzeri 125
1938	Dickey 126	Gehrig 157	Gordon 126
1939	Dickey 126	Dahlgren 144	Gordon 151
1940	Dickey 102	Dahlgren 155	Gordon 155
1941	Dickey 104	Sturm 124	Gordon 131
1942	Dickey 80	Hassett 132	Gordon 147
1943	Dickey 71	Etten 154	Gordon 152
1944	Garback 85	Etten 154	Stirnweiss 154
1945	Garback 59	Etten 152	Stirnweiss 152
1946	Robinson 95	Etten 84	Gordon 108
1947	Robinson 74	McQuinn 142	Stirnweiss 148
1948	Niarhos 82	McQuinn 90	Stirnweiss 141
1949	Berra 109	Henrich 52	Coleman 122
1950	Berra 148	Collins 99	Coleman 152
1951	Berra 141	Collins 114	Coleman 102
1952	Berra 140	Collins 119	Martin 107
1953	Berra 133	Collins 113	Martin 146
1954	Berra 149	Collins 117	McDougald 92
1955	Berra 145	Skowron 74	McDougald 126
1956	Berra 135	Skowron 120	Martin 105
1957	Berra 121	Skowron 115	Richardson 93
1958	Berra 88	Skowron 118	McDougald 115
1959	Berra 116	Skowron 72	Richardson 109
1960	Howard 91	Skowron 142	Richardson 141
1961	Howard 111	Skowron 149	Richardson 161
1962	Howard 129	Skowron 135	Richardson 161
1963	Howard 132	Pepitone 143	Richardson 150
1964	Howard 146	Pepitone 155	Richardson 157
1965	Howard 95	Pepitone 115	Richardson 158
1966	Howard 100	Pepitone 119	Richardson 147
1967	Gibbs 99	Mantle 131	Clarke 140
1968	Gibbs 121	Mantle 131	Clarke 139
1969	Gibbs 66	Pepitone 132	Clarke 156
1970	Munson 125	Cater 131	Clarke 157
1971	Munson 117	Cater 78	Clarke 156
1972	Munson 132	Blomberg 95	Clarke 143
1973	Munson 142	F. Alou 67	Clarke 147
1974	Munson 137	Chambliss 106	Alomar 76
1975	Munson 130	Chambliss 147	Alomar 150
1976	Munson 121	Chambliss 155	Randolph 124
1977	Munson 136	Chambliss 157	Randolph 147
1978	Munson 125	Chambliss 155	Randolph 134
1979	Munson 88	Chambliss 134	Randolph 153
1980	Cerone 147	Watson 104	Randolph 138
1981	Cerone 69	Watson 50	Randolph 93
1982	Cerone 89	Mayberry 64	Randolph 143
1983	Wynegar 94	Griffey 100	Randolph 104
1984	Wynegar 126	Mattingly 133	Randolph 142
1985	Wynegar 96	Mattingly 159	Randolph 143

YANKEES POSITION LEADERS

(By Games)

Year	3rd Base	Shortstop	Designated Hitter
1903	Conroy 123	Elberfeld 90	
1904	Conroy 110	Elberfeld 122	
1905	Yeager 90	Elberfeld 108	
1906	LaPorte 114	Elberfeld 98	
1907	Moriarty 91	Elberfeld 118	
1908	Conroy 119	Ball 130	
1909	Austin 111	Knight 78	
1910	Austin 133	Knight 79	
1911	Hartzell 124	Knight 82	
1912	Hartzell 56	Martin 64	
1913	Midkiff 76	Peckinpaugh 93	
1914	Maisel 148	Peckinpaugh 157	
1915	Maisel 134	Peckinpaugh 142	
1916	Baker 96	Peckinpaugh 146	
1917	Baker 146	Peckinpaugh 148	
1918	Baker 126	Peckinpaugh 122	
1919	Baker 141	Peckinpaugh 121	
1920	Ward 114	Peckinpaugh 137	
1921	Baker 83	Peckinpaugh 147	
1922	Baker 60	Scott 154	
1923	Dugan 146	Scott 152	
1924	Dugan 148	Scott 153	
1925	Dugan 96	Wanninger 111	
1926	Dugan 122	Koenig 141	
1927	Dugan 111	Koenig 122	
1928	Dugan 91	Koenig 125	
1929	Robertson 77	Durocher 93	
1930	Chapman 91	Lary 113	
1931	Sewell 121	Lary 155	
1932	Sewell 122	Crosetti 83	
1933	Sewell 131	Crosetti 133	
1934	Saltzgaver 84	Crosetti 119	
1935	Rolfe 136	Crosetti 87	
1936	Rolfe 133	Crosetti 151	
1937	Rolfe 154	Crosetti 147	
1938	Rolfe 151	Crosetti 157	
1939	Rolfe 152	Crosetti 152	
1940	Rolfe 138	Crosetti 145	
1941	Rolfe 131	Ruzzuto 128	
1942	Crosetti 62	Rizzuto 144	
1943	Johnson 155	Crosetti 90	
1944	Grimes 97	Milosevich 91	
1945	Grimes 141	Crosetti 126	
1946	Stirnweiss 79	Rizzuto 125	
1947	Johnson 132	Rizzuto 151	
1948	Johnson 118	Rizzuto 128	
1949	Brown 86	Rizzuto 152	
1950	Johnson 100	Rizzuto 155	
1951	Brown 90	Rizzuto 144	
1952	McDougald 117	Rizzuto 152	
1953	McDougald 136	Rizzuto 133	
1954	Carey 120	Rizzuto 126	
1955	Carey 135	Hunter 98	
1956	Carey 131	McDougald 92	
1957	Carey 81	McDougald 121	
1958	Carey 99	Kubek 134	
1959	Lopez 76	Kubek 67	
1960	Boyer 99	Kubek 136	
1961	Boyer 141	Kubek 145	
1962	Boyer 157	Tresh 111	
1963	Boyer 141	Kubek 132	
1964	Boyer 123	Kubek 99	
1965	Boyer 147	Kubek 93	
1966	Boyer 85	Clarke 63	
1967	Smith 115	Amaro 123	
1968	Cox 132	Tresh 119	
1969	Kenney 83	Michael 118	
1970	Kenney 135	Michael 123	
1971	Kenney 109	Michael 136	
1972	Sanchez 68	Michael 121	
1973	Nettles 157	Michael 128	Hart 106
1974	Nettles 154	Mason 152	Blomberg 58
1975	Nettles 157	Mason 93	Herrmann 35
1976	Nettles 158	Stanley 110	May 81
1977	Nettles 156	Dent 157	May 51
1978	Nettles 159	Dent 123	Johnson 39
1979	Nettles 144	Dent 141	Spencer 71
1980	Nettles 88	Dent 141	Soderholm 51
1981	Nettles 97	Dent 73	Murcer 33
1982	Nettles 122	Smalley 93	Gamble 74
1983	Nettles 129	Smalley 90	Baylor 136
1984	Harrah 74	Meacham 96	Baylor 127
1985	Pagliarulo 134	Meacham 155	Baylor 140

37

YANKEES POSITION LEADERS
(By Games)

Year	Outfield	Outfield	Outfield
1903	Keeler 128	McFarland 103	Davis 102
1904	Keeler 142	Anderson 112	Dougherty 106
1905	Keeler 139	Fultz 122	Dougherty 108
1906	Keeler 152	Hoffman 98	Delahanty 92
1907	Keeler 107	Hoffman 135	Conroy 100
1908	Keeler 88	Hemphill 142	Stahl 67
1909	Keeler 95	Demmitt 109	Engle 134
1910	Wolter 130	Hemphill 94	Cree 134
1911	Wolter 113	Daniels 120	Cree 137
1912	Zinn 106	Daniels 131	Cree 50
1913	Wolter 121	Daniels 87	Cree 144
1914	Cook 126	Hartzell 128	Cree 76
1915	Cook 131	Hartzell 107	High 117
1916	Gilhooley 57	Magee 128	High 109
1917	Miller 112	Hendryx 107	High 100
1918	Gilhooley 111	Miller 62	Bodie 90
1919	Vick 100	Lewis 141	Bodie 134
1920	Ruth 139	Lewis 99	Bodie 129
1921	Ruth 152	Miller 56	Meusel 147
1922	Ruth 110	Witt 138	Meusel 121
1923	Ruth 148	Witt 144	Meusel 121
1924	Ruth 152	Witt 143	Meusel 143
1925	Ruth 98	Combs 150	Meusel 131
1926	Ruth 149	Combs 145	Meusel 107
1927	Ruth 151	Combs 152	Meusel 131
1928	Ruth 154	Combs 149	Meusel 131
1929	Ruth 133	Combs 141	Meusel 96
1930	Ruth 144	Combs 135	Rice 87
1931	Ruth 142	Combs 129	Chapman 137
1932	Ruth 127	Combs 138	Chapman 149
1933	Ruth 132	Combs 104	Chapman 147
1934	Ruth 111	Byrd 104	Chapman 149
1935	Selkirk 127	Hill 94	Chapman 138
1936	Selkirk 135	Powell 84	DiMaggio 138
1937	Hoag 99	Powell 94	DiMaggio 150
1938	Selkirk 95	Henrich 130	DiMaggio 145
1939	Selkirk 124	Keller 105	DiMaggio 117
1940	Selkirk 111	Keller 136	DiMaggio 130
1941	Henrich 139	Keller 137	DiMaggio 139
1942	Henrich 119	Keller 152	DiMaggio 154
1943	Lindell 122	Keller 141	Metheny 91
1944	Lindell 149	Martin 80	Metheny 132
1945	Stainback 83	Martin 102	Metheny 128
1946	Henrich 111	Keller 149	DiMaggio 131
1947	Henrich 132	Lindell 118	DiMaggio 139
1948	Henrich 102	Lindell 79	DiMaggio 152
1949	Bauer 95	Mapes 108	Woodling 98
1950	Bauer 110	Woodling 118	DiMaggio 137
1951	Bauer 107	Woodling 116	DiMaggio 113
1952	Bauer 139	Woodling 118	Mantle 141
1953	Bauer 126	Woodling 119	Mantle 121
1954	Bauer 108	Noren 116	Mantle 144
1955	Bauer 133	Noren 126	Mantle 145
1956	Bauer 146	Howard 65	Mantle 144
1957	Bauer 135	Howard 71	Mantle 139
1958	Bauer 123	Siebern 133	Mantle 150
1959	Bauer 111	Siebern 93	Mantle 143
1960	Lopez 106	Maris 131	Mantle 150
1961	Berra 87	Maris 160	Mantle 150
1962	Lopez 84	Maris 154	Mantle 154
1963	Lopez 124	Maris 86	Tresh 144
1964	Tresh 146	Maris 137	Mantle 132
1965	Tresh 154	Moschitto 89	Mantle 108
1966	Tresh 84	Maris 95	Mantle 97
1967	Tresh 118	Whitaker 114	Pepitone 123
1968	White 154	Robinson 98	Kosco 95
1969	White 126	Woods 67	Murcer 118
1970	White 161	Blefary 79	Murcer 155
1971	White 145	F. Alou 80	Murcer 143
1972	White 155	Callison 74	Murcer 151
1973	White 162	M. Alou 94	Murcer 160
1974	Piniella 130	Maddox 135	Murcer 156
1975	White 135	Maddox 55	Bonds 129
1976	White 156	Rivers 136	Gamble 104
1977	White 135	Rivers 136	Jackson 127
1978	Piniella 103	Rivers 138	Jackson 104
1979	Piniella 112	Murcer 70	Jackson 125
1980	Piniella 104	Brown 131	Jackson 94
1981	Winfield 102	Mumphrey 79	Jackson 61
1982	Winfield 135	Mumphrey 123	Griffey 127
1983	Winfield 152	Mumphrey 83	Kemp 103
1984	Winfield 140	Moreno 108	Griffey 82
1985	Winfield 152	Henderson 141	Griffey 110

YANKEES PITCHING LEADERS
(By Starts and/or Saves)

Year	Starter	Starter	Starter	Starter	Starter or Reliever
1903	Chesbro-R	Tannehill-L	Griffith-R	Wolfe-R	Howell-R
1904	Chesbro-R	Powell-R	Orth-R	Hughes-R	Griffith-R
1905	Chesbro-R	Powell-R	Orth-R	Hogg-R	Griffith-R
1906	Chesbro-R	Clarkson-R	Orth-R	Hogg-R	Griffith-R
1907	Chesbro-R	Doyle-R	Orth-R	Hogg-R	Keefe-R
1908	Chesbro-R	Manning-R	Lake-R	Hogg-R	Orth-R
1909	Warhop-R	Manning-R	Lake-R	Brockett-R	Hughes-R
1910	Warhop-R	Ford-R	Quinn-R	Vaughn-L	Caldwell-R
1911	Warhop-R	Ford-R	Caldwell-R	Fisher-R	Quinn-R
1912	Warhop-R	Ford-R	Caldwell-R	McConnell-R	Fisher-R
1913	Shultz-L	Ford-R	Keating-R	Fisher-R	McConnell-R
1914	Warhop-R	Caldwell-R	Keating-R	Fisher-R	McHale-R
1915	Warhop-R	Caldwell-R	Brown-R	Fisher-R	Pieh-R
1916	Shawkey-R	Cullop-L	Mogridge-L	Fisher-R	Russell-R
1917	Shawkey-R	Caldwell-R	Mogridge-L	Fisher-R	Russell-R
1918	Love-L	Caldwell-R	Mogridge-L	Russell-R	Finneran-R
1919	Shawkey-R	Quinn-R	Mogridge-L	Thormahlen-L	Russell-R
1920	Shawkey-R	Quinn-R	Mays-R	Collins-R	Thormahlen-L
1921	Shawkey-R	Hoyt-R	Mays-R	Collins-R	Quinn-R
1922	Shawley-R	Hoyt-R	Mays-R	Bush-R	Jones-R
1923	Shawkey-R	Hoyt-R	Jones-R	Bush-R	Pennock-L
1924	Shawkey-R	Hoyt-R	Pennock-L	Bush-R	Jones-R
1925	Shocker-R	Hoyt-R	Pennock-L	Jones-R	Shawkey-R
1926	Shocker-R	Hoyt-R	Pennock-L	Jones-R	Braxton-L
1927	Shocker-R	Hoyt-R	Pennock-L	Ruether-L	Moore-R
1928	Pipgras-R	Hoyt-R	Pennock-L	Johnson-R	Shealy-R
1929	Pipgras-R	Hoyt-R	Pennock-L	Wells-R	Moore-R
1930	Pipgras-R	Ruffing-R	Sheird-R	Wells-R	Johnson-R
1931	Johnson-R	Ruffing-R	Pennock-L	Gomez-L	Pipgras-R
1932	Pipgras-R	Ruffing-R	Pennock-L	Gomez-L	Allen-R
1933	Van Atta-L	Ruffing-R	Allen-R	Gomez-L	Moore-R
1934	Murphy-R	Ruffing-R	Broaca-R	Gomez-L	DeShong-R
1935	Allen-R	Ruffing-R	Broaca-R	Gomez-L	Murphy-R
1936	Pearson-R	Ruffing-R	Broaca-R	Gomez-L	Malone-R
1937	Pearson-R	Ruffing-R	Hadley-R	Gomez-L	Murphy-R
1938	Pearson-R	Ruffing-R	Chandler-R	Gomez-L	Murphy-R
1939	Donald-R	Ruffing-R	Hadley-R	Gomez-L	Murphy-R
1940	Russo-L	Ruffing-R	Chandler-R	Breuer-R	Murphy-R
1941	Russo-L	Ruffing-R	Chandler-R	Gomez-L	Murphy-R
1942	Borowy-R	Ruffing-R	Chandler-R	Bonham-R	Murphy-R
1943	Borowy-R	Wensloff-R	Chandler-R	Bonham-R	Murphy-R
1944	Borowy-R	Donald-R	Dubiel-R	Bonham-R	Turner-R
1945	Borowy-R	Bevens-R	Dubiel-R	Bonham-R	Turner-R
1946	Page-R	Bevens-R	Chandler-R	Bonham-R	Murphy-R
1947	Shea-R	Bevens-R	Chandler-R	Reynolds-R	Page-R
1948	Shea-R	Raschi-R	Lopat-L	Reynolds-R	Page-R
1949	Byrne-L	Raschi-R	Lopat-L	Reynolds-R	Page-R
1950	Byrne-L	Raschi-R	Lopat-L	Reynolds-R	Page-R
1951	Morgan-R	Raschi-R	Lopat-L	Reynolds-R	Ostrowski-L
1952	Sain-R	Raschi-R	Lopat-L	Reynolds-R	Kuzava-L
1953	Sain-R	Raschi-R	Lopat-L	Ford-L	Reynolds-R
1954	Byrd-R	Grim-R	Lopat-L	Ford-L	Sain-R
1955	Turley-R	Byrne-L	Kucks-R	Ford-L	Konstanty-R
1956	Turley-R	Larsen-R	Kucks-R	Ford-L	Morgan-R
1957	Turley-R	Sturdivant-R	Kucks-R	Shantz-L	Grim-R
1958	Turley-R	Larsen-R	Kucks-R	Ford-L	Duren-R
1959	Turley-R	Maas-R	Ditmar-R	Ford-L	Duren-R
1960	Turley-R	Terry-R	Ditmar-R	Ford-L	Shantz-L
1961	Stafford-R	Terry-R	Sheldon-R	Ford-L	Arroyo-L
1962	Stafford-R	Terry-R	Bouton-R	Ford-L	Bridges-L
1963	Downing-L	Terry-R	Bouton-R	Ford-L	Reniff-R
1964	Downing-L	Terry-R	Bouton-R	Ford-L	Mikkelson-R
1965	Downing-L	Stottlemyre-R	Bouton-R	Ford-L	Ramos-R
1966	Downing-L	Stottlemyre-R	Talbot-R	Peterson-L	Ramos-R
1967	Downing-L	Stottlemyre-R	Talbot-R	Peterson-L	Womack-L
1968	Bahnsen-R	Stottlemyre-R	Barber-L	Peterson-L	Hamilton-L
1969	Bahnsen-R	Stottlemyre-R	Burbach-R	Peterson-L	Aker-R
1970	Bahnsen-R	Stottlemyre-R	Kline-R	Peterson-L	McDaniel-R
1971	Bahnsen-R	Stottlemyre-R	Kline-R	Peterson-L	McDaniel-R
1972	Kekick-L	Stottlemyre-R	Kline-R	Peterson-L	Lyle-L
1973	Dobson-R	Stottlemyre-R	Medich-R	Peterson-L	Lyle-L
1974	Dobson-R	Tidrow-R	Medich-R	May-L	Lyle-L
1975	Dobson-R	Hunter-R	Medich-R	May-L	Lyle-L
1976	Figueroa-R	Hunter-R	Ellis-R	Holtzman-L	Lyle-L
1977	Figueroa-R	Guidry-L	Gullett-L	Torrez-R	Lyle-L
1978	Figueroa-R	Guidry-L	Tidrow-R	Beattie-R	Gossage-R
1979	John-L	Guidry-L	Tiant-R	Hunter-R	Gossage-R
1980	John-L	Guidry-L	Tiant-R	Underwood-L	Gossage-R
1981	John-L	Guidry-L	Righetti-L	May-L	Gossage-R
1982	John-L	Guidry-L	Righetti-L	Morgan-R	Gossage-R
1983	Rawley-L	Guidry-L	Righetti-L	Fontenot-L	Gossage-R
1984	Niekro-R	Guidry-L	Rasmussen-L	Fontenot-L	Righetti-L
1985	Niekro-R	Guidry-L	Whitson-R	Cowley-R	Righetti-L

39

ALL-TIME YANKEES—TOP 20
HITTING CATEGORIES

#	Games		At Bats		Runs		Hits	
1.	Mantle	2401	Mantle	8102	Ruth	1959	Gehrig	2721
2.	Gehrig	2164	Gehrig	8001	Gehrig	1888	Ruth	2518
3.	Berra	2116	Berra	7546	Mantle	1677	Mantle	2415
4.	Ruth	2084	Ruth	7217	DiMaggio	1390	DiMaggio	2214
5.	White	1881	DiMaggio	6821	Combs	1186	Berra	2148
6.	Dickey	1789	White	6550	Berra	1174	Dickey	1969
7.	DiMaggio	1736	Dickey	6300	Crosetti	1006	Combs	1866
8.	Crosetti	1682	Crosetti	6277	White	964	White	1803
9.	Rizzuto	1661	Lazzeri	6094	Lazzeri	952	Lazzeri	1784
10.	Lazzeri	1659	Rizzuto	5816	Rolfe	942	Rizzuto	1588
11.	Nettles	1535	Combs	5748	Dickey	930	Pipp	1577
12.	Howard	1492	Pipp	5594	Henrich	901	Meusel	1565
13.	Pipp	1488	Nettles	5519	Rizzuto	877	Munson	1558
14.	Combs	1455	Richardson	5386	Pipp	820	Crosetti	1541
15.	Munson	1423	Munson	5344	RANDOLPH	812	Richardson	1432
16.	Howard	1412	Howard	5044	Bauer	792	Howard	1405
17.	Bauer	1406	Meusel	5032	Meusel	764	Nettles	1396
18.	McDougald	1336	RANDOLPH	4958	Nettles	750	Rolfe	1394
19.	RANDOLPH	1323	Rolfe	4827	Keller	714	RANDOLPH	1365
20.	Meusel	1294	Bauer	4784	McDougald	697	Bauer	1326

#	Doubles		Triples		Home Runs		RBIs	
1.	Gehrig	535	Gehrig	162	Ruth	659	Gehrig	1991
2.	Ruth	424	Combs	154	Mantle	536	Ruth	1970
3.	DiMaggio	389	DiMaggio	131	Gehrig	493	DiMaggio	1537
4.	Mantle	344	Pipp	121	DiMaggio	361	Mantle	1509
5.	Dickey	343	Lazzeri	115	Berra	358	Berra	1430
6.	Meusel	338	Ruth	106	Nettles	250	Dickey	1209
7.	Lazzeri	327	Meusel	87	Maris	203	Lazzeri	1154
8.	Berra	321	Henrich	73	Dickey	202	Meusel	1005
9.	Combs	309	Mantle	72	Keller	184	Nettles	834
10.	White	300	Dickey	72	Henrich	183	Pipp	825
11.	Henrich	269	Keller	69	Murcer	175	Henrich	795
12.	Crosetti	260	Rolfe	67	Lazzeri	169	White	758
13.	Pipp	259	Stirnweiss	66	Pepitone	166	Howard	732
14.	Rolfe	257	Crosetti	65	Skowron	165	Keller	723
15.	Rizzuto	239	Chapman	64	Howard	161	Munson	701
16.	Munson	229	Rizzuto	62	White	160	Murcer	687
17.	Howard	211	Cree	62	Bauer	158	Skowron	672
18.	Bauer	211	Conroy	59	Gordon	153	Bauer	654
19.	Chapman	209	Bauer	56	Meusel	146	Crosetti	649
20.	Nettles	202	Peckinpaugh	53	Jackson	144	Combs	629
			RANDOLPH	53				

BATTING AVERAGE
(500 or more games)

1.	Ruth	.349	6.	Meusel	.311	11.	Skowron	.294
2.	Gehrig	.340	7.	Chapman	.305	12.	Keller	.294
3.	Combs	.325	8.	Mantle	.298	13.	Pecking'gh	.294
4.	DiMaggio	.325	9.	Schang	.297	14.	WINFIELD	.294
5.	Dickey	.312	10.	Piniella	.295	15.		

16.	Cree	.292			
17.	Munson	.292			
18.	Selkirk	.290			
19.	Rolfe	.289			
20.	Keller	.286			

CAPS—Active Yankee Player

STOLEN BASES

1.	Chase	248	6.	Maisel	183	11.	Daniels	145
2.	White	233	7.	Mantle	153	12.	Pecking'gh	143
3.	RANDOLPH	217	8.	Clarke	151	13.	Cree	132
4.	Chapman	184	9.	Rizzuto	149	14.	Meusel	131
5.	Conroy	184	10.	Lazzeri	147	15.	Stirnweiss	130

16.	Keeler	118			
17.	Pipp	114			
18.	Crosetti	113			
19.	Ruth	110			
20.	Gehrig	102			

YANKEE SINGLE SEASON LEADERS
BY POSITION

	HOME RUNS		RBIs		Avg	
Pitcher	5	Ruffing 1936	22	Ruffing . 1936, 41	.339	Ruffing ... 1935
Catcher	30	Berra .. 1952, 56	133	Dickey ... 1937	.362	Dickey ... 1936
First Base	49	Gehrig 1934	184	Gehrig ... 1931	.379	Gehrig... 1930
Second Base	30	Gordon 1940	114	Lazzeri .. 1926	.354	Lazzeri .. 1929
Third Base	37	Nettles 1977	107	Nettles ... 1977	.329	Rolfe 1939
Shortstop	16	Smalley ... 1982	107	Lary 1931	.324	Rizzuto .. 1950
Outfield	61	Maris....... 1961	170	Ruth 1921	.393	Ruth..... 1923

DID YOU KNOW ... that two Yankees have stolen second, third and home in the same game? Bob Meusel on May 16, 1927 and Fritz Maisel on August 17, 1915.

ALL-TIME YANKEES—TOP 20 PITCHING CATEGORIES

	Games			Innings			Wins			Pct. (100 decis.)
1.	Ford, W.	498	Ford, W.	3171	Ford, W.	236	Chandler	.717
2.	Ruffing	426	Ruffing	3169	Ruffing	231	Raschi	.706
3.	Lyle	420	Stottlemyre	2662	Gomez	189	GUIDRY	.694
4.	Shawkey	415	Gomez	2498	Shawkey	168	Ford, W.	.690
5.	Murphy	383	Shawkey	2489	Stottlemyre	164	Reynolds	.686
6.	Gomez	367	Hoyt	2273	Pennock	162	Mays	.670
7.	Hoyt	365	Pennock	2190	Hoyt	157	Lopat	.657
8.	Stottlemyre	360	GUIDRY	2027	GUIDRY	154	Gomez	.652
9.	Pennock	346	Chesbro	1953	Reynolds	131	Ruffing	.651
10.	Hamilton	311	Peterson	1856	Chesbro	126	Pennock	.643
11.	Gossage	308	Caldwell	1718	Raschi	120	Byrne	.643
12.	GUIDRY	304	Reynolds	1700	Lopat	113	Murphy	.637
13.	Reynolds	295	Raschi	1537	Peterson	109	Hoyt	.616
14.	Peterson	288	Lopat	1497	Chandler	109	Bonham	.612
15.	Page	278	Chandler	1485	Caldwell	96	Turley	.612
16.	Chesbro	269	Warhop	1423	Murphy	93	Pipgras	.595
17.	Caldwell	248	Fisher	1380	Pipgras	93	Chesbro	.577
18.	Pipgras	247	Pipgras	1352	Turley	82	Terry	.569
19.	Reniff	247	Quinn	1279	Mays	79	Shawkey	.562
20.	Turley	234	Turley	1269	Bonham	79	Downing	.559

	Strikeouts			Shutouts			Complete Games			ERA (Over 800 Inn.)
1.	Ford, W.	1956	Ford, W.	45	Ruffing	261	Ford, R.	2.54
2.	Ruffing	1526	Stottlemyre	40	Gomez	173	Chesbro	2.58
3.	GUIDRY	1510	Ruffing	40	Chesbro	169	Orth	2.72
4.	Gomez	1468	Gomez	28	Pennock	165	Bonham	2.73
5.	Stottlemyre	1257	Reynolds	27	Shawkey	161	Ford, W.	2.74
6.	Shawkey	1163	Chandler	26	Ford, W.	156	Chandler	2.84
7.	Downing	1028	GUIDRY	26	Hoyt	156	Fisher	2.91
8.	Reynolds	967	Shawkey	24	Stottlemyre	152	Stottlemyre	2.97
9.	Chesbro	913	Raschi	24	Caldwell	151	Caldwell	2.99
10.	Turley	909	Turley	21	Chandler	109	Warhop	3.09
11.	Peterson	893	Lopat	20	Warhop	105	Peterson	3.10
12.	Raschi	832	Pennock	19	Ford, R.	103	Shawkey	3.10
13.	Caldwell	803	Peterson	18	Orth	102	Bahnsen	3.10
14.	Hoyt	713	Bonham	17	Raschi	99	Quinn	3.12
15.	Pennock	656	Chesbro	16	Reynolds	96	GUIDRY	3.17
16.	Pipgras	652	Terry	16	Bonham	91	Lopat	3.25
17.	RIGHETTI	616	Hoyt	15	Lopat	91	Downing	3.25
18.	Terry	615	Pipgras	13	GUIDRY	88	Mays	3.25
19.	Chandler	614	Caldwell	13	Pipgras	84	Reynolds	3.30
20.	Byrne	592	Downing	12	Quinn	82	Gomez	3.34

CAPS—ACTIVE YANKEE PLAYER

LEADING YANKEE RELIEF PITCHERS

Year	Pitcher	W	S	Year	Pitcher	W	S
1943	Murphy	12	8	1965	Ramos	5	19
1944	Turner	4	7	1966	Ramos	3	13
1945	Turner	3	10	1967	Womack	5	18
1946	Murphy	4	7	1968	McDaniel	4	10
1947	Page	14	17*	1969	Aker	8	11
1948	Page	7	16	1970	McDaniel	9	29
1949	Page	13	27*	1971	McDaniel	5	4
1950	Ferrick	8	9	1972	Lyle	9	35*
1951	Kuzava	5	5	1973	Lyle	5	27
1952	Sain	3	7	1974	Lyle	9	15
1953	Reynolds	7	13	1975	Lyle	5	6
1954	Sain	6	22*		Tidrow	6	5
1955	Konstanty	7	11	1976	Lyle	7	23
1956	Morgan	6	11	1977	Lyle	13	26
1957	Grim	12	19*	1978	Gossage	10	27*
1958	Duren	6	20*	1979	Gossage	5	18
1959	Duren	3	14		Davis	14	9
1960	Shantz	5	11	1980	Gossage	6	33*
1961	Arroyo	15	29*	1981	Gossage	3	20
1962	Bridges	8	18	1982	Gossage	4	30
1963	Reniff	4	18	1983	Gossage	13	22
1964	Mikkelson	7	12	1984	Righetti	5	31
				1985	Righetti	12	29

*Denotes League Leader

ALL-TIME YANKEES-TOP 20 SAVE LEADERS

1.	Gossage	150	6.	McDaniel	58	11.	Sain	39	16.	Morgan	26
2.	Lyle	141	7.	Arroyo	43	12.	Hamilton	36	17.	Shawkey	26
3.	Murphy	104	8.	Duren	43	13.	Aker	31	18.	Womack	24
4.	Page	76	9.	Reniff	41	14.	Grim	28	19.	Davis	22
5.	RIGHETTI	61	10.	Reynolds	41	15.	Hoyt	28	20.	Jones	22

ALL-TIME YANKEE TEAM RECORDS

Most players .... 47 in 1979, 1982
Fewest players .... 25 in 1923, 1927
Most games .... 164 in 1964, 1968
Most at-bats .... 5705 in 1964
Most runs .... 1067 in 1931
Fewest runs .... 459 in 1908
Most opponents runs .... 898 in 1930
Most hits .... 1683 in 1930
Fewest hits .... 1137 in 1968
Most singles .... 1157 in 1931
Most doubles .... 315 in 1936
Most triples .... 110 in 1930
Most homers .... 240 in 1961
Most home runs by pinch-hitters, season .... 10 in 1961
Most home runs with bases filled .... 7 in 1948, 1980
Most total bases .... 2703 in 1936
Most sacrifices, (S.H. and S.F.) .... 218 in 1922, 1926
Most sacrifice hits .... 178 in 1906
Most sacrifice flies .... 72 in 1974
Most stolen bases .... 289 in 1910
Most caught stealing .... 82 in 1920
Most bases on balls .... 766 in 1932
Most strikeouts .... 1043 in 1967
Fewest strikeouts .... 420 in 1924
Most hit by pitch .... 50 in 1985
Fewest hit by pitch .... 14 in 1969
Most runs batted in .... 995 in 1936
Most GWRBI .... 96 in 1980
Highest batting average .... .309 in 1930
Lowest batting average .... .214 in 1968
Highest slugging average .... .489 in 1927
Lowest slugging average .... .287 in 1914
Most grounded into double play .... 152 in 1982
Fewest-grounded into double play .... 91 in 1963
Most left on bases .... 1239 in 1934
Fewest left on bases .... 1010 in 1920
Most .300 hitters .... 9 in 1930
Most putouts .... 4520 in 1964
Fewest putouts .... 3993 in 1935
Most assists .... 2086 in 1904
Fewest assists .... 1493 in 1948
Most chances accepted .... 6383 in 1980
Fewest chances accepted .... 5551 in 1935
Most errors .... 386 in 1912
Fewest errors .... 109 in 1947, 1964
Most errorless games .... 91 in 1964
Most consecutive errorless games .... 10 in 1977
Most double plays .... 214 in 1956
Fewest double plays .... 81 in 1912
Most consecutive games, one or more double plays .... 18 (23 double plays), 1941
Most passed balls .... 32 in 1913
Fewest passed balls .... 0 in 1931
Highest fielding average .... .983 in 1964
Lowest fielding average .... .939 in 1912
Most games won .... 110 in 1927
Most games lost .... 103 in 1908
Highest percentage games won .... .714 in 1927
Lowest percentage games won .... .329 in 1912
Most shutouts won, season .... 24 in 1951
Most shutouts lost, season .... 27 in 1914
Most 1-0 games won .... 6 in 1908, 1968
Most 1-0 games lost .... 9 in 1914
Most consecutive games won, season .... 19 in 1947
Most consecutive games lost, season .... 13 in 1913
Most times league champions 33
Most runs, game .... New York 25, Philadelphia 2, May 24, 1936
Most runs, game, by opponent, on road .... Cleveland 24, New York 6, July 29, 1928
Most runs, game, by opponent, at home .... Detroit 19, New York 1, June 17, 1925
                                                                Toronto 19, New York 3, September 10, 1977
Most runs, shutout game .... New York 21, Philadelphia 0,
                                                                Aug. 13, 1939, 2nd game, 8 innings
Most runs shutout game, by opponent .... Chicago 15, N.Y. 0, July 15, 1907
                                                                Chicago 15, N.Y. 0, May 4, 1950
Most runs, doubleheader shutout .... 24, New York vs Philadelphia, September 4, 1944.
Longest 1-0 game won ...... 15 innings, New York 1, Philadelphia 0, July 4, 1925, first game
Longest 1-0 game lost .... 13 innings, Chicago 1, New York 0, July 25, 1941
Most runs, inning .... 14, N.Y. vs. Washington, July 6, 1920, fifth inning
Most hits, game .... 30, New York vs. Boston, September 28, 1923
Most home runs, game .... 8, New York vs. Philadelphia, June 28, 1939, first game
Most consecutive games, one or more home runs .... 25 (40 homers), 1941
Most home runs in consecutive games in which
home runs were made .... 40 (25 games), 1941
Most total bases, game. .... 53, New York vs. Philadelphia, June 28, 1939, first game

ALL-TIME YANKEE BATTING RECORDS
INDIVIDUAL

Most years with Yankees	Yogi Berra	18 (1946-63)
	Mickey Mantle	(1951-68)
Most games, season	Bobby Richardson	162 (1961)
	Roy White	162 (1970)
	Chris Chambliss	162 (1978)
Most at bats, season	Bobby Richardson	692 (1962)
Most runs, season	Babe Ruth	177 (1921)*
Most hits, season	Earle Combs	231 (1927)
Most singles, season	Willie Keeler	166 (1906)
	Earle Combs	166 (1927)
Most doubles, season	Lou Gehrig	52 (1927)
Most triples, season	Earle Combs	23 (1927)
Most home runs, right hander, season	Joe DiMaggio	46 (1937)
Most home runs, left hander, season	Roger Maris	61 (1961)*
	Babe Ruth	60 (1927)*
Most home runs, rookie, season	Joe DiMaggio	29 (1936)
Most grand slam home runs, season	Lou Gehrig	4 (1934)
	Tommy Henrich	4 (1948)
Most grand slam home runs, career	Lou Gehrig	23*
Most home runs, season, at home	Babe Ruth	32 (1921) (PG)*
	Lou Gehrig	30 (1934) (YS)
	Roger Maris	30 (1961) (YS)
Most home runs, season, on the road	Babe Ruth	32 (1927)*
Most home runs, one month, right handed	Joe DiMaggio	15 (7/37)
Most home runs, one month, left handed	Babe Ruth	17 (9/27)*
Most total bases, season	Babe Ruth	457 (1921)*
Most sacrifice hits, season	Willie Keeler	42 (1905)
Most sacrifice flies, season	Roy White	17 (1971)†
Most stolen bases, season	Rickey Henderson	80 (1985)
Most caught stealing, season	Ben Chapman	23 (1931)
Most walks, season	Babe Ruth	170 (1923)*
Most strikeouts, season	Bobby Bonds	137 (1975)
Fewest strikeouts, season	Joe Sewell	3 (1932)
Most hit by pitch, season	Don Baylor	24 (1985)
Most runs batted in, season	Lou Gehrig	184 (1931)†
Most consecutive games with an RBI	Babe Ruth	11 (1931)
Most GWRBI, season	Dave Winfield	21 (1983)
	Don Mattingly	21 (1985)
Highest batting average, season	Babe Ruth	.393 (1923)
Highest slugging average, season	Babe Ruth	.847 (1920)*
Longest hitting streak	Joe DiMaggio	56 (1941)*
Most grounded into double plays, season	Dave Winfield	30 (1983)
Fewest grounded into double plays, season	Mickey Mantle	2 (1961)
	Mickey Rivers	2 (1977)

ALL-TIME YANKEE PITCHING RECORDS
INDIVIDUAL

Most years with Yankees	Whitey Ford	16 (1950, 53-67)
Most games, righthander, season	Pedro Ramos	65 (1965)
	Dooley Womack	65 (1967)
Most games, lefthander, season	Dave Righetti	74 (1985)
Most games started, season	Jack Chesbro	51 (1904)
Most complete games, season	Jack Chesbro	48 (1904)
Most games finished, RHP, season	Rich Gossage	58 (1980)
Most games finished, LHP, season	Sparky Lyle	60 (1977)
	Dave Righetti	60 (1985)
Most innings pitched, season	Jack Chesbro	454 (1904)
Most victories, RHP, season	Jack Chesbro	41 (1904)*
Most victories, LHP, season	Lefty Gomez	26 (1934)
Most 20-victory seasons	Bob Shawkey	4
	Lefty Gomez	4
	Red Ruffing	4
Most losses, season	Al Orth	21 (1907)
	Sam Jones	21 (1925)
	Joe Lake	21 (1908)
	Russ Ford	21 (1912)
Highest winning percentage, season	Ron Guidry (25-3)	.893 (1978)
Most consecutive victories, season	Jack Chesbro	14 (1904)
	Whitey Ford	14 (1961)
Most consecutive losses, season	William Hogg	9 (1908)
	Thad Tillotson	9 (1967)
Most saves, lefthander, season	Sparky Lyle	35 (1972)
Most saves, righthander, season	Rich Gossage	33 (1980)
Most walks, lefthander, season	Tommy Byrne	179 (1949)
Most walks, righthander, season	Bob Turley	177 (1955)
Most strikeouts, season	Ron Guidry	248 (1978)
Most strikeouts, 9-inning game	Ron Guidry	18 (6/17/78)
Most strikeouts, extra-inning game	Whitey Ford	15 (4/22/59)
Most shutouts, season	Ron Guidry	9 (1978)
Most 1-0 shutouts won, career	Bob Shawkey	7
Most shutouts lost, season	Bill Zuber	7 (1945)
Most runs allowed, season	Russ Ford	165 (1912)
Most earned runs allowed, season	Sam Jones	127 (1925)
Most hits allowed, season	Jack Chesbro	337 (1904)
Most hit batsmen, season	John Warhop	26 (1909)
Most wild pitches, season	Al Downing	14 (1964)
Most home runs allowed, season	Ralph Terry	40 (1962)
Lowest E.R.A., season, right handed	Spud Chandler	1.64 (1943)
Lowest E.R.A., season, left handed	Ron Guidry	1.74 (1978)

*Major League Record   †American League Record

TOP TEN YANKEES, SINGLE SEASON

	At Bats			Runs Scored			Hits			Doubles	
1.	Rich'dson	692 1962	Ruth		177 1921	Combs	231 1927	Gehrig		52 1927
2.	Clarke	686 1970	Gehrig		167 1936	Gehrig	220 1930	MATTINGLY		48 1985
3.	Rich'dson	679 1964	Ruth		163 1928	Gehrig	218 1927	Gehrig		47 1926
4.	Rich'dson	664 1965	Gehrig		163 1931	DiMaggio	215 1937	Meusel		47 1927
5.	Rich'dson	662 1961	Ruth		158 1920	Rolfe	213 1939	Gehrig		47 1928
6.	Crosetti	656 1939	Ruth		158 1927	Gehrig	211 1931	Rolfe		46 1939
7.	MATTINGLY	652 1985	Ruth		151 1923	MATTINGLY	211 1985	Ruth		45 1923
8.	Combs	648 1927	DiMaggio		151 1937	Gehrig	210 1928	Meusel		45 1928
9.	Rolfe	648 1939	Ruth		150 1930	Gehrig	210 1934	Ruth		44 1921
10.	Dugan	644 1923	Gehrig		149 1927	Rich'dson	209 1962	DiMaggio		44 1936
			Ruth		149 1931			MATTINGLY		44 1984

	Triples			Home Runs			Runs Batted In			Total Bases	
1.	Combs	23 1927	Maris		61 1961	Gehrig	184 1931	Ruth		457 1921
2.	Combs	22 1930	Ruth		60 1927	Gehrig	175 1927	Gehrig		447 1927
3.	Stirnweiss	22 1945	Ruth		59 1921	Gehrig	174 1930	Gehrig		419 1931
4.	Cree	22 1911	Ruth		54 1928	Ruth	170 1921	DiMaggio		418 1937
5.	Combs	21 1928	Ruth		54 1920	DiMaggio	167 1937	Ruth		417 1927
6.	Gehrig	20 1926	Mantle		54 1961	Gehrig	165 1934	Gehrig		410 1931
7.	Pipp	19 1924	Mantle		52 1956	Ruth	164 1927	Gehrig		409 1934
8.	Gehrig	18 1927	Ruth		49 1930	Ruth	163 1931	Ruth		403 1936
9.	Gehrig	17 1930	Gehrig		49 1934	Gehrig	159 1937	Ruth		399 1923
10.	4 tied	16	Gehrig		49 1936	Ruth	155 1926	Ruth		391 1924
						DiMaggio	155 1948			

	Stolen Bases			Walks			Strikeouts (Batter)			Batting Average	
1.	HENDERSON	80 1985	Ruth		170 1923	Bonds	137 1975	Ruth		.393 1923
2.	Maisel	74 1914	Ruth		148 1920	R. Jackson	133 1978	DiMaggio		.381 1939
3.	Chapman	61 1931	Mantle		146 1957	R. Jackson	129 1977	Gehrig		.379 1930
4.	Stirnweiss	55 1944	Ruth		144 1921	Mantle	126 1959	Ruth		.378 1921
5.	Maisel	51 1915	Ruth		144 1926	Mantle	125 1960	Ruth		.378 1924
6.	Cree	48 1911	Ruth		142 1924	R. Jackson	122 1980	Ruth		.376 1920
7.	Fultz	44 1905	Ruth		138 1927	Mantle	120 1958	Gehrig		.374 1928
8.	Rivers	43 1976	Ruth		136 1930	Mantle	111 1952	Ruth		.373 1927
9.	Hemphill	42 1908	Ruth		135 1928	Mantle	107 1954	Ruth		.373 1931
10.	Conroy	41 1907	Gehrig		132 1935	R. Jackson	107 1979	Ruth		.372 1925
	Daniels	41 1910								

	Hitting Streaks			Games Pitched			Complete Games			Wins	
1.	DiMaggio	56 1941	RIGHETTI		74 1985	Chesbro	48 1904	Chesbro		41 1904
2.	Peckinpaugh	29 1919	Lyle		72 1977	Powell	38 1904	Orth		27 1908
3.	Combs	29 1931	Lyle		66 1974	Orth	36 1906	Mays		27 1921
4.	Gordon	29 1942	Arroyo		65 1961	Chesbro	33 1903	R. Ford		26 1910
5.	Chase	27 1907	Ramos		65 1965	R. Ford	32 1912	Mays		26 1920
6.	Ruth	26 1921	Womack		65 1967	Mays	30 1921	Bush		26 1922
7.	DiMaggio	23 1940	Lyle		64 1976	Hunter	30 1975	Gomez		26 1934
8.	DiMaggio	22 1937	Gossage		64 1980	R. Ford	29 1910	GUIDRY		25 1978
9.	DiMaggio	20 1937	RIGHETTI		64 1984	Orth	26 1905	W. Ford		25 1961
10.	Hassett	20 1942	Gossage		63 1978	Mays	26 1920	Chesbro		24 1906
	Rivers	20 1976	Frazier		63 1982			Shawkey		24 1916
	WINFIELD	20 1984						Pipgras		24 1928
	MATTINGLY	20 1985						W. Ford		24 1963

	Shutouts			Strikeouts (Pitcher)			Earned Run Average			Saves	
1.	GUIDRY	9 1978	GUIDRY		248 1978	Chandler	1.64 1943	Lyle		35 1972
2.	R. Ford	8 1910	Chesbro		239 1904	R. Ford	1.65 1910	Gossage		33 1980
3.	W. Ford	8 1964	Downing		217 1964	GUIDRY	1.74 1978	RIGHETTI		31 1984
4.	Reynolds	7 1951	Turley		210 1955	Chesbro	1.82 1904	Gossage		30 1982
5.	W. Ford	7 1958	R. Ford		209 1910	Vaughn	1.83 1910	Arroyo		29 1961
6.	Stottlemyre	7 1971	W. Ford		209 1961	Lake	1.88 1909	McDaniel		29 1970
7.	Stottlemyre	7 1972	Powell		202 1904	Caldwell	1.94 1914	RIGHETTI		29 1985
8.	Hunter	7 1975	GUIDRY		201 1979	W. Ford	2.01 1958	Page		27 1949
9.	John, tied	6 1980	Ruffing		194 1937	Cullop	2.05 1916	Lyle		27 1973
	12 others					Bahnsen	2.06 1968	Gossage		27 1978
10.			Ruffing		190 1932					

CAPS—Active Yankee Player

LONGEST YANKEE WINNING STREAKS		LONGEST YANKEE LOSING STREAKS	
19	 1947	13 (1 tie)	... 1913
18	 1953	12	 1908
16	 1926	11	 1911
15	 1906	9	.... 1912 (twice)
15	 1960	9	 1916
14	 1941	9	 1945
13	 1954	9	 1953
13	 1961	9	 1982

NEW YORK YANKEES TWENTY-GAME WINNERS

Year	Pitcher	W	L	Year	Pitcher	W	L
1903—	Jack Chesbro	21	15	1938—	Red Ruffing	21	7
1904—	Jack Chesbro	41	12	1939—	Red Ruffing	21	7
	Jack Powell	23	19	1942—	Ernie Bonham	21	5
1906—	Albert Orth	27	17	1943—	Spud Chandler	20	4
	Jack Chesbro	24	16	1946—	Spud Chandler	20	8
1910—	Russell Ford	26	6	1949—	Vic Raschi	21	10
1911—	Russell Ford	22	11	1950—	Vic Raschi	21	8
1916—	Bob Shawkey	23	14	1951—	Eddie Lopat	21	9
1919—	Bob Shawkey	20	13		Vic Raschi	21	10
1920—	Carl Mays	26	11	1952—	Allie Reynolds	20	8
	Bob Shawkey	20	13	1954—	Bob Grim	20	6
1921—	Carl Mays	27	9	1958—	Bob Turley	21	7
1922—	Joe Bush	26	7	1961—	Whitey Ford	25	4
	Bob Shawkey	20	12	1962—	Ralph Terry	23	12
1923—	Sad Sam Jones	21	8	1963—	Whitey Ford	24	7
1924—	Herb Pennock	21	9		Jim Bouton	21	7
1926—	Herb Pennock	23	11	1965—	Mel Stottlemyre	20	9
1927—	Waite Hoyt	22	7	1968—	Mel Stottlemyre	21	12
1928—	George Pipgras	24	13	1969—	Mel Stottlemyre	20	14
	Waite Hoyt	23	7	1970—	Fritz Peterson	20	11
1931—	Lefty Gomez	21	9	1975—	Catfish Hunter	23	14
1932—	Lefty Gomez	24	7	1978—	Ron Guidry	25	3
1934—	Lefty Gomez	26	5		Ed Figueroa	20	9
1936—	Red Ruffing	20	12	1979—	Tommy John	21	9
1937—	Lefty Gomez	21	11	1980—	Tommy John	22	9
	Red Ruffing	20	7	1983—	Ron Guidry	21	9
				1985—	Ron Guidry	22	6

THE NO-HITTERS

NO-HIT GAMES BY YANKEE PITCHERS

1910—Thomas L. Hughes, vs. Cleveland, August 30 (9 innings lost in 11th) 0-5
1917—*George A. Mogridge, at Boston, April 24 2-1
1923—Samuel P. Jones, at Philadelphia, September 4 2-0
1938—M. Monte Pearson, vs. Cleveland, August 27 (2nd game) 13-0
1951—Allie P. Reynolds, at Cleveland, July 12 (night) 1-0
      Allie P. Reynolds, vs. Boston, September 28 (1st game) 8-0
1956—Don J. Larsen, vs. Brooklyn, October 8 (Fifth Game of World
      Series—only PERFECT GAME in Series history) 2-0
1983—*David A. Righetti, vs. Boston, July 4 4-0

*Left-handed pitcher.

NO-HIT GAMES PITCHED AGAINST YANKEES

1908—Cy Young, Boston at New York, June 30 8-0
1916—George Foster, Boston vs. New York at New York, June 21 2-0
1919—Raymond B. Caldwell, Cleveland at New York,
      September 10 (1st game) 3-0
1946—Robert W. A. Feller, Cleveland at New York, April 30 1-0
1952—Virgil O. Trucks, Detroit at New York, August 25 1-0
1958—James Hoyt Wilhelm, Baltimore vs. New York at Baltimore,
      September 20 1-0

ABOUT ONE-HITTERS

Yankee pitchers have hurled 48 one-hitters over the years, the most recent being by Luis Tiant on July 8, 1979 at Oakland in which Rickey Henderson had a 4th inning single. Bob Turley and Whitey Ford each hurled 3 for the Yanks, and both men participated in a fourth. Luis Tiant had 2 previously, now three overall. Bob Shawkey, Rip Collins, Lefty Gomez, Vic Raschi and Floyd Bevens, each threw two one-hitters, with one of Bevens' coming in a World Series.

The Yankees have been one-hit 44 times. The last time was June 29, 1985 at New York by Milwaukee's Moose Haas. Don Mattingly's seventh inning double ruined the no-hit bid for Haas. The Yankees have been one-hit 16 times since they were last no-hit in 1958. Joe Wood, Earl Hamilton, and Nolan Ryan are the only men with a pair of one-hitters against New York, both of Hamilton's coming in 1913. No-hit pitcher Hoyt Wilhelm also one-hit the Yankees in 1959.

Horace Clarke and Don Mattingly are the only Yankees to twice serve as spoilers. Clarke had the only hit in no-hit bids by Jim Palmer and Joe Niekro. In 1970 Clarke broke up three no-hitters in the 9th inning in one month, two of which wound up being more than one-hitters. On May 2, 1984 Mattingly ruined a perfect game at Chicago for LaMarr Hoyt with a wind-blown single in the 7th inning and last year broke up Moose Haas' no-hit bid.

Of recent vintage, Bob Ojeda of Boston took a no-hitter into the 9th inning at Yankee Stadium 9/12/81 only to have Rick Cerone leadoff with a double followed by a Dave Winfield double.

YANKEE ALL-TIME PACE-SETTERS

BATTING CHAMPIONS

Babe Ruth 1924
Lou Gehrig 1934
Joe DiMaggio 1939, 1940
Geo. Stirnweiss 1945
Mickey Mantle 1956
Don Mattingly 1984

HOME RUN CHAMPIONS

Wally Pipp 1916, 1917
Babe Ruth 1920, 1921, 1923
1924, 1926, 1927
1928, 1929, 1930, 1931
Bob Muesel 1925
Lou Gehrig 1931, 1934, 1936
Joe DiMaggio 1937, 1948
Nick Etten 1944
Mickey Mantle 1955, 1956, 1958, 1960
Roger Maris 1961
Graig Nettles 1976
Reggie Jackson 1980

A. L. ROOKIE OF YEAR AWARDS

Gil McDougald, 3b 1951
Bob Grim, p 1954
Tony Kubek, inf-of 1957
Tom Tresh, ss-of 1962
Stan Bahnsen, p 1968
Thurman Munson, c 1970
Dave Righetti, p 1981

R.B.I. LEADERS

Wally Pipp 1916
Babe Ruth 1920, 1921, 1923
1926, 1928
Bob Meusel 1925
Lou Gehrig 1927, 1928, 1930
1931, 1934
Joe DiMaggio 1941, 1948
Nick Etten 1945
Mickey Mantle 1956
Roger Maris 1960, 1961
Don Mattingly 1985

MOST VALUABLE PLAYER

Babe Ruth 1923
Lou Gehrig 1927, 1936
Joe DiMaggio 1939, 1941, 1947
Joe Gordon 1942
Spud Chandler 1943
Phil Rizzuto 1950
Yogi Berra 1951, 1954, 1955
Mickey Mantle 1956, 1957, 1962
Roger Maris 1960, 1961
Elston Howard 1963
Thurman Munson 1976
Don Mattingly 1985

CY YOUNG AWARD

Bob Turley 1958
Whitey Ford 1961
Sparkey Lyle 1977
Ron Guidry 1978

OUTSTANDING YANKEE BATTING FEATS

FOUR HOME RUNS ONE GAME

Lou Gehrig 6/3/32

THREE HOME RUNS ONE GAME

Tony Lazzeri 1927, 1936
Lou Gehrig 1927, 1929, 1930
Babe Ruth 1930
Ben Chapman 1932
Joe DiMaggio 1937, 1948, 1950
Bill Dickey 1939
Charlie Kerr 1940
Johnny Mize 1950
Mickey Mantle 1955
Tom Tresh 1965
Bobby Murcer 1970, 1973
Cliff Johnson 1977

HOME RUN, FIRST M.L. AT BAT

John Miller 1966

SWITCH-HITTING HR, ONE GAME

Mickey Mantle .... *10 times
Roy White .... 5 times
Tom Tresh .... 3 times
Roy Smalley .... 1 time

HOME RUN, FIRST TWO M.L. GAMES

Joe Lefebvre 1980

TRIPLE CROWN WINNERS

Lou Gehrig 1934
Mickey Mantle 1956

TWO HOME RUNS ONE INNING

Joe DiMaggio 1936
Joe Pepitone 1962
Cliff Johnson 1977

FOUR CONSECUTIVE HOME RUNS

Lou Gehrig 1932
John Blanchard 1961
Mickey Mantle 1962
Bobby Murcer 1970

TWO CONSECUTIVE PINCH HRs

Ray Caldwell 1915
Charlie Keller 1948
John Blanchard 1961
Ray Barker 1965

200 HITS ROOKIE SEASON

Earle Combs .... (203) 1925
Joe DiMaggio .... (206) 1936

SIX HITS ONE GAME

Myril Hoag .... 6/6/34 (1st game)

CENTERFIELD BLEACHER HOME RUNS, NEW YANKEE STADIUM

Singleton, Baltimore 1977
Jackson, New York (World Series) 1977
Jackson, New York 1981

NEW YORK YANKEE A.L. BATTING CHAMPIONS

Year	Yankee	AVG	G	AB	R	H	2B	3B	HR	RBI
1924	Babe Ruth	.378*	153	529	143*	200	39	7	46*	121
1934	Lou Gehrig	.363*	154	579	128	210	40	6	49*	165*
1939	Joe DiMaggio	.381*	120	462	108	176	32	6	30	126
1940	Joe DiMaggio	.352*	132	508	93	179	28	9	31	133
1945	George Stirnweiss	.309*	152	632*	107*	195*	32	22*	10	64
1956	Mickey Mantle	.353*	150	533	132*	188	22	5	52*	130*
1984	Don Mattingly	.343*	153	603	91	207*	44*	2	23	110

#3—BABE RUTH

Born, February 6, 1895, died, August 16, 1948. Threw and batted left-handed. Boston-New York, A.L.; Boston, N.L., 1914-1935. The greatest drawing card, the Yankees' greatest home run hitter, an outstanding pitcher and the most colorful figure in the history of baseball. Hit 714 home runs in addition to 15 World Series homers. The "Babe" compiled a lifetime average of .342, won 92 games as a pitcher and played in 10 World Series during his action-packed 22 years. Elected to Hall of Fame 1936.

#4—LOU GEHRIG

Born, June 19, 1903, died, June 2, 1941. Threw and batted lefthanded. New York Yankees 1923-1939. The "Iron-Horse" played in 2130 consecutive games, a virtually unapproachable record, hit 493 home runs, 10 World Series homers, compiled a lifetime average of .340, was named the American League's Most Valuable Player 3 times, and amassed more than a score of major and league records. Elected to Hall of Fame 1939.

#5—JOE DIMAGGIO

Born, November 25, 1914. Threw and batted righthanded. New York Yankees 1936-1951. The "Yankee Clipper" considered the greatest centerfielder of modern baseball, hit in 56 consecutive games, a major league record, in 1941; hit 361 home runs, 8 World Series homers, compiled a lifetime average of .325, was named the American League's Most Valuable Player three times and holder of numerous batting and World Series records. Elected to Hall of Fame 1955.

#7—MICKEY MANTLE

Born, October 20, 1931. Switch-hitter threw right. New York Yankees, 1951-68. The most popular player of his era, a man cheered in every ballpark he played in. Winner of the Triple Crown in 1956. Led league in home runs four times, ending career with 536, third highest in history at the time. Holds record for most World Series homers with 18, accomplished in 12 World Series. Selected for 20 All-Star Games. 3-times MVP (1956-57-62). Won Hickock Belt in 1956. Played more games (2401) than any Yankee despite injury plagued career. Elected to Hall of Fame 1974.

JOE DIMAGGIO'S HITTING STREAK

Starting on Thursday, May 15, 1941 in Yankee Stadium and continuing until Thursday night, July 17 in Cleveland's Municipal Stadium, where he was finally stopped by pitchers Al Smith and Jim Bagby, DiMaggio piled up this amazing mark:

Consecutive games hit safely	56	Home Runs	15
At bats	223	Triples	4
Hits	91	Doubles	16
Average for streak	.408	Singles	56
Total bases for streak	160	Strikeouts	7
Runs scored	56	Bases on Balls	21
RBIs	55	Hit by pitcher	2

> **HOME RUNS, ONE MONTH** ... Babe Ruth hit 17 homers in September, 1927. Mickey Mantle hit 16 in May, 1956. Ruth had 15 in a month three times, DiMaggio once, and Maris once.

> **DID YOU KNOW** ... that when Joe DiMaggio hit safely in 56 consecutive games in 1941, he collected 56 singles and also scored 56 runs during the streak?

> **DID YOU KNOW** ... that when Babe Ruth hit his 60 homers in 1927, 19 were made off lefthanders? He hit two grand slams and batted in 100 runs with his homers.

NEW YORK YANKEES 200 HIT CLUB

Year	Yankee	AVG	AB	H	Year	Yankee	AVG	AB	H
1921	Babe Ruth	.378	540	204	1934	Lou Gehrig	.363*	579	210
1923	Babe Ruth	.393	522	205	1936	Joe DiMaggio	.323	637	206
1924	Babe Ruth	.378*	529	200		Lou Gehrig	.354	579	205
1925	Earle Combs	.342	593	203	1937	Joe DiMaggio	.346	621	215
1927	Earle Combs	.356	648*	231*		Lou Gehrig	.351	569	200
	Lou Gehrig	.373	584	218	1939	Red Rolfe	.329	648	213*
1928	Lou Gehrig	.374	562	210	1944	George Stirnweiss	.319	643	205*
1929	Earle Combs	.345	586	202	1950	Phil Rizzuto	.324	617	200
1930	Lou Gehrig	.379	581	220	1962	Bobby Richardson	.302	692*	209*
1931	Lou Gehrig	.341	619	211*	1984	Don Mattingly	.343*	603	207*
1932	Lou Gehrig	.349	596	208	1985	Don Mattingly	.324	652	211

YANKEE ALL-STAR GAME SELECTIONS
(1933 to 1985)

1933—Chapman, of; Dickey, c; Gehrig, 1b; Gomez, p; Lazzeri, 2b; Ruth, of.

1934—Chapman, of; Dickey, c; Gehrig, 1b; Gomez, p; Ruffing, p; Ruth, of.

1935—Chapman, of; Gehrig, 1b; Gomez, p.

1936—Crosetti, ss; Dickey, c; DiMaggio, of; Gehrig, 1b; Gomez, p; Pearson, p; Selkirk, of.

1937—Dickey, c; DiMaggio, of; Gehrig, 1b; Gomez, p; Murphy, p; Rolfe, 3b.

1938—Dickey, c; DiMaggio, of; Gehrig, 1b; Gomez, p; Rolfe, 3b; Ruffing, p.

1939—Crosetti, ss; Dickey, c; DiMaggio, of; Gomez, p; Gordon, 2b; Murphy, p; Rolfe, 3b; Ruffing, p; Selkirk, of.

1940—Dickey, c; DiMaggio, of; Gordon, 2b; Keller, of; Pearson, p; Rolfe, 3b; Ruffing, p.

1941—Dickey, c; DiMaggio, of; Gordon, 2b; Keller, of; Ruffing, p; Russo, p.

1942—Bonham, p; Chandler, p; Dickey, c; DiMaggio, of; Gordon, 2b; Henrich, of; Rizzuto, ss; Rosar, c; Ruffing, p.

1943—Bonham, p; Chandler, p; Dickey, c; Gordon, 2b; Keller, of; Lindell, of.

1944—Borowy, p; Hemsley, c; Page, p.

1945—NO GAME

1946—Chandler, p; Dickey, c; DiMaggio, of; Gordon, 2b; Keller, of; Stirnweiss, 3b.

1947—Chandler, p; DiMaggio, of; Henrich, of; Johnson, 3b; McQuinn, 1b; Page, p; Robinson, c; Shea, p; Keller, of.

1948—Berra, c; DiMaggio, of; Henrich, of; McQuinn, 1b; Page, p; Raschi, p.

1949—Berra, c; DiMaggio, of; Henrich, of; Raschi, p; Reynolds, p.

1950—Berra, c; Byrne, p; Coleman, 2b; DiMaggio, of; Henrich, 1b; Raschi, p; Reynolds, p.; Rizzuto, ss.

1951—Berra, c; DiMaggio, of; Lopat, p; Rizzuto, ss.

1952—Bauer, of; Berra, c; Mantle, of; Raschi, p; Reynolds, p; Rizzuto, ss; McDougald, 2b.

1953—Bauer, of; Berra, c; Mantle, of; Mize, 1b; Reynolds, p; Rizzuto, ss; Sain, p.

1954—Bauer, of; Berra, c; Ford, p; Mantle, of; Noren, of; Reynolds, p.

1955—Berra, c; Ford, p; Mantle, of; Turley, p.

1956—Berra, c; Ford, p; Kucks, p; Mantle, of; Martin, 2b; McDougald,ss.

1957—Berra, c; Grim, p; Howard, c; Mantle, of; McDougald, ss; Richardson, 2b; Shantz, p; Skowron, 1b.

1958—Berra, c; Duren, p; Ford, p; Howard, c; Kubek, inf; Mantle, of; McDougald, 2b; Skowron, 1b; Turley, p.

1959—Berra, c; Duren, p; Ford, p; Mantle, of; McDougald, ss; Richardson, 2b; Skowron, 1b; Howard, c; Kubek, ss.

1960—Berra, c; Coates, p; Ford, p; Howard, c; Mantle, of; Maris, of; Skowron, 1b.

1961—Arroyo, p; Berra, of; Ford, p; Howard, c; Kubek, ss; Mantle, of; Maris, of; Skowron, 1b.

1962—Berra, c; Howard, c; Mantle, of; Maris, of; Richardson, 2b; Terry, p; Tresh, ss.

1963—Bouton, p; Howard, c; Mantle, of; Pepitone, 1b; Richardson, 2b; Tresh, of.

1964—Ford, p; Howard, c; Mantle, of; Pepitone, 1b; Richardson, 2b.

1965—Howard, c; Mantle, of; Pepitone, 1b; Richardson, 2b; Stottlemyre, p.

1966—Richardson, 2b; Stottlemyre, p.

1967—Downing, p; Mantle, 1b.

1968—Mantle, 1b; Stottlemyre, p.

1969—Stottlemyre, p; White, of.

1970—Peterson, p; Stottlemyre, p; White, of.

1971—Munson, c; Murcer, of.

1972—Murcer, of.

1973—Lyle, p; Munson, c; Murcer, of.

1974—Munson, c; Murcer, of.

1975—Bonds, of; Hunter, p; Munson, c; Nettles, 3b.

1976—Chambliss, 1b; Hunter, p; Lyle, p; Munson, c; Randolph, 2b; Rivers, of.

1977—Jackson, of; Lyle, p; Munson, c; Nettles, 3b; Randolph, 2b.

1978—Gossage, p; Guidry, p; Nettles, 3b.

1979—Guidry, p; Jackson, of; John, p; Nettles, 3b.

1980—Dent, ss; Gossage, p; Jackson, of; John, p; Nettles, 3b; Randolph, 2b

1981—Davis, p; Dent, ss; Gossage, p; Jackson, of; Randolph, 2b; Winfield, of.

1982—Gossage, p; Guidry, p; Winfield, of.

1983—Guidry, p; Winfield, of.

1984—Niekro, p; Mattingly, 1b; Winfield, of.

1985—Henderson, of; Mattingly, 1b; Winfield, of.

The Yankees (then Highlanders), played their first game on April 22, 1903 in Washington, losing 3-1 before 11,950 fans. The first lineup was: Lefty Davis (lf), Willie Keeler (rf), Dave Fultz (cf), Jimmy Williams (2b), John Ganzel (1b), Wid Conroy (3b), Herman Long (ss), Jack O'Connor (c) and Jack Chesbro (p.

ALL-STAR GAMES IN YANKEE STADIUM

July 11, 1939
NL 001 000 000 - 1 7 1
AL 000 210 000 - 3 6 1
Derringer, Lee (4), Fette (7) &
Lombardi.
Ruffing, Bridges (4), Feller (6) & Dickey

WP-Bridges; LP-Lee
HR-DiMaggio.
Att-62,892

July 13, 1960 (2nd game)
NL 021 000 102 - 6 10 0
AL 000 000 000 - 0 8 0
Law, Podres (3), Williams (5), Jackson
(7), Henry (8), McDaniel (9) &
Crandall, Bailey, Burgess.
Ford, Wynn (4), Staley (5), Lary (8),
Bell (9) & Berra, Lollar.

WP-Law; LP-Ford
HR-Mathews, Mays, Musial, Boyer
Att-38,362

July 19, 1977
NL 401 000 020 - 7 9 1
AL 000 002 102 - 5 8 0
Sutton, LaVelle (4), Seaver (6), R.
Reuschel (8), Gossage (9) & Bench,
Simmons, Stearns.
Palmer, Kern (3), Eckersley (4),
LaRoche (6), Campbell (7), Lyle (8)
& Fisk, Wynegar.

WP-Sutton; LP-Palmer
HR-Morgan, Luzinski, Garvey, Scott.
Att-56,683

YANKEES ON SPORTING NEWS ALL-STAR TEAMS

Selected at Conclusion of Season

1926—Ruth, Pennock
1927—Ruth, Gehrig
1928—Ruth, Gehrig, Hoyt
1929—Ruth
1930—Ruth
1931—Gehrig, Ruth
1932—Lazzori, Dickey
1933—Dickey
1934—Gehrig, Gomez
1936—Gehrig, Dickey
1937—Gehrig, DiMaggio, Rolfe, Ruffing
1938—Rolfe, DiMaggio, Dickey, Ruffing
1939—Gordon, DiMaggio, Rolfe, Dickey
  Ruffing
1940—Gordon, DiMaggio
1941—Gordon, DiMaggio, Dickey
1942—Gordon, DiMaggio, Bonham
1943—Johnson, Chandler
1945—Stirnweiss
1946—A. Robinson
1947—DiMaggio
1948—DiMaggio
1949—Rizzuto, Henrich, Page
1950—Rizzuto, Berra, Raschi
1951—Rizzuto, Reynolds
1952—Rizzuto, Mantle, Berra, Reynolds

1954—Berra
1955—Ford
1956—Mantle, Berra, Ford
1957—Mantle, McDougald, Berra
1958—Turley
1960—Skowron, Maris
1961—Richardson, Kubek, Mantle, Maris,
  Howard, Ford
1962—Richardson, Tresh, Mantle, Terry
1963—Richardson, Pepitone, Howard, Ford
1964—Richardson, Mantle, Howard
1965—Richardson, Stottlemyre
1966—Richardson
1971—Murcer
1972—Murcer
1973—Munson, Murcer
1974—Munson
1975—Munson, Nettles
1976—Munson, Chambliss, Rivers
1977—Nettles, Randolph
1978—Guidry, Nettles
1980—Randolph, Jackson, Cerone, John
1981—Guidry
1982—Winfield
1983—Guidry, Winfield
1984—Mattingly, Winfield
1985—Baylor, Guidry, Henderson, Mattingly

BABE RUTH AWARD WINNERS

(World Series MVP)

1949	Joe Page	1958	Elston Howard
1950	Jerry Coleman	1961	Whitey Ford
1951	Phil Rizzuto	1962	Ralph Terry
1952	Johnny Mize	1977	Reggie Jackson
1953	Billy Martin	1978	Bucky Dent
1956	Don Larsen		

The Yankees were the first team to wear uniform numbers regularly (1929), and their numbers have always been a source of fascination. More are retired than on any other team ... Did you know that Joe DiMaggio was #9 as a rookie? Yogi Berra was #35? Mickey Mantle #6? Bobby Richardson #29? Roy White #48?

1986 NEW YORK YANKEES ROSTER

MANAGER: Lou Piniella (14)
COACHES: Joe Altobelli (48), Sammy Ellis (41), Stump Merrill (42), Gene Michael (40), Jeff Torborg (44), Roy White (6)
TRAVELING SECRETARY: Bill Kane
DIRECTOR OF MEDIA RELATIONS: Harvey Greene   **TEAM PHYSICIAN:** Dr. John Bonamo   **TEAM TRAINER:** Gene Monahan

No.	Pitchers (17)	B	T	Ht.	Wt.	Born	Birthplace	Residence	1985 Club	W-L	ERA	G	GS	CG	SV	IP	H	BB	SO	ML Ser
53	ALLEN, Neil	R	R	6-2	190	1/24/58	Kansas City, KS	Syosset, NY	St. Louis	1-4	5.59	23	1	0	2	29.0	32	17	10	
									New York (AL)	1-0	2.76	17	0	0	1	29.1	26	13	16	7.000
36	ARMSTRONG, Mike	R	R	6-3	195	3/17/54	Glen Cove, NY	Halifax, VA	Columbus	2-2	6.64	21	3	0	2	40.2	49	26	40	
									New York (AL)	0-0	3.07	9	0	0	0	14.2	9	2	11	4.044
43	BURNS, Britt	L	L	6-5	231	6/08/59	Houston, TX	Homewood, AL	Chicago (AL)	18-11	3.96	36	34	8	0	227.0	206	79	172	6.042
50	BYSTROM, Marty	R	R	6-5	210	7/26/58	Coral Gables, FL	Hawthorne, NJ	Columbus	2-0	1.88	4	4	0	0	24.0	13	9	16	
									New York (AL)	3-2	5.71	8	8	0	0	41.0	44	19	16	5.019
62	DRABEK, Doug	R	R	6-1	185	7/25/62	Victoria, TX	Victoria, TX	Albany	13-7	2.99	26	26	9	0	192.2	153	55	153	
									Columbus	0-0	2.38	7	0	0	0	11.1	8	7	12	0.000
54	FISHER, Brian	R	R	6-4	210	3/18/62	Honolulu, HI	Aurora, CO	New York (AL)	4-4	2.38	55	0	0	14	98.1	77	29	85	0.159
64	FULTON, Bill	R	R	6-3	195	10/22/63	Pittsburgh, PA	Pittsburgh, PA	Ft. Lauderdale	11-2	1.61	15	15	9	0	112.0	91	30	71	0.000
52	GEORGE, Steve	S	L	6-0	160	10/18/61	St. Louis, MO	Pompano Beach, FL	Ft. Lauderdale	13-7	1.75	24	24	12	0	164.2	120	76	141	0.000
49	GUIDRY, Ron	L	L	5-11	157	8/28/50	Lafayette, LA	Lafayette, LA	New York (AL)	22-6	3.27	33	33	11	0	259.0	243	42	143	10.004
47	NIEKRO, Joe	R	R	6-1	195	11/07/44	Martins Ferry, OH	Lakeland, FL	Houston	9-12	3.72	32	32	4	0	213.0	197	99	117	
									New York (AL)	2-1	5.84	3	3	0	0	12.1	14	8	4	17.138
35	NIEKRO, Phil	R	R	6-1	193	4/01/39	Blaine, OH	Lilburn, GA	New York (AL)	16-12	4.09	33	33	7	0	220.0	203	120	149	20.154
45	RASMUSSEN, Dennis	L	L	6-7	225	4/18/59	Los Angeles, CA	Omaha, NE	Columbus	0-3	3.80	7	7	1	0	45.0	41	25	43	
									New York (AL)	3-5	3.98	22	16	2	0	101.2	97	42	63	1.124
19	RIGHETTI, Dave	L	L	6-3	198	11/28/58	San Jose, CA	San Jose, CA	New York (AL)	12-7	2.78	74	0	0	29	107.0	96	45	92	4.151
28	SCURRY, Rod	L	L	6-2	195	3/17/56	Sacramento, CA	Reno, NV	Pittsburgh	0-1	3.21	30	0	0	1	47.2	42	28	43	
									New York (AL)	1-0	2.84	5	0	0	2	12.2	5	10	17	6.032
29	SHIRLEY, Bob	L	R	6-0	180	6/25/54	Cushing, OK	Tulsa, OK	New York (AL)	5-5	2.64	48	2	0	0	109.0	103	26	55	9.000
75	TEWKSBURY, Bob	R	R	6-4	180	11/30/60	Concord, NH	Penacook, NH	Albany	6-5	3.54	17	17	4	0	106.2	101	19	63	0.000
38	WHITSON, Ed	R	R	6-3	195	5/19/55	Johnson City, TN	Dublin, OH	Columbus	3-0	1.02	6	6	1	0	44.0	27	5	21	
									New York (AL)	10-8	4.88	30	30	2	0	158.2	201	43	89	7.159

No.	Catchers (5)	B	T	Ht.	Wt.	Born	Birthplace	Residence	1985 Club	AVG	G	AB	R	H	2B	3B	HR	RBI	BB	SO	SB	ML Ser
34	BRADLEY, Scott	L	R	5-11	185	3/22/60	Essex Fells, NJ	Essex Fells, NJ	Albany	.125	6	24	2	3					2	2	1	0

Catchers (continued)

No.	Name	Birthplace	Residence	Born	B	T	Ht.	Wt.	1985 Club	AVG	G	AB	R	H	2B	3B	HR	RBI	BB	SO	SB	ML Ser
58	ESPINO, Juan	Bonao, DR	Bonao, DR	3/16/56	R	R	6-1	190	Columbus	.301	43	163	17	49	10	0	0	27	8	12	2	
									New York (AL)	.163	19	49	4	8	1	0	0	1	1	5	0	0.155
63	LOMBARDI, Phil	Abilene, TX	Granada Hills, CA	2/20/63	R	R	6-2	200	Columbus	.250	76	224	30	56	11	2	5	20	22	36	0	
									New York (AL)	.364	9	11	0	4	1	0	2	5	2	5	0	0.122
59	LYDEN, Mitch	Portland, OR	Beaverton, OR	12/14/64	R	R	6-3	200	Ft. Lauderdale	.255	116	400	44	102	21	1	10	58	39	93	1	0.000
27	WYNEGAR, Butch	York, PA	Longwood, FL	3/14/56	S	R	6-1	192	New York (AL)	.223	102	309	27	69	15	0	5	32	64	43	0	10.000

Infielders (10)

No.	Name	Birthplace	Residence	Born	B	T	Ht.	Wt.	1985 Club	AVG	G	AB	R	H	2B	3B	HR	RBI	BB	SO	SB	ML Ser
2	BERRA, Dale	Ridgewood, NJ	Glen Ridge, NJ	12/13/56	R	R	6-0	190	New York (AL)	.229	48	109	8	25	5	1	0	20	7	20	1	7.060
61	DESTRADE, Orestes	Havana, CUBA	Miami, FL	5/08/62	S	R	6-4	210	Albany	.253	136	471	81	119	24	5	23	72	86	129	0	0.000
22	FISCHLIN, Mike	Sacramento, CA	Tucson, AZ	9/13/55	R	R	6-1	165	Cleveland	.200	73	60	12	12	4	1	0	2	5	7	0	5.006
23	MATTINGLY, Don	Evansville, IN	Evansville, IN	4/20/61	L	L	6-0	175	New York (AL)	.324	159	652	107	211	48	3	35	145	56	41	2	2.163
20	MEACHAM, Bobby	Los Angeles, CA	Glen Rock, NJ	8/25/60	S	R	6-1	180	New York (AL)	.218	156	481	70	105	16	2	0	47	54	102	25	1.162
12	PAGLIARULO, Mike	Medford, MA	Melrose, MA	6/15/60	L	R	6-2	195	New York (AL)	.239	138	380	55	91	16	2	19	62	45	88	0	1.086
30	RANDOLPH, Willie	Holly Hill, SC	Franklin Lakes, NJ	7/06/54	R	R	5-11	166	New York (AL)	.276	143	497	75	137	21	2	5	40	85	39	16	10.064
18	ROBERTSON, Andre	Orange, TX	Orange, TX	10/02/57	R	R	5-10	162	Columbus	.393	9	28	3	11	0	0	0	1	1	3	1	
									New York (AL)	.328	50	125	16	41	5	0	2	17	6	24	5	3.044
55	SOPER, Mike	Miami, FL	Miami, FL	5/23/65	R	R	6-1	165	Glens Falls	.296	132	480	50	142	16	0	4	49	26	51	5	0.000
56	SOSA, Miguel	La Romana, DR	La Romana, DR	5/15/60	R	R	5-10	165	Richmond	.192	119	433	49	83	13	2	14	49	13	75	7	0.000

Outfielders (8)

No.	Name	Birthplace	Residence	Born	B	T	Ht.	Wt.	1985 Club	AVG	G	AB	R	H	2B	3B	HR	RBI	BB	SO	SB	ML Ser
25	BAYLOR, Don	Austin, TX	Cresskill, NJ	6/28/48	R	R	6-1	210	New York (AL)	.231	142	477	70	110	24	1	23	91	52	90	0	14.030
46	COTTO, Henry	Bronx, NY	Caguas, PR	1/05/61	R	R	6-2	178	Columbus	.257	75	272	38	70	16	2	7	36	19	61	10	
									New York (AL)	.304	34	56	4	17	1	0	1	6	3	12	1	1.123
33	GRIFFEY, Ken	Donora, PA	Westchester, OH	4/10/50	L	L	6-0	200	New York (AL)	.274	127	438	68	120	28	0	10	69	41	51	7	11.171
24	HENDERSON, Rickey	Chicago, IL	Oakland, CA	12/25/58	R	L	5-10	195	Ft. Lauderdale	.167	3	18	5	3	0	0	0	3	5	7	1	
									New York (AL)	.314	143	547	146	172	28	5	24	72	99	65	80	6.101
17	MATA, Vic	Santiago, DR	Santo Domingo, DR	6/17/61	R	R	6-1	165	Columbus	.261	104	375	39	98	14	2	3	27	27	58	2	
									New York (AL)	.143	6	7	1	1	0	0	0	0	0	2	0	0.098
21	PASQUA, Dan	Yonkers, NY	Ridgewood, NJ	10/17/61	L	L	6-0	203	Columbus	.321	78	287	52	92	16	5	18	69	48	62	2	
									New York (AL)	.209	60	148	17	31	3	1	9	25	16	38	0	0.098
11	ROENICKE, Gary	Covina, CA	Phoenix, MD	12/05/54	R	R	6-3	200	Baltimore	.218	113	225	36	49	9	0	15	43	44	36	2	7.164
31	WINFIELD, Dave	St. Paul, MN	Teaneck, NJ	10/03/51	R	R	6-6	220	New York (AL)	.275	155	633	105	174	34	6	26	114	52	96	19	12.105

NON-ROSTER PLAYERS

No.	Pitchers	B	T	Ht.	Wt.	Born	Birthplace	Residence	1985 Club	W-L	ERA	G	GS	CG	SV	IP	H	BB	SO	ML Ser
68	ARNSBERG, Brad	R	R	6-4	210	8/20/63	Seattle, WA	Medford, OR	Albany	14-2	1.59	20	20	9	0	141.1	105	35	82	0.000
60	BALABON, Rick	R	R	6-2	175	4/26/67	Philadelphia, PA	Wayne, PA	Oneonta	5-2	1.74	12	12	3	0	72.1	50	39	68	0.000
67	CHRISTIANSEN, Clay	R	R	6-5	220	6/28/58	Wichita, KS	Columbus, KS	Columbus	10-6	3.66	28	18	3	1	137.2	128	59	67	0.075
65	DERSIN, Eric	R	R	6-1	200	1/06/64	Cumberland, MD	Ft. Ashby, WV	Ft. Lauderdale	4-3	4.05	8	8	0	0	46.2	52	24	29	0.000
									Daytona Beach	5-5	4.40	17	17	5	0	108.0	101	45	80	
57	FAULK, Kelly	R	R	6-2	195	4/23/59	Crowley, LA	Worthington, OH	Columbus	4-7	5.42	18	16	1	0	84.2	90	48	40	0.000
									Albany	3-0	4.50	6	5	0	0	35.0	32	14	24	
	*HOLLAND, Al	R	L	5-11	210	8/16/52	Roanoke, VA	Voorhees, NJ	Philadelphia	0-1	3.38	3	0	0	0	4.0	5	4	1	6.058
									Pittsburgh	1-3	1.48	38	0	0	4	58.2	48	17	47	
									California	0-1	4.70	15	0	0	0	24.1	17	10	14	
	JOHN, Tommy	R	L	6-3	200	5/22/43	Terre Haute, IN	Anaheim, CA	California	2-4	6.19	12	6	0	0	38.1	51	15	17	21.113
									Oakland	2-6		9	7	0	0	48.0	66	13	8	
26	MONTEFUSCO, John	R	R	6-1	192	5/25/50	Keansburg, NJ	Colts Neck, NJ	New York	0-0	10.29	3	1	0	0	7.0	12	2	2	11.070
	PULIDO, Alfonso	L	L	5-11	175	1/23/59	Vera Cruz, MX	Vera Cruz, MX	Columbus	11-8	3.39	31	20	4	1	149.0	154	34	67	0.053

No.	Catchers	B	T	Ht.	Wt.	Born	Birthplace	Residence	1985 Club	AVG	G	AB	R	H	2B	3B	HR	RBI	BB	SO	SB	ML Ser
69	GEREN, Bob	R	R	6-3	205	9/22/61	San Diego, CA	San Diego, CA	Louisville	.357	5	14	2	5	2	0	1	3	0	1	0	0.000
									Arkansas	.225	103	315	38	71	18	1	5	40	31	74	3	

No.	Infielders	B	T	Ht.	Wt.	Born	Birthplace	Residence	1985 Club	AVG	G	AB	R	H	2B	3B	HR	RBI	BB	SO	SB	ML Ser
71	MARTINEZ, Carlos	R	R	6-5	175	8/11/65	La Guaira, VZ	La Guaira, VZ	Ft. Lauderdale	.248	93	311	39	77	15	7	6	44	14	65	8	0.000
13	SMITH, Keith	B	R	6-1	185	10/20/61	Los Angeles, CA	Canyon County, CA	New York	—	4	0	1	0	0	0	0	0	0	0	0	0.034
									Columbus	.241	123	307	40	74	9	1	4	21	39	66	10	

No.	Outfielders	B	T	Ht.	Wt.	Born	Birthplace	Residence	1985 Club	AVG	G	AB	R	H	2B	3B	HR	RBI	BB	SO	SB	ML Ser
70	BUHNER, Jay	R	R	6-3	205	8/13/64	Louisville, KY	Houston, TX	Ft. Lauderdale	.296	117	409	65	121	18	10	11	76	65	76	6	0.000
73	McNEALY, Derwin	L	L	6-2	165	4/25/60	Los Angeles, CA	Los Angeles, CA	Syracuse	.265	135	472	49	125	13	6	1	42	36	74	22	0.000
72	REED, Derwin	R	R	6-1	190	10/16/65	Ventura, CA	Ventura, CA	Ft. Lauderdale	.317	100	369	63	117	21	4	10	61	36	56	13	0.000
74	STEGMAN, Dave	R	R	5-11	175	7/21/65	Inglewook, CA	Lompoc, CA	Syracuse	.319	89	257	36	82	15	4	10	45	35	35	1	2.038

*Late addition to 40-man roster.

YANKEE STADIUM MONUMENTS

MILLER JAMES HUGGINS
MANAGER OF THE NEW YORK YANKEES. 1918-1929
PENNANT WINNERS 1921-22-23-26-27-28
WORLD CHAMPIONS 1923, 1927 AND 1928
AS A TRIBUTE TO A SPLENDID CHARACTER WHO
MADE PRICELESS CONTRIBUTIONS TO BASEBALL
AND ON THIS FIELD BROUGHT GLORY TO THE
NEW YORK CLUB OF THE AMERICAN LEAGUE.
THIS MEMORIAL ERECTED BY COL. JACOB RUPPERT
AND BASEBALL WRITERS OF NEW YORK
MAY 30, 1932

TO THE MEMORY OF JACOB RUPPERT
1867-1939
GENTLEMAN • AMERICAN • SPORTSMAN
THROUGH WHOSE VISION AND COURAGE THIS
IMPOSING EDIFICE, DESTINED TO BECOME
THE HOME OF CHAMPIONS, WAS ERECTED
AND DEDICATED TO THE
AMERICAN GAME OF BASEBALL

HENRY LOUIS GEHRIG
JUNE 19, 1902-JUNE 2nd, 1941
A MAN, A GENTLEMAN AND A GREAT BALL PLAYER
WHOSE AMAZING RECORD OF 2,130 CONSECUTIVE
GAMES SHOULD STAND FOR ALL TIME
THIS MEMORIAL IS A TRIBUTE FROM THE YANKEE
PLAYERS TO THEIR BELOVED CAPTAIN AND
TEAM MATE
JULY THE FOURTH 1941

GEORGE HERMAN "BABE" RUTH
1895-1948
A GREAT BALL PLAYER
A GREAT MAN
A GREAT AMERICAN
ERECTED BY THE YANKEES AND
THE NEW YORK BASEBALL WRITERS
APRIL 19, 1949

EDWARD GRANT BARROW
1868-1953
MOULDER OF TRADITION OF VICTORY
UNDER WHOSE GUIDANCE THE YANKEES
WON FOURTEEN AMERICAN LEAGUE PENNANTS
AND TEN WORLD CHAMPIONSHIPS AND
BROUGHT TO THIS FIELD SOME OF THE
GREATEST BASEBALL STARS OF ALL TIME.
THIS MEMORIAL IS A TRIBUTE FROM THOSE
WHO SEEK TO CARRY ON HIS GREAT WORKS
ERECTED APRIL 15, 1954

JOE DiMAGGIO
NEW YORK YANKEES 1936-1951
THE YANKEE CLIPPER
HIT IN 56 CONSECUTIVE GAMES
"GREATEST LIVING PLAYER" IN BASEBALL'S
CENTENNIAL YEAR
IN RECOGNITION OF HIS SINGULAR EXCELLENCE
AND FOR HIS LEGACY OF GREATNESS
THIS PLAQUE DEDICATED TO JOE DiMAGGIO
BY MICKEY MANTLE IN A CEREMONY AT
YANKEE STADIUM ON JUNE 8, 1969

MICKEY MANTLE
A MAGNIFICENT YANKEE
536 HOME RUNS
THE MOST POPULAR PLAYER OF HIS ERA
IN RECOGNITION OF HIS TRUE GREATNESS
IN THE YANKEE TRADITION AND
FOR HIS UNEQUALED COURAGE
THIS PLAQUE PRESENTED TO MICKEY MANTLE
BY JOE DiMAGGIO IN A CEREMONY AT
YANKEE STADIUM ON JUNE 8, 1969

JOSEPH VINCENT McCARTHY
MANAGER NEW YORK YANKEES 1931-1946
ONE OF BASEBALL'S MOST BELOVED AND
RESPECTED LEADERS
LED YANKEES TO 8 PENNANTS AND
7 WORLD CHAMPIONSHIPS INCLUDING
4 CONSECUTIVE 1936-1939, COMPILING A
.627 WINNING PERCENTAGE
ERECTED BY NEW YORK YANKEES
APRIL 21, 1976

CHARLES DILLON "CASEY" STENGEL
1880-1975
BRIGHTENED BASEBALL FOR OVER 50 YEARS
WITH SPIRIT OF ETERNAL YOUTH
YANKEE MANAGER 1949-1960 WINNING
10 PENNANTS AND 7 WORLD CHAMPIONSHIPS
INCLUDING A RECORD 5 CONSECUTIVE 1949-1953
ERECTED BY NEW YORK YANKEES
JULY 30, 1976

THURMAN MUNSON
NEW YORK YANKEES
June 7, 1947-August 2, 1979
YANKEE CAPTAIN
"OUR CAPTAIN AND LEADER HAS NOT LEFT US
TODAY, TOMORROW, THIS YEAR, NEXT . . .
OUR ENDEAVORS WILL REFLECT OUR
LOVE AND ADMIRATION FOR HIM."
ERECTED BY THE NEW YORK YANKEES
SEPTEMBER 20, 1980

ROGER EUGENE MARIS
AGAINST ALL ODDS
IN 1961 HE BECAME THE ONLY PLAYER TO HIT
MORE THAN 60 HOME RUNS IN A SINGLE SEASON
IN BELATED RECOGNITION OF ONE OF BASEBALL'S
GREATEST ACHIEVEMENTS EVER
HIS 61 in '61
THE YANKEES SALUTE HIM AS A GREAT PLAYER
AND AS AUTHOR OF ONE OF THE MOST
REMARKABLE CHAPTERS IN THE HISTORY
OF MAJOR LEAGUE BASEBALL
ERECTED BY NEW YORK YANKEES
JULY 21, 1984

ELSTON GENE HOWARD
1929-1980
"A MAN OF GREAT GENTLENESS AND DIGNITY"
ONE OF ALL-TIME YANKEE GREATS
AMERICAN LEAGUE MVP IN 1963
WINNER OF TWO GOLD GLOVES
A FITTING LEADER TO BE FIRST BLACK PLAYER
TO WEAR THE YANKEE UNIFORM
"IF, INDEED, HUMILITY IS A TRADEMARK
OF MANY GREAT MEN—ELSTON HOWARD WAS
ONE OF THE TRULY GREAT YANKEES"
ERECTED BY NEW YORK YANKEES
JULY 21, 1984

PHILIP FRANCIS RIZZUTO
"A MAN'S SIZE IS MEASURED BY HIS HEART"
SCOOTER SPARKED YANKEES TO 10
PENNANTS AND 8 WORLD CHAMPIONSHIPS
1950 MAJOR LEAGUE PLAYER OF YEAR
MVP OF WORLD SERIES IN 1951
HAS ENJOYED TWO OUTSTANDING CAREERS
ALL-TIME YANKEE SHORTSTOP
ONE OF GREAT YANKEE BROADCASTERS
"HOLY COW"
ERECTED BY NEW YORK YANKEES
AUGUST 4, 1985

IN COMMEMORATION
OF THE SOLEMN MASS
FOR PEACE OFFERED
BY HIS
HOLINESS POPE PAUL VI
OCTOBER 4, 1965
HERE IN YANKEE STADIUM
GIFT OF
KNIGHTS of COLUMBUS

IN COMMEMORATION
OF THE MASS FOR
WORLD JUSTICE AND PEACE
OFFERED BY
HIS HOLINESS
POPE JOHN PAUL II
OCTOBER 2, 1979
HERE IN YANKEE STADIUM
GIFT OF
KNIGHTS of COLUMBUS

DID YOU KNOW ... the Yankees lineup when Dave Righetti no-hit the Red Sox on July 4, 1983? Campaneris 3b, Mattingly 1b, Winfield cf, Piniella lf, Baylor dh, Wynegar c, Kemp rf, Smalley ss, Robertson 2b, Righetti p.

1985 FINAL SPRING TRAINING STATISTICS

Batter	AVG	G	AB	R	H	2B	3B	HR	RBI	GW RBI	BB	SO	SB
Baylor	.233	23	73	12	17	3	0	4	14	0	6	16	0
Berra	.327	24	55	10	18	5	0	0	5	2	8	9	0
Bonilla	.179	15	28	2	5	0	0	0	2	1	1	1	0
Bradley	.265	24	68	6	18	2	1	1	12	0	3	0	0
Cotto	.291	23	55	5	16	3	1	0	11	1	0	7	0
Espino	.000	13	14	0	0	0	0	0	0	0	0	4	0
Griffey	.429	16	42	8	18	4	0	1	4	0	1	4	1
Hassey	.220	20	41	5	9	5	0	0	4	0	3	6	0
Henderson	.333	8	21	3	7	2	0	0	1	0	3	2	1
Hudler	.280	16	25	5	7	1	0	0	2	0	1	6	2
Mata	.208	15	24	2	5	0	0	0	1	0	0	3	0
Mattingly	.409	9	22	3	9	2	1	1	4	1	1	1	0
Meacham	.197	24	66	7	13	1	1	0	5	1	5	19	1
Moreno	.312	23	77	15	24	3	2	0	6	0	3	10	4
Pagliarulo	.286	14	42	2	12	2	1	0	5	0	4	9	0
Randolph	.255	18	51	9	13	4	0	1	7	1	5	3	0
Robertson	.348	11	23	4	8	0	1	2	3	1	0	4	0
Sample	.321	25	53	10	17	3	1	2	8	0	7	8	2
Smith	.500	6	4	2	2	0	0	0	1	0	1	1	0
Winfield	.103	12	29	3	3	1	0	0	1	1	4	2	0
Wynegar	.192	21	52	4	10	3	0	1	11	1	5	7	0
DH Hitters	.269		78	12	21	4	0	4	13	0	5	17	0
PH Hitters	.067		15	0	1	0	0	0	0	0	1	5	0
Others	.161		62	2	10	4	0	0	3	0	2	13	0
Totals	.260		940	119	244	48	9	13	106	11	63	136	10
Opponents	.281		958	131	269	22	8	21	126	9	64	139	11

Pitcher		W-L	ERA	G	GS	CG	Sho	SV	IP	H	R	ER	BB	SO
Armstrong	R	0-2	8.18	9	0	0	0	0	11.0	14	11	10	7	5
Bordi	R	2-0	1.88	9	0	0	0	3	14.1	14	3	3	1	8
Cowley	R	2-2	6.00	7	2	0	0	0	24.0	31	19	16	8	23
Fisher	R	2-1	3.38	6	1	0	0	0	16.0	14	9	6	5	7
Guidry	L	0-0	2.25	3	3	0	0	0	12.0	11	3	3	7	7
Montefusco	R	1-3	6.32	4	4	0	0	0	15.2	17	12	11	6	9
Murray	R	1-1	5.68	8	0	0	0	0	12.2	17	12	8	5	3
Niekro	R	1-1	4.00	6	6	0	0	0	27.0	22	13	12	6	14
Pulido	L	0-0	2.38	5	0	0	0	1	11.1	14	5	3	2	2
Rasmussen	L	0-0	3.20	6	6	0	0	0	25.1	28	12	9	4	20
Righetti	L	2-0	1.80	11	0	0	0	3	15.0	19	3	3	4	12
Shirley	L	2-0	1.77	9	0	0	0	0	20.1	16	4	4	4	7
Silva	R	0-0	.00	2	0	0	0	0	2.0	0	0	0	1	2
Whitson	R	2-1	3.90	6	6	0	0	0	27.2	35	15	12	4	15
Williams	R	0-0	5.40	2	0	0	0	0	5.0	7	3	3	0	1
Others		0-1	11.25	3	0	0	0	0	4.0	8	5	5	0	4
Totals		15-12	4.05	96	28	0	0	7	244.1	269	131	110	64	139
Opponents		12-15	4.25	72	28	0	0	5	239.1	244	119	113	63	136

FINAL HOME ATTENDANCE   91,219   14 dates
1985 Spring Training   6,516   avg. attendance

1985 SPRING ATTENDANCE

Home Attendance in Ft. Lauderdale (14 dates) 91,219
Road Attendance (14 dates)... 74,726
Overall Spring Attendance Totals...................................... 165,945

James P. Dawson Award

The James P. Dawson Award was established in honor of the late sportswriter of the New York Times who died while covering the Yankees during spring training. It is presented annually to the outstanding rookie in spring training. Two former winners of the award, Tony Kubek in 1957 and Tom Tresh in 1962, went on to win American League Rookie of the Year honors. The award was first presented to rookie Norm Siebern by manager Casey Stengel in St. Petersburg at the conclusion of spring training in 1956. Media personnel who regularly cover the Yankees vote to decide the winner.

1956	Norm Siebern, of	1971	none selected
1957	Tony Kubek, ss	1972	Rusty Torres, of
1958	John Blanchard, c	1973	Otto Velez, of
1959	Gordon Windhorn, of	1974	Tom Buskey, p
1960	John James, p	1975	Tippy Martinez, p
1961	Roland Sheldon, p	1976	Willie Randolph, 2b
1962	Tom Tresh, ss	1977	George Zeber, inf
1963	Pedro Gonzalez, 2b	1978	Jim Beattie, p
1964	Pete Mikkelsen, p	1979	Paul Mirabella, p
1965	Arturo Lopez, of	1980	Mike Griffin, p
1966	Roy White, of	1981	Gene Nelson, p
1967	Bill Robinson, of	1982	Andre Robertson, ss
1968	Mike Ferraro, 3b	1983	Don Mattingly, 1b-of
1969	Jerry Kenney, of	1984	Jose Rijo, p
	Bill Burbach, p	1985	Scott Bradley, c
1970	John Ellis, 1b-c		

NEW YORK YANKEES
1986 SPRING TRAINING SCHEDULE

SPRING HEADQUARTERS: Fort Lauderdale Stadium, 5301 N.W. 12th Ave. 33309 Telephone (305) 776-1921.

HOTEL HEADQUARTERS: King Neptune Hotel, 1208 N. Ocean Blvd., Pompano Beach, FL 33062, Telephone: (305) 782-5300.

Day/Date	Opponent	Site	Time	Score NYY	OPP
Saturday, March 8	Baltimore	Ft. Lauderdale	1:30 p.m.	___	___
Sunday, March 9	Baltimore	Miami	1:30 p.m.	___	___
Monday, March 10	Texas	Ft. Lauderdale	7:30 p.m.	___	___
Tuesday, March 11	Toronto	Ft. Lauderdale	7:30 p.m.	___	___
Wednesday, March 12	Workout		10:30 a.m.		
Thursday, March 13	Montreal	Ft. Lauderdale	7:30 p.m.	___	___
Friday, March 14	Baltimore	Ft. Lauderdale	7:30 p.m.	___	___
Saturday, March 15	Univ. of Fla.	Gainesville	2:30 p.m.	___	___
Sunday, March 16	Toronto	Dunedin	1:30 p.m.	___	___
	Chicago	Sarasota	1:30 p.m.	___	___
Monday, March 17	Toronto	Dunedin	1:30 p.m.	___	___
Tuesday, March 18	Chicago	Sarasota	1:30 p.m.	___	___
Wednesday, March 19	Baltimore	Miami	7:30 p.m.	___	___
Thursday, March 20	Montreal	W. Palm Beach	1:30 p.m.	___	___
Friday, March 21	Texas	Pompano	1:30 p.m.	___	___
	White Sox	Ft. Lauderdale	7:30 p.m.	___	___
Saturday, March 22	Baltimore	Miami	7:30 p.m.	___	___
Sunday, March 23	Texas	Ft. Lauderdale	1:30 p.m.	___	___
Monday, March 24	OFF DAY				
Tuesday, March 25	Kansas City	Ft. Lauderdale	7:30 p.m.	___	___
Wednesday, March 26	Montreal	Ft. Lauderdale	7:30 p.m.	___	___
Thursday, March 27	Texas	Pompano	1:30 p.m.	___	___
Friday, March 28	Baltimore	Ft. Lauderdale	7:30 p.m.	___	___
Saturday, March 29	Atlanta	Ft. Lauderdale	1:30 p.m.	___	___
Sunday, March 30	Texas	Ft. Lauderdale	1:30 p.m.	___	___
Monday, March 31	Baltimore	Miami	1:30 p.m.	___	___
Tuesday, April 1	Kansas City	Ft. Myers	1:30 p.m.	___	___
Wednesday, April 2	White Sox	Ft. Lauderdale	7:30 p.m.	___	___
Thursday, April 3	Baltimore	Ft. Lauderdale	1:30 p.m.	___	___
Friday, April 4	Toronto	Denver	1:30 p.m.	___	___
Saturday, April 5	Toronto	Denver	1:30 p.m.	___	___
Tuesday, April 8	**Opening Day** vs.Kansas City				

Reporting Dates For Invited Players:
  Batterymen—Thu., Feb. 20/First Workout Fri., Feb. 21
  Remainder of Squad—Tue., Feb. 25/First Workout Wed., Feb. 26

ITINERARY FOR SPRING TRAINING—1986

March 15-17 Bay Harbor Inn, Tampa, FL—(813) 885-2541
April 3-4 Westin Hotel, Denver, CO—(303) 572-4247

RECENT SPRING TRAINING RECORDS

1962—17-10	1967—13-17	1972—11-15-1	1977—11-13	1982—9-16
1963—12-17-1	1968—14-14-1	1973—18-11	1978—10-13	1983—16-8
1964—12-16	1969—16-9	1974—14-14-1	1979—7-18	1984—10-16
1965—12-18	1970—18-9	1975—14-17	1980—10-8-1	1985—15-12
1966—17-11	1971—8-23	1976—10-7	1981—13-13-1	

YANKEE SPRING TRAINING SITES

1903-04	Atlanta, GA	1919-20	Jacksonville, FL
1905	Montgomery, AL	1921	Shreveport, LA
1906	Birmingham, AL	1922-24	New Orleans, LA
1907-08	Atlanta, GA	1925-42	St. Petersburg, FL
1909	Macon, GA	1943	Asbury Park, NJ
1910-11	Athens, GA	1944-45	Atlantic City, NJ
1912	Atlanta, GA	1946-50	St. Petersburg, FL
1913	Hamilton, Bermuda	1951	Phoenix, AZ
1914	Houston, TX	1952-61	St. Petersburg, FL
1915	Savannah, GA	1962-	Ft. Lauderdale, FL
1916-18	Macon, GA		

FORT LAUDERDALE STADIUM

(opened 1962)

TOTAL SEATING—7,461		DIAMOND DIMENSIONS	
Box Seats	1,923	Left field foul line	335 feet
Reserved Seats	2,538	Center Field	401 feet
Bleacher Seats	3,000	Right Field foul line	325 feet

Facilities for press, radio and television atop grandstand—capacity, 82. Parking facilities for 3,000 cars.

THE MANAGER AND HIS COACHES

PINIELLA, LOUIS VICTOR "Lou" (Manager)   #14

6-2, 200. Born 8/28/43 in Tampa, FL. Age 42, turns 43 August 28. Resides in Temple Terrace, FL. BR. TR. Married: Anita Garcia 4/12/67. Children: Lou, Jr. (16), Kristi (13) and Derrick (7). College: University of Tampa.

Lou was named as the Yankees Manager October 17, 1985 ... Retired officially on June 17, 1984 and was named a Yankee coach ... honored with Lou Piniella Day on August 5 ... a consistent player, recognized as one of baseball's "most professional hitters" ... has always been extremely tough for Yankees in clutch ... his .295 lifetime batting average with Yankees ranks him in top 10 all-time as Yankee ... missed most of 1975 season with inner ear problem that required mid-season surgery ... returned to regular duty in '76 and was runner-up to teammate Dock Ellis for Comeback Player of the Year ... originally signed by Cleveland scout and former Yankee Spud Chandler ... has always been excellent post-season performer ... in '77 hit safely in 5 ALCS games ... in '78 hit safely in all 6 W.S. games ... hit in 1st 3 games of 1981 W.S. to extend his personal W.S. hitting streak to 9 consecutive games ... led all Yankee hitters with .438 average in '81 W.S. ... in 1981 led A.L. DHs (50 or more games as DH) in batting average, .344 and was 2nd in league as pinch hitter (25 or more at bats) with .360 average ... on August 24 was asked to help Yankee coaching staff as batting instructor, working with his teammates on the fine art of hitting ... always one of Yankees most exciting players ... fans welcome each of his at bats with chants of "Lou, Lou" ... a lifetime native of Tampa, FL area and is of Spanish ancestry ... enjoys the stock market ... operates 2 restaurants in New York-Metropolitan area.

Tied major league record for most assists by outfielder, inning (2), May 27, 1974 (third inning).

Named by Baseball Writers Association as American League Rookie of Year, 1969.

CAREER PLAYING RECORD

YR	Club	AVG	G	AB	R	H	2B	3B	HR	RBI	BB	SO	SB
1962	Selma-a	.270	70	278	40	75	10	5	8	44	10	57	4
1963	Peninsula	.310	143	548	71	170	29	4	16	77	34	70	8
1964	Aberdeen-b	.270	20	74	8	20	8	3	0	12	6	9	1
	BALTIMORE	.000	4	1	0	0	0	0	0	0	0	0	0
1965	Elmira-c	.249	126	490	64	122	29	6	11	64	22	57	5
1966	Portland	.289	133	457	47	132	22	3	7	52	20	52	6
1967	Portland	.308	113	396	46	122	20	1	8	56	23	47	2
1968	Portland	.317	88	331	49	105	15	3	13	62	19	31	0
	CLEVELAND-de	.000	6	5	1	0	0	0	0	1	0	0	1
1969	KANSAS CITY	.282	135	493	43	139	21	6	11	68	33	56	2
1970	KANSAS CITY	.301	144	542	54	163	24	5	11	88	35	42	3
1971	KANSAS CITY-f	.279	126	448	43	125	21	5	3	51	21	43	5
1972	KANSAS CITY	.312	151	574	65	179	33*	4	11	72	34	59	7
1973	KANSAS CITY-g	.250	144	513	53	128	28	1	9	69	30	65	5
1974	YANKEES	.305	140	518	71	158	26	0	9	70	32	58	1
1975	YANKEES-h	.196	74	199	7	39	4	1	0	22	16	22	0
1976	YANKEES	.281	100	327	36	92	16	6	3	38	18	34	0
1977	YANKEES	.330	103	339	47	112	19	3	12	45	20	31	2
1978	YANKEES	.314	130	472	67	148	34	5	6	69	34	36	3
1979	YANKEES	.297	130	461	49	137	22	2	11	69	17	31	3
1980	YANKEES	.287	116	321	39	92	18	0	2	27	29	20	0
1981	YANKEES-i	.277	60	159	16	44	9	0	5	18	13	9	0
1982	YANKEES	.307	102	261	33	80	17	1	6	37	18	18	0
1983	YANKEES-j	.291	53	148	19	43	9	1	2	16	11	12	1
1984	YANKEES	.302	29	86	8	26	4	1	1	6	7	5	0
Minor League Totals		**.290**	**693**	**2574**	**325**	**746**	**133**	**25**	**63**	**367**	**134**	**323**	**26**
N.Y.Y. Totals		**.295**	**1037**	**3291**	**392**	**971**	**178**	**20**	**57**	**417**	**215**	**276**	**10**
M.L. Totals		**.291**	**1747**	**5867**	**651**	**1705**	**305**	**41**	**102**	**766**	**368**	**541**	**33**

GWRBI: 1980-2; 1981-2; 1982-3; 1983-2; 1984-2. Total-11.

Signed as free agent by Cleveland Indians' organization, June 9, 1962.

a-Drafted by Washington Senators from Jacksonville (Cleveland Indians' organization), November 26, 1962.

b-Reinstated from Military List by Washington Senators, July 20, 1964 and assigned to Baltimore Orioles to complete deal for pitcher Lester (Buster) Narum, August 4, 1964; Orioles optioned him to Aberdeen.

c-Traded by Baltimore Orioles to Cleveland Indians' organization for catcher Cam Carreon, March 10, 1966.

d-Selected by Seattle Pilots from Cleveland Indians in expansion draft, October 15, 1968.

e-Traded by Seattle Pilots to Kansas City Royals for outfielder Steve Whitaker and pitcher John Gelnar (latter assigned to Vancouver), April 1, 1969.
f-On disabled list May 5 through June 8, 1971.
g-Traded with pitcher Ken Wright to New York Yankees for pitcher Lindy McDaniel, December 7, 1973.
h-On disabled list, June 17 to July 6, 1975.
i-On disabled list, August 23, 1981 to September 7, 1981.
j-On disabled list, April 4 to April 22, 1983 with sore left shoulder.
k-Retired June 17, 1984.
Player/batting instructor, 1981-1984; Coach, New York Yankees, 1984-85.

DIVISION SERIES RECORD

YR	Club, Opp.	AVG	G	AB	R	H	2B	3B	HR	RBI	BB	SO	SB
1981 N.Y. vs Mil.		.200	4	10	1	2	1	0	1	3	0	0	0

CHAMPIONSHIP SERIES RECORD

YR	Club, Opp.	AVG	G	AB	R	H	2B	3B	HR	RBI	BB	SO	SB
1976 N.Y. vs K.C.		.273	4	11	1	3	1	0	0	0	0	1	0
1977 N.Y. vs K.C.		.333	5	21	1	7	3	0	0	2	0	1	0
1978 N.Y. vs K.C.		.235	4	17	2	4	0	0	0	0	0	3	0
1980 N.Y. vs K.C.		.200	2	5	1	1	0	0	1	1	2	1	0
1981 N.Y. vs Oak.		.600	3	5	2	3	0	0	1	3	0	0	0
L.C.S. Totals		.305	18	59	7	18	4	0	2	6	2	6	0

WORLD SERIES RECORD

Tied World Series record for one or more hits, each game, six-game series, 1978.

YR	Club, Opp.	AVG	G	AB	R	H	2B	3B	HR	RBI	BB	SO	SB
1976 N.Y. vs Cin.		.333	4	9	1	3	1	0	0	0	0	0	0
1977 N.Y. vs L.A.		.273	6	22	1	6	0	0	0	3	0	3	0
1978 N.Y. vs L.A.		.280	6	25	3	7	0	0	0	4	0	0	1
1981 N.Y. vs L.A.		.438	6	16	2	7	1	0	0	3	0	1	1
W.S. Totals		.319	22	72	7	23	2	0	0	10	0	4	2

ALL-STAR GAME RECORD

YR	Club, Site	AVG	G	AB	R	H	2B	3B	HR	RBI	BB	SO	SB
1972 A.L., Atl.		.000	1	1	0	0	0	0	0	0	0	0	0

ALL TIME YANKEE MANAGER ROSTER (26)

Yogi Berra 1964, 1984-85
Frank Chance 1913-14
Hal Chase 1910-11
Bill Dickey 1946
Bill Donovan 1915-17
Norm Elberfeld 1908
Art Fletcher 1929
Clark Griffith 1903-08
Bucky Harris 1947-48
Ralph Houk 1961-63, 1966-73
Dick Howser 1980
Miller Huggins 1918-29
Johnny Keane 1965-66

Clyde King 1982
Bob Lemon 1978-79, 1981-82
Billy Martin 1975-78, 1979, 1983, 1985
Joe McCarthy 1931-46
Gene Michael 1981, 1982
Johnny Neun 1946
Roger Peckinpaugh 1914
Lou Piniella 1986
Bob Shawkey 1930
George Stallings 1909-10
Casey Stengel 1949-60
Bill Virdon 1974-75
Harry Wolverton 1912

ALTOBELLI, JOSEPH SALVATORE "Joe" "Alto"   (Coach)   #48

6-0, 180. Born 5/26/32 in Detroit, MI. Age 53, turns 54 May 26. Resides in Rochester, NY. BL TL Married: Patsy Wooten, 5/3/52. Children: Mike (33), Mark (31), Jody (29), Jackie (26), Terry (23) and Joe (17).

Returns to Yankees' organization in 1986 as Lou's bench coach ... originally joined organization for 1980 season, taking Gene Michael's position as Columbus manager ... guided Clippers to league championship and named I.L. Manager of the Year for third time ... in 1981 and 1982 served as Yankees third base coach ... in 1983 as Baltimore Oriole manager, led team to World Championship, becoming just 9th manager to win World Series in his first year as manager of that club ... Joe had replaced the legendary Earl Weaver, who retired after the 1982 season after managing the O's for 14-1/2 seasons ... ironically Earl was called out of retirement to replace Joe last summer ... played professionally for 15 seasons as first baseman/outfielder ... in 1951 set Florida State League record that still stands, hitting safely in 36 consecutive games ... was manager in the Oriole system for 11 seasons, including 6 years at AAA Rochester where he won four pennants, finished second once and averaged 84 wins.

ALTOBELLI (continued)

CAREER PLAYING RECORD

Led American Association 1st basemen in fielding with .987% in 1958; in putouts with 1247 in 1962; in assists with 89 in 1962; and in double plays with 146 in 1954, 126 in 1955, and 160 in 1962.

Led International League 1st basemen in double plays with 143 in 1960.

Led Eastern League 1st basemen in assists with 83 in 1953 and in errors with 40 in 1952.

Led Florida State League 1st basemen in putouts with 1259, in assists with 90 and in errors with 45 in 1951.

YR	Club	AVG	G	AB	R	H	2B	3B	HR	RBI	BB	SO	SB
1951	Daytona Beach	.341	140†	598	118	204	40*	19	8	101	47	45	16
1952	Reading	.271	128	436	49	118	9	7	2	37	33	39	3
1953	Reading	.294	148	528	76	155	28	9	4	65	73	35	15
1954	Indianapolis	..287	149	551	73	158	31	10	6	79	41	59	4
1955	Indianapolis	.271	98	395	58	107	24	1	7	53	38	42	3
	CLEVELAND	.200	42	·75	8	15	3	0	2	5	5	14	0
1956	Indianapolis	.254	145	528	69	134	18	10	19	81	36	67	8
1957	Columbus	.234	22	77	16	18	5	1	2	10	9	16	0
	CLEVELAND	.207	83	87	9	18	3	2	0	9	5	14	3
1958	Indianapolis-a	.287	133	463	60	133	24	4	12	74	34	57	3
1959	Toronto-b	.253	148	518	71	131	17	6	17	61	43	68	3
1960	Montreal	.255	154	552	79	141	25	5	31*	105*	55	78	1
1961	Syracuse-c	.256	96	351	50	90	11	4	10	47	34	46	0
	MINNESOTA-d	.221	41	95	10	21	2	1	3	14	13	14	0
1962	Omaha-e	.271	141	502	81	136	23	7	13	67	72	63	3
1963	Rochester-f	.244	97	315	45	77	13	0	15	44	39	41	0
1964	Rochester	.249	122	345	35	86	11	1	11	52	36	45	0
1965	Rochester-g	.295	117	393	51	116	11	3	20	59	44	59	0
1966	Rochester-g	.233	25	60	5	14	5	0	1	5	4	13	0
1967	Elmira	.143	3	7	0	1	0	0	0	2	1	2	0
1970	Dallas-Ft. Worth	.364	11	11	1	4	0	0	0	3	2	1	0
Minor League Totals		**.275**	**1877**	**6630**	**937**	**1823**	**295**	**87**	**178**	**945**	**642**	**776**	**59**
M.L. Totals		**.210**	**166**	**257**	**27**	**54**	**8**	**3**	**5**	**28**	**23**	**42**	**3**

Signed as free agent by Cleveland Indians' organization in 1950.

a-Sold by Cleveland Indians' organization to Toronto (International League), January 13, 1959.

b-Traded to Los Angeles Dodgers' organization for third baseman Clyde Parris, April 1, 1960.

c-Purchased by Minnesota Twins' organization from Syracuse (International League), July 31, 1961.

d-Released outright to Los Angeles Dodgers' organization, October 12, 1961.

e-Outrighted from Omaha (American Association) to Rochester (International League), October 12, 1962.

f-On disabled list, May 13 to May 29 and July 19 to August 14, 1963.

g-Player-coach.

PITCHING RECORD

YR	CLUB	W-L	ERA	G	GS	CG	Sho	SV	IP	H	R	ER	BB	SO
1970	Dallas-Ft. Worth	0-0	13.50	2	0	0	0	0	4	5	8	6	3	1

RECORD AS MANAGER

Named American League Manager of the Year by U.PI., 1983.

Named National League Manager of the Year by A.P., 1978.

Named Minor League Manager of the Year by T.S.N., 1974.

Named International League Manager of the Year, 1971, 1976 and 1980.

Named Appalachian League Manager of the Year, 1967.

YR	CLUB	Position	W	L	YR	CLUB	Position	W	L
1966	Bluefield	Third	38	33	1975	Rochester	Second	85	56
1967	Bluefield	First	42	25	1976	Rochester-d	First	88	50
1968	Stockton	Seventh	29	41	1977	SAN FRAN.	Fourth (W)	75	87
	(Second Half)	Second	38	32	1978	SAN FRAN.	Third (W)	89	73
1969	Dallas-Ft. Worth	Second (W)	75	58	1979	SAN FRAN.-e	Fourth (W)	61	79
1970	Dallas-Ft. Worth	Third (W)	63	73	1980	Columbus-f	First	83	57
1971	Rochester-a	First	86	54	1983	BALTIMORE	First (E)	98	64
1972	Rochester	Fourth	76	68	1984	BALTIMORE	Fifth (E)	85	77
1973	Rochester-b	First (A)	79	67	1985	BALTIMORE-g	Fourth (E)	28	26
1974	Rochester-c	First (N)	88	56					

	W	L
Minor League Totals	870	670
N.L. Totals	225	239
A.L. Totals	211	167
M.L. Totals	436	406

a-Won playoffs defeating Syracuse, three games to one and Tidewater, three games to two; won Junior World Series against Denver (American Association), four games to three.

b-Lost championship playoff to Charleston, three games to none.

c-Won Governor's Cup defeating Syracuse, four games to three; won League Championship defeating Memphis, four games to two.

d-Lost semifinal playoff series to Richmond, three games to one.

e-Replaced by Dave Bristol, September 5, 1979.

g-Replaced by Earl Weaver, June 12, 1985 with team in fourth, 8 games back.
Coach, New York Yankees, 1981, 1982, 1986; Manager, American League All-Star Team, 1984; Coach, American League All-Star Team, 1983.

		CHAMPIONSHIP SERIES RECORD					WORLD SERIES RECORD		
YR	CLUB	OPP.	W	L	YR	Club	OPP.	W	L
1983	Bal.	vs Chi.	3	1	1983	Bal.	vs Phi.	4	1

ELLIS, SAMUEL JOSEPH "Sammy" (Coach) #41

6-1, 182. Born 2/11/41 in Youngstown, OH. Age 45, turned 45 February 11. Resides in Temple Terrace, FL, BR, TL.

Back again as Yankee Pitching Coach ... last several seasons has served Yankees in many roles: as Major League Pitching Coach, Columbus Pitching Coach and as Organizational Pitching Instructor ... highly touted from Mississippi State University, received large bonus, breaking in with Reds' organization in 1961 as young fireballer at Columbia, SC ... joined Cincinnati staff as regular in 1964 ... had biggest season in 1965 winning more than 20 games ... also played for Angels and White Sox and had his 6-year big league career cut short by arm problems ... joined Yankees organization as pitching coach at Ft. Lauderdale in 1978 ... largely credited with much of Dave Righetti's success.

Pitched 4-0 no-hit victory against Tacoma, August 19, 1962.
Led Pacific Coast League pitchers with .667 winning percentage in 1962.
Led National League in home runs allowed with 35 in 1966.

CAREER PLAYING RECORD

YR	CLUB	W-L	ERA	G	GS	CG	Sho	SV	IP	H	R	ER	BB	SO
1961	Columbia	10-3	1.89	16	15	10	5	—	114	84	28	24	62	129
	Indianapolis	0-0	0.00	1	0	0	0	—	2	0	0	0	0	0
1962	San Diego	12-6	3.53	27	25	10	4	—	171	129	73	67	98*	162
	CINCINNATI	2-2	6.75	8	4	0	0	0	28	29	25	21	29	27
1963	San Diego	12-10	2.62*	27	27	10	1	0	192	142	69	56	101*	192
1964	CINCINNATI	10-3	2.58	52	5	2	0	14	122	101	38	35	28	125
1965	CINCINNATI	22-10	3.78	44	39	15	2	2	264	222	119	111*	104	183
1966	CINCINNATI	12-19	5.29	41	36	7	0	0	221	226	135	130*	78	154
1967	CINCINNATI-a	8-11	3.84	32	27	8	1	0	176	197	86	75	67	80
1968	CALIFORNIA-b	9-10	3.95	42	24	3	0	2	164	150	80	72	56	93
1969	CHICAGO (AL)	0-3	5.90	10	5	0	0	0	29	42	20	19	16	15
	Portland	4-8	4.41	16	16	5	0	0	102	106	54	50	49	62
1970	Tulsa	0-4	6.55	7	7	0	0	0	33	42	28	24	14	15
1971	Birmingham	11-15	3.72	28	28	11	0	0	208	192	110	86	82	125
A.L. Totals		**9-13**	**4.24**	**52**	**29**	**3**	**0**	**2**	**193**	**192**	**100**	**91**	**72**	**108**
N.L. Totals		**54-45**	**4.13**	**177**	**111**	**32**	**3**	**16**	**811**	**775**	**403**	**372**	**306**	**569**
M.L. Totals		**63-58**	**4.15**	**229**	**140**	**35**	**3**	**18**	**1004**	**967**	**503**	**463**	**378**	**677**

a-Traded to California Angels for pitchers Jorge Rubio and Bill Kelso, November 30, 1967.
b-Traded to Chicago White Sox for outfielder Bill Voss (assigned to Hawaii) and pitcher Andy Rubilotta (assigned to El Paso), January 20, 1969.
Pitching Coach, Ft. Lauderdale, 1978-79; Columbus, 1980-82; Organizational Pitching Instructor, 1983; Pitching Coach, New York Yankees, 1982-86.

ALL-STAR GAME RECORD

YR	CLUB	W-L	ERA	G	GS	CG	Sho	SV	IP	H	R	ER	BB	SO
1965	N.L. Min.						(Did not play)							

MERRILL, CARL HARRISON "Stump" (Coach) #42

5-8, 185. Born 2/25/44 in Brunswick, ME. Age 42, turned 42 February 25. BL. TR. Resides in Topsham, ME. Married: Carole. Children: Leslie and Carin. College: Bachelor and Masters Degrees in Physical Education from University of Maine, Orono.

Began 1985 season as Yankee 1st base coach ... switched positions with Doug Holmquist, going to Columbus as manager on May 7 when Billy Martin returned as manager ... After spending his entire six year playing career as catcher in Phillies' farm system, Carl joined the Yankees' organization in 1977 as pitching coach at West Haven ... prior to beginning of professional coaching and managerial career he spent time at his college alma

MERRILL (continued)

mater as assistant baseball coach under the late Jack Butterfield ... joined managerial ranks in 1978 at West Haven and has led his clubs to the playoffs or outright championship in five of the last seven years ... guided his 1978 and 1982 teams to league championships ... named manager of Eastern League All-Star team in 1978 ... in 1980 was Southern League Manager of the Year and All-Star Manager and led Nashville to a league record 97 wins ... spends fall and winter months as offensive backfield coach for Bowdoin College football team in Brunswick and also enjoys officiating high school basketball.

CAREER PLAYING RECORD

YR	Club	AVG	G	AB	R	H	2B	3B	HR	RBI	BB	SO	SB
1966	Portsmouth	.182	6	11	1	2	0	0	0	0	6	3	0
	Batavia	.233	46	142	13	33	5	0	0	11	34	47	1
1967	Bakersfield	.254	29	59	12	15	1	0	0	6	23	17	1
	Eugene	.213	46	122	19	26	4	2	0	12	29	20	4
1968	Reading	.189	42	95	8	18	4	0	0	5	22	16	0
	San Diego	.091	4	11	1	1	0	0	0	1	1	3	0
1969	Reading	.252	80	226	35	57	9	2	1	29	50	23	1
1970	Eugene	.261	55	111	12	29	4	0	0	12	27	12	1
1971	Eugene	.242	77	157	21	38	9	1	1	15	40	27	2
Minor League Totals		**.234**	**385**	**934**	**122**	**219**	**36**	**5**	**2**	**91**	**232**	**168**	**10**

RECORD AS A MANAGER

YR	Club	Position	W	L	YR	Club	Position	W	L
1978	West Haven-a	Second	82	57	1982	Ft. Lauderdale-e	First (S)	82	50
1979	West Haven-b	First	83	56	1983	Ft. Lauderdale-f	Second (S)	77	54
1980	Nashville-c	First (W)	97	46	1984	Columbus-g	First	82	57
1981	Nashville-d	First (W)	81	62	1985	Columbus-h	Fourth	65	52
					Minor League Totals			**649**	**434**

a-Finished second in both halves, not in playoffs; finished with best composite record.

b-Won both halves for league championship; no playoffs.

c-Finished second in first half; won second half; lost 1st round of playoffs to Memphis, three games to one; finished with best composite record; set league record with 97 wins.

d-Finished second in first half; won second half; won 1st round of playoffs defeating Memphis, three games to none; lost championship series to Orlando, three games to one; finished with best composite record.

e-Won first half; finished second in second half; won 1st round of playoffs defeating Vero Beach, two games to one; won league championship series defeating Tampa, three games to two; finished with best composite record.

f-Finished second in first half; finished third in second half.

g-Lost 1st round of playoffs to Pawtucket, three games to one.

h-Replaced Doug Holmquist on May 7. Won 1st round of playoffs from Syracuse, three games to one; lost final round of playoffs to Tidewater, three games to one.

Coach, West Haven, 1977; New York Yankees, 1985, 1986.

MICHAEL, EUGENE RICHARD "Gene" "Stick" (Coach) #40

6-2, 185. Born 6/2/38 in Kent, OH. Age 47, turns 48 June 2. Resides in Closter, NJ. BS. TR. Children: Sandra (23), Mark (21), Matthew (18). College: Graduate of Kent State University.

Will be 3rd base coach again this year ... has been field manager twice ... Michael was originally named Yankee manager on November 21, 1980 ... in 1981 under Michael, Yankees were 34-22, leading eastern division of AL by 2 games, on June 11 when players' strike occurred and Yankees were eventually declared 1st half winners, qualifying for the Division Series in October ... replaced by Bob Lemon as manager, September 6, 1981 ... named manager of Yankees for 2nd time, April 25, 1982 replacing Bob Lemon ... under Michael team was 44-42 when Clyde King was named manager, August 4, 1982 ... previously had been Yankees General Manager, being named to that post on November 1, 1979, after serving as field manager of AAA Columbus Clippers for 1979 ... guided Clippers to regular season and post-season International League titles after starting season with 10 straight wins ... Clippers finished 85-54 under Michael ... coached first base for Yankees in 1978 after he had been a front office Administrative Assistant in 1977 ... upon his retirement as player, he was hired as Yankee coach ... one of most popular Yankees during his playing career ... was regular shortstop from 1969-1973 ... mastered the hidden ball trick, pulling it off 5 times with Yankees ... was close friend and roommate of the late Thurman Munson ... graduated from Kent State with a B.S. in Education ... also played basketball at Kent State and was pursued by NY Knicks to play pro basketball.

CAREER PLAYING RECORD

Led Northern League shortstops with 225 putouts, 87 double plays and 56

60

errors in 1959; led Northern League shortstops with 232 putouts, 90 double plays and 55 errors in 1960; led Sophomore League shortstops with 195 putouts, 391 assists and 85 double plays in 1961; and led International League shortstops with 254 putouts and 78 double plays in 1965.

Led International League in sacrifice hits with 16 in 1965.

Led American League shortstops with 28 errors in 1970.

YR	Club	AVG	G	AB	R	H	2B	3B	HR	RBI	BB	SO	SB
1959	Grand Forks	.227	124	480	54	109	11	3	1	43	51	83	11
1960	Savannah	.100	3	10	1	1	1	0	0	0	—	—	—
	Grand Forks	.206	121	428	47	88	15	2	2	41	44	75	8
1961	Hobbs	.324	121	513	121	166	25	7	5	79	62	67	36
1962	Kinston	.215	138	474	58	102	11	3	1	36	64	92	10
1963	Kinston	.304	125	421	73	128	17	6	1	57	51	49	10
1964	Columbus	.221	131	407	43	90	13	3	3	19	37	77	7
1965	Columbus	.217	138	443	53	96	14	0	1	30	61	84	5
1966	Columbus	.289	78	227	38	80	9	2	3	21	31	42	3
	PITTSBURGH-a	.152	30	33	9	5	2	1	0	2	0	7	0
1967	LOS ANGELES-b	.202	98	223	20	45	3	1	0	7	11	30	1
1968	YANKEES	.198	61	116	8	23	3	0	1	8	2	23	3
1969	YANKEES	.272	119	412	41	112	24	4	2	31	43	56	7
1970	YANKEES	.214	134	435	42	93	10	1	2	38	50	93	3
1971	YANKEES	.224	139	456	36	102	15	0	3	35	48	64	3
1972	YANKEES	.233	126	391	29	91	7	4	1	32	32	45	4
1973	YANKEES	.225	129	418	30	94	11	1	3	47	26	51	1
1974	YANKEES-c	.260	81	177	19	46	9	0	0	13	14	24	0
1975	DETROIT-d	.214	56	145	15	31	2	0	3	13	8	28	0
1976	BOSTON-e					(Did not play)							
Minor League Totals		**.253**	**979**	**3403**	**488**	**860**	**116**	**26**	**17**	**326**	**401**	**569**	**90**
N.Y.Y. Totals		**.233**	**789**	**2405**	**205**	**561**	**79**	**10**	**12**	**204**	**215**	**356**	**21**
A.L. Totals		**.232**	**845**	**2550**	**220**	**592**	**81**	**10**	**15**	**217**	**223**	**384**	**21**
N.L. Totals		**.195**	**128**	**256**	**29**	**50**	**5**	**2**	**0**	**9**	**11**	**37**	**1**
M.L. Totals		**.229**	**973**	**2806**	**249**	**642**	**86**	**12**	**15**	**226**	**234**	**421**	**22**

a-Traded with third baseman Bob Bailey to Los Angeles Dodgers for shortstop Maury Wills, December 1, 1966.

b-Sold to New York Yankees, November 30, 1967.

c-Unconditionally released, January 21, 1975; signed as free agent by Detroit Tigers, January 28, 1975.

d-Released, October 22, 1975; signed as free agent by Boston Red Sox, February 15, 1976.

e-Released, May 8, 1976.

PITCHING RECORD

YR	CLUB	W-L	ERA	G	GS	CG	Sho	SV	IP	H	R	ER	BB	SO
1962	Kinston	0-0	0.00	1	0	0	0	—	2	0	0	0	0	1
1963	Kinston	1-3	6.79	16	4	3	0	—	53	71	47	40	36	48
1964	Columbus	0-0	9.00	2	0	0	0	—	4	5	4	4	1	2
1968	YANKEES	0-0	0.00	1	0	0	0	—	3	5	5	0	0	3
M.L. Totals		**0-0**	**0.00**	**1**	**0**	**0**	**0**	**—**	**3**	**5**	**5**	**0**	**0**	**3**

RECORD AS A MANAGER

YR	Club	Position	W	L		YR	Club	Position	W	L
1979	Columbus-a	First	85	54		1982	YANKEES-c,d	Fifth (E)	44	42
1981	YANKEES-b	First (E)	34	22		**M.L. Totals**			**92**	**76**
	(Second Half)		14	12						

a-Won playoff against Tidewater, three games to one; won championship playoff from Syracuse, four games to three.

b-Replaced by Bob Lemon, September 6.

c-Replaced Bob Lemon, April 26, with team 6-8, tied for fourth place, 3-1/2 games back.

d-Replaced by Clyde King, August 3, with team 50-50, tied for fifth place, 8 games back.

Coach, New York Yankees, June 4, 1976 through June 13, 1977 and 1978; General Manager, New York Yankees, 1980; Scout, New York Yankees, 1981-1983; Coach, New York Yankees, 1984-1986.

TORBORG, JEFFREY ALLEN "Jeff"   (Coach)   #44

6-0, 195. Born 11/26/41 in Westfield, NJ. Age 44, turns 45 November 26. Resides in Mountainside, NJ. BR. TR. Married: Sue Barber 6/6/63. Children: Doug (21), Greg (18) and Dale (14).

Joined Yankee coaching staff August 1, 1979 after his dismissal as manager of the Indians on July 23rd ... had managed the Tribe from June 19, 1977 ... prior to that, he was a coach for the Indians beginning with the 1975 season, serving under Frank Robinson ... Jeff played 10 years in the majors, 7 with the Dodgers and 3

TORBORG (continued)

with the Angels ... played on the World Champion Dodgers in 1965 and N.L. pennant winner in 1966 ... caught two no-hitters with the Dodgers, by Sandy Koufax in 1965 and Bill Singer in 1970 ... also caught a Nolan Ryan no-hitter with the Angels in 1973 ... major league record is 4 by Ray Schalk ... Jeff was also behind the plate when Don Drysdale threw his 5th consecutive shutout in 1968 ... and caught Koufax and Ryan when they set single season strikeout records ... retired after '73 season ... a native of northern Jersey, Jeff earned a B.S. in Education from Rutgers, and has a Master's degree in Athletic Administration from Montclair State ... his thesis was on the effects of platooning in baseball ... in his senior year at Rutgers, Jeff hit .537 to lead the NCAA in batting and setting a record that still stands.

CAREER PLAYING RECORD

YR	Club	AVG	G	AB	R	H	2B	3B	HR	RBI	BB	SO	SB
1963	Albuquerque	.223	64	184	19	41	10	3	1	18	15	37	0
1964	LOS ANGELES	.233	28	43	4	10	1	1	0	4	3	8	0
1965	LOS ANGELES	.240	56	150	8	36	5	1	3	13	10	26	0
1966	LOS ANGELES	.225	46	120	4	27	3	0	1	13	10	23	0
1967	LOS ANGELES	.241	76	196	11	42	4	1	2	12	13	31	1
1968	LOS ANGELES	.161	37	93	2	15	2	0	0	4	6	10	0
1969	LOS ANGELES	.185	51	124	7	23	4	0	0	7	9	17	1
1970	LOS ANGELES-a	.231	64	134	11	31	8	0	1	17	14	15	1
1971	CALIFORNIA-b	.203	55	123	6	25	5	0	0	5	3	6	0
1972	CALIFORNIA-c	.209	59	153	5	32	3	0	0	8	14	21	0
1973	CALIFORNIA-de	.220	102	255	20	56	7	0	1	18	21	32	0
A.L. Totals		.213	216	531	31	113	15	0	1	31	38	59	0
N.L. Totals		.214	358	860	47	184	27	3	7	70	65	130	3
M.L. Totals		.214	574	1391	78	297	42	3	8	101	103	189	3

a-Sold to California Angels, March 13, 1971.
b-On disabled list, June 25 through July 27.
c-On disabled list, May 21 through June 13.
d-On disabled list, July 13 to August 10, 1973.
e-Traded to St. Louis Cardinals for pitcher John Andrews, December 6, 1973; released by St. Louis, March 25, 1974.

RECORD AS A MANAGER

YR	Club	Position	W	L	YR	Club	Position	W	L
1977	CLEVELAND-a	Fifth (E)	45	59	1979	CLEVELAND-b	Sixth (E)	43	52
1978	CLEVELAND	Sixth (E)	69	90	M.L. Totals			157	201

a-Replaced Frank Robinson with club in sixth place, June 19, 1977.
b-Replaced by Dave Garcia, July 23, 1979.
Coach, Cleveland Indians, 1975 to June, 1977; coach, New York Yankees, 1979 to 1986.

WHITE, ROY HILTON (Coach)   #6

5-10, 171. Born on 12/27/43 in Los Angeles, CA. Age 42, turns 43 December 27. Resides in Upper Saddle River, NJ. BS. TR. Married: Linda Hoxie 12/15/66. Children: Loreena (17) and Reade (14½). College: Compton J.C.

Returns to coaching lines after 1-1/2 years in front office ... one of all time Yankee favorites, returned in 1983 to Yankees as coach, after 3 year "second career" in Japan ... ranks among all time top 20 Yankees in stolen bases (2nd with 233), games played (6th with 1,881), runs scored (8th with 964), hits (8th with 1,803), doubles (10th with 300), RBI's (12th with 758) and HR's (16th with 160) ... career spans several distinct eras of Yankee history ... scouted and signed by Yankee organization in 1961 at height of Yankee dynasty ... after several impressive minor league seasons, received first taste of major leagues in 1965, the beginning of the "lean years" for the Yankees ... career matured and blossomed as Yankees were rebuilding and developing into A.L. pennant winners of '76, '77, and '78 and World Series champions of '77 and '78 ... played 3 years with Yorimuri Giants of Tokyo in Japan's Central League ... only Yankee outfielder ever to field 1,000 for a season ... originally signed as an infielder, but Bobby Richardson's presence brought about the switch ... hit switch home runs in a game 5 times ... also switch hit triples in a game once ... raised in Compton, CA with such future big leaguers as Reggie Smith, Dock Ellis, Dave Nelson, Don Wilson and Bobby Tolan.

CAREER PLAYING RECORD

Tied major league records for most times switch hitting two triples, game, Season (1), September 8, 1970; fewest triples, season, 150 or more games (0),

1972; highest fielding average by outfielder, season, 100 or more games (1.000), 1975; fewest double plays by outfielder, season, for leader in double plays (4), 1977; fewest double plays by outfielder, season, 150 or more games (0), 1973.

Tied modern major league record for most at bats, game (7), August 31, 1974.

Established American League record for most sacrifice flies, season, 17, 1971.

Switch-hit homers in one game on five occasions: May 7, 1970, August 13, 1973, April 23, 1975, August 18, 1976 and June 13, 1978.

Led American League in sacrifice flies with 11 in 1969.

Led American League outfielders in double plays with 4 in 1977.

Tied for American League lead among outfielders in fielding, 1.000, 1971.

Named Most Valuable Player in Southern League, 1965.

YR	Club	AVG	G	AB	R	H	2B	3B	HR	RBI	BB	SO	SB
1962	Greensboro	.204	25	93	17	19	5	0	1	1	19	19	6
	Ft. Lauderdale	.286	98	367	54	105	12	6	3	41	49	37	15
1963	Greensboro	.309	146*	554	117*	171	25	10	9	66	100	66	8
1964	Columbus-a	.257	110	370	55	95	13	6	9	41	47	54	6
1965	Columbus	.300	139	560*	103*	168*	26	14*	19	56	85	71	22
	YANKEES	.333	14	42	7	14	2	0	0	3	4	7	2
1966	YANKEES-b	.225	115	316	39	71	13	2	7	20	37	43	14
1967	Spokane	.343	84	306	49	105	24	4	6	48	40	23	9
	YANKEES	.224	70	214	22	48	8	0	2	18	19	25	10
1968	YANKEES	.267	159	577	89	154	20	7	17	62	73	50	20
1969	YANKEES-c	.290	130	448	55	130	30	5	7	74	81	51	18
1970	YANKEES	.296	162+	609	109	180	30	6	22	94	95	66	24
1971	YANKEES	.292	147	524	86	153	22	7	19	84	86	66	14
1972	YANKEES	.270	155	516	76	150	29	0	10	54	99+	60	23
1973	YANKEES	.246	162+	639*	88	157	22	3	18	60	78	81	15
1974	YANKEES	.275	136	473	68	130	19	8	7	43	67	44	15
1975	YANKEES	.290	148	556	81	161	32	5	12	59	72	50	16
1976	YANKEES	.286	156	626	104*	179	29	3	14	65	83	52	31
1977	YANKEES	.268	143	519	72	139	25	2	14	52	74	58	18
1978	YANKEES-d	.269	103	346	44	93	13	3	8	43	42	35	10
1979	YANKEES-e	.215	81	205	24	44	6	0	3	27	23	21	2
1980	TOKYO-Giants	.284	128	469	—	133	—	—	29	75	64	64	13
1981	TOKYO-Giants	.273	127	422	—	115	—	—	13	55	71	68	18
1982	TOKYO-Giants-f	.296	107	338	—	100	—	—	12	41	—	—	—
N.Y.Y. Totals		.271	1881	6650	964	1803	300	51	160	758	933	709	233

*denotes league leader; + denotes tied for league lead.

Signed as free-agent by New York Yankees' organization, July 1, 1961.
a-On disabled list, July 7 through July 29, 1964.
b-Optioned to Spokane as part of deal in which New York Yankees traded pitcher Jack Cullen, outfielder-infielder John Miller and $25,000 to Los Angeles Dodgers for infielder John Kennedy, April 3, 1967.
c-On military list, June 27 through July 12, 1969.
d-On supplemental disabled list, May 19 to June 3, 1978.
e-Granted free agency, November 1, 1979.
f-Named coach of Yankees, January 6, 1983.
Coach, New York Yankees, 1983-84, 1986.

CHAMPIONSHIP SERIES RECORD

Tied Championship Series record for most bases on balls, five-game Series (5), 1976.
Tied American League Championship Series record for most two-base hits, total Series (6).

YR	Club, Opp.	AVG	G	AB	R	H	2B	3B	HR	RBI	BB	SO	SB
1976	N.Y. vs K.C.	.294	5	17	4	5	3	0	0	3	5	1	1
1977	N.Y. vs K.C.	.400	4	5	2	2	2	0	0	0	1	0	0
1978	N.Y. vs K.C.	.313	4	16	5	5	1	0	1	1	1	2	0
L.C.S. Totals		.316	13	38	11	12	6	0	1	4	7	3	1

WORLD SERIES RECORD

Tied World Series record for most at bats, game, no hits (5), October 21, 1976; one or more hits, each game, six-game Series, 1978.

YR	Club, Opp.	AVG	G	AB	R	H	2B	3B	HR	RBI	BB	SO	SB
1976	N.Y. vs Cin.	.133	4	15	0	2	0	0	0	0	3	0	0
1977	N.Y. vs L.A.	.000	2	2	0	0	0	0	0	0	0	0	0
1978	N.Y. vs L.A.	.333	6	24	9	8	0	0	1	4	4	5	2
W.S. Totals		.244	12	41	9	10	0	0	1	4	7	5	2

ALL-STAR GAME RECORD

YR	Club, Site	AVG	G	AB	R	H	2B	3B	HR	RBI	BB	SO	SB
1969	A.L., Was.	.000	1	1	0	0	0	0	0	0	0	1	0
1970	A.L., Cin.					(Selected, did not play)							

THE PLAYERS

ALLEN, NEIL PATRICK (RHP) #53

6-2, 190. Born 1/24/58 in Kansas City, KS. Age 28, turned 28 on January 24. Resides in Syosset, NY. BR. TR. Married: Linda. Children: Neil Robert (4) and Courtney Leigh (2).

MAJOR LEAGUE SERVICE: 7 years.

CONTRACT STATUS: Signed multi-year contract with Cardinals ... extends through 1987 season.

1985 SEASON: Acquired on July 17 in attempt to bolster the bullpen ... Making only 1 start in 23 games for St. Louis, he was 1-4 with 2 saves, 5.59 ERA upon his arrival in NY ... Was 1-0 w/1 save, 2.76 ERA in 17 relief appearances with Yankees, finishing 10 games ... Only save as Yankee came 8/23 @ Seattle ... Only win came 9/30 vs. Baltimore, pitching 1.1 perfect innings w/2 Ks ... Did not allow a run his last 4 outings, 9.2 IP ... Opposing batters hit just .234 against him.

CAREER: 1984—Neil was used as a late inning reliever, replacing Bruce Sutter as the stopper for the Cardinals ... Pitched 17 consecutive scoreless innings from May 7-May 25, allowing only 5 hits in 7 appearances ... His longest outing was 5.2 scoreless innings in an August 31 victory over Houston's Nolan Ryan ... 1983—Began season as a reliever with the Mets ... Became a starter for the first time since his rookie year in 1979 ... Neil was moved back to the bullpen by the Mets, and was later traded to the Cardinals in a mid-season trade ... He began his career with the Cardinals as a starter, posting a 5-1 record, but after four consecutive losses was again moved to the pen ... His relief record was 3-0 with a 1.88 ERA in 7 games with the Cardinals ... 1982—Was 6th in NL in saves, despite missing much of the season with illness and injury ... Recorded his 15th save on June 14, before being sidelined for 11 days with a bacterial infection of the colon ... Appeared in only 5 games after August 1, and was diagnosed on August 8 as having a slight strain of the elbow ... 1981—Was third in N.L. in saves ... From August 11-August 27, he didn't allow a run in eight consecutive appearances (14 IP) and recorded a pair of wins and six saves ... 1980—Finished fourth in NL in saves ... Saved 22 games and didn't permit a run in 37 of his 59 appearances ... 1979—Began first five games of his career as a starter, and after going 0-4 was converted to a reliever ... Went on the DL on May 31 with an injured rib cage, and became the number one reliever after being activated on June 25 ... From that point made 38 appearances, with a record of 5-5 with 8 saves ... First save was July 28, 1979, vs. Cubs at NY.

PERSONAL/MISCELLANEOUS: In 1983 became first NL pitcher since 1976 to shut out same twice while pitching for two different clubs, blanking the Dodgers 4-0 on May 20 while with the Mets and then 3-0 on July 24 while with the Cardinals ... Earned varsity letters in baseball, football and basketball at Bishop Ward High School in Kansas City ... Had football scholarships from all Big Eight Conference schools, and signed a letter of intent with Kansas State, but concentrated on baseball after being signed by the Mets ... Is an active volunteer for Muscular Dystrophy.

YR	CLUB	W-L	ERA	G	GS	CG	Sho	SV	IP	H	R	ER	BB	SO
1976	Marion	2-0	1.91	6	4	2	1	1	33	23	8	7	6	29
	Wausau	4-2	3.75	6	6	2	0	0	48	51	27	20	20	34
1977	Lynchburg-a	10-2	2.79	20	20	11†	2	0	142	136	55	44	43	126*
1978	Jackson	5-9	2.10	16	16	8	3	0	120	88	38	28	38	111
	Tidewater	2-7	4.42	10	10	2	0	0	57	65	35	28	12	30
1979	NEW YORK (N)-b	6-10	3.55	50	5	0	0	8	99	100	46	39	47	65
1980	NEW YORK (N)	7-10	3.71	59	0	0	0	22	97	87	43	40	40	70
1981	NEW YORK (N)	7-6	2.96	43	0	0	0	18	67	64	26	22	26	50
1982	NEW YORK (N)	3-7	3.06	50	0	0	0	19	64.2	65	22	22	30	59
1983	NEW YORK (N)-c	2-7	4.50	21	4	1	1	2	54.0	57	29	27	36	32
	ST. LOUIS	10-6	3.70	25	18	4	2	0	121.2	122	55	50	48	74
1983	Totals	12-13	3.94	46	22	5	3	2	175.2	179	84	77	84	106
1984	ST. LOUIS	9-6	3.55	57	1	0	0	3	119.0	105	54	47	49	66
1985	ST. LOUIS-d	1-4	5.59	23	1	0	0	2	29.0	32	22	18	17	10
	YANKEES	1-0	2.76	17	0	0	0	1	29.1	26	9	9	13	16
1985	Totals	2-4	4.17	40	1	0	0	3	58.1	58	31	27	30	26
Minor League Totals		**23-20**	**2.86**	**58**	**56**	**25**	**6**	**1**	**400**	**363**	**163**	**127**	**119**	**330**
N.L. Totals		**45-56**	**3.64**	**328**	**29**	**5**	**3**	**74**	**655.1**	**632**	**297**	**265**	**293**	**426**
M.L. Totals		**46-56**	**3.60**	**345**	**29**	**5**	**3**	**75**	**684.2**	**658**	**306**	**274**	**306**	**442**

Selected by New York Mets' organization in 11th round of free-agent draft, June 8, 1976.
a-On disabled list, July 26 to September 1.
b-On disabled list, June 1 to June 25.

c-Traded with pitcher Rick Ownbey to St. Louis Cardinals for first baseman Keith Hernandez, June 15, 1983.

d-Traded to New York Yankees for a player to be named later, July 17, 1985.

		1985						CAREER				
ERA	W-L-S	G	IP	H	ER	Club	ERA	W-L-S	G	IP	H	ER
0.00	1-0-0	1	1.1	0	0	**Baltimore**	0.00	1-0-0	1	1.1	0	0
—	—	—	—	—	—	**Boston**	—	—	—	—	—	—
2.45	0-0-0	2	3.2	3	1	**California**	2.45	0-0-0	2	3.2	3	1
0.00	0-0-0	1	1.0	0	0	**Chicago**	0.00	0-0-0	1	1.0	0	0
5.06	0-0-0	3	5.1	5	3	**Cleveland**	5.06	0-0-0	3	5.1	5	3
0.00	0-0-0	1	1.0	0	0	**Detroit**	0.00	0-0-0	1	1.0	0	0
0.00	0-0-0	1	1.0	1	0	**Kansas City**	0.00	0-0-0	1	1.0	1	0
—	—	—	—	—	—	**Milwaukee**	—	—	—	—	—	—
—	—	—	—	—	—	**Minnesota**	—	—	—	—	—	—
—	—	—	—	—	—	**Oakland**	—	—	—	—	—	—
7.71	0-0-1	4	4.2	7	4	**Seattle**	7.71	0-0-1	4	4.2	7	4
2.25	0-0-0	2	4.0	4	1	**Texas**	2.25	0-0-0	2	4.0	4	1
0.00	0-0-0	2	7.1	6	0	**Toronto**	0.00	0-0-0	2	7.1	6	0
2.76	1-0-1	17	29.1	26	9	**Total**	2.76	1-0-1	17	29.1	26	9
2.70	1-0-0	7	10.0	8	3	**Home**	—	—	—	—	—	—
2.79	0-0-1	10	19.1	18	6	**Road**	—	—	—	—	—	—

		Low Hit	—
3—8/31/85 vs California		**K-High**	7—three times
1—		**Win Streak**	4—1983

S = SAVES

ARMSTRONG, MICHAEL DENNIS "Mike"   (RHP)   #36

6-3, 195. Born 3/7/54 in Glen Cove, NY. Age 32, turned 32 on March 7. Resides in Halifax, VA. BR. TR. Married: Diane. College: University of Miami.

MAJOR LEAGUE SERVICE: 4 years and 44 days.

CONTRACT STATUS: Signed 1-year contract for 1986.

1985 SEASON: Assigned to Columbus April 6, two days prior to Opening Day ... appeared in 13 games @ Columbus, doing 1-0 w/1 save, 20.2 IP, 23 Ks ... recalled to Yankees June 3 ... made first appearance of '85 6/6 @ Milwaukee ... made 6 appearances until again being optioned to Columbus 7/17 ... was again recalled 8/5 ... made no appearances before another trip to the AAA affiliate 8/16 where he remained until 9/5 ... made just 3 appearances in September allowing 1 run in 8.0 IP ... threw 5.0 IP 9/24 vs. Detroit, his longest outing as Yankee ... opposing batters hit just .173 against him ... 9 games were fewest outings of career.

CAREER: Began career as Reds' 1st round selection in January, 1974 ... traded to Padres organization in 1979 ... and to Royals in 1981 ... made major league debut with Padres vs. Cincinnati on August 12, 1980, pitching 1.0 innings, allowing a walk ... in 1982, made his A.L. debut on May 19 vs. Yankees, allowing only 2 hits over three scoreless innings ... posted first ML win on May 23 vs. Texas ... recorded first ML save June 29 vs. Oakland ... had his first full ML season in 1983 ... finished 32 of 58 games appeared in ... was #2 man in KC bullpen, often preceding Dan Quisenberry who set a ML record with 45 saves (45 saves tied in '84 by Bruce Sutter) ... in 1984, used primarily in middle inning relief, he notched his first Yankee win July 16th.

PERSONAL/MISCELLANEOUS: Native of Long Island, NY ... played college ball at the University of Miami in Coral Gables, FL.

YR	CLUB	W-L	ERA	G	GS	CG	Sho	SV	IP	H	R	ER	BB	SO
1974	Tampa	0-2	9.56	6	2	0	0	0	16	26	17	17	18	14
	Seattle	6-7	2.65	15	15	6	1	0	102	85	45	30	47	86
1975	Three Rivers	5-10	2.70	25	24	5	1	0	150	116	55	45	44	86
1976	Three Rivers	10-10	3.51	24	24	5	0	0	146	146	77	57	52	91
1977	Three Rivers	*16-10	3.77	30	29*	7	3	1	184	185	91	77	83	107
1978	Indianapolis	1-2	6.65	16	1	0	0	1	23	26	18	17	17	17
	Chattanooga	9-6	3.04	31	3	0	0	7	74	61	34	25	37	54
1979	Nashville-a	5-1	3.38	32	0	0	0	3	64	58	30	24	29	53
	Amarillo	2-3	3.48	7	4	1	0	0	31	32	15	12	14	34
	Hawaii	0-0	2.57	3	0	0	0	1	7	6	2	2	5	4
1980	Hawaii	4-4	1.95	42	0	0	0	16	74	48	18	16	26	67
	SAN DIEGO	0-0	5.79	11	0	0	0	0	14.0	16	10	9	13	14
1981	Hawaii	5-2	1.50	22	0	0	0	6	36	21	7	6	12	39
	SAN DIEGO-b	0-2	6.00	10	0	0	0	0	12.0	14	9	8	11	9
1982	Omaha	4-2	3.21	15	0	0	0	3	28	19	12	10	19	28
	KANSAS CITY	5-5	3.20	52	0	0	0	6	112.2	88	45	40	43	75

		ERA	G					IP	H	R	ER	BB	SO
1983	KANSAS CITY-c	10-7	3.86	58	0	0	0	3	102.2	86	53	44	45	52
1984	Ft. Lauderdale	1-0	0.77	8	0	0	0	2	11.2	9	2	1	5	15
	YANKEES-d	3-2	3.48	36	0	0	0	1	54.1	47	21	21	26	43
1985	Columbus	2-2	6.64	21	3	0	0	2	40.2	49	31	30	26	40
	YANKEES	0-0	3.07	9	0	0	0	0	14.2	9	5	5	2	11
Minor League Totals		**70-61**	**3.36**	**297**	**105**	**24**	**5**	**42**	**987.1**	**887**	**454**	**369**	**434**	**735**
N.Y.Y. Totals		**3-2**	**3.39**	**45**	**0**	**0**	**0**	**1**	**69.0**	**56**	**26**	**26**	**28**	**54**
A.L. Totals		**18-14**	**3.19**	**155**	**0**	**0**	**0**	**10**	**310.1**	**230**	**124**	**110**	**116**	**181**
N.L. Totals		**0-2**	**5.88**	**21**	**0**	**0**	**0**	**0**	**26.0**	**30**	**19**	**17**	**24**	**23**
M.L. Totals		**18-16**	**3.40**	**176**	**0**	**0**	**0**	**10**	**336.1**	**260**	**143**	**127**	**140**	**204**

Selected by Cleveland Indians' organization in 9th round of free-agent draft, June 6, 1972.
Selected by Cincinnati Reds' organization in 1st round (24th player selected) of free-agent draft, January 9, 1974.
a-Traded to San Diego Padres' organization for third baseman Paul O'Neill, July 25, 1979.
b-Traded to Kansas City Royals' organization for player to be named later, April 4, 1982.
c-Traded to New York Yankees with catcher Duane Dewey for first baseman Steve Balboni and pitcher Roger Erickson, December 8, 1983.
d-On disabled list, March 27 to June 16, 1984; included rehabilitation assignment to Ft. Lauderdale from May 31 to June 16, 1984.

		1985				Club		**CAREER**			
ERA	W-L-S	G	IP	H	ER		ERA	W-L-S	G	IP	H	ER
—	—	—	—	—	—	Baltimore	5.64	0-2-1	12	22.1	20	14
—	—	—	—	—	—	Boston	2.89	1-2-0	8	18.2	14	6
—	—	—	—	—	—	California	1.50	4-1-1	11	30.0	22	5
—	—	—	—	—	—	Chicago	5.11	2-1-1	16	24.2	24	14
—	—	—	—	—	—	Cleveland	0.82	3-1-0	11	22.0	9	2
1.29	0-0-0	3	7.0	1	1	Detroit	1.66	2-0-1	12	21.2	14	4
—	—	—	—	—	—	Kansas City	7.71	0-0-0	3	4.2	9	4
7.36	0-0-0	3	3.2	5	3	Milwaukee	4.11	0-1-1	10	15.1	14	7
0.00	0-0-0	1	2.0	1	0	Minnesota	5.87	0-2-0	14	23.0	23	15
—	—	—	—	—	—	Oakland	1.39	2-0-3	12	26.0	17	4
—	—	—	—	—	—	Seattle	2.76	0-0-2	11	16.1	15	5
9.00	0-0-0	1	1.0	2	1	Texas	4.13	3-1-0	15	24.0	18	11
0.00	0-0-0	1	1.0	0	0	Toronto	7.16	0-2-0	10	16.1	17	13
3.07	0-0-0	9	14.2	9	5	Total	—	—	—	—	—	—
1.80	0-0-0	5	10.0	5	2	Home	—	—	—	—	—	—
5.79	0-0-0	4	4.2	4	3	Road	—	—	—	—	—	—

—			Low Hit	—
6— 9/24/85 vs. Det.			K-High	6— 9/24/85 vs. Det.
—			Win Streak	6— 1983-84

S = SAVES

BAYLOR, DON EDWARD (DH) #25

6-1, 210. Born 6/28/49 in Austin, TX. Age 36, turns 37 June 28. Resides in Cresskill, NJ. BR. TR. Single. Child: Don, Jr. (12)

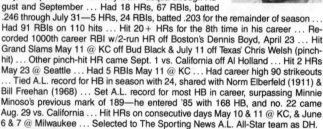

MAJOR LEAGUE SERVICE: 14 years and 30 days.

CONTRACT STATUS: Signed 4-year contract (with option for 5th) on December 1, 1982 ... contract extends through 1986 season ('87 with option).

1985 SEASON: The regular DH from April through July, was platooned with lefty Dan Pasqua through August and September ... Had 18 HRs, 67 RBIs, batted .246 through July 31—5 HRs, 24 RBIs, batted .203 for the remainder of season ... Had 91 RBIs on 110 hits ... Hit 20+ HRs for the 8th time in his career ... Recorded 1000th career RBI w/2-run HR off Boston's Dennis Boyd, April 23 ... Hit Grand Slams May 11 @ KC off Bud Black & July 11 off Texas' Chris Welsh (pinch-hit) ... Other pinch-hit HR came Sept. 1 vs. California off Al Holland ... Hit 2 HRs May 23 @ Seattle ... Had 5 RBIs May 11 @ KC ... Had career high 90 strikeouts ... Tied A.L. record for HB in season with 24, shared with Norm Elberfeld (1911) & Bill Freehan (1968) ... Set A.L. record for most HB in career, surpassing Minnie Minoso's previous mark of 189—he entered '85 with 168 HB, and no. 22 came Aug. 29 vs. California ... Hit HRs on consecutive days May 10 & 11 @ KC, & June 6 & 7 @ Milwaukee ... Selected to The Sporting News A.L. All-Star team as DH.

CAREER: Enjoyed best season in 1979, being named American League MVP—leading league with 139 RBI, 120 runs, 162 games, and batting a career high of .296, 186 hits, 33 doubles and 36 HR ... during 6 seasons with California, hit 141 HRs, becoming Angels all-time HR leader ... ranks among Angels' top 10 in 10 different offensive categories ... following 1979, he played only 90 games, slowed by fractured left wrist and dislocated middle toe on his left foot ... in 1982 helped lead California to A.L. West Division title when he led A.L. with 21 GWRBI ... had successful premier season with Yankees in 1983 ... used primarily as DH, led team in doubles, stolen bases, & hit-by-pitch ... hit over .300—a career first ... won Silver Bat as A.L. DH. In 1984 led club being hit by pitch 23 times, and came within 1 of A.L. single season record of 24 ... Hit career HR 250 June 26, 1984, off Detroit's Sid Mange. Originally signed to Oriole's system in 1967 ... named Minor League Player of the Year in 1970 ... after 4 seasons with Baltimore, was traded to Oakland as part of deal including Reggie Jackson ... played out option with A's in 1976, signing a 6-year contract with California that fall ... served as Angel player representative for 3 seasons ... has been hit-by-pitch a record 192 times in his career, breaking the previous A.L. record of 189 held by Minnie Minoso.

PERSONAL/MISCELLANEOUS: Native of Austin, TX ... attended Miami Dade Junior College and Blinn Junior College (Brenham, TX) ... has raised money for Cystic Fibrosis Foundation the last 6 seasons ... 1985 winner of Roberto Clemente Award.

Established major league record for most times caught stealing, inning, (2), June 15, 1974 (9th inning).

Tied major league records for most long hits, opening game of season (4), April 6, 1973 (2 doubles, 1 triple, 1 home run); most consecutive home runs, two consecutive games (4), July 1 and 2, 1975 (bases on balls included).

Tied modern major league record for most at bats, game (7), August 25, 1979.

Tied American League record for most hits, two consecutive games (9), August 13 and 14, 1973.

Hit three home runs in a game, July 2, 1975.

Led American League in sacrifice flies with 12 in 1978.

Led American League in being hit by pitch with 13 in 1973, 20 in 1976, 18 in 1978, 23 in 1984, 24 in 1985 and tied for lead with 13 in 1975.

Major League hit by pitch: 1970-0, 1971-1, 1972-9, 1973-13*, 1974-10, 1975-13+, 1976-20*, 1977-12, 1978-18*, 1979-11, 1980-11, 1981-7, 1982-7, 1983-13, 1984-23*, and 1985-24*. Total-192.

Led International League in being hit by pitch with 19 in 1970 and 16 in 1971.

Led International League in total bases with 296 in 1970.

Led Texas League in being hit by pitch with 13 in 1969.

Led Appalachian League with 135 total bases and tied for caught stealing with 6 in 1967.

Named American League Most Valuable Player by Baseball Writers' Association of America, 1979.

Named American League Player of the Year by Sporting News, 1979.

Named Appalachian League Player of Year, 1967.

Named Minor League Player of the Year by Sporting News, 1970.

YR	Club	AVG	G	AB	R	H	2B	3B	HR	RBI	BB	SO	SB
1967	Bluefield	.346*	67†	246	50	85*	10	8*	8	47	35	52	26*
1968	Stockton	.369	68	244	52	90	6	3	7	40	35	65	14
	Elmira	.333	6	24	4	8	1	1	1	3	3	4	1
	Rochester	.217	15	46	4	10	2	0	0	4	3	17	1
1969	Miami	.375	17	56	13	21	5	4	3	24	7	8	3
	Dallas-Ft. Worth	.300	109	406	71	122	17	10†	11	57	48	77	19
1970	Rochester	.327	140†	508	127*	166	34*	15*	22	107	76	99	26
	BALTIMORE	.235	8	17	4	4	0	0	0	4	2	3	1
1971	Rochester	.313	136	492	104	154	31†	10	20	95	79	73	25
	BALTIMORE	.000	1	2	0	0	0	0	0	1	2	1	0
1972	BALTIMORE	.253	102	320	33	81	13	3	11	38	29	50	24
1973	BALTIMORE	.286	118	405	64	116	20	4	11	51	35	48	32
1974	BALTIMORE	.272	137	489	66	133	22	1	10	59	43	56	29
1975	BALTIMORE-a	.282	145	524	79	148	21	6	25	76	53	64	32
1976	OAKLAND-b	.247	157	595	85	147	25	1	15	68	58	72	52
1977	CALIFORNIA	.251	154	561	87	141	27	0	25	75	62	76	26
1978	CALIFORNIA	.255	158	591	103	151	26	0	34	99	56	71	22
1979	CALIFORNIA	.296	162†	628	120*	186	33	3	36	139*	71	51	22
1980	CALIFORNIA-c	.250	90	340	39	85	12	2	5	51	24	32	6
1981	CALIFORNIA	.239	103	377	52	90	18	1	17	66	42	51	3
1982	CALIFORNIA-d	.263	157	608	80	160	24	1	24	93	57	69	10
1983	YANKEES	.303	144	534	82	162	33	3	21	85	40	53	17
1984	YANKEES	.262	134	493	84	129	29	1	27	89	38	68	1
1985	YANKEES	.231	142	477	70	110	24	1	23	91	52	90	0
Minor League Totals		**.324**	**558**	**2022**	**425**	**656**	**106**	**51**	**72**	**377**	**286**	**395**	**115**
N.Y.Y. Totals		**.267**	**420**	**1504**	**236**	**401**	**86**	**5**	**94**	**265**	**130**	**211**	**18**
M.L. Totals		**.263**	**1912**	**6961**	**1048**	**1843**	**327**	**6**	**284**	**1085**	**664**	**855**	**277**

GWRBI: 1980-4; 1981-11; 1982-21*; 1983-8; 1984-13; 1985-10. Total-67.

Selected by Baltimore Orioles' organization in 2nd round of free-agent draft, June 6, 1967.
a-Traded with pitchers Mike Torrez and Paul Mitchell to Oakland A's for outfielder Reggie Jackson and pitchers Ken Holtzman and Bill Van Bommel, April 2, 1976.
b-Played out option year and granted free agency, November 1, 1976; signed as free agent by California Angels, November 16, 1976.
c-On disabled list with fractured left wrist, May 11 to June 26, 1980.
d-Granted free agency, November 10, 1982; signed by New York Yankees, December 1, 1982.

BAYLOR (continued)

CHAMPIONSHIP SERIES RECORD

Established Championship Series record for most runs batted in, five-game Series (10), 1982.

Tied Championship Series records for most home runs with bases filled, game (1), October 9, 1982; most runs batted in, game (5), October 5, 1982; most runs batted in, inning (4), October 9, 1982 (8th inning).

Tied American League Championship Series record for most times on losing club (4).

YR	Club, Opp.	AVG	G	AB	R	H	2B	3B	HR	RBI	BB	SO	SB
1973	Bal. vs Oak.	.273	4	11	3	3	0	0	0	1	3	5	0
1974	Bal. vs Oak.	.267	4	15	0	4	0	0	0	0	0	2	0
1979	Cal. vs Bal.	.188	4	16	2	3	0	0	1	2	1	2	0
1982	Cal. vs Mil.	.294	5	17	2	5	1	1	1	10	2	0	0
L.C.S. Totals		.254	17	59	7	15	1	1	2	13	6	9	0

ALL-STAR GAME RECORD

YR	Club, Site	AVG	G	AB	R	H	2B	3B	HR	RBI	BB	SO	SB
1979	A.L., Sea.	.500	1	4	2	2	1	0	0	1	0	0	0

1985 vs. OPPONENTS

Club	AB	H	HR	RBI	AVG
Baltimore	39	7	2	9	.179
Boston	41	11	1	12	.268
Cleveland	44	9	3	7	.205
Detroit	38	6	1	3	.158
Milwaukee	35	7	2	4	.200
Toronto	34	7	1	5	.206
California	39	8	1	4	.205
Chicago	37	9	1	3	.243
Kansas City	36	13	3	14	.361
Minnesota	40	11	2	12	.275
Oakland	31	6	1	5	.194
Seattle	33	9	3	6	.273
Texas	30	7	2	7	.233
1st Half	270	64	15	60	.237
2nd Half	207	46	8	31	.222
vs. LHP	194	49	11	39	.253
vs. RHP	283	61	12	52	.216
Home	231	50	12	50	.216
Away	246	60	11	41	.244

BAYLOR'S BESTS

Season

AVG.	.303–1983
H	186–1979
HR	36–1979
RBI	139–1979
SB	52–1976
Hit Strk	14 games–1976

Game

H	5–at Tex. 8-14-73
	vs. Bos. 9-4-75
	vs. Sea. 4-13-82
HR	3–at Det. 7-2-75
RBI	8–at Tor. 8-25-79
SB	4–at Minn. 5-17-76

BERRA, DALE ANTHONY (INF)   #2

6-0, 190. Born: 12/13/56 in Ridgewood, NJ. Age 29, turns 30 December 13. Resides in Glen Ridge, NJ. BR. TR. Married.

MAJOR LEAGUE SERVICE: 7 years, 60 days.

CONTRACT STATUS: Signed through 1988.

1985 SEASON: Used primarily at third base vs. left-handed pitchers, playing in 28 games through May ... From June on, he totalled just 20 games played ... Played 4 games in July, going 1/9 ... Played 3 games in August, going 0/3 ... Caught at homeplate Aug. 2 vs. Chicago along with teammate Bobby Meacham on the same play ... Had only 1 AB from 8/31 on, getting a pinch-hit RBI single Sept. 15 vs. Toronto ... Only HR came June 11 vs. Toronto—a solo 9th inning shot off Gary LaValle tying the game ... Only GWRBI came June 8 @ Milwaukee.

CAREER: 1984—Hit safely in a career high 11 games July 13 to July 21 ... hit his second career grand slam August 8th at St. Louis, driving in a career high five runs (3rd time) ... 1983—Set career highs for games, at bats, and walks ... tied career highs in doubles and homeruns ... started all but two games, and was the Pirates' shortstop in all but 29 innings, playing more than any other N.L. shortstop ... batted .333 with 10 doubles in final 29 games ... established new major league record by reaching first on catcher's interference seven times (personal total through '84 is 18) ... 1982—Became the fulltime Pirate shortstop, playing 153 games at the position ... combined with Johnny Ray to give Pittsburgh the best offensive D.P. combination in the league ... 1981—opened the season as the regular second baseman due to an injury to Phil Garner ... filled in at second, short, and third the remainder of the year ... stole 11 bases in 12 attempts ... 1980—first full season in the majors ... hit first career grand slam off Mets' Mark Bomback, June 1 ... filled in at shortstop for Tim Foli (injured) and third base for Bill Madlock (suspended) ... 1979—came north with the Pirates in April ... saw action at both short and third ... sent to Portland (AAA) in mid-season ... recalled September 1, hitting .286 down the stretch run ... 1978—recalled from Columbus July 29 ... hit first M.L. homerun August 20 off Houston's Tom Dixon ... with Columbus, tied for club lead in homers and stolen bases ... top vote getter for International League All-Star team ... 1977—made major league debut August 22 vs. San Diego ... had first big league hit and RBI September 4 at Los Angeles ... at Columbus, tied for team lead with 18 HRs ... 1976—Led Western Carolinas League (A) in games, sixth in batting ... made WCL All-Star team ... 1975—led New York-Penn League with 49 RBI, making the league's All-Star team.

PERSONAL/MISCELLANEOUS: Wife's name is Leigh ... graduate of Montclair (NJ) High School where he was two time All-State at shortstop ... was All-State and captain of both the high school football and hockey teams ... played semi-pro, American Legion, and Little League in Montclair ... the son of Yankee manager and Hall of Fame catcher, Yogi Berra, Dale and dad form the first significant father/son, manager/player combination in baseball history ... brother Tim played NFL football, and brother Larry was a catcher in the Mets' organization for two years.

Tied for National League lead in errors by shortstops with 30 in 1984.
Established major league record for most times awarded first base on catcher's interference, season (7), 1983.
Led National League in intentional bases on balls received with 19 in 1983.
Led International League third basemen in errors with 29 in 1977.
Led Western Carolinas League third basemen in assists with 269, double plays with 27 and errors with 41 in 1976.
Led New York-Pennsylvania League third basemen with 137 assists and 24 errors in 1975.
Led New York-Pennsylvania League in sacrifice flies with 8 in 1975.
Tied for New York-Pennsylvania League lead in double plays by third basemen with 13 in 1975.

YR	Club	AVG	G	AB	R	H	2B	3B	HR	RBI	BB	SO	SB
1975	Niagara Falls	.257	67	269*	36	69	6	4	3	49*	19	47	9
1976	Charleston	.298	139*	527	78	157	28	5	16	89	41	98	7
1977	Columbus	.290	125	438	68	127	18	7	18	54	44	67	12
	PITTSBURGH	.175	17	40	0	7	1	0	0	3	1	8	0
1978	Columbus	.280	99	361	58	101	18	5	18	63	30	73	9
	PITTSBURGH	.207	56	135	16	28	2	0	6	14	13	20	3
1979	Portland	.324	56	210	37	68	13	2	6	32	19	29	2
	PITTSBURGH	.211	44	123	11	26	5	0	3	15	11	17	0
1980	PITTSBURGH	.220	93	245	21	54	8	2	6	31	16	52	2
1981	PITTSBURGH	.241	81	232	21	56	12	0	2	27	17	34	11
1982	PITTSBURGH	.263	156	529	64	139	25	5	10	61	33	83	6
1983	PITTSBURGH	.251	161	537	51	135	25	1	10	52	61	84	8
1984	PITTSBURGH-ab	.222	136	450	31	100	16	0	9	52	34	78	1
1985	YANKEES	.229	48	109	8	25	5	1	1	8	7	20	1
Minor League Totals		**.289**	**486**	**1806**	**277**	**522**	**83**	**23**	**61**	**287**	**153**	**314**	**39**
N.L. Totals		**.238**	**744**	**2291**	**215**	**545**	**94**	**8**	**46**	**255**	**186**	**376**	**31**
M.L. Totals		**.238**	**792**	**2400**	**223**	**570**	**99**	**9**	**47**	**263**	**193**	**396**	**32**

GWRBI: 1980-4; 1981-2; 1982-6; 1983-4; 1984-9; 1985-1. Total-26.

Selected by Pittsburgh Pirates' organization in 1st round (20th player selected) of free-agent draft, June 4, 1975.
a-On disabled list, August 30 to September 14, 1984, due to elbow injury.
b-Traded to New York Yankees with pitcher Alfonso Pulido and outfielder Jay Buhner for outfielder Steve Kemp, infielder Tim Foli and cash, December 20, 1984.

1985 vs. OPPONENTS

Club	AB	H	HR	RBI	AVG
Baltimore	3	0	0	0	.000
Boston	9	4	0	0	.444
Cleveland	18	5	0	0	.278
Detroit	4	0	0	0	.000
Milwaukee	3	1	0	1	.333
Toronto	6	2	1	2	.333
California	2	1	0	0	.500
Chicago	16	3	0	1	.188
Kansas City	17	3	0	0	.176
Minnesota	7	0	0	0	.000
Oakland	6	1	0	2	.167
Seattle	11	1	0	0	.091
Texas	7	4	0	2	.571
1st Half	98	23	1	7	.235
2nd Half	11	2	0	1	.182
vs. LHP	90	22	1	7	.244
vs. RHP	19	3	0	1	.158
Home	52	15	1	5	.288
Away	57	10	0	3	.175

BERRA'S BESTS

Season

AVG.	.263–1982
H	161–1983
HR	10–1982, 1983
RBI	61–1982
SB	11–1981
Hit Strk	11 games–1984

Game

H	4–5 times
HR	2–5/30/83 vs Atlanta
RBI	5–3 times
SB	2–3 times

DID YOU KNOW ... that the Yankees had seven doubleplays in a single game against the Philadelphia Athletics on August 14, 1942?

BRADLEY, SCOTT WILLIAM "Scott" (C/OF) #34

5-11, 185. Born: 3/22/60 in Essex Fells, NJ. Age 25, turns 26 March 22. Resides in Essex Fells, NJ. BL. TR. Single. College: University of North Carolina.

MAJOR LEAGUE SERVICE: 155 days.

CONTRACT STATUS: Signed 1-year contract for 1985.

1985 SEASON: Having survived final Spring Training cuts, he began season with parent club ... Made first start April 21 vs. Cleveland, suffering a fractured right pinky in a home plate collision with Brook Jacoby—was first M.L. start as back-stop ... Placed on 15-day DL, April 24 ... Transferred to 21-day DL, May 6 ... Assigned to Sarasota for rehabilitation, June 5 ... Assigned to Albany to continue rehabilitation, June 9, playing in 6 games, hitting .125 ... Reinstated from DL, June 17 ... Played in 14 games (starting 9 as DH) from June 28 to July 3 ... Had first career 3-hit game June 18 @ Baltimore ... Optioned to Columbus July 11 as Dan Pasqua was recalled ... Recalled to big club, July 22, replacing injured Butch Wynegar ... Played just 4 games, going 1/10—started 2 at catcher—before being optioned to Columbus, Aug. 2 ... Again recalled to NY Sept. 14, making only 1 PH appearance (9/15 vs. Toronto) the remainder of season ... At Columbus he hit .301 in 43 games, playing 17 games at third base, and 24 at catcher.

CAREER: 1984—At Columbus, he hit .335 with the Clippers to win the International League Batting Crown ... was voted IL Rookie of the Year and Most Valuable Player ... made ML debut September 9 in Boston ... his first hit in the Majors was a single, at Toronto, off Luis Leal on September 13 ... his first RBI was a game winner vs. Baltimore, September 19 ... 1983—He led the Southern League's Nashville Sounds (AA) in at-bats (525), runs (83), hits (142), & doubles (33) ... was second in games (137) & RBI (76) ... 1982—with Ft. Lauderdale, tied for the Florida State League (A) lead with 13 GWRBI ... led Ft. Lauderdale in batting (.296), at bats (439), doubles (28), & RBI (66) ... was starting catcher on FSL All-Star team ... 1981—led the Oneonta Yankees in hits (85) & RBI (54) ... Named to New York-Penn League All-Star team.

PERSONAL/MISCELLANEOUS: Born and raised in Essex Fells, NJ attended West Essex Regional High School, North Caldwell, NJ ... played basketball and was All-State in football ... holds a BS in Business Administration from the University of North Carolina ... has two brothers; Jeff, 22 and Bob, 27—Bob is head soccer coach at Princeton ... played for the U.S.A. National baseball team ... likes uniform number 5 for Joe DiMaggio and George Brett ... signed by Yankee scout Jim Gruzdis.

Named International League Most Valuable Player and Rookie of the Year, 1984.
Tied for International League lead in game winning RBI with 14 in 1984.
Tied for Florida State League lead in game winning RBI with 13 in 1982.

YR	Club	AVG	G	AB	R	H	2B	3B	HR	RBI	BB	SO	SB
1981	Oneonta	.308	71	276	48	85	17	4	4	54	22	15	7
1982	Nashville	.105	5	19	2	2	1	0	0	0	1	0	0
	Ft. Lauderdale	.296	121	439	52	130	28	4	3	66	26	13	5
1983	Nashville	.270	137	525	83	142	33	4	8	76	40	16	3
1984	Columbus	.335*	138*	538*	84	180*	31	2	6	84†	33	31	1
	YANKEES	.286	9	21	3	6	1	0	0	2	1	1	0
1985	Albany	.125	6	24	2	3	1	0	0	2	2	1	0
	Columbus	.301	43	163	17	49	10	0	4	27	8	12	2
	YANKEES-a	.163	19	49	4	8	2	1	0	1	1	5	0
Minor League Totals		**.298**	**521**	**1984**	**288**	**591**	**121**	**14**	**25**	**309**	**132**	**88**	**18**
M.L. Totals		**.233**	**28**	**60**	**7**	**14**	**3**	**1**	**0**	**3**	**2**	**6**	**0**

GWRBI: 1984-1; 1985-0.

Selected by Minnesota Twins' organization in 12th round of free-agent draft, June 6, 1978.
Selected by New York Yankees' organization in 3rd round of free-agent draft, June 8, 1981.
a-Placed on 15-day disabled list with fractured right finger, April 24; assigned to Sarasota on rehabilitation assignment, June 5; transferred to Albany, June 9; reinstated off disabled list June 17.

DID YOU KNOW ... Lou Gehrig was pinch-hit for eight times in his career, but only twice after 1925—by Earle Combs in 1932 and by Myril Hoag in 1935. Babe Ruth was pinch-hit for by Bobby Veach on Aug. 9, 1925.

DID YOU KNOW ... that when the Yankees and Royals resumed play of the "Pine Tar" game on August 18, 1983 that Ron Guidry played in centerfield and Don Mattingly at second base for the Yankees?

1985 vs. OPPONENTS

Club	AB	H	HR	RBI	AVG
Baltimore	14	4	0	1	.286
Boston	1	0	0	0	.000
Cleveland	8	0	0	0	.000
Detroit	5	1	0	0	.200
Milwaukee	6	1	0	0	.167
Toronto	9	1	0	0	.111
California	—	—	—	—	—
Chicago	—	—	—	—	—
Kansas City	2	1	0	0	.500
Minnesota	—	—	—	—	—
Oakland	—	—	—	—	—
Seattle	—	—	—	—	—
Texas	4	0	0	0	.000
1st Half	38	7	0	1	.184
2nd Half	11	1	0	0	.091
vs. LHP	10	1	0	0	.100
vs. RHP	39	7	0	1	.179
Home	15	1	0	0	.067
Away	34	7	0	1	.206

BRADLEY'S BESTS

Season

AVG.	.286–1984
H	8–1985
HR	0–
RBI	2–1984, 1985
SB	0–
Hit Strk	3 games–1985

Game

H	3–@ Baltimore, 6/18/85
HR	0–
RBI	1–
SB	0–

BURNS, ROBERT BRITT "Burnsy" (LHP) #43

6-5, 217. Born 6/8/59 in Houston, Tex. Age 26, turns 27 June 8. Resides in Homewood, Al. BR. TL. Married: Julie Umphrey October 30, 1982.

MAJOR LEAGUE SERVICE: 6 years, 42 days.

CONTRACT STATUS: Signed multi-year contract with White Sox ... extends through 1986 season.

1985 SEASON: Finished tied for third in the AL in victories with a team leading, and personal high (18) ... tied for second in the league with 4 shutouts, three of which were 4-hitters, the forth being a 5-hit performance ... finished 6th in strikeouts with a career high 172 ... started a career high 34 games, appearing only twice in relief ... had four outings in which achieved double figures in strikeouts, setting a personal single season high with 12 at Baltimore on May 1 ... had three shutouts vs. Cleveland, ending season with 33.2 consecutive scoreless innings against the Indians.

CAREER: 1984—Volunteered to start the season in the bullpen due to the quantity of White Sox starting pitching ... was placed back in the starting rotation 6 weeks into the season, his first start a May 13 8-1 win over Texas ... then went 0-8 in next 11 starts, and returned to bullpen on July 5 ... made three relief appearances before developing a bacterial infection, going on the 15 day disabled list on July 19 ... after brief rehabilitative work at two farm clubs ("A" Appleton and "AAA" Denver) Burns' next appearance with the Sox came on August 20 ... returned to starting rotation September 7 and snapped 10-game losing streak on September 12 with a 4-2 win at Oakland ... his 10-game losing streak was longest in AL in 1984 ... best game was on September 23 at Comiskey when he beat Seattle 4-0, allowing 3 hits in 8.2 innings ... recorded three 7 strikeout games ... 1983—Began season on DL after being sidelined in spring training with a viral infection in his pitching arm ... didn't pitch in a game until May 9, and was inconsistent early ... returned to form late in year, and won several key games in Sox pennant race ... pitched a one-hit shutout against Angels on September 9 in Chicago and followed that with a 2-hit blanking of Angels in California on September 24 ... despite only 26 starts, his four shutouts were second best in AL ... 1982—Led Sox in wins (13), and won-loss percentage .722, despite missing final weeks of season with shoulder injury ... 1981—Hurled 30 consecutive scoreless innings in August ... won six straight mid-season games ... named to AL All-Star team, but didn't appear in game ... his success was tempered when his father was struck by an automobile near Birmingham, Ala. on July 16, and passed away without regaining consciousness on September 12 ... over his father's two-month fight for life, Burns commuted between his father's bedside and his starting rotations ... 1980—Struck out 133 batters in rookie season 2nd best in career ... had 15-13 record with 2.84 ERA in only 32 starts.

PERSONAL/MISCELLANEOUS: Named Sporting News rookie pitcher of the Year in 1980 ... "discovered" by former Chicago Tribune book critic Robert Cromie, who read an article about Burns' high school heroics while in Birmingham on business ... Cromie clipped the article and mailed it to White Sox president Bill Veeck, a friend of Cromie ... Burns' sensational prep career included a 0.12 ERA, a 35-2 record, 30 hits, 30 walks, and 292 strikeouts in 139 innings ... included was an 18-game winning streak.

BURNS (continued)

Tied for American League lead in balks with 4 in 1980.
Named American League Rookie Pitcher of the Year by TSN, 1980.

YR	CLUB	W-L	ERA	G	GS	CG	Sho	SV	IP	H	R	ER	BB	SO
1978	Appleton	3-2	2.40	6	6	1	0	0	30	25	8	8	2	28
	CHICAGO (AL)	0-2	13.75	2	2	0	0	0	8	14	12	11	3	3
	Knoxville	1-1	4.29	4	4	0	0	0	21	24	16	10	4	17
1979	Knoxville	6-10	4.83	20	19	4	1	1	110	126	68	59	37	92
	Iowa	2-3	3.29	7	6	1	0	1	41	41	17	15	15	34
	CHICAGO (AL)	0-0	5.40	6	0	0	0	0	5	10	5	3	1	2
1980	CHICAGO (AL)	15-13	2.84	34	32	11	1	0	238	213	83	75	63	133
1981	CHICAGO (AL)	10-6	2.64	24	23	5	1	0	156.2	139	52	46	49	108
1982	CHICAGO (AL)	13-5	4.04	28	28	5	1	0	169.1	168	89	76	67	116
1983	CHICAGO (AL)-a	10-11	3.58	29	26	8	4	0	173.2	165	79	69	55	115
1984	CHICAGO (AL)-b	4-12	5.00	34	16	2	0	3	117.0	130	74	65	45	85
	Appleton	1-0	1.80	1	1	0	0	0	5.0	4	1	1	1	5
	Denver	1-0	4.50	1	1	0	0	0	6.0	6	3	3	3	5
1985	CHICAGO (AL)-c	18-11	3.96	36	34	8	4	0	227.0	206	105	100	79	172
Minor League Totals		**14-16**	**4.06**	**39**	**37**	**6**	**1**	**2**	**213.0**	**226**	**113**	**96**	**62**	**181**
M.L. Totals		**70-60**	**3.66**	**193**	**161**	**39**	**11**	**3**	**1095.0**	**1045**	**499**	**445**	**362**	**734**

Selected by Chicago White Sox' organization in 3rd round of free-agent draft, June 6, 1978.
a-On disabled list, March 29 to May 9, 1983.
b-On disabled list, July 19 to August 20, 1984; including rehabilitation assignment to Appleton,
August 10 to August 15, and to Denver, August 16 to August 20.
c-Traded to New York Yankees with shortstop Mike Soper, outfielder Glen Braxton and two players to be named later for catcher Ron Hassey and pitcher Joe Cowley, December 12, 1985.

CHAMPIONSHIP SERIES RECORD

YR	CLUB, Opp.	W-L	ERA	G	GS	CG	Sho	SV	IP	H	R	ER	BB	SO
1983	Chi. vs. Bal.	0-1	0.96	1	1	0	0	0	9.1	6	1	1	5	8

ALL-STAR GAME RECORD

YR	CLUB, Site	W-L	ERA	G	GS	CG	Sho	SV	IP	H	R	ER	BB	SO
1981	A.L., Cle.	(Selected, did not play)												

	1985					CAREER				
ERA	W-L-S	G	IP	H	ER	Club	ERA	W-L-S	G	IP	H	ER
6.20	1-2-0	3	24.1	23	17	**Baltimore**	3.96	5-4-0	15	84.0	77	37
4.50	2-0-0	3	20.0	21	10	**Boston**	3.61	5-1-0	11	67.1	66	27
3.86	1-1-0	3	18.2	19	8	**California**	3.58	8-6-2	21	110.2	95	44
—	—	—	—	—	—	**Chicago**	—	—	—	—	—	—
0.00	4-0-3	4	32.0	16	0	**Cleveland**	2.80	6-3-3	12	70.2	55	22
2.81	1-0-0	2	16.0	12	5	**Detroit**	4.50	4-4-0	15	86.0	85	43
9.64	0-1-0	1	4.2	5	5	**Kansas City**	5.37	4-8-0	13	72.0	77	43
5.11	1-1-0	2	12.1	12	7	**Milwaukee**	3.88	2-4-0	13	65.0	55	28
0.76	2-1-1	3	23.2	10	2	**Minnesota**	3.62	4-6-1	14	87.0	85	35
12.50	0-1-0	3	7.2	15	10	**Oakland**	3.15	4-4-1	11	71.1	65	25
—	—	—	—	—	—	**Seattle**	4.06	5-5-1	13	71.0	64	32
5.25	2-2-0	4	24.0	28	14	**Texas**	3.26	7-4-0	14	85.2	85	31
4.66	2-1-0	3	19.1	20	10	**Toronto**	3.70	8-6-1	15	104.2	118	43
3.96	18-11-4	36	227.0	206	100	**Total**	3.66	70-60-11	193	1095.2	1045	445
3.91	10-6-3	18	117.1	102	51	**Home**	—	—	—	—	—	—
4.02	8-5-1	18	109.2	104	49	**Road**	—	—	—	—	—	—

4—3 times		Low Hit	1—vs Cal 9/9/83
12—@ Balt. 5/1/85		K-High	12—@ 5/1/85
5—		Win Streak	6—

S = Shutouts

BYSTROM, MARTIN EUGENE "Marty"   (RHP)   #50

6-5, 210. Born 7/26/58 in Coral Gables, FL. Resides
in Hawthorne, NJ. Age 27, turns 28 July 26. BR. TR.
Married: Meg MacLean, 2/2/85. College: Miami-Dade
South Junior College.

MAJOR LEAGUE SERVICE: 5 years, 19 days.

CONTRACT STATUS: Signed 1-year contract (with
option for 2nd), October 31, 1985 ... contract extends
through 1986 (option year).

1985 SEASON: After undergoing ulnar nerve surgery
on his right elbow in November 1984 he spent most of
'85 rehabilitating ... he was placed on the 60-day Emergency DL April 8, remaining
in Ft. Lauderdale to work ... was assigned to Columbus on injury rehab, 6/16

where he remained until being brought to NY to continue rehab 7/75 ... the right-hander was reinstated from the DL 7/23, making his first start of '85 7/28 @ Texas allowing 7 runs (4 ER) in 1.2 IP ... he won his next 3 decisions (5 starts), 8/2-24 ... gave up 8 HRs in 41.0 IP allowing 2 HRs in 3 of his 8 starts ... elbow tenderness prevented him from pitching after his 9/9 start.

CAREER: 1984—Traded to the Yankees June 30, joining the team on July 2 in Arlington ... made and won first A.L. start, July 3 at Texas ... was 2-0 in first five Yankee starts ... placed on disabled list August 3 with tender right elbow ... activated on September 3, he made only one appearance the remainder of the season ... underwent Ulnar nerve surgery on right elbow, November 11 ... 1983—began season on DL with strained rib cage muscle ... activated May 3 ... sidelined again August 21 with tender right elbow ... pitched one game at Peninsula as part of injury rehabilitation program ... threw second career shutout after returning from the DL, blanking Montreal 5-0 ... 1982—also began year on the DL, this time due to a recurring shoulder problem carried over from 1981 ... activated June 7 ... used primarily as starter, but made three relief appearances ... missed two starts in July with shoulder stiffness ... 1981—bothered by shoulder injury, appeared in only 11 games between Philadelphia and Reading ... 1980—threw shutout in first ML start, September 10 at New York ... was 5-0 in September, winning Pitcher of the Month honors ... Phillies won every game he started, including World Series Game #5 ... started season on DL at Oklahoma City with a hamstring pull, did not pitch until May 18 ... 1979—jumped from A to AAA where he tied for American Association lead in games started and ninth in ERA ... 1978—led the Carolina League in IP and SO, while sharing league high 15 wins ... pitched 3-0 perfect game victory against Winston-Salem, August 12.

PERSONAL/MISCELLANEOUS: Graduated Killian (Miami) High School ... played baseball at Miami-Dade Junior College ... played American Legion baseball ... originally signed by scouts Hugh Alexander and Catfish Smith ... has lifetime batting totals of: .161 BA, 18/112, with 0 HR & 5 RBI.

Led National League in hit batsmen with 7 in 1983.
Led American Association in balks with 5 in 1979.

YR	CLUB	W-L	ERA	G	GS	CG	Sho	SV	IP	H	R	ER	BB	SO
1977	Spartanburg	13-11	3.38	27†	27	12	2	0	184	199*	83	69	49	99
1978	Peninsula	†15-7	2.83	26	26	13†	5†	0	197*	170	71	62	46	159*
1979	Okla. City	9-5	4.08	26	26†	7	0	0	172	174	102	78	69	108
1980	Okla. City-a	6-5	3.66	14	14	4	1	0	91	89	49	37	27	68
	PHILADELPHIA	5-0	1.50	6	5	1	1	0	36	26	6	6	9	21
1981	PHILADELPHIA	4-3	3.33	9	9	1	0	0	54	55	21	20	16	24
	Reading	0-0	4.50	2	2	0	0	0	4	5	2	2	1	2
1982	PHILADELPHIA-b	5-6	4.85	19	16	1	0	0	89	93	53	48	35	50
1983	PHILADELPHIA-cd	6-9	4.60	24	23	1	1	0	119.1	136	75	61	44	87
	Peninsula	1-0	0.00	1	1	0	0	0	6.0	5	1	0	1	9
1984	Portland	0-2	5.56	5	5	0	0	0	23.0	26	17	14	9	10
	PHILADELPHIA-e	4-4	5.08	11	11	0	0	0	56.2	66	36	32	22	26
	YANKEES-f	2-2	2.97	7	7	0	0	0	39.1	34	16	13	13	24
1984	Totals	6-6	4.22	18	18	0	0	0	96.0	100	52	45	35	50
1985	Columbus	2-0	1.88	4	4	0	0	0	24.0	13	7	5	9	16
	YANKEES-g	3-2	5.71	8	8	0	0	0	41.0	44	29	26	19	16
Minor League Totals		46-30	3.43	105	105	36	8	0	701.0	681	332	267	211	471
N.Y.Y. Totals		5-4	4.37	15	15	0	0	0	80.1	78	45	39	32	40
N.L. Totals		24-22	4.23	69	64	4	2	0	355.0	376	191	167	126	208
M.L. Totals		29-26	4.26	84	79	4	2	0	435.1	454	236	206	158	248

Signed as free agent by Philadelphia Phillies' organization, December 15, 1976.
a-On disabled list, April 14 to May 16 and May 27 to June 12, 1980.
b-On disabled list, March 22 to June 8, 1982.
c-On Philadelphia disabled list, March 27 to May 3, 1983; included rehabilitation assignment to Peninsula, April 28 to May 3, 1983.
d-On disabled list, August 21 to September 11, 1983.
e-Traded to New York Yankees with minor league outfielder Keith Hughes for pitcher Shane Rawley, June 30, 1984.
f-On disabled list, August 3 to September 3, 1984 with tender right elbow.
g-On disabled list recovering from elbow surgery, April 8 to July 23, including rehabilitation assignment to Columbus, June 16 to July 5.

CHAMPIONSHIP SERIES RECORD

YR	CLUB, Opp.	W-L	ERA	G	GS	CG	Sho	SV	IP	H	R	ER	BB	SO
1980	Phi. vs. Hous.	0-0	1.69	1	1	0	0	0	5.1	7	2	1	2	1

WORLD SERIES RECORD

YR	CLUB	W-L	ERA	G	GS	CG	Sho	SV	IP	H	R	ER	BB	SO
1980	Phi. vs. K.C.	0-0	5.40	1	1	0	0	0	5.0	10	3	3	1	4
1983	Phi. vs. Bal.	0-0	0.00	1	0	0	0	0	1.0	0	0	0	0	1
W.S. Totals		0-0	4.50	2	1	0	0	0	6.0	10	3	3	1	5

BYSTROM (continued)

1985 ERA	W-L-S	G	IP	H	ER	Club	CAREER ERA	W-L-S	G	IP	H	ER
—	—	—	—	—	—	Baltimore	—	—	—	—	—	—
6.43	1-0-0	1	7.0	6	5	Boston	7.56	1-1-0	2	8.1	10	7
9.00	0-1-0	1	4.0	6	4	California	9.00	0-1-0	1	4.0	6	4
4.26	0-0-0	2	12.2	10	6	Chicago	5.09	0-1-0	3	17.2	17	10
1.80	1-0-0	1	5.0	5	1	Cleveland	1.80	1-0-0	1	5.0	5	1
—	—	—	—	—	—	Detroit	—	—	—	—	—	—
—	—	—	—	—	—	Kansas City	0.00	1-0-0	1	7.0	5	0
5.79	0-0-0	1	4.2	5	3	Milwaukee	3.09	0-0-0	2	11.2	8	4
—	—	—	—	—	—	Minnesota	2.77	0-0-0	2	13.0	10	4
—	—	—	—	—	—	Oakland	—	—	—	—	—	—
4.50	1-0-0	1	6.0	6	3	Seattle	4.50	1-0-0	1	1.2	6	4
21.60	0-1-0	1	1.2	6	4	Texas	7.04	1-1-0	2	7.2	11	6
—	—	—	—	—	—	Toronto	—	—	—	—	—	—
5.71	3-2-0	8	41.0	44	26	Total	4.37	5-2-0	15	80.1	78	39
5.32	2-1-0	4	22.0	24	13	Home	—	—	—	—	—	—
6.16	1-1-0	4	19.0	20	13	Road	—	—	—	—	—	—

—
4—2 times
3—
S = SHUTOUTS

Low Hit	3—5/3/81 vs San Francisco
K-High	9—5/3/81 vs San Francisco
Win Streak	7—Start of Career, 1980-81.

COTTO, HENRY (OF)   #46

6-2, 178. Born 1/5/61 in Bronx, New York. Age 25, turned 25 Jan. 5. Resides in Caguas, Puerto Rico. BR. TR.

MAJOR LEAGUE SERVICE: 1 year and 123 days.

CONTRACT STATUS: Signed 1-year contract for 1986 season.

1985 SEASON: Opened '85 with Yankees due to Rickey Henderson's injured ankle ... after Henderson's late April return, Henry was used as a late inning defensive replacement in both left and center fields ... went 8/28, .286, 21 games before being optioned to Columbus, July 5 ... played 75 games in the Columbus OF, hitting .257, making just 2 errors ... recalled to NY September 3 ... played in 13 games, starting his last 6 in leftfield, through season's end ... went 2/4 with 4 RBIs, hitting his 1st M.L. HR October 6 @ Toronto off Bill Caudill.

CAREER: 1984—Earned reputation as excellent outfielder ... appeared in 88 games in the Cubs' outfield, and his .984 fielding average was team high for Cubs who appeared in more than 50 games ... inserted into three games of the NLCS as late inning defensive replacement, two in leftfield and one in right ... went 1/1 in only official at bat in game 1 of NLCS vs. Padres ... appeared in game 4 of NLCS as a pinch runner, and scored a run ... showed good speed on the bases as well as the outfield, stealing 9 bases in 12 attempts ... traded to Yankees in Dec. '84 ... 1983—tied for the American Association lead in caught stealing with 17 ... spent 20 days on DL, May 10-30 ... 1982—led Texas League in stolen bases with 52 ... in the outfield Henry led the league in total chances (333) and putouts (310) ... 1981—displayed a good arm, leading the Midwest League in assists.

PERSONAL/MISCELLANEOUS: Henry has a perfect 1.000 percentage in both batting (1/1) and fielding (2/2) in post season play.

Tied for American Association lead in caught stealing with 17 in 1983.
Led Texas League outfielders in putouts with 310 and total chances with 333 in 1982.
Led Midwest League outfielders in assists with 23 in 1981.

YR	Club	AVG	G	AB	R	H	2B	3B	HR	RBI	BB	SO	SB
1980	Sarasota	.283	43	166	24	47	7	5	0	30	12	15	12
	Quad Cities	.282	19	78	9	22	1	1	0	5	4	10	8
1981	Quad Cities	.292	128	493	80	144	15	6	1	46	59	62	52
1982	Midland	.307	130	524	103	161	12	5	1	36	59	79	52
1983	Iowa-a	.261	104	426	52	111	7	10	0	35	35	67	32
1984	Iowa	.200	8	30	3	6	2	0	0	0	2	3	1
	CHICAGO (NL)-b	.274	105	146	24	40	5	0	0	8	10	23	9
1985	Columbus	.257	75	272	38	70	16	2	7	36	19	61	10
	YANKEES-c	.304	34	56	4	17	1	0	1	6	3	12	1
Minor League Totals		**.282**	**507**	**1989**	**309**	**561**	**60**	**29**	**9**	**188**	**190**	**297**	**167**
M.L. Totals		**.282**	**139**	**202**	**28**	**57**	**6**	**0**	**1**	**14**	**13**	**35**	**10**

Signed as free agent by Chicago Cubs' organization, June 7, 1980.
a-On disabled list, May 10 to May 30, 1983.

b-Traded with catcher Ron Hassey and pitchers Rich Bordi and Porfi Altamirano to New York Yankees for pitchers Ray Fontenot and outfielder Brian Dayett, December 4, 1984.

c-On disabled list with punctured left eardrum, May 30 to July 5, including rehabilitation assignment to Columbus, June 25 to July 5.

1985 vs. OPPONENTS

Club	AB	H	HR	RBI	AVG
Baltimore	11	5	0	0	.455
Boston	1	0	0	0	.000
Cleveland	10	4	0	2	.400
Detroit	1	0	0	0	.000
Milwaukee	4	1	0	0	.250
Toronto	7	2	1	4	.286
California	1	0	0	0	.000
Chicago	6	1	0	0	.167
Kansas City	1	1	0	0	1.000
Minnesota	6	2	0	0	.333
Oakland	3	0	0	0	.000
Seattle	0	0	0	0	—
Texas	5	1	0	0	.200
1st Half	28	8	0	0	.286
2nd Half	28	9	1	6	.321
vs. LHP	51	15	0	4	.294
vs. RHP	5	2	1	2	.400
Home	37	11	0	2	.297
Away	19	6	1	4	.316

COTTO'S BESTS

	Season	
AVG.	.304–1985	
H	40–1984	
HR	1–1985	
RBI	8–1985	
SB	9–1984	
Hit Strk		
	Game	
H		
HR		
RBI		
SB		

DESTRADE, ORESTES (1B)   #61

6-4, 210. Born 5/8/62 in Havanna, Cuba. Age 23, turns 24 May 8. Resides in Miami, FL. BS. TR.

CONTRACT STATUS: Signed 1-year contract for 1986 season.

1985 SEASON: Led Albany in games (136), ABs (564), runs (82), hits (119), doubles (24), HRs (23), RBIs (72) and slugging percentage (.471) ... named Eastern League All-Star DH, despite leading circuit in games played @ first base (134) ... DPs (99), putouts (1103), total chances (1194) ... Finished 2nd in EL in HRs and total bases (222), tied 2nd walks (86) and 3rd in runs.

CAREER: Has progressed steadily through the minors while showing the ability to play both first and outfield ... In 1981 at Paintsville he led the Appalachian League in home runs with 14 ... he was named the 1981 Appalachian League All-Star first baseman ... In 1983 at Ft. Lauderdale he led the Florida State League in walks with 82 ... was named the Florida State Leagues All-Star first baseman ... he was second on the Lauderdale Club in Homers and RBI with 18 and 74 respectively ... In 1984 he led the Lauderdale team with 12 HR ... A switch hitter, he hits the ball to all fields from both sides, but makes better contact from the right side.

PERSONAL/MISCELLANEOUS: Attended Coral Park H.S. and Christopher Columbus H.S. in Miami where he graduated in 1980 ... signed by Fred Ferreira.

Led Eastern League first basemen with 134 games, 1194 total chances, 1103 putouts and 99 double plays in 1985.

Tied for Florida State League lead with 15 GWRBI in 1983.

Tied for Appalachian League lead in double plays by first basemen with 42 in 1981.

YR	Club	AVG	G	AB	R	H	2B	3B	HR	RBI	BB	SO	SB
1981	Paintsville	.274	63	208	51	57	12	1	14*	46	48	49	2
1982	Greensboro	.180	43	122	9	22	4	1	1	14	27	42	1
	Oneonta	.232	64	194	44	45	12	1	4	30	38	56	11
1983	Ft. Lauderdale	.292	127	425	61	124	24	5	18	74	82†	86	3
1984	Nashville	.240	35	121	15	29	6	0	6	12	15	36	1
	Ft. Lauderdale	.221	95	308	40	68	14	2	12	57	64	82	4
1985	Albany	.253	136	471	82	119	24	5	23	72	86	129*	9
Minor League Totals		**.251**	**563**	**1849**	**302**	**464**	**96**	**15**	**78**	**305**	**360**	**480**	**31**

Selected by California Angels' organization in 23rd round of free-agent draft, June 3, 1980.
Signed as free agent by New York Yankees' organization, May 17, 1981.

> **LUIS TIANT** is the only pitcher to defeat the Yankees five times in one season since expansion in 1961. In fact, when he was 5-1 against the Yankees in 1974, he was the first to do it since 1959, when Frank Lary, Don Mossi and Cal McLish all accomplished it.

DRABEK, DOUGLAS DEAN (RHP) #62

6-1, 185. Born and resides in Victoria, TX. Age 23, turns 24 July 25. BR. TR. College: University of Houston.

CONTRACT STATUS: Signed 1-year contract for 1986 season.

1985 SEASON: Spent first full season in Yankee organization at Albany (AA Eastern League) ... Topped Eastern League with 153 strikeouts and 192.2 innings pitched ... 13 wins was second in league ... Tied first on team with 9 complete games and 2 shutouts; second in wins and games started; third with 2.99 ERA (pitchers with at least 15 games) ... Had mere .218 batting average against ... A fastball pitcher with good control and good move to first.

CAREER: 1983—Was drafted by the White Sox in the 12th round of the June '83 draft ... second in the New York-Penn League in strikeouts with 103 ... 1984—was second in ERA (2.24) in the Eastern League before being acquired by the Yankees with Kevin Hickey for Roy Smalley on July 18, 1984.

PERSONAL/MISCELLANEOUS: A graduate of St. Joseph High School where he was All-State in Baseball, Football & Track.

YR	CLUB	W-L	ERA	G	GS	CG	Sho	SV	IP	H	R	ER	BB	SO
1983	Niagara Falls	6-7	3.65	16	13	3	0	0	103.0	99	52	42	48	103
1984	Appleton	1-0	1.80	1	1	0	0	0	5.0	3	1	1	3	6
	Glens Falls-a	12-5	2.24	19	17	7	0	0	125.0	90	34	31	44	75
	Nashville	1-2	2.32	4	4	2	0	0	31.0	30	11	8	10	22
1985	Albany	13-7	2.99	26	26	9	2	0	192.2*	153	71	64	55	153*
Minor League Totals		**33-21**	**2.88**	**66**	**61**	**21**	**2**	**0**	**456.2**	**375**	**169**	**146**	**160**	**359**

Selected by Cleveland Indians' organization in 4th round of free-agent draft, June 3, 1980.
Selected by Chicago White Sox' organization in 11th round of free-agent draft, June 6, 1983.
a-Traded with pitcher Kevin Hickey to New York Yankees' organization, August 13, 1984, completing deal in which New York traded infielder Roy Smalley to Chicago White Sox for two players to be named later, July 18, 1984.

ESPINO, JUAN REYES (C) #58

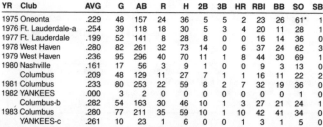

6-1, 190. Born 3/16/56 in Bonao, Dominican Republic, where he resides. Age 30, turned 30 on March 16. BR. TR.

MAJOR LEAGUE SERVICE: 122 days.

CONTRACT STATUS: Signed 1-year contract for 1986 season.

1985 SEASON: Had his contract purchased from Columbus, June 21 ... played in 6 games between June 23 & July 2, all at catcher, starting 3 games ... outrighted to Columbus July 3 ... went 2-for-4 June 23 @ Detroit, and 2-for-3 June 26 @ Baltimore—the only games in which he hit safely in, having only 4 ABs after ... contract was again purchased from Columbus August 20 ... appeared in only 3 games through October ... at Columbus he hit .250 in 74 games, playing in 73 at catcher.

CAREER: 1984—Had been in the Yankee organization for nine seasons before being sold to the Cleveland Indians' organization in March of 1984 ... named to International League All-Star team as catcher for Maine ... first major league hit on May 24, 1983 at California ... first major league homer on September 7 at Milwaukee vs. Cocanower.

PERSONAL/MISCELLANEOUS: Was signed by Epy Guerrero for 1975 season.

Led Eastern League catchers in fielding with .987 pct. in 1978.

YR	Club	AVG	G	AB	R	H	2B	3B	HR	RBI	BB	SO	SB
1975	Oneonta	.229	48	157	24	36	5	5	2	23	26	61*	1
1976	Ft. Lauderdale-a	.254	39	118	18	30	5	3	4	20	11	28	1
1977	Ft. Lauderdale	.199	52	141	8	28	8	0	0	16	14	36	0
1978	West Haven	.280	82	261	32	73	14	0	6	37	24	62	3
1979	West Haven	.236	95	296	40	70	11	1	8	44	30	69	1
1980	Nashville	.161	17	56	3	9	1	0	0	9	3	13	0
	Columbus	.209	48	129	11	27	7	1	1	16	11	22	2
1981	Columbus	.233	80	253	22	59	8	2	7	32	19	36	0
1982	YANKEES	.000	3	2	0	0	0	0	0	0	0	1	0
	Columbus-b	.282	54	163	30	46	10	1	3	27	21	24	1
1983	Columbus	.280	77	211	35	59	10	1	10	42	41	34	0
	YANKEES-c	.261	10	23	1	6	0	0	1	3	1	5	0

	AVG	G	AB	R	H	2B	3B	HR	RBI	BB	SO	SB
1984 Maine-d	.251	97	327	38	82	6	1	7	41	36	64	0
1985 Columbus	.250	74	224	30	56	11	0	3	20	22	36	0
YANKEES	.364	9	11	0	4	0	0	0	0	0	0	0
Minor League Totals	**.246**	**763**	**2336**	**291**	**575**	**96**	**13**	**51**	**327**	**258**	**485**	**9**
M.L. Totals	**.278**	**22**	**36**	**1**	**10**	**0**	**0**	**1**	**3**	**1**	**6**	**0**

Signed as free agent by New York Yankees' organization, December 26, 1974.
a-On disabled list, May 26 to June 9, 1976.
b-On disabled list, August 3 to August 23, 1982.
c-Sold to Cleveland Indians' organization, March 31, 1984.
d-Sold to New York Yankees' organization, January 8, 1985.

1985 vs. OPPONENTS

Club	AB	H	HR	RBI	AVG
Baltimore	3	2	0	0	.667
Boston	—	—	—	—	—
Cleveland	0	0	0	0	—
Detroit	4	2	0	0	.500
Milwaukee	1	0	0	0	.000
Toronto	3	0	0	0	.000
California	—	—	—	—	—
Chicago	—	—	—	—	—
Kansas City	—	—	—	—	—
Minnesota	—	—	—	—	—
Oakland	—	—	—	—	—
Seattle	—	—	—	—	—
Texas	—	—	—	—	—
1st Half	11	4	0	0	.364
2nd Half	0	0	0	0	—
vs. LHP	10	4	0	0	.400
vs. RHP	1	0	0	0	.000
Home	4	2	0	0	.500
Away	7	2	0	0	.286

ESPINO'S BESTS

Season

AVG.	.364–1985
H	6–1983
HR	1–1983
RBI	3–1983
SB	0
Hit Strk	2 games–1983

Game

H	3 @ CAL 5-24-83
HR	1–
RBI	1–
SB	0

FISCHLIN, MICHAEL THOMAS "Mike" (IF) #22

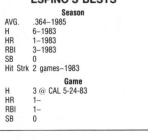

6-1, 165. Born 9/13/55 in Sacramento, CA. Age 30, turns 31 September 13. Resides in Tucson, AZ. BR. TR. Married: Sandra Ann Kremen 11/7/81. Children: James Matthew (16) and Ryan Wade (14). College: Graduated Cosumnes River Junior College.

MAJOR LEAGUE SERVICE: 5 years and 6 days.

CONTRACT STATUS: Signed 1-year contract for 1986 season.

1985 SEASON: With Cleveland all year . . . used primarily as a utility infielder playing in 30 games at SS, 20 at 2B, four at 3B and two at 1B . . . hit .571 in the month of July going 4-for-7 with a double and triple . . . saw the most action in September appearing in 17 games without committing an error.

CAREER: Originally signed by the Yankees in the 7th round of the June draft, 1975 . . . has played with both Houston and Cleveland organization . . . a utility man, has played second, third, shortstop, and caught one game . . . was the Indians starting second baseman the final month of the 1984 season . . . collected his first Major League hit off Charlie Hough of the Dodgers in 1977 . . . has good speed, had a team high 40 steals for Charleston (AAA) in 1981.

PERSONAL/MISCELLANEOUS: Graduated from Elk Grove High School (CA), where he played baseball and basketball, 1973 . . . was team captain and All-League second baseman his senior year . . . graduated from Cosumnes River Junior College (Sacramento, CA) in 1975, where he was team captain and All-Conference shortstop . . . was Honor Roll student both years of JC.

Led International League in sacrifice hits with 15 in 1981.

Led Pacific Coast League shortstops in putouts with 200, assists with 437, errors with 40, fielding with .941 percentage, and doubleplays with 88 in 1980.

Tied National League record for fewest chances offered by shortstop, two consecutive games (1), June 18 and 20, 1978.

YR	Club	AVG	G	AB	R	H	2B	3B	HR	RBI	BB	SO	SB
1975	Oneonta	.230	35	135	22	31	4	3	0	6	15	26	6
	Ft. Lauderdale	.183	29	104	7	19	4	0	0	7	10	16	1
1976	West Haven	.153	61	248	16	38	7	1	2	20	25	50	5
	Oneonta	.255	14	55	13	14	3	0	0	5	8	6	3
1977	Ft. Lauderdale-a	.294	53	201	28	59	6	4	0	20	27	27	4
	Columbus, GA	.242	66	223	23	54	5	0	1	16	37	40	4
	HOUSTON	.200	13	15	0	3	0	0	0	0	0	2	0

FISCHLIN (continued)

1978 Charleston	.211	82	280	38	59	10	2	0	19	38	49	6
HOUSTON	.116	44	86	3	10	1	0	0	0	4	9	1
1979 Charleston-b	.255	44	138	13	31	4	1	0	8	11	17	4
1980 Tucson	.281	131	417	65	117	24	7	3	49	57	65	30
HOUSTON-c	.000	1	0	0	0	0	0	0	0	0	1	0
1981 Charleston	.238	136	463	83	110	14	7	5	43	89	97	40
CLEVELAND	.233	22	43	3	10	1	0	0	5	3	6	3
1982 CLEVELAND	.268	112	276	34	74	12	1	0	21	34	36	9
1983 CLEVELAND	.209	95	225	31	47	5	2	2	23	26	32	9
1984 CLEVELAND	.226	85	133	17	30	4	2	1	14	12	20	2
1985 CLEVELAND-d	.200	73	60	12	12	4	1	0	2	5	7	0
Minor League Totals	.235	651	2264	308	532	81	25	11	193	317	393	103
N.L. Totals	.127	58	102	3	13	1	0	0	0	4	12	1
A.L. Totals	.235	387	737	97	173	26	6	3	65	80	101	23
M.L. Totals	.222	445	839	100	186	27	6	3	65	84	113	24

GWRBI: 1981-1; 1982-4; 1983-2; 1984-0; 1985-0. Total-7.

Selected by New York Yankees' organization in 7th round of free-agent draft, June 4, 1975.

a-Traded with pitcher Randy Niemann and a player to be named later to Houston Astros' organization for catcher-first baseman Cliff Johnson, June 15, 1977; Houston acquired first baseman-outfielder Dave Bergman to complete deal, November 23, 1977.

b-On disabled list, June 18 to August 28, 1979.

c-Traded to Cleveland Indians' organization for cash and a player to be named later, April 3, 1981; Houston Astros' organization acquired outfielder Jim Lentine to complete deal, September 28, 1981.

1985 vs. OPPONENTS

Club	AB	H	HR	RBI	AVG
Baltimore	8	2	0	1	.250
Boston	7	1	0	0	.143
Cleveland	—	—	—	—	—
Detroit	1	0	0	0	.000
Milwaukee	0	0	0	0	—
Toronto	0	0	0	0	—
California	1	1	0	0	1.000
Chicago	4	2	0	0	.500
Kansas City	0	0	0	0	—
Minnesota	6	0	0	0	.000
Oakland	10	2	0	0	.100
Seattle	7	2	0	1	.286
Texas	1	1	0	0	1.000
1st Half	36	8	0	2	.222
2nd Half	24	4	0	0	.167
vs. LHP	31	7	0	0	.226
vs. RHP	29	5	0	2	.172
Home	40	10	0	2	.250
Away	20	2	0	0	.100

FISCHLIN'S BESTS

	Season
AVG.	.268–1982
H	74–1982
HR	2–1983
RBI	23–1983
SB	9–1982, 1983
Hit Strk	10 games–1982

	Game
H	3–4 times
HR	1–3 times
RBI	4–9-20-83 vs. Milw.
SB	2–9-10-83 vs. Bost.

FISHER, BRIAN KEVIN (RHP)   #54

6-4, 210. Born 3/18/62 in Honolulu, HI. Resides in Aurora, CO. Age 24, turned 24 March 18. BR. TR.

MAJOR LEAGUE SERVICE: 159 days.

CONTRACT STATUS: Signed 1-year contract for 1986.

1985 SEASON: One of Yankees' final cuts out of Spring Training where he made an impressive showing . . . Initial plans were for Fisher to be middle reliever, but quickly established himself as Yankees' righthand stopper . . . at Columbus relieved in 7 games (11.1 IP, 8 H, 4 R, 3 ER, 7 BB, 12 K, 2.38 ERA) . . . purchased by Yankees on May 1 when Rich Bordi was disabled . . . made first major league appearance on May 7 @ Minnesota . . . earned first ML win in relief of Montefusco on May 14 vs. Minnesota . . . picked up first ML save on May 18 at California . . . since May 25, kept ERA under 3.00 thru remainder of season . . . struck out season high of 6 batters on 3 occasions (June 15 vs. Det., June 30 vs. Milw. and August 21 @ Cal.) . . . from August 24 @ Seattle to September 14 vs. Toronto, didn't allow any runs (10 AP, 15.1 IP, 2 BB, 19 K), lowering ERA from 2.41 to 2.00 . . . allowed just 4 HRs in 98.1 IP, 1 HR every 89 ABs . . . From 7/29 thru season's end: 29 app., 47.2 IP, 11 ER, 2.08 ERA (6 ER came in 1 app.; 9/16 vs. Cleveland allowing 7 hits in 1.1 IP) 2-2, 10 saves, K:W ratio of 2.9:1 . . . Opposing hitters batted a mere .216 vs. Fisher.

CAREER: Was strictly a starter in his five years with the Braves minor league system . . . in 111 minor league games relieved only twice . . . achieved 100+ strikeouts four consecutive years, 1981-84 . . . was acquired from Atlanta for Rick Cerone, December 5, 1984 . . . tied Carolina League record held by Rudy May by striking out 20 batters in one game, issued no walks in game, vs. Salem in 1982.

78

PERSONAL/MISCELLANEOUS: Graduated from Hinkley (Aurora Col) High School in 1980 . . . was high school all-American in baseball and all-league in football.

Tied for South Atlantic League lead in balks with 4 in 1981.

YR	CLUB	W-L	ERA	G	GS	CG	Sho	SV	IP	H	R	ER	BB	SO
1980	Bradenton	5-3	3.84	12	12	0	0	0	61	55	34	26	53*	48
1981	Anderson	6-8	4.26	25	23	6	1	0	152	139	96	72	94	152
1982	Durham-a	6-6	2.77	18	18	3	0	0	104.0	72	43	32	43	129
1983	Savannah	8-11	5.22	27	27	3	1	0	150.0	172	101	87	56	103
1984	Richmond-b	9-11	4.28	29	29*	4	0	0	183.0	188	101†	87*	100†	122
1985	Columbus	0-0	2.38	7	0	0	0	0	11.1	8	4	3	7	12
	YANKEES	4-4	2.38	55	0	0	0	14	98.1	77	32	26	29	85
Minor League Totals		**34-39**	**4.18**	**118**	**109**	**16**	**2**	**0**	**661.1**	**634**	**379**	**307**	**353**	**566**
M.L. Totals		**4-4**	**2.38**	**55**	**0**	**0**	**0**	**14**	**98.1**	**77**	**32**	**26**	**29**	**85**

Selected by Atlanta Braves' organization in 2nd round of free-agent draft, June 3, 1980.
a-On disabled list, May 18 to July 1, 1982.
b-Traded to New York Yankees for catcher Rick Cerone, December 5, 1984.

	1985							CAREER				
ERA	W-L-S	G	IP	H	ER	Club	ERA	W-L-S	G	IP	H	ER
3.86	0-0-3	4	7.0	6	3	**Baltimore**	3.86	0-0-3	4	7.0	6	3
0.00	0-0-3	4	5.0	2	0	**Boston**	0.00	0-0-3	4	5.0	2	0
0.96	0-0-2	3	9.1	1	1	**California**	0.96	0-0-2	3	9.1	1	1
10.80	1-1-0	4	3.1	9	5	**Chicago**	10.80	1-1-0	4	3.1	9	5
6.75	1-1-0	4	8.0	9	6	**Cleveland**	6.75	1-1-0	4	8.0	9	6
2.89	0-0-0	3	9.1	7	3	**Detroit**	2.89	0-0-0	3	9.1	7	3
0.00	0-0-0	5	6.1	2	0	**Kansas City**	0.00	0-0-0	5	6.1	2	0
1.84	0-1-1	6	14.2	9	3	**Milwaukee**	1.84	0-1-1	6	14.2	9	3
2.57	1-0-1	6	14.0	12	4	**Minnesota**	2.57	1-0-1	6	14.0	12	4
4.50	0-0-1	5	4.0	3	2	**Oakland**	4.50	0-0-1	5	4.0	3	2
0.00	1-0-2	4	11.1	13	0	**Seattle**	0.00	1-0-2	4	11.1	13	0
0.00	0-0-0	2	2.0	0	0	**Texas**	0.00	0-0-0	2	2.0	0	0
0.00	0-1-1	5	4.0	4	0	**Toronto**	0.00	0-1-1	5	4.0	4	0
2.38	4-4-14	55	98.1	77	26	**Total**	2.38	4-4-14	55	98.1	77	26
2.75	3-3-8	32	55.2	49	17	**Home**	—	—	—	—	—	—
1.90	1-1-6	23	42.2	28	9	**Road**	—	—	—	—	—	—

	Low Hit	—
6—3 times	**K-High**	6—3 times
1—	**Win Streak**	1—

S = SAVES

FULTON, WILLIAM DAVID "Bill" (RHP) #57

6-3, 195. Born 10/22/63 in Pittsburgh, PA where he now resides. Age 22, turns 23 October 22. BR. TR. College: Pensacola Junior College.

CONTRACT STATUS: Signed 1-year contract for 1986 season.

1985 SEASON: Started season in Florida Instructional League . . . Moved to Ft. Lauderdale May 29 . . . Hurled a seven inning no-hitter vs. Lakeland, July 2 . . . Tied for second in Florida State League with nine complete games; third with 1.61 ERA . . . Had .217 batting average against . . . Has riding fastball which can sink, also outstanding curve.

CAREER: Acquired by 2nd round pick in the secondary phase of the June, 1983 free agent draft . . . had been selected by the Baltimore Orioles in the 1st round of January, 1983 free agent draft . . . On July 25, 1983 pitched a no-hitter against Geneva Cubs as Oneonta won the game 1-0.

PERSONAL/MISCELLANEOUS: Bill was signed by Murray Cook.

Pitched 5-0 no-hit victory against Lakeland, July 2, 1985.
Pitched 1-0 no-hit victory against Geneva, July 25, 1983.

YR	CLUB	W-L	ERA	G	GS	CG	Sho	SV	IP	H	R	ER	BB	SO
1983	Oneonta	4-7	3.74	14	13	4	1	0	84.1	73	49	35	35	77
1984	Greensboro	2-3	4.15	10	8	3	0	0	52.0	45	26	24	26	29
1985	Ft. Lauderdale	11-2	1.61	15	15	9	1	0	112.0	91	31	20	30	71
Minor League Totals		**17-12**	**2.86**	**39**	**36**	**16**	**2**	**0**	**248.1**	**209**	**106**	**79**	**91**	**177**

Selected by Baltimore Orioles' organization in 1st round of free-agent draft, January, 1983.
Selected by New York Yankees' organization in 2nd round (secondary phase) of free-agent draft, 1983.

GEORGE, STEPHEN EDWARD "Steve"   (LHP)   #52

6-0, 160. Born 10/18/61 in St. Louis, MO. Age 24, turns 25 October 18. Resides in Pompano Beach, FL. BS. TL. College: Florida Southern.

CONTRACT STATUS: Signed 1-year contract for 1986 season.

1985 SEASON: Led Florida State League with five shutouts and 12 complete games ... Finished second in FSL with 141 Ks ... Threw five inning no hitter vs. Miami, August 14 ... Named to FSL All-Star team ... Led Ft. Lauderdale with 13 wins, 164.2 innings pitched, 14 strikeouts; second with 24 games started ... Has sneaky fastball and good slider ... Had .201 batting average against.

CAREER: The lefty was used primarily as a reliever in his first three minor league seasons ... led the Greensboro club in games with 35 in 1983 ... was signed by Fred Ferreira.

PERSONAL/MISCELLANEOUS: Graduated from Deerfield Senior H.S. in 1979 before attending Florida Southern College.

YR	CLUB	W-L	ERA	G	GS	CG	Sho	SV	IP	H	R	ER	BB	SO
1982	Paintsville	3-4	4.97	13	7	2	0	1	63.1	62	45	35	38	64
1983	Greensboro	5-4	5.04	35	9	0	0	4	84.0	93	65	47	64	78
1984	Greensboro	2-4	5.18	24	3	0	0	0	48.2	30	31	28	55	46
1985	Ft. Lauderdale	13-7	1.75	24	24	12*	5*	0	164.2	120	48	32	76	141
Minor League Totals		**23-19**	**3.54**	**96**	**43**	**14**	**5**	**5**	**360.2**	**305**	**189**	**142**	**233**	**329**

Selected by New York Yankees' organization in 15th round of free-agent draft, June, 1982.

GRIFFEY, GEORGE KENNETH "Ken"   (OF-1B)   #33

6-0, 200. Born 4/10/50 in Donora, PA. Age 35, turns 36 April 10. Resides in Westchester, OH. BL. TL. Married: Alberta Littleton 9/4/69. Children: George, Jr. (16½), Craig (15).

MAJOR LEAGUE SERVICE: 11 years and 171 days.

CONTRACT STATUS: Signed 6-year contract (with option for 7th) in 1981 ... contract extends thru 1987 season ('88 with option).

1985 SEASON: His 1985 season was an overall improvement over '84, posting better numbers in most offensive categories ... Although his season BA was .274, he remains one of only 12 active lifetime .300 hitters (with at least 10 seasons or 1000 hits), now at .2996, or .300 ... His 1985 may be best remembered for "the catch of the year", robbing Boston's Marty Barrett of a game tying, 9th inning HR August 19 at Yankee Stadium, leaping high above the leftfield wall and landing in a somersault ... Placed on 15-day DL with sprained left wrist, June 1, retroactive to May 28, activated June 12 ... Played in 1500th career game August 12 @ Chicago ... Final HR of year, September 22 @ Baltimore off Ken Dixon, was career no. 100 ... 5 of his 10 HRs were hit off Minnesota pitching ... Hit two 3-run HRs July 7 (2nd game) vs. Minnesota—the 6 RBIs matched his career high, and equalled Winfield for the team single game high ... Also had 5 RBIs May 8 @ Minnesota ... Hit 3rd career Grand Slam, 2nd as Yankee, May 14 off Minnesota's Curt Wardle ... Hit 6th inning pinch-hit HR May 5 off K.C.'s Joe Beckwith ... Had 11 game hit streak July 4-18 ... Had 35 multiple hit games—5th high on team.

CAREER: In 1984 recorded 1,500th hit of his career, June 12 at Boston ... In 1983 was simply outstanding in his 2nd season as Yankee ... batted over .300 entire year, ranking among league leaders ... In 1982, batted .277 in his 1st season in pinstripes, 30 points below his previous major league average ... however, turned things around at the plate in his last 38 games, batting .341 (47-138) with 7 HRs and 29 RBI, raising his batting average from .251 on August 17th ... on August 18 started on 13 game hitting streak in which he raised his batting average 20 points, the 13 game streak being the longest by a Yankee in 1982 ... in 1980 was Reds' MVP and MVP of All-Star game ... missed end of 1979 season with mid-August operation on left knee and thigh bone ... '72 named to Eastern League All-Star team and in '73 to American Association All-Star team.

PERSONAL/MISCELLANEOUS: Born and grew up in Donora, PA, birthplace of Stan Musial.

Tied Major League record for most at-bats, game, since 1900, 7, June 13, 1975.

Tied for Eastern League lead in double plays by outfielders with 6 and tied for lead in errors by outfielders with 15 in 1972.
Led Gulf Coast League outfielders in errors with 10 in 1969.

YR	Club	AVG	G	AB	R	H	2B	3B	HR	RBI	BB	SO	SB
1969	Bradenton	.281	49	153	22	43	11*	1	1	12	18	35	11
1970	Sioux Falls	.244	51	164	20	40	2	1	2	24	23	41	10
1971	Tampa	.342	88	281	60	96	7	11	3	33	43	54	25
	Three Rivers	.406	9	32	1	13	1	2	0	4	1	10	4
1972	Three Rivers	.318	128	472	96*	150	21	3	14	52	55	93	31
1973	Indianapolis	.327	107	397	88	130	18	5	10	58	51	84	43*
	CINCINNATI	.384	25	86	19	33	5	1	3	14	6	10	4
1974	Indianapolis	.333	43	162	34	54	6	4	5	18	18	26	12
	CINCINNATI	.251	88	227	24	57	9	5	2	19	27	43	9
1975	CINCINNATI	.305	132	463	95	141	15	9	4	46	67	67	16
1976	CINCINNATI	.336	148	562	111	189	28	9	6	74	62	65	34
1977	CINCINNATI	.318	154	585	117	186	35	8	12	57	69	84	17
1978	CINCINNATI	.288	158	614	90	177	33	8	10	63	54	70	23
1979	CINCINNATI-a	.316	95	380	62	120	27	4	8	32	36	39	12
1980	CINCINNATI	.294	146	544	89	160	28	10	13	85	62	77	23
1981	CINCINNATI-b	.311	101	396	65	123	21	6	2	34	39	42	12
1982	YANKEES	.277	127	484	70	134	23	2	12	54	39	58	10
1983	YANKEES-c	.306	118	458	60	140	21	3	11	46	34	45	5
1984	YANKEES	.273	120	399	44	109	20	1	7	56	29	32	2
1985	YANKEES-d	.274	127	438	68	120	28	4	10	69	41	51	7
Minor League Totals		.317	475	1661	321	526	71	27	35	201	209	343	136
N.Y.Y. Totals		.283	492	1779	242	503	92	10	40	225	143	186	24
N.L. Totals		.307	1047	3857	672	1186	201	60	60	424	422	397	150
M.L. Totals		.300	1539	5636	914	1689	293	70	100	649	565	583	174

GWRBI: 1980-13; 1981-3; 1982-9; 1983-7; 1984-5; 1985-6. Total-43.

Selected by Cincinnati Reds' organization in 29th round of free-agent draft, June 5, 1969.
a-On disabled list, August 14 to September 7, 1979.
b-Traded to New York Yankees for pitcher Brian Ryder and a player to be named later, November 4, 1981. Cincinnati Reds' organization acquired pitcher Fred Toliver to complete deal, December 10, 1981.
c-On disabled list, July 2 to August 2 with pulled hamstring.
d-On disabled list, May 28 to June 12, with sprained left wrist.

CHAMPIONSHIP SERIES RECORD

Tied Championship Series record for most stolen bases, game (3), October 5, 1975.

YR	Club, Opp.	AVG	G	AB	R	H	2B	3B	HR	RBI	BB	SO	SB
1973	Cin. vs N.Y.	.143	3	7	0	1	1	0	0	0	0	1	0
1975	Cin. vs Pitt.	.333	3	12	3	4	1	0	0	4	0	3	3
1976	Cin. vs Phil.	.385	3	13	2	5	0	1	0	2	2	1	2
L.C.S. Totals		.313	9	32	5	10	2	1	0	6	2	5	5

WORLD SERIES RECORD

Tied World Series record for fewest chances accepted by outfielder, extra-inning game (9), October 21, 1975 (12 innings); most at-bats, game no hits (5), October 21, 1976.

YR	Club, Opp.	AVG	G	AB	R	H	2B	3B	HR	RBI	BB	SO	SB
1975	Cin. vs Bos.	.269	7	26	4	7	3	1	0	4	4	2	2
1976	Cin. vs N.Y.	.059	4	17	2	1	0	0	0	1	0	1	1
W.S. Totals		.186	11	43	6	8	3	1	0	5	4	3	3

ALL-STAR GAME RECORD

YR	Club, Site	AVG	G	AB	R	H	2B	3B	HR	RBI	BB	SO	SB
1976	N.L., Phil.	1.000	1	1	1	1	0	0	0	1	0	0	0
1977	N.L., N.Y. (AL)				(Selected, did not play)								
1980	N.L., S.D.	.667	1	3	1	2	0	0	1	1	0	0	0
A.S.G. Totals		.750	2	4	2	3	0	0	1	2	0	0	0

YANKEE PLAYER REPRESENTATIVES

1946	Johnny Murphy	1974	Bobby Murcer
1947-54	Allie Reynolds	1975	George Medich
1955-57	Jerry Coleman		Ed Herrmann
1958-60	Bob Turley	1976	Larry Gura
1960-61	Bobby Richardson		Dock Ellis
1962	Whitey Ford	1977	Ken Holtzman
1963-66	Clete Boyer	1978-81	Reggie Jackson
1967	Mel Stottlemyre	1982	Tommy John,
1967-70	Steve Hamilton		Dave Winfield
1970-72	Jack Aker	1983-84	Don Baylor
1972-73	Bernie Allen	1985	Dave Winfield
1973-74	Mike Hegan		

1985 vs. OPPONENTS

Club	AB	H	HR	RBI	AVG
Baltimore	33	11	2	7	.333
Boston	45	17	0	7	.378
Cleveland	34	7	0	0	.206
Detroit	41	12	0	7	.293
Milwaukee	23	5	1	4	.217
Toronto	28	3	1	3	.107
California	33	8	0	1	.242
Chicago	36	11	0	6	.306
Kansas City	27	10	1	5	.370
Minnesota	52	17	5	17	.327
Oakland	21	4	0	3	.190
Seattle	22	3	0	5	.136
Texas	43	12	0	4	.279
1st Half	228	59	6	37	.259
2nd Half	210	61	4	32	.290
vs. LHP	108	26	2	18	.241
vs. RHP	330	94	8	51	.285
Home	195	57	6	32	.292
Away	243	63	4	37	.259

GRIFFEY'S BESTS

	Season
AVG.	.336–1976
H	189–1976
HR	13–1980
RBI	85–1980
SB	34–1976
Hit Strk	16 games–1977

	Game
H	5–vs. Chi. (N) 7-28-77
HR	2–last time: vs. Minn.(2) 7-7-85
RBI	6–last time: vs. Minn.(2) 7-7-85
SB	4–5-30-76 (1st game)

GUIDRY, RONALD AMES
"Ron" "Louisiana Lightning" (LHP)   #49

5-11, 157. Born 8/28/50 in Lafayette, LA, where he resides. Age 35, turns 36 August 28. BL. TL. Married: Bonnie Rutledge 9/23/72. Children: Jamie (9), Brandon (6), Danielle (1). College: University of Southwestern Louisiana.

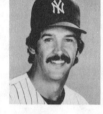

MAJOR LEAGUE SERVICE: 10 years and 4 days.

CONTRACT STATUS: Signed 4-year contract (with option for 5th) on December 15, 1981 ... contract extends thru 1986 season.

1985 SEASON: In 1985, answered questions raised by his 10-11 season of '84 and re-established himself as the staff ace ... began season with 6-3 win at Cleveland on April 13, first win of '85 for Yankees who had dropped 3-game series in Boston ... lost next 3 starts, but on May 4 vs. KC, pitched complete game 5-2 win, starting him on a 12-game win streak that upped his record to 13-3 on July 20 ... over the 12-game win streak: 16 G, 15 GS, 123.2 IP, 94 H, 34 R, 30 ER, 8 HR, 16 W, 58 Ks, 2.18 ERA ... win streak ended w/ 6-5 loss @ Cleveland 7/31 ... would have been selected to All-Star team but declined because he would have been unavailable to pitch in game ... on June 17 @ Baltimore, pitched his 25th career shutout ... in next appearance threw another shutout, June 22 @ Detroit ... struckout season high 10, 10/3 vs. Baltimore ... made one relief appearance, May 17 @ California, retiring Reggie Jackson, and was part of combo shutout with Phil Niekro and Don Cooper ... won 20th game on September 22 @ Baltimore, 1st in AL in '85 and became only 7th Yankee to win 20 games 3 times ... Guidry won 9 of last 11 decisions, 6 of last 7 including the last three straight ... allowed 5 HRs 9/17 @ Detroit a career high (gave up 4 HR 5/28/82 @ Minnesota) ... opposing hitters combined for a .248 BA vs. Guidry ... had .976 fielding percentage committing just 1 E in 41 TC ... authored 3 4-hitters: 5/4 vs. KC, 6/22 @ Detroit, 7/14 vs. Texas ... 9-4 3.77 ERA on road w/ .243 BA against, 20 W, 65 Ks, 13-2, 2.82 ERA; at YS with .252 BA against 22 W, 78 Ks, 10-0, 2.42 ERA ... during day .220 BA against, 12 W, 48 Ks, 12-6, 3.63 ERA ... night, .259 BA against, 30 W, 95 K's ... K's 100+ batters for 9th straight year ... pitched 2000th career inning, 9/17 @ Detroit (3rd inning) ... notched 1500th career K, 9/28 vs. Baltimore 7 inning, K of Lee Lacy ... on Yankee All-Time Lists: moved to 12th with 304 games; 8th with 2027 IP; remains 8th with 154 wins; now 3rd with .700 W/L percentage; now 3rd with 1510 Ks; T 6th with 26 shutouts; 17th 88 CG; 15th 3.17 ERA.

CAREER: 1984—Moved into 4th place on the All-Time Yankee strikeout list, when he K'd his 1258th batter during a 4-1 CG victory over Texas, April 20 ... his best performance came in a highlight filled August 7 game, when Ron blanked the White Sox 7-0 on 4-hits, striking out a season high 13 (also team season high, later tied by Joe Cowley). The win was Gator's career #132, moving him up to 8th on that All-Time Yankee list, and career shutout #24, which tied him for 7th on that Yankee list. He ended this game of personal milestones by striking out the side in the ninth on nine pitches, tying a major league record ... placed on DL, for the first time in his career, with an inflamed rib cartilage ... made first relief appearance since July 21, 1982 on September 17 vs. Baltimore ... 1983—led A.L. with 21 CG (most of his career), 3rd with 21 wins, T4th with 3 shutouts, T5th with .700 W-L%, 6th with 156 K's, 7th with 250.1 IP, and 12th with 3.42 ERA ... won 6 straight starts

August 19 to September 14 ... named to 4th A.L. All-Star team, but did not play due to lower back strain ... won second consecutive Gold Glove Award with 1.000 fielding pct.... played center-field for 1/3 inning in the August 18 conclusion of the "Pine Tar" game ... also named to Sporting News All-Star team ... 1982—jumped off to fast start, posting 8-1 record by June 14 ... won his 100th M.L. game August 31 at Minnesota ... 1981—was A.L. Pitcher of the Month in August (4-0, 0.37 ERA) ... broke little finger on right hand on comebacker, 8/23, but played with splint, not missing any starts ... 1980—reached 100th career decision (72-28), matching Maglie, Raschi, Chandler, & Reulbach behind Ford's 74-26 for second best record ever through 1st 100 decisions ... 1979—won second straight ERA title ... named to UPI All-Star team ... played inning in centerfield vs Toronto, 9/29//79 ... 1978— a dream season for any pitcher ... won Cy Young Award, finished second in MVP voting (to Jim Rice), and set numerous records (see below) ... set Yankee record for most consecutive wins to start season, winning first 13, breaking record of Atley Donald, the scout that signed Guidry ... his 9 shutouts tied Babe Ruth's A.L. record for most by lefty, set in 1916 ... Yankees won 30 of 35 games he started, scoring only 7 runs in the 5 losses ... opposing batters hit only .193 ... struckout 10 or more in 8 games, including a club record 18 vs California, 6/17, breaking Bob Shawkey's record of 15 set in 1919 ... 248 strikeouts is a club record ... his 1.75 ERA was lowest by major leaguer since Koufax' 1.73 in '66 ... 15 wins followed Yankee losses ... was unanimous choice for Cy Young Award (only other unanimous choice was Denny McLain in 1968) ... named Sporting News Man of the Year, TSN Player of the Year, A.P. Male Athlete of the Year, Baseball Quarterly Performer of the Year ... named to A.L., A.P., UPI, & TSN All-Star teams ... 1977— was first full year with Yankees ... used in relief in 6 of first 7 appearances, but ended year with 24 straight starts ... has 5th best All-Time Yankee W-L% (.680, 132-62) among pitchers with 100 or more wins.

PERSONAL/MISCELLANEOUS: Named Outstanding Track Man for 2 years at Northside High where they had no baseball team ... hurled no-hitter and named to Gulf States All-Stars at Southwestern Louisiana where he majored in architecture ... named 1984 Roberto Clemente Award winner as player who "best exemplifies the game of baseball both on and off the field" ... has been active in the Special Olympics program, assisting their chapters around the country ... was Honorary Fund Raising Chairman for 1983 International Summer Olympic Games ... points to his service to humanity as being the best work of his life ... enjoys hunting, chess, studying chess, and is quite proficient at playing the drums ... biggest thrill was 18 strikeout game ... grew up a Yankee and Whitey Ford fan.

Won Cy Young Award (by unanimous vote), 1978.

Established major league record for highest winning percentage, lifetime (minimum; 200 decisions), .694.

Established major league record for highest winning percentage, season, 20 or more wins (.893), 1978.

Established American League record for most strikeouts by lefthanded pitcher, game (18), June 17, 1978.

Tied American League record for most shutouts by lefthander, season, (9), 1978.

Won American League Gold Glove as pitcher, 1983, 1984, 1985.

YR	CLUB	W-L	ERA	G	GS	CG	Sho	SV	IP	H	R	ER	BB	SO
1971	Johnson City	2-2	2.11	7	7	2	2	0	47	34	13	11	27	61
1972	Ft. Lauderdale-a	2-4	3.82	15	13	1	1	0	66	53	35	28	50	61
1973	Kinston-b	7-6	3.21	20	16	2	1	1	101	85	53	36	70	97
1974	West Haven-c	2-4	5.26	37	8	1	0	2	77	80	48	45	53	79
1975	Syracuse	6-5	2.90	42	0	0	0	14	62	46	24	20	37	76
	YANKEES	0-1	3.38	10	1	0	0	0	16	15	6	6	9	15
1976	Syracuse	5-1	0.68	22	0	0	0	9	40	16	5	3	13	50
	YANKEES	0-0	5.63	7	0	0	0	0	16	20	12	10	4	12
1977	YANKEES	16-7	2.82	31	25	9	5	1	211	174	72	66	65	176
1978	YANKEES	*25-3	1.74*	35	35	16	9*	0	274	187	61	53	72	248
1979	YANKEES-a	18-8	2.78*	33	30	15	2	2	236	203	83	73	71	201
1980	YANKEES	17-10	3.56	37	29	5	3	1	220	215	97	87	80	166
1981	YANKEES-d	11-5	2.76	23	21	0	0	0	127	100	41	39	26	104
1982	YANKEES	14-8	3.81	34	33	6	1	0	222	216	104	94	69	162
1983	YANKEES	21-9	3.42	31	31	21	3	0	250.1	232	99	95	60	156
1984	YANKEES-e	10-11	4.51	29	28	5	1	0	195.2	223	102	98	44	127
1985	YANKEES	*22-6	3.27	34	33	11	2	0	259.0	243	104	94	42	143
Minor League Totals		**24-22**	**3.27**	**143**	**44**	**6**	**3**	**26**	**393.0**	**314**	**178**	**143**	**250**	**424**
M.L. Totals		**154-68**	**3.17**	**304**	**266**	**88**	**26**	**4**	**2027.0**	**1828**	**781**	**715**	**542**	**1510**

Selected by New York Yankees' organization in 3rd round of free-agent draft, June 8, 1971.
a-Played in one game as an outfielder.
b-On temporary inactive list, July 13 to August 3, 1973.
c-Appeared as an outfielder.
d-Granted free agency, November 13, 1981; Signed by New York Yankees, December 15, 1981.
e-On disabled list, August 16 to September 3, 1984.

DID YOU KNOW ... that the Yankees hit 13 homeruns in a doubleheader against the Philadelphia Athletics on June 28, 1939?

DIVISION SERIES RECORD

YR	CLUB, Opp.	W-L	ERA	G	GS	CG	Sho	SV	IP	H	R	ER	BB	SO
1981	N.Y. vs Mil.	0-0	5.40	2	2	0	0	0	8.1	11	5	5	3	8

CHAMPIONSHIP SERIES RECORD

YR	CLUB, Opp.	W-L	ERA	G	GS	CG	Sho	SV	IP	H	R	ER	BB	SO
1976	N.Y. vs K.C.			(Appeared in one game as pinch runner)										
1977	N.Y. vs K.C.	1-0	3.97	2	2	1	0	0	11.1	9	5	5	3	8
1978	N.Y. vs K.C.	1-0	1.12	1	1	0	0	0	8.0	7	1	1	1	7
1980	N.Y. vs K.C.	0-1	12.00	1	1	0	0	0	3.0	5	4	4	4	2
1981	N.Y. vs Oak.			(Eligible, did not appear)										
L.C.S. Totals		2-1	4.03	5	4	1	0	0	22.1	21	10	10	8	17

WORLD SERIES RECORD

YR	CLUB, Opp.	W-L	ERA	G	GS	CG	Sho	SV	IP	H	R	ER	BB	SO
1976	N.Y. vs Cin.			(Eligible, did not appear)										
1977	N.Y. vs L.A.	1-0	2.00	1	1	1	0	0	9.0	4	2	2	3	7
1978	N.Y. vs L.A.	1-0	1.00	1	1	1	0	0	9.0	8	1	1	7	4
1981	N.Y. vs L.A.	1-1	1.93	2	2	0	0	0	14.0	8	3	3	4	15
W.S. Totals		3-1	1.69	4	4	2	0	0	32.0	20	6	6	14	26

ALL-STAR GAME RECORD

YR	CLUB, Site	W-L	ERA	G	GS	CG	Sho	SV	IP	H	R	ER	BB	SO
1978	A.L., S.D.	0-0	0.00	1	0	0	0	0	.1	0	0	0	0	0
1979	A.L., Sea.	0-0	0.00	1	0	0	0	0	.1	0	0	0	1	0
1982	A.L., Mont.			(Selected, did not appear)										
1983	A.L., Chi. (AL)			(Selected, replaced due to injury)										
A.S.G. Totals		0-0	0.00	2	0	0	0	0	.2	0	0	0	1	0

		1985						CAREER					
ERA	W-L-S	G	IP	H	ER	Club	ERA	W-L-S	G	IP	H	ER
3.12	3-0-1	3	26.0	23	9	Baltimore	3.66	10-7-1	27	164.2	142	67
3.13	2-1-0	3	23.0	24	8	Boston	3.20	13-5-2	27	183.0	178	65
2.16	0-0-0	2	8.1	8	2	California	2.93	7-6-4	22	126.0	107	41
3.00	1-0-0	1	9.0	9	3	Chicago	3.46	11-4-3	23	150.2	134	58
3.74	1-2-0	3	21.2	22	9	Cleveland	2.96	10-6-1	21	146.0	133	48
4.20	1-1-1	2	15.0	12	7	Detroit	3.53	16-9-4	31	206.2	195	81
2.92	3-0-0	3	24.2	21	8	Kansas City	3.27	14-4-2	20	129.1	113	47
3.66	2-0-0	3	19.2	22	8	Milwaukee	3.89	8-7-2	21	134.1	136	58
2.50	2-0-0	2	18.0	13	5	Minnesota	2.97	16-4-2	26	200.0	188	66
1.88	2-1-0	3	24.0	22	5	Oakland	2.56	17-4-2	23	165.1	140	47
3.27	3-0-0	3	22.0	19	8	Seattle	3.04	11-3-0	22	124.1	108	42
4.73	1-1-0	4	32.1	31	17	Texas	2.81	12-4-1	21	157.0	134	49
2.93	1-0-0	2	15.1	17	5	Toronto	2.93	9-5-2	20	141.1	122	46
3.27	22-6-2	34	259.0	243	94	Total						
2.82	13-2-0	17	137.1	132	43	Home						
3.77	9-4-2	17	121.2	111	51	Road						

4—3 times
10—10/3/86 vs Balt.
12—

Low Hit	2—6 Times
K-High	18—6/17/78 vs. California
Win Streak	13—1978

S = SHUTOUTS

HENDERSON, RICKEY HENLEY (OF) #24

5-10, 195. Born 12/25/58 at Chicago, IL. Age 27, turns 28 on December 25. Resides in Oakland, CA. BR. TL. Single.

MAJOR LEAGUE SERVICE: 6 years and 101 days.

CONTRACT STATUS: Signed 5-year contract on December 8, 1984 ... contract extends through 1989 season.

1985 SEASON: More than the perfect lead-off hitter, a slugging dimension was added to his game ... Began 1985 on the 15-day disabled list with a sprained left ankle, suffered in an exhibition game vs. Boston, March 31—activated April 22, missing 10 games ... Set new career highs in HRs (24) & RBIs (72) ... His .314 BA was 4th in A.L. ... Led A.L. in runs scored for a second time (146)—the highest single season M.L. total since Ted Williams scored 150 runs in 1949—most runs by a Yankee since Joe DiMaggio scored 151 in 1937 ... 80 stolen bases led A.L. for 6th straight season (see STOLEN BASE section) ... 99 walks was 4th in A.L. and most by a Yankee since Willie Randolph led the league with 119 in 1980 .... .419 on base pct.—4th in A.L., a career high ... .516 slugging pct.—7th in A.L., also a career high ... Had 1st career 5-hit game, June 17 @ Baltimore (matched league high) ... Scored 4 runs in game for 2nd & 3rd times in career: July 10 vs. K.C. & September 25 vs. Detroit (also equalled A.L. high)—he and Oakland's Mike Davis were only players with two 4-run games ... Set A.L. single season record with 7 leadoff HRs ... Is first player in A.L. history to hit 20+ HRs and steal 50+ bases ... Had first career 2-HR games: June 21 @ Detroit & July 30 (2nd game) @ Cleveland ... Played one game as DH, going 0-for-4, July 23 @ K.C. ... 0-for-1 as PH ... Lined into a triple play, May 3 vs. K.C. ... Had two 11-game hitting streaks: April 29-May 12, 18-for-44, .409 BA, with 13 runs, 4 doubles, 1 HR, 5 RBIs; August 5-21, 17-for-46, .370 BA, with 13 runs, 2 doubles, 4 HRs, 11 RBIs ... Also had 10 game hit streak, September 18-29, 14-for-38, .368 BA, with 15 runs, 6 doubles, 1 triple, 1 HR ... His season BA peaked @ .361, July 10—the conclusion of a 7-game hitting streak which began July 4, going 12-for-26, .462 BA ... Was A.L. Player of the Month for June: 27 games, 47-for-113, .416 BA, 31 runs, 4 doubles, 2 triples, 6 HRs, 17 RBIs, 22 SBs—failed to hit in just 4 of the 27 games ... Homered in consecutive games: June 20-21 (3 HRs in 2 games); July 27-28; August 19-21 (3 HRs, 3 games) ... Scored at least 1 run in 101 of 143 games played ... Hit only .200 through his first 10 games ... Was hitting .357 at All-Star break (July 13), with 77 runs, 11 HRs, 37 RBIs, 41 SBs ... Post ASB hit .270, with 69 runs, 13 HRs, 35 RBIs, 39 SBs ... From August 22 through September 7, played 16 games, 9-for-51, .176, with 14 runs, 1 double, 0 HRs, 2 RBIs—dropping BA from .350 to .327 ... Went 2-for-24, .083 over last 7 games, BA falling from .325 to .314.

HENDERSON'S STOLEN BASES: Set a new Yankee single season stolen base record when he collected SB no. 75, September 25 vs. Detroit (Lance Parrish catching), breaking the record of 74 set by Fritz Maisel in 1914 ... Stole 500th career base May 10 @ K.C.—youngest player to reach this goal ... If he maintains his current average of 82 SBs per season, would be youngest player to reach 600 mark, during '86 ... Moved from 31st to 19th on All-Time SB list, with 573 for career ... Passed Cesar Cedeno as current active leader ... Improved career SB success ratio to 79% (148 career CS) ... Stole 4 bases June 26 vs. Baltimore ... Was successful in first 13 SB attempts before being caught by California's Bob Boone, May 29—went on to steal 22 straight before next CS, June 26 ... CS only three times by catchers: Boone, May 29; Carlton Fisk, August 12 @ Chicago; & Rich Gedman, August 19 vs. Boston ... Successful 14 of 16 attempts stealing third base ... Set new A.L. record for most consecutive years, 50+ stolen bases (6) ... Was 29-for-33 with none out; 30-for-34 with 1-out; 21-for-23 with 2-out ... Was 61-for-66 with NY ± 0, 1 or 2 runs and 15-for-16 with NY ± 0, 1 or 2 runs after the 6th inning.

1985 ALL-STAR TEAMS & AWARDS

Seagram's A.L. All-Star Team
The Sporting News A.L. All-Star Team
The Sporting News Silver Slugger Team
Associated Press A.L. All-Star Team
1985 American League All-Star Team

CAREER: 1976—reported to Boise after June draft, hitting .336 with 29 steals in 36 attempts ... **1977**—at Modesto, led the California League with a then record 95 steals ... was third with .345 BA, and 104 walks ... led league outfielders in total chances (313) ... named to league All-Star team, and was Modesto MVP ... became fourth player in professional baseball to steal 7 bases in one game, May 26 at Fresno ... **1978**—led Eastern League with 81 steals ... led league outfielders in double plays (4), and assists (15) ... named to Eastern League All-Star team ... **1979**—stole 44 bases in only 71 PCL games with Ogden, finishing fourth ... immediately stepped into Oakland's starting lineup when called up June 23 ... led A's with 33 steals ... **1980**—became the first A.L. player and third big leaguer to steal 100 bases in a season ... broke Ty Cobb's A.L. mark of 96 that year ... was second in league with 117 walks, third in on-base pct. (.422), and fourth in runs scored (111) ... **1981**—named to Sporting News All-Star team, and won his first Gold Glove Award ... led A.L. in hits (135), runs (89), and steals (56) ... finished fourth in league batting race (.319) ... third in on-base-pct. (.411) ... hit .364 against new mates in League Championship Series ... **1982**—he broke Lou Brock's remarkable record of 118 stolen bases on August 27th at Milwaukee—went on to steal 130 total bases ... led A.L. in walks (116) ... third in one-base-pct. (.399) ... walked 5 times vs. Angels April 8—a career best ... **1983**—went over the 100 steal mark for the third time in his career (108)—Rickey is the only player to do it more than once in a career ... stole 66 bases in 77 attempts after the All-Star break, winning his fourth consecutive title ... also hit .327 after the break to wind up at .292 ... .415 on-base-pct. was second to Wade Boggs ... fourth in runs (105) ... tied A.L. mark by stealing 7 bases in 2 straight games, July 3-4, vs. Texas ... became youngest player in baseball to steal 400 bases, August 21 in Milwaukee ... **1984**—his 66 stolen bases led the American League for a fifth straight year ... He was second in the A.L. with 113 runs, and third in on-base-pcts., .339.

PERSONAL/MISCELLANEOUS: Averaged 82 stolen bases per year over 6 major league seasons, and has a career success rate of 78% ... 31st on the All-Time

HENDERSON (continued)

stolen base list & with Joe Morgan's retirement, becomes the active leader with 493 base thefts ... 3 stolen bases would move him to 30th on the All-Time list, and 7 swipes will make him only the 30th player to reach the 500 plateau—he would also be the youngest player to achieve this height ... a Rickey Henderson/Willie Randolph 1-2 batting combination, has averaged 104 stolen bases, and 163 walks a season ... graduated from Oakland's Technical High School in 1976 ... played baseball, basketball, and football ... was All-Oakland Athletic League for 3 years in baseball ... as a senior hit .465 and stole 30 bases ... that year played for the North team in California's annual high school All-Star game at Anaheim Stadium ... in football, rushed for 1,100 yards his senior year, and received a reported two dozen scholarship offers to play football ... hobbies include swimming and fishing ... an Oakland, CA resident, Rickey is not married.

YANKEES' STOLEN BASE NOTES: Most stolen bases by a Yankee, career, is 248—Hal Chase, 1905-1913.

Established modern major league record for most stolen bases, season (130), 1982.

Established major league record for most times caught stealing, season (42), 1982.

Established American League record for most home runs as leadoff batter, season, 7, 1985.

Tied American League record for most stolen bases, two consecutive games (7), July 3, 4, 1983.

Major League caught stealing: 1979–11, 1980–26*, 1981–22*, 1982–42*, 1983–19*, 1984–18*, and 1985-3. Total–141.

Led American League outfielders in putouts with 327 and total chances with 341 in 1981.

Led Eastern League outfielders in double plays with 4 and tied for lead in assists with 15 in 1978.

Led California League outfielders in errors with 20 in 1977.

Led Northwest League outfielders in errors with 12 in 1976.

Won American League Gold Glove as outfielder in 1981.

Won American League Silver Bat as outfielder in 1981.

YR	Club	AVG	G	AB	R	H	2B	3B	HR	RBI	BB	SO	SB
1976	Boise	.336	46	140	34	47	13	2	3	23	33	32	29
1977	Modesto	.345	134	481	120	166	18	4	11	69	104	67	95*
1978	Jersey City	.310	129	439	80	136	13	4	0	33	83	65	81*
1979	Ogden	.309	71	259	66	80	11	8	3	26	53	41	44
	OAKLAND	.274	89	351	49	96	13	3	1	26	34	39	33
1980	OAKLAND	.303	158	591	111	179	22	4	9	53	117	54	100*
1981	OAKLAND	.319	108	423	89*	135*	18	7	6	35	64	68	56*
1982	OAKLAND	.267	149	536	119	143	24	4	10	51	116*	94	130*
1983	OAKLAND	.292	145	513	105	150	25	7	9	48	103*	80	108*
1984	OAKLAND-a	.293	142	502	113	147	27	4	16	58	86	81	66*
1985	Ft. Lauderdale	.167	3	6	5	1	0	1	0	3	5	2	1
	YANKEES-b	.314	143	547	146	172	28	5	24	72	99	65	80*
Minor League Totals		**.325**	**383**	**1325**	**305**	**430**	**55**	**19**	**17**	**154**	**278**	**207**	**250**
M.L. Totals		**.295**	**934**	**3463**	**732**	**1022**	**157**	**34**	**75**	**343**	**619**	**481**	**573**

GWRBI: 1980-4; 1981-7; 1982-5; 1983-6; 1984-4; 1985-6. Total-32.

Selected by Oakland A's organization in 4th round of free-agent draft, June 8, 1976.
a-Traded to Oakland Athletics with pitcher Bert Bradley to New York Yankees for pitchers Jay Howell, Jose Rijo, Eric Plunk and Tim Birtsas and outfielder Stan Javier, December 8, 1984.
b-On disabled list, March 30 through April 22; including rehabilitation assignment to Ft. Lauderdale, April 19 through 22 with sprained left ankle.

DIVISION SERIES RECORD

YR	Club, Opp.	AVG	G	AB	R	H	2B	3B	HR	RBI	BB	SO	SB
1981	Oak. vs K.C.	.182	3	11	3	2	0	0	0	0	2	0	2

CHAMPIONSHIP SERIES RECORD

YR	Club, Opp.	AVG	G	AB	R	H	2B	3B	HR	RBI	BB	SO	SB
1981	Oak. vs N.Y.	.364	3	11	0	4	2	1	0	1	1	2	2

ALL-STAR GAME RECORD

YR	Club, Site	AVG	G	AB	R	H	2B	3B	HR	RBI	BB	SO	SB
1980	A.L., L.A.	.000	1	1	0	0	0	0	0	0	0	1	0
1982	A.L., Mon.	.750	1	4	1	3	0	0	0	0	0	0	1
1983	A.L., Chi. (A)	.000	1	1	0	0	0	0	0	1	0	0	0
1984	A.L., S.F.	.000	1	2	0	0	0	0	0	0	0	1	0
1985	A.L., Min.	.333	1	3	1	1	0	0	0	0	0	1	1
A.S.G. Totals		**.364**	**5**	**11**	**2**	**4**	**0**	**0**	**0**	**1**	**0**	**2**	**2**

DID YOU KNOW ... that the 1936 Yankees had five players with 100 or more RBI? (Gehrig 152, DiMaggio 125, Lazzeri 109, Dickey 107 and Selkirk 107)

1985 vs. OPPONENTS

Club	AB	H	HR	RBI	AVG
Baltimore	50	23	1	10	.460
Boston	36	9	1	4	.250
Cleveland	23	7	2	4	.304
Detroit	46	15	4	8	.326
Milwaukee	55	12	2	5	.218
Toronto	46	12	2	5	.261
California	40	8	2	6	.200
Chicago	38	11	2	8	.289
Kansas City	48	18	1	6	.375
Minnesota	36	15	2	3	.417
Oakland	45	13	1	2	.289
Seattle	48	16	2	7	.333
Texas	36	13	2	4	.361
1st Half	277	99	11	37	.357
2nd Half	270	73	13	35	.270
vs. LHP	181	65	12	25	.359
vs. RHP	366	107	12	47	.292
Home	246	75	8	22	.305
Away	301	97	16	50	.322

HENDERSON'S BESTS

Season

AVG.	.319–1981
H	179–1980
HR	24–1985
RBI	72–1985
SB	130–1982
Hit Strk	14 games–1980

Game

H	5–at Balt. 6/17/85
HR	2–last time at Clev. (2) 7/30/85
RBI	4—last time at Sea. 5/21/85
SB	4–10 times-Last time vs. Balt. 6/26/85
BB	5–vs. California 4-8-82

LOMBARDI, PHILLIP ARDEN "Phil" (C)   #63

6-2, 200. Born 2/20/63 in Abilene, TX. Age 23, turned 23 February 20. Resides in Granada Hills, CA. BR. TR.

CONTRACT STATUS: Signed 1-year contract for 1986 season.

1985 SEASON: A young catcher on the horizon, he plays his sixth year in the Yankee organization . . . was unable to play a full season in '85, suffering an injured ligament in his left knee which required surgery to repair . . . Also played with broken finger in early '85 . . . Caught 65 games, played 10 in OF, 1 @ SS.

CAREER: Yankees' 3rd round selection (4th overall) of the free agent draft, June 8, 1981 . . . has also played outfield, first base and third . . . Stole 22 of 26 bases in 1984 while leading the Lauderdale club in RBI (70) . . . strong arm, good speed and can hit for power.

PERSONAL/MISCELLANEOUS: Graduated from Kennedy H.S. in Granada Hills, CA . . . was signed by Don Lindeberg.

YR	Club	AVG	G	AB	R	H	2B	3B	HR	RBI	BB	SO	SB
1981	Bradenton	.245	20	53	9	13	3	0	0	6	9	7	1
1982	Paintsville	.250	50	180	26	45	8	0	0	14	16	23	3
1983	Ft. Lauderdale	.224	17	49	1	11	2	0	0	3	7	8	1
	Greensboro	.300	94	330	63	99	15	0	7	43	49	44	5
1984	Ft. Lauderdale	.293	127	393	58	115	20	2	8	70	85	37	22
1985	Albany	.256	76	250	44	64	13	2	5	32	39	29	5
Minor League Totals		**.276**	**384**	**1255**	**201**	**347**	**61**	**4**	**20**	**168**	**205**	**148**	**37**

Selected by New York Yankees' organization in 3rd round of free-agent draft, June, 1981.

LYDEN, MITCHELL SCOTT "Mitch" (C)   #59

6-3, 200. Born 12/14/64 in Portland, OR. Age 21, turns 22 December 14. Resides in Beverton, OR. BR. TR.

CONTRACT STATUS: Signed 1-year contract for 1986 season.

1985 SEASON: Another catching prospect, Mitch played a full season @ Ft. Lauderdale . . . Second on club in games (116) and ABs (438); tied 2nd doubles (21) and HRs (10); third in total bases (155) and RBIs (58) . . . Caught 101 games . . . Led FSL catchers in fielding pct. (.988), assists (63), putouts (607) and total changes (678) . . . Named to FSL All-Star team.

CAREER: Yankees 1st pick (4th round) free agent draft, June 1983 . . . exclusively a catcher as a professional . . . led NY-Penn League catchers with .991 fielding pct. in 1983 . . . has a good arm and quick release . . . showing improvement as a hitter, using all fields.

PERSONAL/MISCELLANEOUS: Graduated from Beaverton High School in 1983 . . . was signed by Whitey DeHart.

LYDEN (continued)

Led New York-Pennsylvania League catchers in fielding with .991 percentage in 1983.

Led Florida State League catchers with 101 games, 607 putouts and in fielding with .988 percentage, 1985.

YR	Club	AVG	G	AB	R	H	2B	3B	HR	RBI	BB	SO	SB
1983	Oneonta	.148	47	128	14	19	1	0	0	7	12	36	3
1984	Sarasota	.235	54	200	21	47	4	0	1	21	13	36	3
	Greensboro	.219	14	32	3	7	1	0	1	2	1	9	0
1985	Ft. Lauderdale	.255	116	400	43	102	21	1	10	58	27	93	1
Minor League Totals		**.230**	**231**	**760**	**81**	**175**	**27**	**1**	**12**	**88**	**79**	**174**	**7**

Selected by New York Yankees' organization in 4th round of free-agent draft, June, 1983.

MATA, VICTOR J. (Vic) (OF) #17

6-1, 165. Born 6/17/61 in Santiago, DR. Age 24, turns 25 June 17. Resides: Santo Domingo, DR. BR. TR. Married.

MAJOR LEAGUE SERVICE: 98 days.

CONTRACT STATUS: Signed 1-year contract for 1986.

1985 SEASON: Came north with Yankees at season's outset due to injury to Rickey Henderson ... Made just two appearances (RF, April 10 @ Boston & PH/CF, April 16 vs. Chicago) before being optioned to Columbus April 22, making room for Henderson's return ... Recalled from Columbus June 2 when Ken Griffey was placed on the 15-day D.L. with a sprained left wrist ... Played four games, going 1-for-5, with 1 run ... Optioned to Columbus to make room for Griffey, June 12 ... Made only one start, June 11 vs. Toronto ... Played in 104 games at Columbus, hitting .261 ... Was 4th on team with 375 ABs & 98 hits ... Played 103 games in outfield.

CAREER: Now entering his ninth season in the Yankees' organization, Vic progressed at each minor league level ... Strictly an outfielder in his first three pro seasons, he played first, second, and third base in addition to outfield chores the following three years (playing 56 games at 2B in 1983, while 74 as an outfielder) ... Named to the 1982 South Atlantic League All-Star team as an outfielder ... Made Major league debut July 22 vs. Minnesota, going 2 for 4 ... First Yankee homerun August 5 off Indians Neal Heaton ... Signed by Willie Calvino for the 1978 season.

PERSONAL/MISCELLANEOUS: One of eight children ... married Miguelina Tejeda, February 23, 1984 ... remembers most about his first ML game his first error (on first ball hit to him), and first hit ... Graduated in 1977 from San Pablo High School, Santo Domingo, DR.

Led South Atlantic League outfielders with 259 putouts in 1982.

Tied for South Atlantic League lead in double plays by outfielders with 4 in 1981.

YR	Club	AVG	G	AB	R	H	2B	3B	HR	RBI	BB	SO	SB
1978	Oneonta	.228	34	57	9	13	0	0	0	3	3	11	1
1979	Oneonta	.268	60	224	36	60	6	1	2	23	23	31	11
1980	Greensboro	.277	101	346	43	96	11	2	5	47	23	47	8
1981	Greensboro	.261	102	353	59	92	11	4	2	39	26	56	8
1982	Greensboro	.314	123	481	89	151	25	5	5	64	32	52	8
1983	Nashville	.303	130	465	79	141	19	5	10	63	43	63	6
1984	Columbus	.277	87	314	42	87	13	5	10	49	25	59	4
1985	Columbus	.261	104	375	39	98	14	2	3	27	27	58	2
	YANKEES	.143	6	7	1	1	0	0	0	0	0	0	0
Minor League Totals		**.282**	**741**	**2615**	**396**	**738**	**99**	**24**	**37**	**315**	**202**	**377**	**48**
M.L. Totals		**.312**	**36**	**77**	**9**	**24**	**5**	**0**	**1**	**6**	**0**	**12**	**1**

GWRBI: 1984-1.

Signed by New York Yankees' organization as free-agent for 1978 season.

YANKEE FREE AGENT SIGNINGS

C. Hunter	12/31/74	B. Watson	11/8/79	B. Shirley	12/15/82
D. Gullett	11/18/76	D. Winfield	12/15/80	D. Murray	11/21/83
R. Jackson	11/29/76	B. Castro	2/15/81	P. Niekro	1/6/84
R. Gossage	11/22/77	R. Guidry	12/15/81	E. Whitson	12/27/84
R. Eastwick	12/9/77	D. Collins	12/23/81	J. Niekro	1/8/86
L. Tiant	11/13/78	D. Baylor	12/1/82	P. Niekro	1/8/86
T. John	11/22/78	S. Kemp	12/9/82	B. Wynegar	1/8/86
R. May	11/8/79				

1985 vs. OPPONENTS

Club	AB	H	HR	RBI	AVG
Baltimore	—	—	—	—	—
Boston	1	0	0	0	.000
Cleveland	—	—	—	—	—
Detroit	—	—	—	—	—
Milwaukee	1	0	0	0	.000
Toronto	4	1	0	0	.250
California	—	—	—	—	—
Chicago	1	0	0	0	.000
Kansas City	—	—	—	—	—
Minnesota	—	—	—	—	—
Oakland	0	0	0	0	—
Seattle	—	—	—	—	—
Texas	—	—	—	—	—
1st Half	7	1	0	0	.143
2nd Half	0	0	0	0	—
vs. LHP	7	1	0	0	.143
vs. RHP	—	—	—	—	—
Home	5	1	0	0	.200
Away	2	0	0	0	.000

MATA'S BESTS

Season

AVG.	.329–1984
H	23–1984
HR	1–1984
RBI	6–1984
SB	1–1984
Hit Strk	4 games-1984

Game

H	3–2 times
HR	1–once
RBI	1–6 times
SB	1–once

MATTINGLY, DONALD ARTHUR "Don"   (1B)   #23

6-0, 175. Born 4/20/61 in Evansville, IN where he resides. Age 24, turns 25 April 20. BL. TL. Married: Kim Sexton 9/8/79. Son Taylor.

MAJOR LEAGUE SERVICE: 2 years, 163 days.

CONTRACT STATUS: Signed for 1986 season.

1985 SEASON: Phenomenal season, displaying prowess with bat and glove ... Led majors with 145 RBIs, 48 doubles, 15 sacrifice flies ... Led A.L. with 370 total bases, 21 GW-RBI, 86 extra-base hits ... Second in A.L. with 211 hits, .567 slugging pct., 66 multiple hit games ... Third in A.L. with .324 BA ... Fourth in A.L. with 107 runs ... Led A.L. firstbasemen with .995 fielding pct. ... 145 RBIs were most by a Yankee since Joe DiMaggio had 155 in 1948 ... First Yankee to lead A.L. in RBIs since Roger Maris in 1961 ... Reached 100 RBI plateau August 20—earliest by Yankee since recorded #100 August 4 & Mickey Mantle August 6, 1961 ... 211 hits were most by a Yankee since Red Rolfe's 213 in 1939—sixth highest total in Yankee history ... First Yankee to collect 200 + hits in consecutive seasons since Joe DiMaggio, 1936-37 ... First A.L. player to lead majors in doubles, consecutive seasons since Tris Speaker, 1920-23 ... Pete Rose was the last player to lead the majors in doubles, consecutive seasons, 1975-76 ... First player to lead A.L. in doubles, consecutive seasons, since Tony Oliva, 1969-70 ... 48 doubles is second highest single season total in Yankee history—Lou Gehrig holds the club record with 52 in 1927 ... 652 at-bats—seventh highest total in Yankee history ... First Yankee to have 600+ at-bats, consecutive seasons, since Chris Chambliss, 1977-78 ... 159 games led team, most ever played by a Yankee in a single season at firstbase ... Suffered a minor tear of the medial meniscus cartilage in his right knee in February, while working out with weights at Evansville, IN home ... Underwent arthroscopic surgery to repair damage February 22 ... Rehabilitation caused him to miss the first 18 Spring Training games ... Made spectacular Spring debut, homering in first at bat, March 26 ... April 18-May 3, went 19-for-51, .373 BA with 5 doubles, 13 RBIs, raising BA from .267 to .325 ... Didn't hit 1st HR until May 5, off K.C.'s Bud Black ... BA tailed to .285 June 8, following an 0-for-19 streak (longest 0-for of '85) ... Had 20-game hitting streak, June 22-July 12—longest of '85 by Yankee, longest of Mattingly's career—went 32-for-81, .395 BA with 11 runs, 9 doubles, 3 HRs, 21 RBIs ... Committed first error July 7 (1st game) vs. Minnesota, breaking streak of 153 games (1371 total chances), dating back to June 22, 1984, of not committing an error at firstbase ... Had 19-game hitting streak August 1-21, going 35-for-79, .443 BA with 25 runs, 7 doubles, 10 HRs, 21 RBIs ... Drove in Rickey Henderson with 56 of his 145 RBIs ... Batting second: 58 games, 86-for-242, .355, 20 HRs, 50 RBIs—NY record, 39-19 ... Batting third: 98 games, 124-for-399, .311 BA, 15 HRs, 91 RBIs—NY record, 55-44 ... Batted 4th twice, going 2-for-6, 0 HRs, 3 RBI—NY record, 1-1 ... Yankees went 1-1 in 2-games Mattingly did not play (5/26-27 @ Oakland), suffering from a sore groin ... Had five 2-HR games: first (of season & career) came August 2 off Chicago's Britt Burns; last came September 29 (1st game) off Baltimore's Scott McGregor ... Hit HRs in consecutive games: July 24 & 26; August 2-3 (3 HRs); August 13-14; September 6-7; & September 24-25 ... Most HRs off single pitcher: 3, Britt Burns, Chicago ... Had 10 RBIs in 5 games, May 13-17 ... Had 11 RBIs in 5 games, July 9-13 ... Had 12 RBIs in 5 games, September 6-10 ... Drove in at least 1-run in 10 straight games, September 20-30—16 RBIs total ... Drove in 4-runs four times ...

MATTINGLY (continued)

First player to lead majors in RBIs and strikeout as few as 41 times since Ted Kluszewski led majors with 141 RBIs in 1954, striking out 35 times ... underwent minor surgery November 12 to correct a catch in the extensor tendon of the right hand's little finger—little-to-no rehabilitation required.

American League Most Valuable Player—1985
Rawlings Gold Glove Award Firstbaseman—1985
American League All-Star—1985
American League Player of the Month (August & September)—1985
American League Player of the Week (August 5-11)—1985
New York Daily News Player of the Month (July, August & September)—1985
Yankees Magazine Most Popular Yankee—1985
Mercedes Benz/Yankees Magazine Player of the Month (July, August & September)—1985
SportsChannel Most Valuable Player—1985
The Sporting News A.L. Player of the Year—1985
The Sporting News A.L. All-Star Team—1985
Seagrams 7-Crown of Sports All-Star Team—1985
Associated Press All-Star Team—1985
United Press International All-Star Team—1985
The Sporting News Silver Slugger Team—1985
Player of the Year Award-N.Y. Chapter BBWAA—1985

CAREER: 1984—Became the first Yankee to win A.L. batting championship since Mickey Mantle in 1956, battling teammate Dave Winfield to last day of season, winning .343 to .340 ... Named to his first A.L. All-Star team in his first full Major League season ... Led A.L. with 207 hits, 44 doubles and 59 multiple hit games, and was second with a .537 Slg% ... At .364, was top road hitter in A.L. ... Was first lefthanded hitter to hit .340 since Lou Gehrig, hit .351 in 1937 ... Led A.L. first basemen with .996 fielding pct., making only 5 errors in 1236 total chances ... 1983—Terrific rookie season ... won James P. Dawson Award as top rookie at spring training ... was in starting line-up for Yankee home opener ... optioned to Columbus April 14 ... hit 8 HRs, with 39 RBI and .346 BA with Clippers and was recalled June 20 when Bobby Murcer retired ... hit first M.L. homer off John Tudor, June 24 at Fenway Park ... hit in 24 of 25 games, July 13 to August 11, going hitless (0-2) in both ends (7/24 & 8/18) of "Pine Tar" game ... played 1/3 inning at second base in August 18 conclusion of "Pine Tar" game ... 1982—named International League All-Star as outfielder ... his outstanding season earned promotion to Yankee in September ... 1981—named Yankees Minor League Player of the Year ... led Southern League in doubles ... named to Southern League and Topps AA All-Star teams as outfielder ... drafted late as teams expected him to accept college scholarships ... 1980 named South Atlantic League MVP ... signed by Yankee scouts Jax Robertson and Gust Poulos ... has .332 (611-1842) career minor league BA.

PERSONAL/MISCELLANEOUS: Attended Evansville Memorial High where he played baseball, basketball and football ... played Little League, Babe Ruth League, and American Legion in Evansville ... his brother Randy was a pro football player ... enjoys racquetball. Named American League Most Valuable Player, 1985.

Named American League Most Valuable Player by B.W.A.A., 1985.
Won A.L. Batting Championship, .343 B.A.-1984.
Named American League Player of the Year by Sporting News, 1984.
Led American League 1st basemen in fielding with .996 percentage in 1984, and with .995 percentage in 1985.
Tied for American League lead in double plays by first baseman with 154 in 1985.
Named South Atlantic League Most Valuable Player, 1980.
Named New York Yankees' Minor League Player of the Year, 1981.

YR	Club	AVG	G	AB	R	H	2B	3B	HR	RBI	BB	SO	SB
1979	Oneonta	.349	53	166	20	58	10	2	3	31	30	6	2
1980	Greensboro	.358*	133	494	92	177*	32	5	9	105	59	33	8
1981	Nashville	.314	141	547	74	172	35*	4	7	98	64	55	4
1982	Columbus	.315	130	476	67	150	24	2	10	75	50	24	1
	YANKEES	.167	7	12	0	2	0	0	0	1	0	1	0
1983	Columbus	.340	43	159	35	54	11	3	8	37	29	14	2
	YANKEES	.283	91	279	34	79	15	4	4	32	21	31	0
1984	YANKEES	.343*	153	603	91	207*	44*	2	23	110	41	33	1
1985	YANKEES	.324	159	652	107	211	48*	3	35	145*	56	41	2
Minor League Totals		**.332**	**500**	**1842**	**288**	**611**	**112**	**16**	**37**	**346**	**323**	**132**	**17**
M.L. Totals		**.323**	**410**	**1546**	**232**	**499**	**107**	**9**	**62**	**288**	**118**	**106**	**3**

GWRBI: 1983-3; 1984-12; 1985-21*. Total-36

Selected by New York Yankees' organization in 19th round of free-agent draft, June 5, 1979.

YR	Club, Site	AVG	G	AB	R	H	2B	3B	HR	RBI	BB	SO	SB
1984	A.L., S.F.	.000	1	1	0	0	0	0	0	0	0	0	0
1985	A.L., Min.	.000	1	1	0	0	0	0	0	0	0	0	0
A.S.G. Totals		.000	2	2	0	0	0	0	0	0	0	0	0

1985 vs. OPPONENTS

Club	AB	H	HR	RBI	AVG
Baltimore	51	17	3	17	.333
Boston	54	18	0	7	.333
Cleveland	47	18	2	9	.383
Detroit	49	14	3	6	.286
Milwaukee	54	13	0	9	.241
Toronto	57	19	2	5	.333
California	51	11	4	8	.216
Chicago	52	22	6	13	.423
Kansas City	47	15	2	9	.319
Minnesota	51	16	3	16	.314
Oakland	43	18	3	13	.419
Seattle	51	15	4	16	.294
Texas	45	15	3	17	.333
1st Half	337	104	9	69	.309
2nd Half	315	107	26	76	.340
vs. LHP	264	76	18	67	.288
vs. RHP	388	135	17	78	.348
Home	318	107	22	87	.336
Away	334	104	13	58	.311

MATTINGLY'S BESTS

Season

AVG.	.343–1984
H	211–1985
HR	35–1985
RBI	145–1985
SB	2–1985
Hit Strk	20 games–1985

Game

H	5–3 times
HR	2–5 times
RBI	5–2 times
SB	1–3 times

MEACHAM, ROBERT ANDREW "Bobby" (SS) #20

6-1, 180. Born 8/25/60 in Los Angeles, CA. Age 25, turns 26 on August 25. Resides in Glen Rock, NJ. BS. TR. Married: Gari Breeze, September 11, 1982, Child: Brooke Nicole. College: San Diego State University.

MAJOR LEAGUE SERVICE: 1 year 162 days

CONTRACT STATUS: Signed 1-year contract for 1986.

1985 SEASON: Despite injury plagued season, played consistent shortstop ... Played 155 games at shortstop–most by a Yankee since Bucky Dent played 157 in 1977 ... .9630 fielding pct. was 7th best among A.L. shortstops with at least 100 games ... 4th among A.L. shortstops in games and DPs (103) ... Suffered a dislocated tendon in his left hand, July 28 at Texas–the condition was corrected with post-season surgery ... The injury hampered his lefthanded swing, forcing him to bat righthanded vs. righthanded pitchers on a number of occasions ... Set new career highs for hits (105), RBIs (47), and stolen bases (25) ... Had two 3-RBI games (career highs); May 26 @ Oak. & Aug. 21 @ Cal. ... Went 4-for-4, April 13 @ Clev. & May 26 @ Oak., matching his career highs ... Hit .264 with 32 RBIs on road; .169 with 15 RBIs in NY ... Was hitting .273 through May 29, when he suffered a slight hamstring pull ... Missed next 3 games, and went 2-for-44 June 2-16, dropping BA from .273 to .222 ... Only HR came Aug. 31–a solo off California's Ron Romanick ... Hit would-be HR April 29 @ Texas off Frank Tanana, but passed Willie Randolph near firstbase and was called out–both Randolph and Wynegar scored ... led majors with 23 sacrifice hits.

CAREER: 1984—Appeared in 96 games at shortstop after being called up from Columbus on June 15 ... 1983—Began season at Columbus after fine showing at Spring Training ... brought up to Yankees June 29 when Willie Randolph was disabled ... played shortstop as defensive replacement June 30 at Yankee Stadium vs Baltimore in major league debut ... sent back to Columbus on July 12 ... recalled to Yankees on July 16 but returned to Columbus later the same day when Yankees purchased Larry Milbourne from Philadelphia ... recalled from Columbus on August 19 when Andre Robertson was disabled and returned to Columbus on August 20 when Bert Campaneris was activated off disabled list ... was recalled to Yankees on September 2 ... had 1st major league at bat on September 3 at Seattle ... had 1st major league hit and RBI at Cleveland on September 18 ... 1982—named Florida State League All-Star shortstop ... 1981—was top draft pick of St. Louis playing two seasons at Class A before its trade to Yankees ... in 1981 named South Atlantic League All-Star shortstop.

PERSONAL/MISCELLANEOUS: Graduated from Mater Dei (Santa Ana, CA) High School in 1978—was All-Orange County and All-State in baseball; All-League in basketball and football ... attended San Diego State University for 3 years majoring in business finance ... was named All-American in baseball ... signed first pro contract by Marty Keough (Cardinals) ... enjoys music, golf, and reading the Bible.

MEACHAM (continued)

Led A.L. with 14 sacrifice hits in 1984.
Led Florida State League shortstops with 47 errors in 1982.

YR	Club	AVG	G	AB	R	H	2B	3B	HR	RBI	BB	SO	SB
1981	Gastonia	.182	74	272	24	50	8	2	1	18	37	47	11
1982	St. Petersburg-a	.259	120	421	57	109	15	4	0•	37	43	62	21
1983	Columbus	.262	120	423	58	111	18	3	9	60	35	74	13
	YANKEES	.235	22	51	5	12	2	0	0	4	4	10	8
1984	Nashville	.290	8	31	3	9	0	0	0	3	5	8	9
	Columbus	.283	46	187	35	53	13	6	2	13	19	35	6
	YANKEES	.253	99	360	62	91	13	4	2	25	32	70	9
1985	YANKEES	.218	156	481	70	105	16	2	1	47	54	102	25
Minor League Totals		**.249**	**368**	**1334**	**177**	**332**	**54**	**15**	**12**	**131**	**136**	**226**	**60**
M.L. Totals		**.233**	**277**	**892**	**137**	**208**	**31**	**6**	**3**	**76**	**90**	**182**	**42**

GWRBI: 1984-4; 1985-3. Total 7.

Selected by Chicago White Sox' organization in 14th round of free agent draft, June 6, 1978.
Selected by St. Louis Cardinals' organization in 1st round (8th player selected) of free-agent draft, June 8, 1981.
a-Traded with outfielder Stan Javier to New York Yankees' organization for pitchers Marty Mason and Steve Fincher and outfielder Bob Helsom, December 14, 1982.

1985 vs. OPPONENTS

Club	AB	H	HR	RBI	AVG
Baltimore	43	13	0	4	.302
Boston	39	9	0	5	.231
Cleveland	32	10	0	1	.313
Detroit	34	4	0	2	.118
Milwaukee	39	6	0	3	.154
Toronto	43	9	0	4	.209
California	35	13	1	6	.371
Chicago	35	4	0	2	.114
Kansas City	35	12	0	4	.343
Minnesota	37	6	0	3	.162
Oakland	40	8	0	6	.200
Seattle	32	2	0	1	.063
Texas	45	15	3	17	.333
1st Half	253	58	0	30	.229
2nd Half	228	47	1	17	.206
vs. LHP	181	38	0	16	.210
vs. RHP	300	67	1	31	.223
Home	231	39	1	15	.169
Away	250	66	0	32	.264

MEACHAM'S BESTS

Season

AVG.	.253–1984	
H	105–1985	
HR	2–1985	
RBI	47–1985	
SB	25–1985	
Hit Strk	7 games—1984	

Game

H	4–3 times	
HR	1–3 times	
RBI	3–2 times	
SB	2–3 times	

NIEKRO, JOSEPH FRANKLIN "Joe" (RHP)   #47

6-1, 195. Born 11/7/44 in Martins Ferry, OH. Age 41, turns 42 November 7. Resides in Lakeland, FL. BR. TR. Married: Nancy, two children—Natalie and Lance. College: West Liberty (W.VA) College

MAJOR LEAGUE SERVICE: 17 years, 138 days.

CONTRACT STATUS: Signed 3-year contract, January 8, 1986 . . . contract extends through 1988 season.

1985 SEASON: A veteran of 19 major league seasons, Joe came to the Yankees with minor league infielder Neder Horta from Houston in exchange for minor league LHP Jim Deshaies and RHP Dody Rather, September 15 . . . his acquisition reunited him with brother Phil, as the two played for Atlanta, 1973-'74 . . . made three starts after joining the Yankees: lasted only 1.2 innings in first start, 9/19 @ Detroit, losing 10-3; Combined for 10.2 IP over last two starts, yielding only 2 ER, besting Detroit, Sept. 25 & Milw., Sept. 1 . . . was 9-12, 3.72 ERA in '85 with Houston, completing an 11-year career . . . had 100+ strikeouts for the 5th straight year, and 9th time in career . . . notched 200th career win July 2 @ San Diego, winning 3-2 . . . became Houston's all-time winningest pitcher at 144 wins . . . a free agent after the '85 season, as was older brother Phil, both resigned with New York hours prior to midnight January 8th deadline.

CAREER: has obtained double figures in the wins 9 of last 10 seasons . . . ranks 9th on the Active Player Career Victory list with 204 . . . had a career high 153 strikeouts in 1983 . . . was second in the National League in ERA, (2.47), in 1982 . . . also, tied for second in shutouts (5), third in CG (16), and fourth in innings (270) . . . was 11th in the N.L. in ERA in 1981 (2.82) . . . recorded back-to-back 20-win seasons with the Astros, as he was 21-11 in 1979 and 20-12 in 1980 . . . was the winning pitcher in the one-game play-off for the N.L. West Title in 1980 vs. the Dodgers . . . was the runner-up in the Cy Young balloting in 1979 and was fourth in 1980 . . . tied for the NL lead in shutouts (5) in 1979 . . . named to the 1979 N.L. all-star team as well as the post-season all-star squads as selected by AP and UPI . . . picked as the N.L. Pitcher of the Year by the Sporting News in 1979 . . . had a one-hitter for Detroit against the Yankees on July 2, 1970 as Horace Clark broke up the no-hit bid with a single after 8.1 innings . . . won a four-hitter while hitting a homer off brother Phil on May 26, 1976 . . . holds a 5-4 edge over Phil with the last decision being a 5-3 triumph for Joe at Atlanta on Sept. 13, 1982.

PERSONAL/MISCELLANEOUS: Graduate of Bridgeport (OH) High School . . . attended West Liberty (W. VA) College where he won All-American laurels in baseball . . . very active nationally with the Spina Bifida Association and has received many honors for his contributions.

Pitched seven-inning, 2-0 perfect game against Tidewater, July 16, 1972 (second game).

Led National League in wild pitches with 19 in 1982, 14 in 1983 and tied for lead with 19 in 1979.

YR	CLUB	W-L	ERA	G	GS	CG	Sho	SV	IP	H	R	ER	BB	SO
1966	Caldwell	0-0	0.00	1	1	0	0	0	4	4	0	0	1	7
	Quincy	1-2	1.08	4	3	1	0	—	25	17	7	3	6	14
	Dallas-Ft. Worth	5-4	2.51	12	10	3	2	—	79	71	28	22	15	50
1967	CHICAGO (NL)	10-7	3.34	36	22	7	2	0	170	171	68	63	32	77
1968	CHICAGO (NL)	14-10	4.32	34	29	2	1	2	177	204	93	85	59	65
1969	CHICAGO (NL)-a	0-1	3.79	4	3	0	0	0	19	24	9	8	6	7
	SAN DIEGO-b	8-17	3.70	37	31	8	3	0	202	213	91	83	45	55
	1969 Totals	8-18	3.71	41	34	8	3	0	221	237	100	91	51	62
1970	DETROIT	12-13	4.06	38	34	6	2	0	213	221	107	96	72	101
1971	DETROIT	6-7	4.28	31	15	0	0	1	122	136	62	61	49	43
1972	Toledo-c	2-0	0.64	2	2	2	1	0	14	6	1	1	3	11
	DETROIT	3-2	3.83	18	7	1	0	1	47	62	20	20	8	24
1973	Toledo-d	7-10	3.71	26	20	8	0	0	143	148	74	59	47	77
	ATLANTA	2-4	4.13	20	0	0	0	3	24	23	11	11	11	12
1974	Richmond	8-1	2.08	30	0	0	0	7	52	44	14	12	18	50
	ATLANTA-e	3-2	3.56	27	2	0	0	0	43	36	19	17	18	31
1975	Iowa	1-0	5.00	7	0	0	0	1	9	7	6	5	7	9
	HOUSTON	6-4	3.07	40	4	1	1	4	88	79	32	30	39	54
1976	HOUSTON	4-8	3.36	36	13	0	0	0	118	107	60	44	56	77
1977	HOUSTON	13-8	3.03	44	14	9	2	5	181	155	66	61	64	101
1978	HOUSTON	14-14	3.86	35	29	10	1	0	203	190	97	87	73	97
1979	HOUSTON +	21-11	3.00	38	38	11	5+	0	264	221	102	88	107	119
1980	HOUSTON	20-12	3.55	37	36	11	2	0	256	268	119	101	79	1—7
1981	HOUSTON	9-9	2.82	24	24	5	2	0	166	150	60	52	47	77
1982	HOUSTON	17-12	2.47	35	35	16	5	0	270.0	224	79	74	64	130
1983	HOUSTON	15-14	3.48	38	38*	9	1	0	263.2	238	115	102	101	152
1984	HOUSTON	16-12	3.04	38	38*	6	1	0	248.1	223	104	84	89	127
1985	HOUSTON-f	9-12	3.72	32	32	4	1	0	213.0	197	100	88	99	117
	YANKEES-g	2-1	5.84	3	3	0	0	0	12.1	14	8	8	8	4
	1985 Totals	11-13	3.83	35	35	4	1	0	225.1	211	108	96	107	121
Minor League Totals		**24-17**	**2.82**	**82**	**36**	**14**	**3**	**8**	**326**	**297**	**130**	**102**	**97**	**218**
A.L. Totals		**23-23**	**4.22**	**90**	**59**	**7**	**2**	**2**	**394.1**	**433**	**197**	**185**	**137**	**172**
N.L. Totals		**181-157**	**3.34**	**555**	**388**	**99**	**27**	**12**	**2906.0**	**2723**	**1125**	**1078**	**989**	**1425**
M.L. Totals		**204-180**	**3.44**	**645**	**447**	**106**	**29**	**14**	**3300.1**	**3156**	**1422**	**1263**	**1126**	**1597**

Selected by Cleveland Indians' organization in 7th round of free agent draft, January, 1966.
Selected by Chicago Cubs' organization in 3rd round of free agent draft, June, 1966.
a-Traded with pitcher Gary Ross and infielder Francisco Libran to San Diego Padres for pitcher Dick Selma, April 24, 1969.
b-Traded to Detroit Tigers for pitcher Pat Dobson and shortstop-outfielder Dave Campbell, December 4, 1969.
c-On disabled list, August 7 to September 1, 1972.
d-Sold on waivers to Atlanta Braves, August 7, 1973.
e-Sold to Houston Astros, April 5, 1975.
f-Traded to the New York Yankees for pitcher Jim Deshaies and a player to be named later, September 15, 1985. Pitcher Dody Rather assigned to Houston to complete deal, January 11, 1986.
g-Granted free agency, November, 1985; resigned with New York Yankees, January 8, 1986.

DIVISION SERIES RECORD

YR	CLUB, Opp.	W-L	ERA	G	GS	CG	Sho	SV	IP	H	R	ER	BB	SO
1981	Hou. vs. L.A.	0-0	0.00	1	1	0	0	0	8.0	7	0	0	3	4

CHAMPIONSHIP SERIES RECORD

Established National League Championship Series record for most innings pitched, game (10), October 10, 1980.

YR	CLUB	W-L	ERA	G	GS	CG	Sho	SV	IP	H	R	ER	BB	SO
1980	Hou. vs. Phi.	0-0	0.00	1	1	0	0	0	10.0	6	0	0	1	2

> **DID YOU KNOW . . .** that Babe Ruth did not win the MVP award in 1927 despite hitting 60 homeruns? He had previously won the award in 1923 and a rule at the time prohibited players from winning it twice.

JOE NIEKRO (continued)

1985						Club	CAREER					
ERA	W-L-S	G	IP	H	ER		ERA	W-L-S	G	IP	H	ER
—	—	—	—	—	—	Baltimore	5.03	2-2-0	13	53.2	58	30
—	—	—	—	—	—	Boston	4.86	2-3-0	10	50.0	52	27
—	—	—	—	—	—	California	4.01	2-2-0	6	33.2	31	15
—	—	—	—	—	—	Chicago	4.42	0-3-0	7	18.1	25	9
—	—	—	—	—	—	Cleveland	4.40	3-2-0	8	30.2	32	15
9.45	1-1-0	2	6.2	11	7	Detroit	9.45	1-1-0	2	6.2	11	7
—	—	—	—	—	—	Kansas City	3.40	3-1-0	6	42.1	45	16
1.59	1-0-0	1	5.2	3	1	Minnesota	2.06	4-0-0	8	35.0	32	8
—	—	—	—	—	—	Minnesota	4.66	2-4-0	7	36.2	52	19
—	—	—	—	—	—	Oakland	4.35	1-1-0	9	31.0	36	15
—	—	—	—	—	—	Seattle	—	—	—	—	—	—
—	—	—	—	—	—	Texas	—	—	—	—	—	—
—	—	—	—	—	—	Toronto	—	—	—	—	—	—
5.84	2-1-0	3	12.1	14	8	Total	4.22	23-23-2	90	394.2	433	185
1.69	2-0-0	2	10.2	7	2	Home	—	—	—	—	—	—
32.40	0-1-0	1	1.2	7	6	Road	—	—	—	—	—	—

—		
2—9/25/85 vs. Det.	Low Hit	1—7/2/80
2—	K-High	9—3 times
	Win Streak	9—1979

S = SHUTOUTS

NIEKRO, PHILIP HENRY "Phil" "Knucksie"   (RHP)   #35

6-1, 193. Born 4/1/39 in Blaine, OH. Age 46, turns 47 April 1. Resides in Lilburn, GA. BR. TR. Married: Nancy Lee Farrand, 8/6/66. Children: Philip (18), John (17), and Michael (13).

MAJOR LEAGUE SERVICE: 20 years, 154 days.

CONTRACT STATUS: Signed 1-year contract on January 8, 1986 ... contract extends thru 1986 season.

1985 SEASON: The future Hall of Famer became the 18th player to win 300 games, and the oldest pitcher to throw a shutout, beating Toronto 8-0 on 4-hits, October 6 in Canada ... won career #299 September 8th vs. Oakland, and failed in his next four attempts to win #300: Sept. 13 vs. Toronto, lost 3-2; Sept. 18 @ Detroit, lost 5-2; Sept. 24 vs. Detroit, lost 9-1; Sept. 30 vs. Baltimore, lost 5-4 ... Oct. 6 shutout was career no. 45 ... was starter in two combined shutouts: May 17 @ California; Aug. 29 vs. the Angels ... has two-year Yankee record of 32-20 ... struckout a season high 9 batters twice: April 14 @ Cleveland; April 25 vs. Boston ... walked season high 7, Sept. 3 vs. Seattle ... allowed 3 HRs in single start three times ... was 5-2 in first 8 starts; 7-3 in first 11; then lost 5 consecutive decisions (6 starts), June 9 through July 8; went 8-1 in next 11 starts, July 13 to September 8 ... led club with 149 Ks ... K'd 100+ batters for 18th of last 19 years ... 3197 career strikeouts places him 7th on the All-Time list ... has combined with brother Joe for 504 career wins, second as a brother combo to Jim & Gaylord Perry's 529 ... Phil became the oldest pitcher to win better than 9 games in a season (Jack Quinn won 9 games for Philadelphia at age 46 in 1930 ... along with brother Joe, and catcher Butch Wynegar, resigned with New York just before the midnight January 8th deadline for clubs to sign their own free-agents ... will be entering his 23rd major league season, and will turn 47 just prior to opening day.

CAREER: 1984—Started the season as oldest player ever to appear in a game for the Yankees ... K'd Larry Parrish at Texas on July 4 for his 3000th career strikeout ... named to his fifth All-Star game ... pitched no-hitter against San Diego, August 5, 1973 ... also has 1 one-hitter and 8 two-hitters in career ... recorded 200th career win May 1, 1979 vs Pittsburgh ... Phil and his younger brother Joe of Houston are baseball's second winningest pitching brothers with 504 career wins behind the Perrys, Gaylord and Jim (529) ... continues to move up on all-time lists (see separate chart) ... holds most of Braves all-time pitching records ... has been named to 4 National League All-Star teams ... went on post-season tour of Japan following 1979 season as member of N.L. team that played A.L. All-Stars ... was voted the outstanding pitcher on the trip and was the only two-game winner... has won 5 gold gloves.

PERSONAL/MISCELLANEOUS: Graduated from Bridgeport (Ohio) High School in 1957 where he was teammate of John Havlicek, former Boston Celtic great ... his brother Joe is a 15 year veteran on the major leagues and currently pitching with Houston ... greatest thrill as ballplayer is still the signing of his first pro contract with Bill Maughn ... a great humanitarian, Phil formed Phil Niekro Roasts, Inc. to help raise funds for Spina Bifida, the second most common birth defect ... has aided March of Dimes, Big Brothers Association and the Empty Stocking Fund ... recognized for his community service by being named winner of the Brian Piccolo Award in 1977 and Roberto Clemente Award in 1980 . . . in 1979 was voted baseball's Lou Gehrig Memorial Award, given annually to the player who most exemplifies the ability and character of Gehrig . . . served as Braves' player representative . . . was candidate for Braves' managerial post that was eventually filled by Bobby Cox after 1977 season and Joe Torre in 1981 . . . in off-season enjoys hunting, fishing, table tennis, bowling and poetry writing.

CAREER RECORD

Established major league records for fewest sacrifice flies allowed, season, most innings (0 and 284), 1969; most seasons and most consecutive seasons leading major leagues, runs allowed (3); most wild pitches, lifetime (207).

Tied major league records for most strikeouts, inning (4), July 29, 1977 (sixth inning); most seasons and most consecutive seasons leading league, runs allowed (3); most wild pitches, inning (4), August 4, 1979, second game (fifth inning); most seasons and most consecutive seasons leading league, games lost (4).

Tied modern major league record for most wild pitches, game (6), August 4, 1979, second game.

Established National League records for most putouts by pitcher, lifetime (340); most games started, no relief appearances, season (44), 1979.

Pitched 9-0 no-hit victory against San Diego Padres, August 5, 1973.

Led National League in winning percentage with .810 in 1982.

Led National League in home runs allowed with 41 in 1979 and 30 in 1980.

Led National League in hit batsmen with 11 in 1979.

Led National League in wild pitches with 19 in 1967 and 17 in 1977.

Led National League in sacrifice hits with 18 in 1968.

Named Gold Glove for N.L. pitchers, 1978 through 1980 and 1982, 1983.

YR	CLUB	W-L	ERA	G	GS	CG	Sho	SV	IP	H	R	ER	BB	SO
1959	Wellsville	2-1	7.46	10	2	0	0	—	35	47	38	29	24	16
	McCook	7-2	3.12	23*	0	0	0	—	52	35	20	18	29	48
1960	Jacksonville	6-4	2.77	38	3	0	0	—	84	66	36	26	52	52
	Louisville	1-0	3.60	6	0	0	0	—	10	11	5	4	9	2
1961	Austin	4-4	2.95	51*	1	0	0	—	110	100	45	36	53	84
1962	Louisville	9-6	3.86	49	1	1	0	—	98	111	50	42	41	48
1963	Denver				(In Military Service)									
1964	Denver	11-5	3.45	29	21	13	1	—	172	172	79	66	45	119
	MILWAUKEE	0-0	4.80	10	0	0	0	0	15	15	10	8	7	8
1965	MILWAUKEE	2-3	2.88	41	1	0	0	6	75	73	32	24	26	49
1966	ATLANTA	4-3	4.14	28	0	0	0	2	50	48	32	23	23	17
	Richmond	3-4	3.67	17	4	2	0	—	43	43	27	22	16	36
1967	ATLANTA	11-9	1.87*	46	20	10	1	9	207	164	64	43	55	129
1968	ATLANTA	14-12	2.59	37	34	15	5	2	257	228	83	74	45	140
1969	ATLANTA	23-13	2.57	40	35	21	4	1	284	235	93	81	57	193
1970	ATLANTA	12-18	4.27	34	32	10	3	0	230	222	124	109	68	168
1971	ATLANTA	15-14	2.98	42	36	18	4	2	269	248	112	89	70	173
1972	ATLANTA	16-12	3.06	38	36	17	1	0	282	254	112	96	53	164
1973	ATLANTA	13-10	3.31	42	30	9	1	4	245	214	103	90	89	131
1974	ATLANTA	†20-13	2.38	41	39	18*	6	1	302*	249	91	80	88	195
1975	ATLANTA	15-15	3.20	39	37	13	1	0	276	285	115	98	72	144
1976	ATLANTA	17-11	3.29	39	37	10	2	0	271	249	116	99	101	173
1977	ATLANTA	16-20†	4.04	44	43*	20*	2	0	330*	315*	166*	148*	164*	262*
1978	ATLANTA	19-18*	2.88	44	42*	22*	4	0	334*	295*	129*	107†	102	248
1979	ATLANTA	†21-20*	3.39	44	44*	23*	1	0	342*	311*	160*	129	113*	208
1980	ATLANTA	15-18*	3.63	40	38†	11	3	1	275	256	119	111	85	176
1981	ATLANTA	7-7	3.11	22	22	3	3	0	139	120	56	48	56	62
1982	ATLANTA-a	17-4	3.61	35	35	4	2	0	234.1	225	106	94	73	144
1983	ATLANTA-b	11-10	3.97	34	33	2	0	0	201.2	212	94	89	105	128
1984	YANKEES	16-8	3.09	32	31	5	1	0	215.2	219	85	74	76	136
1985	YANKEES	16-12	4.09	33	33	7	1	0	220.0	203	110	100	120	149
Minor League Totals		**43-26**	**3.62**	**223**	**32**	**16**	**0**	**0**	**604**	**585**	**300**	**243**	**269**	**405**
N.Y.Y. Totals		**32-20**	**3.59**	**65**	**64**	**12**	**2**	**0**	**435.2**	**422**	**195**	**174**	**196**	**285**
N.L. Totals		**268-230**	**3.20**	**739**	**594**	**226**	**43**	**29**	**4619.0**	**4218**	**1917**	**1640**	**1452**	**2912**
M.L. Totals		**300-250**	**3.23**	**804**	**658**	**238**	**45**	**29**	**5054.2**	**4640**	**2112**	**1814**	**1648**	**3197**

Signed as free agent by Milwaukee Braves' organization, July 19, 1958.

a-On disabled list, March 31 to April 21, 1982 with rib injury.

b-Released by Atlanta Braves, October 7, 1983; signed as free agent by New York Yankees, January 6, 1984.

CHAMPIONSHIP SERIES RECORD

Established Championship Series record for most runs allowed, game (9), October 4, 1969.

Tied Championship Series record for most runs allowed, three-game Series (9), 1969.

Tied National League Championship Series record for most runs allowed, inning (5), October 4, 1969 (fifth inning).

YR	CLUB, Opp.	W-L	ERA	G	GS	CG	Sho	SV	IP	H	R	ER	BB	SO
1969	Atl. vs N.Y.	0-1	4.50	1	1	0	0	0	8	9	9	4	4	4
1982	Atl. vs St.L.	0-0	3.00	1	1	0	0	0	6	6	2	2	4	5
N.L.C.S. Totals		**0-1**	**3.86**	**2**	**2**	**1**	**0**	**0**	**14**	**15**	**11**	**6**	**8**	**9**

PHIL NIEKRO (continued)

ALL-STAR GAME RECORD

YR	CLUB, Site	W-L	ERA	G	GS	CG	Sho	SV	IP	H	R	ER	BB	SO
1969 N.L., Was.		0-0	0.00	1	0	0	0	0	1.0	0	0	0	0	2
1975 N.L., Mil.							(Did not play)							
1978 N.L., S.D.		0-0	0.00	1	0	0	0	0	0.1	0	0	0	0	0
1982 N.L., Mon.							(Did not play)							
1984 A.L., S.F.							(Did not play)							
A.S.G. Totals		0-0	0.00	2	0	0	0	0	1.1	0	0	0	0	2

1985 / CAREER

ERA	W-L-S	G	IP	H	ER	Club	ERA	W-L-S	G	IP	H	ER
4.70	0-0-0	1	7.2	12	4	Baltimore	7.27	0-0-0	3	17.1	28	14
4.00	1-1-0	3	18.0	14	8	Boston	3.46	2-1-0	4	26.0	24	10
0.00	3-0-0	3	22.2	8	0	California	2.47	4-2-0	7	47.1	39	13
3.00	1-0-0	1	9.0	7	3	Chicago	8.04	1-1-0	3	15.2	24	14
4.95	2-1-0	4	20.0	22	11	Cleveland	2.85	5-1-0	8	41.0	41	13
10.38	0-4-0	4	21.2	34	25	Detroit	7.71	1-4-0	5	30.1	37	26
4.03	1-1-0	3	22.1	21	10	Kansas City	3.08	4-2-1	7	52.2	54	18
10.00	0-2-0	2	9.0	13	10	Milwaukee	3.75	1-3-0	5	36.0	33	15
2.00	1-0-0	1	9.0	7	2	Minnesota	1.77	2-0-0	3	20.1	19	4
3.21	2-0-0	2	14.0	9	5	Oakland	2.45	3-0-0	3	22.0	13	6
4.15	2-1-0	3	21.2	17	10	Seattle	3.48	4-2-0	6	44.0	32	17
4.50	2-1-0	3	20.0	22	10	Texas	4.50	3-2-0	5	34.0	40	17
0.72	1-1-1	3	25.0	17	2	Toronto	1.52	2-2-1	6	47.1	38	8
4.09	16-12-0	33	220.0	203	100	Total	3.59	32-20-2	65	435.2	422	174
3.85	9-5-0	17	110.0	98	47	Home	—	—	—	—	—	—
4.34	7-7-0	16	110.0	105	53	Road	—	—	—	—	—	—

4—10/6/84 @ Tor.
9—4/14/84 @ Clev.
5—

Low Hit   0—8/5/73 vs San Diego
K-High   —
Win Streak   —

S = SHUTOUTS

NIEKRO ON ALL-TIME LISTS
(All Caps Indicates Still Active)

WINS

	Pitcher	W	L	Pct.
1	Cy Young	511	313	.620
2	Walter Johnson	416	279	.599
3	Christy Mathewson	373	188	.665
	Grover Alexander	373	208	.642
5	Warren Spahn	363	245	.597
6	Kid Nichols	361	208	.634
	Pud Galvin	361	309	.539
8	Tim Keefe	342	224	.604
9	John Clarkson	327	176	.650
10	STEVE CARLTON	314	215	.596
	Gaylord Perry	314	265	.542
12	Old Hoss Radbourn	308	191	.617
13	Mickey Welch	307	209	.595
14	Eddie Plank	305	181	.628
15	TOM SEAVER	304	192	.613
16	Lefty Grove	300	141	.680
	Early Wynn	300	244	.551
	PHIL NIEKRO	300	250	.546
19	DON SUTTON	295	228	.564

STRIKEOUTS

1	NOLAN RYAN	4083
2	STEVE CARLTON	3920
3	TOM SEAVER	3537
4	Gaylord Perry	3534
5	Walter Johnson	3508
6	DON SUTTON	3315
7	PHIL NIEKRO	3197

GAMES STARTED

1	Cy Young	818
2	Gaylord Perry	690
3	Pud Galvin	682
4	DON SUTTON	672
5	Walter Johnson	666
6	Warren Spahn	665
7	PHIL NIEKRO	658
8	STEVE CARLTON	655

GAMES PITCHED		INNINGS PITCHED	
1 Hoyt Wilhelm	1070	1 Cy Young	7377
3 ROLLIE FINGERS	944	5 Warren Spahn	5246
9 Tug McGraw	824	6 Grover Alexander	5188
10 PHIL NIEKRO	804	7 Kid Nichols	5067
11 GENE GARBER	782	8 PHIL NIEKRO	5054.2
12 KENT TEKULVE	780	9 STEVE CARLTON	4879.0
		10 DON SUTTON	4795.2

PAGLIARULO, MICHAEL TIMOTHY "Mike" "Pags"   (3B) #12

6-2, 195. Born 3/15/60 in Medford, MA. Age 26, turned 26 March 15. Resides in Melrose, MA. BL. TR. Married: Karen D'Ettore, 10/16/83. College: University of Miami.

MAJOR LEAGUE SERVICE: 1 year, 86 days.

CONTRACT STATUS: Signed 1-year contract for 1986.

1985 SEASON: Became NY's regular third baseman as season progressed, in his first full major league season ... set career highs in almost every offensive category ... averaged 1 HR every 20 ABs ... went 4 for 6, 9/9 @ Milwaukee—first career 4-hit game ... had first career 2 HR game 7/27 @ Texas, hitting a pair of 2-run homers good for 4 RBIs which equalled his career game high ... matched career long hitting streak 7 games, 7/14-24 ... hitting only .165 through 6/9 (15/91) with 2 HRs and 16 RBIs, went 76/289, .263 with 17 HRs, 46 RBIs through remainder of season ... hit 7 HRs in August ... sent to bat righthanded vs. Mickey Mahler, September 18 @ Detroit, striking out with runners @ 2nd & 3rd, two out, score tied @ 2 ... played 134 games @ 3rd base, most by Yankee since Graig Nettles played 144 in 1979 ... 3rd fewest errors for third basemen with at least 100 games ... 22 PH appearances, 2nd highest on club, hitting .278 ... hit .254 in 126 games vs. righthanders; .151 in just 12 games vs. southpaws ... 62 RBIs ranked 6th on club.

CAREER: 1984—Made major league debut July 7, when called up from Columbus to replace injured Toby Harrah ... first big league homer July 13 (2nd game) off KC's Brett Saberhagen ... first grand-slam September 18 off Baltimore's Dennis Martinez ... 1983—played full season at AA Nashville ... led Southern League 3rd basemen in fielding with .954 pct., 133 games, 433 total chances (98 putouts and 315 assists) ... 1982—named utility infielder on South Atlantic League All-Star team ... signed in 1981 by Yankee scout Fred Ferreira.

PERSONAL/MISCELLANEOUS: Graduated from Medford (MA) High School in 1978 where he played baseball, basketball, soccer, and track... in baseball and soccer, was All-State 2 years, MVP and captain ... attended University of Miami in Coral Gables, FL—was Finance major ... his father, Charles Pagliarulo, was an infielder in the Chicago Cubs organization in 1958 ... enjoys golf, and going to Boston Celtics and Bruins games ... played for South Medford, LL, Medford Babe Ruth League, and Medford Post #45-American Legion baseball.

Led Southern League third basemen in fielding with .954 pct., games with 133, total chances with 433, putouts with 98 and assists with 315 in 1983.
Led South Atlantic League third basemen with 278 assists in 1982.
Led New York-Pennsylvania League in intentional bases on balls received with 8 and led third basemen in total chances with 214 and in assists with 159 in 1981.

YR	Club	AVG	G	AB	R	H	2B	3B	HR	RBI	BB	SO	SB
1981	Oneonta	.216	72	245	32	53	9	4	2	28	38	47	13
1982	Greensboro	.280	123	403	79	113	22	0	22	79	83	76	7
1983	Nashville	.260	135	450	82	117	19	4	19	80	59	100	8
1984	Columbus	.212	58	146	24	31	5	1	7	25	18	30	0
	YANKEES	.239	67	201	24	48	15	3	7	34	15	46	0
1985	YANKEES	.239	138	380	55	91	16	2	19	62	45	86	0
Minor League Totals		**.252**	**388**	**1244**	**217**	**314**	**55**	**9**	**50**	**212**	**198**	**253**	**28**
M.L. Totals		**.239**	**406**	**581**	**79**	**139**	**31**	**5**	**26**	**96**	**60**	**132**	**0**

GWRBI: 1984-5; 1985-5. Total-10.

Selected by New York Yankees' organization in 6th round of free agent draft, June 8, 1981.

DID YOU KNOW ... that on August 1, 1937, the Yankees beat the St. Louis Browns, 14-5 and in the game Lou Gehrig and Joe DiMaggio for the Yankees and Wally Schang for the Browns each hit for the cycle?

PAGLIARULO (continued)

1985 vs. OPPONENTS

Club	AB	H	HR	RBI	AVG
Baltimore	30	11	0	2	.324
Boston	30	8	2	4	.267
Cleveland	23	5	0	4	.217
Detroit	29	6	2	3	.207
Milwaukee	35	11	2	7	.314
Toronto	32	6	1	4	.188
California	37	10	4	13	.270
Chicago	23	6	1	4	.261
Kansas City	20	8	1	2	.400
Minnesota	29	9	2	5	.310
Oakland	32	4	1	3	.125
Seattle	24	3	1	6	.125
Texas	32	4	2	5	.125
1st Half	188	41	6	29	.218
2nd Half	192	50	13	33	.260
vs. LHP	53	8	2	7	.151
vs. RHP	327	83	17	55	.254
Home	178	43	8	29	.242
Away	202	48	11	33	.238

PAGLIARULO'S BESTS

Season

AVG.	.239–1984, 1985
H	91–1985
HR	19–1985
RBI	62–1985
SB	0–
Hit Strk	7 games–1984, 1985

Game

H	4–@ MILW 9/9/85
HR	2–@ TEX 7/27/85
RBI	4–2 times
SB	0–

PASQUA, DANIEL ANTHONY "Dan" (OF) #21

6-0, 203. Born 10/17/61 in Yonkers, NY. Resides in Harrington Park, NJ. BL. TL. Single. College: William Paterson College.

MAJOR LEAGUE SERVICE: 98 days

CONTRACT STATUS: Signed 1-year contract for 1986.

1985 SEASON: Playing only 78 games at Columbus, was named International League Rookie of the Year and Most Valuable Player, hitting .321, with 18 HRs, 69 RBIs ... After starting the season with the Clippers, was recalled to Yankees May 30, when Henry Cotto was placed on the 21-day D.L. with a punctured left eardrum ... First major league hit was a homerun in second at-bat of first big league game–5th inning, May 30 @ California off Ron Romanick ... Remained with NY until optioned to Columbus, June 17 ... Again recalled July 11 ... Hit 2 HRs in second game after recall, July 12 vs. Texas–both upper deck blasts to rightfield at Yankee Stadium off Dave Rozema and Dave Stewart ... Demoted to Columbus for final time August 5, only to be recalled after the minimum 10 days, August 16 ... Went 3-for-4 with 1 double, and 3-run HR, and 4 RBIs, August 25 at Seattle ... Hit 4 HRs in six games, Sept. 3-10, with 10 RBIs ... Averaged 1 HR every 16.4 at-bats (Mattingly averaged 1 HR every 18.6 ABs) ... has too many at-bats to be considered a "rookie" in 1986.

CAREER: 1984—Played entire year at Nashville, performing at AA level for the first time ... led the Sounds in HRs (33), total bases (231), RBI (91) and SLG % (.502) ... 1983—led Ft. Lauderdale Yankees in games, at-bats, runs, doubles, triples, homeruns, & RBI ... second in walks ... third in batting (players with 100 + games) and hits ... 1982—named to Applachian League All-Star team and winner of league MVP award ... led league in homeruns with 16.

PERSONAL/MISCELLANEOUS: Attended Old Tappan (NJ) High School where he played football and baseball ... was All-County baseball, 1979 ... was All-American in baseball at William Patterson College, '81 & '82 ... played Little League in Congers, NY and Harrington Park, NJ ... originally a centerfielder, was changed to rightfield at Ft. Lauderdale in 1983 ... would like to own his own business after his career.

Named International League Rookie of the Year and Most Valuable Player, 1985.

Named Appalachian League Player of the Year, 1982.

YR	Club	AVG	G	AB	R	H	2B	3B	HR	RBI	BB	SO	SB
1982	Paintsville	.301	60	239	43	72	10	2	16*	63+	22	42	1
	Oneonta	.294	4	17	3	5	1	0	2	4	2	3	1
1983	Ft. Lauderdale	.273	131	451	83	123	25	10	19	84	80	125	12
	Columbus	.000	1	3	0	0	0	0	0	0	1	2	0
1984	Nashville	.243	136	460	78	112	14	3	33*	91	95	148*	5
1985	Columbus	.321	78	287	52	92	16	5	18	69	48	62	5
	YANKEES	.209	60	148	17	31	3	1	9	25	16	38	0
Minor League Totals		**.277**	**410**	**1457**	**259**	**404**	**66**	**20**	**88**	**311**	**248**	**382**	**24**
M.L. Totals		**.209**	**60**	**148**	**17**	**31**	**3**	**1**	**9**	**25**	**16**	**38**	**0**

GWRBI: 1985-1.

Selected by New York Yankees' organization in 3rd round of free-agent draft, June 7, 1982.

1985 vs. OPPONENTS

Club	AB	H	HR	RBI	AVG
Baltimore	5	2	0	0	.400
Boston	9	2	0	0	.222
Cleveland	9	2	0	2	.222
Detroit	2	0	0	0	.000
Milwaukee	18	3	1	2	.167
Toronto	18	2	0	0	.111
California	15	2	1	2	.133
Chicago	9	3	1	3	.333
Kansas City	7	2	0	0	.286
Minnesota	4	0	0	0	.000
Oakland	20	4	2	7	.200
Seattle	19	5	2	6	.263
Texas	13	4	2	3	.308
1st Half	36	7	3	4	.194
2nd Half	112	24	6	21	.214
vs. LHP	15	2	0	2	.133
vs. RHP	133	29	9	23	.218
Home	87	19	7	16	.218
Away	61	12	2	9	.197

PASQUA'S BESTS

Season

AVG.	.209–1985
H	31–1985
HR	9–1985
RBI	25–1985
SB	0–
Hit Strk	3 games–1985

Game

H	3–@ SEA 8/25/85
HR	2–vs. TEX 7/12/85
RBI	4–@ SEA 8/25/85
SB	0–

RANDOLPH, WILLIE LARRY (2B) #30

5-11, 166. Born 7/6/54 in Holly Hill, SC. Age 31, turns 32 July 6. Resides in Upper Saddle River, NJ. Married: Gretchen Foster 2/1/75. Children: Taniesha (10), Chantre (7), Andre (6) and Ciara (1½).

MAJOR LEAGUE SERVICE: 10 years and 64 days.

CONTRACT STATUS: Signed 5-year contract in 1979 ... contract was extended for 2 more years thru 1986 season.

1985 SEASON: Had another consistent year ... Among A.L. second basemen: second with 739 total chances and 104 double plays; third with 425 assists ... 40 RBIs were his most since driving in 46 in 1980 ... Most games played, GW-RBIs, and stolen bases since 1982 ... Had 5,000th career at-bat, September 29 vs. Baltimore ... Hit 200th career double, October 3, off Milwaukee's Tim Leary ... Broke into Yankee All-Time lists in big way: now 15th on runs scored list, with 812; 18th on hit list, with 1,365; 18th with 4,958 at-bats; 19th with 1,323 games played; and tied with Roger Peckinpaugh for 20th at 53 triples ... Had 10 game hitting streak, June 30-July 11, going 15/36, .417 BA ... 5 HRs were most since smacking 7 in 1980 ... Had 3 doubles in 1st game of DH, July 30 @ Cleveland ... Scored 4 runs, July 27 @ Texas ... Had first career 2-HR game, September 5 vs. Oakland, going 4-for-4 .... .382 on-base %, 6th in A.L., 14th in majors ... 85 walks were tied 7th in A.L., 13th in majors ... Had 36 multiple hit games ... Received "Good Guy" Award—N.Y. Press Photographers Association.

CAREER: Has been on 4 All-Star teams in his 9 full seasons ... was leading International League in hitting when called up in '75 to Pirates ... named James P. Dawson Award Winner as top rookie in 1976 Yankee camp ... was rookie on All-Star ballot ... named to Topps All-Rookie team in 1976 ... hampered by right shoulder injury, and injury to outside of right knee that required minor surgery ... in 1977 named to AP, UPI, and TSN All-Star teams ... had 5 RBI game vs. Boston on 9/7/78 ... despite bruised left knee and pulled left hamstring, still made AP and UPI All-Star teams ... hamstring kept him out of post-season play ... in 1979 his 13 triples were 3rd in A.L. and most by a Yankee since Henrich's 14 in 1948 ... committed only 13 errors and his .985 pct. was just .003 behind league leader Duane Kuiper ... in 1980 had his best season ever as Yankee leadoff hitter ... led A.L. in walks, 119, most by Yankees since Mantle's 122 in 1962 ... had 13-game hitting streak in May, longest of his career ... named to UPI and TSN All-Star teams and won TSN Silver Bat Award for A.L. second basemen ... his solo HR in Game #3 of 1981 ALCS was the game winner to win AL pennant ... in 1982 led Yankees in games played (144), AB (553), runs scored (85), hits (155), and walks (75) ... 1984—Flirted with a .300 average all season before finishing at .287, second highest in his career ... stole 200th base of Yankee career on July 16 vs. Texas ... ranks 3rd on All-Time Yankee stolen base list.

PERSONAL/MISCELLANEOUS: Although born in South Carolina, Willie's family moved to Brownsville section of Brooklyn when he was a baby ... played stickball in streets and fields of Canarsie and at Tilden H.S. ... has 3 brothers and a sister ... his brother Terry was drafted by the Green Bay Packers in 1977 and also played for the Jets.

Tied major league record for most assists by second baseman in extra-inning game since 1900 with 13, August 25, 1976 (19 innings).

RANDOLPH (continued)

Established American League record for most chances accepted by second baseman in extra-inning game with 20, August 25, 1976 (19 innings).

Led American League second basemen in putouts (355), assists (478), and doubleplays (128) in 1979.

YR	Club	AVG	G	AB	R	H	2B	3B	HR	RBI	BB	SO	SB
1972	Bradenton	.317	44	167	21	53	6	5	0	10	24	23	10
1973	Charleston	.280	121	428	93	120	25	6	8	51	90*	54	43
1974	Thetford Mines	.254	135	461	103*	117	28	6	12	53	110*	78	38
1975	Charleston	.339	91	313	41	106	13	5	7	42	37	29	14
	PITTSBURGH-a	.164	30	61	9	10	1	0	0	3	6	1	1
1976	YANKEES	.267	125	430	59	115	15	4	1	40	58	39	37
1977	YANKEES	.274	147	551	91	151	28	11	4	40	64	53	13
1978	YANKEES-b	.279	134	499	87	139	18	6	3	42	82	51	36
1979	YANKEES	.270	153	574	98	155	15	13	5	61	95	39	32
1980	YANKEES	.294	138	513	99	151	23	7	7	46	119*	45	30
1981	YANKEES	.232	93	357	59	83	14	3	2	24	57	24	14
1982	YANKEES	.280	144	553	85	155	21	4	3	36	75	35	16
1983	YANKEES-c	.279	104	420	73	117	21	1	2	38	53	32	12
1984	YANKEES	.287	142	564	86	162	24	2	2	31	86	42	10
1985	YANKEES	.276	143	497	75	137	21	2	5	40	85	39	16
Minor League Totals		**.289**	**391**	**1369**	**258**	**396**	**72**	**22**	**27**	**156**	**261**	**184**	**105**
N.Y.Y. Totals		**.275**	**1323**	**4958**	**812**	**1365**	**200**	**53**	**34**	**398**	**774**	**397**	**217**
M.L. Totals		**.274**	**1353**	**5019**	**821**	**1375**	**201**	**53**	**34**	**401**	**780**	**398**	**218**

GWRBI: 1980-5; 1981-2; 1982-6; 1983-1; 1984-5; 1985-6. Total-25.

Selected by Pittsburgh Pirates' organization in 7th round of free-agent draft, June 6, 1972.
a-Traded with pitchers Ken Brett and Dock Ellis to New York Yankees for pitcher Doc Medich, December 11, 1975.
b-On disabled list, June 23 to July 14, 1978.
c-On disabled list, June 27 to July 11 and July 13 to August 5, 1983.

DIVISION SERIES RECORD

YR	Club, Opp.	AVG	G	AB	R	H	2B	3B	HR	RBI	BB	SO	SB
1981	N.Y. vs Mil.	.200	5	20	0	4	0	0	0	1	1	4	0

CHAMPIONSHIP SERIES RECORD

YR	Club, Opp.	AVG	G	AB	R	H	2B	3B	HR	RBI	BB	SO	SB
1975	Pit. vs Cin.	.000	2	2	1	0	0	0	0	0	0	1	0
1976	N.Y. vs K.C.	.118	5	17	0	2	0	0	0	1	3	1	1
1977	N.Y. vs K.C.	.278	5	18	4	5	1	0	0	2	1	0	0
1978	N.Y. vs K.C.				(Eligible, replaced due to injury)								
1980	N.Y. vs K.C.	.385	3	13	0	5	2	0	0	1	1	3	0
1981	N.Y. vs Oak.	.333	3	12	2	4	0	0	1	2	0	1	0
L.C.S. Totals		**.258**	**18**	**62**	**7**	**16**	**3**	**0**	**1**	**6**	**5**	**6**	**1**

WORLD SERIES RECORD

Established World Series record for most bases on balls, six-game Series (9), 1981.

Tied World Series record for fewest chances accepted by second baseman, game (0), October 25, 1981.

YR	Club, Opp.	AVG	G	AB	R	H	2B	3B	HR	RBI	BB	SO	SB
1976	N.Y. vs Cin.	.071	4	14	1	1	0	0	0	0	1	3	0
1977	N.Y. vs L.A.	.160	6	25	5	4	2	0	1	1	2	2	0
1978	N.Y. vs L.A.				(Eligible, replaced due to injury)								
1981	N.Y. vs L.A.	.222	6	18	5	4	1	1	2	3	9	0	1
W.S. Totals		**.158**	**16**	**57**	**11**	**9**	**3**	**1**	**3**	**4**	**12**	**5**	**1**

ALL-STAR GAME RECORD

Established All-Star Game record for most assists by second baseman, nine-inning game (6), July 19, 1977.

Tied All-Star Game record for most at bats, nine-inning game (5), July 19, 1977; most errors, game (2), July 8, 1980.

YR	Club, Site	AVG	G	AB	R	H	2B	3B	HR	RBI	BB	SO	SB
1976	A.L., Phil				(Selected, replaced due to injury)								
1977	A.L., N.Y. (AL)	.200	1	5	0	1	0	0	0	1	0	2	0
1980	A.L., L.A.	.500	1	4	0	2	0	0	0	0	0	0	0
1981	A.L., Cle.	.333	1	3	0	1	0	0	0	0	0	1	0
A.S.G. Totals		**.333**	**3**	**12**	**0**	**4**	**0**	**0**	**0**	**1**	**0**	**3**	**0**

DID YOU KNOW ... The 1927 Yankees, Murderer's Row, considered by many the greatest team in baseball history, went through the entire 154 game schedule that year using only 25 men.

1985 vs. OPPONENTS

Club	AB	H	HR	RBI	AVG
Baltimore	25	6	0	4	.240
Boston	51	9	0	1	.176
Cleveland	30	12	0	5	.400
Detroit	27	8	0	1	.296
Milwaukee	40	7	0	2	.175
Toronto	32	10	0	2	.313
California	41	13	0	3	.317
Chicago	48	13	0	1	.271
Kansas City	39	8	0	0	.205
Minnesota	40	17	0	4	.425
Oakland	43	11	3	5	.256
Seattle	35	9	0	3	.257
Texas	46	14	2	9	.304
1st Half	291	82	2	24	.282
2nd Half	206	55	3	16	.267
vs. LHP	185	58	2	11	.314
vs. RHP	312	79	3	29	.253
Home	221	58	3	21	.262
Away	276	79	2	19	.286

RANDOLPH'S BESTS

Season

AVG.	.294–1980
H	162–1984
HR	7–1980
RBI	61–1979
SB	37–1976
Hit Strk	16 games–1983

Game

H	4–10 times
HR	2–vs. Oak 9/5/85
RBI	5–@ Bost. 9-7-78
SB	3–@ Cal. 6-11-80

RASMUSSEN, DENNIS LEE (LHP) #45

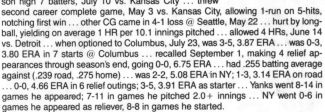

6-7, 225. Born 4/18/59 in Los Angeles, CA. Age 26, turns 27 April 18. Resides in Omaha, NE. BL. TL. Married: Sharon Wesely 2/6/82. Child: Ashley (2). College: Creighton University.

MAJOR LEAGUE SERVICE: 1 year, 124 days

CONTRACT STATUS: Signed 1-year contract for 1986.

1985 SEASON: Started season with major league team for first time in five years as pro ... struck out season high 7 batters, July 10 vs. Kansas City ... threw second career complete game, May 3 vs. Kansas City, notching first win ... other CG came in 4-1 loss @ Seattle, May 22 ... hurt by long-ball, yielding on average 1 HR per 10.1 innings pitched ... allowed 4 HRs, June 14 vs. Detroit ... when optioned to Columbus, July 23, was 3-5, 3.87 ERA ... was 0-3, 3.80 ERA in 7 starts @ Columbus ... recalled September 1, making 4 relief appearances through season's end, going 0-0, 6.75 ERA ... had .255 batting average against (.239 road, .275 home) ... was 2-2, 5.08 ERA in NY; 1-3, 3.14 ERA on road ... 0-0, 4.66 ERA in 6 relief outings; 3-5, 3.91 ERA as starter ... Yanks went 8-14 in games he appeared; 7-11 in games he pitched 2.0+ innings ... NY went 0-6 in games he appeared as reliever, 8-8 in games he started.

CAREER: Known as fastball pitcher, but gets many of his strikeouts with big breaking curveball ... 1982—finished second in PCL with 162 K's for Spokane ... 1983—was ace of Columbus staff, leading I.L. in K's and tying for league lead in wins and starts ... struckout 14 batters in a game at Charleston ... made his first major league start on May 23 striking out a career high 10 batters, in 8 innings of 2-hit shutout to gain his first M.L. win.

PERSONAL/MISCELLANEOUS: Grew up in Lakewood, CO. where he was a baseball and basketball star at Bear Creek H.S. ... played college baseball and basketball at Creighton University in Omaha, NE ... played with Kevin McKenna (Indiana Pacers '83-'84) and against Larry Bird and Dave Corzine ... is grandson of Wilbur Lee (Bill) Brubaker, infielder with Pittsburgh Pirates and Boston Braves, 1932-40 and 1943.

Led Eastern League in wild pitches with 18 in 1981.

YR	CLUB	W-L	ERA	G	GS	CG	Sho	SV	IP	H	R	ER	BB	SO
1980	Salinas,	4-6	5.45	11	11	4	1	0	76	69	51	46	52	63
1981	Holyoke	8-12	3.98	24	24	6	1	0	156	134	95	69	99	125
1982	Spokane-a	11-8	5.03	27	27	4	2	0	171.2	166	110	96	113	162
1983	Columbus-b	†13-10	4.57	28	28†	8	1	0	181	161	106	92	108	187*
	SAN DIEGO-c	0-0	1.98	4	1	0	0	0	13.2	10	5	3	8	13
1984	Columbus	4-1	3.09	6	6	3	1	0	43.2	24	15	15	27	30
	YANKEES	9-6	4.57	24	24	1	0	0	147.2	127	79	75	60	110
1985	Columbus	0-3	3.80	7	7	1	0	0	45.0	41	24	19	25	43
	YANKEES	3-5	3.98	22	16	2	0	0	101.2	97	56	45	42	63
Minor League Totals		40-40	4.50	103	103	26	6	0	673.1	595	361	337	424	610
N.Y.Y. Totals		15-11	3.73	46	40	3	0	0	289.1	224	135	120	102	173
M.L. Totals		12-11	4.21	50	41	3	0	0	263.0	234	140	123	110	186

Selected by Pittsburgh Pirates' organization in 18th round of free-agent draft, June 7, 1977.
Selected by California Angels' organization in 1st round (17th player selected) of free-agent draft, June 3, 1980.

RASMUSSEN (continued)

a- Traded to New York Yankees, November 24, 1982, completing deal in which New York traded pitcher Tommy John to California Angels for a player to be named later, August 31, 1982.

b- Traded with second baseman Edwin Rodriguez to San Diego Padres, September 12, 1983, completing deal in which San Diego traded pitcher John Montefusco to New York Yankees for two players to be named later, August 26, 1983.

c- Traded with a player to be named later to New York Yankees from San Diego Padres for third baseman Graig Nettles, March 30, 1984. Yankees acquired pitcher Darin Cloninger to complete deal, April 26, 1984.

1985							CAREER					
ERA	W-L-S	G	IP	H	ER	Club	ERA	W-L-S	G	IP	H	ER
10.80	0-0-0	1	1.2	3	2	**Baltimore**	5.48	0-2-0	4	23.0	24	14
9.00	0-1-0	1	6.0	10	6	**Boston**	8.27	0-2-0	3	16.1	25	15
—	—	—	—	—	—	**California**	6.97	0-1-0	2	10.1	7	8
0.00	0-0-0	2	13.0	11	0	**Chicago**	1.80	1-0-0	3	20.0	13	4
—	—	—	—	—	—	**Cleveland**	4.50	1-0-0	1	6.0	4	3
4.63	0-1-0	4	11.2	17	6	**Detroit**	4.10	1-1-0	6	26.1	29	12
4.28	2-1-0	4	27.1	15	13	**Kansas City**	3.78	3-1-0	5	33.1	20	14
2.19	0-0-0	2	12.1	15	3	**Milwaukee**	2.05	2-0-0	4	26.1	15	6
2.35	1-0-0	2	7.2	4	2	**Minnesota**	3.05	2-0-0	4	20.2	13	7
1.04	0-0-0	1	8.2	4	1	**Oakland**	2.63	0-0-0	2	13.2	10	4
6.10	0-2-0	2	10.1	9	7	**Seattle**	2.36	2-3-0	5	34.1	20	9
18.00	0-0-0	1	2.0	6	4	**Texas**	12.60	0-0-0	2	5.0	10	7
9.00	0-0-0	2	1.0	3	1	**Toronto**	10.90	0-1-0	5	14.0	24	17
3.98	3-5-0	22	101.2	97	45	**Total**	4.33	12-11-0	46	249.1	224	120
5.08	2-2-0	10	44.1	46	25	**Home**						
3.14	1-3-0	12	57.1	51	20	**Road**						

5—5/3/85 vs. K.C.		**Low Hit**	5—2 times
7—7/10/85 vs. K.C.		**K-High**	10—5/23/84 @ Seattle
2—		**Win Streak**	6—1984

S = SHUTOUTS

RIGHETTI, DAVID ALLEN "Dave" "Rags" (LHP) #19

6-3, 198. Born 11/28/58 in San Jose, CA where he resides. Age 27 turns 28 on November 28. TL. BL. Single. College: San Jose City College.

MAJOR LEAGUE SERVICE: 4 years and 151 days.

CONTRACT STATUS: Signed 4-year contract (with option for 5th) in 1982 ... contract extends thru 1986 season ('87 with option).

1985 SEASON: As debate continued on whether he should start or relieve, Dave once again proved to be one of baseball's premier relievers ... 74 appearances set a new Yankee record, breaking Sparky Lyle's mark of 72 games set in 1977 ... began season impressively, not allowing any runs in his first 7 outings, going 1-0 with 4 saves, throwing 8.1 innings ... struck out a season high 4 batters three times: May 30 vs. California; June 30 vs. Milwaukee; & September 5 vs. Oakland ... had rough stint from May 25 through June 20, going 1-4, with just 2 saves (17.1 IP, 14 ER, 7.27 ERA) ... beginning with next appearance, went 8-1 with 18 saves through season's end (14 ER, 60.1 IP, 2.09 ERA), lowering ERA from 3.66 to 2.78 ... was 29-for-43 in "save situations", failing: April 27; May 12 & 25; June 7, 12, 18 & 20; July 26 & 30 (2nd game); August 18, 21 & 24; September 5 & 9 ... from July 29 through September 29, went 5-0, with 10 saves ... did not allow an ER in 13 consecutive outings, August 9 to 31 (17.2 IP, 5 BB, 17 Ks), lowering ERA from 3.26 to 2.62 ... was named A.L. Player of the Month in August (4-0, with 5 saves, 1.17 ERA, finishing 11 of 16 games, 23.0 IP, 14 hits, 3 ER, & 22 Ks) ... allowed just 5 HRs in 107.0 IP ... recorded saves in last 4 straight games ... combined with teammate Brian Fisher for one of the Yankees' best relief tandems—the combined stats: 16-11, with 43 saves, 205.1 IP, 59 ER, 2.59 ERA ... Dave finished 60 of 74 appearances—81% ... was 9-1, 2.24 ERA at Yankee Stadium ... opposing batters combined for .231 batting average against.

CAREER: 1984—Moved to the bullpen where he saved 31 of 40 save situations ... only Lyle (35 in 1972) and Gossage (33 in 1980) had better seasons as Yankees ... got his 500th career strikeout vs. Angel's Brian Downing on September 1 at California ... 1983—pitched his July 4th no-hitter against the Red Sox at Yankee Stadium ... was 10-3 in 1st half of season ... struckout 11 vs Chicago on August 15 ... struckout 7 or more on 12 occasions ... 1982—suffered slight sophomore jinx, but still led Yankee staff in K's with 163 (3rd in A.L.) ... 1981—American League Rookie of the Year, narrowly missing the ERA crown with 2.06 (fell 1.2 innings short) ... in post-season started and won game 2 of Division Series vs Milwaukee ... relieved game 5 and earned deciding win ... won clinching game (#3) of A.L.C.S. at Oakland ... started and lost game #3 of World Series ... 1979—made major league debut September 16 vs Detroit at Yankee Stadium on

Catfish Hunter Day with no decision . . . named to Topps National Association Class AAA All-Star team . . . 1978—July 16 for Tulsa, struck out 21 batters at Midland, striking out the side 4 times and having stretch of 7 straight K's.

PERSONAL/MISCELLANEOUS: Grew up in San Jose where he was All-League in baseball at Pioneer H.S. . . . also played basketball . . . attended San Jose City College where he was a teammate of Blue Jays pitcher Dave Stieb . . . won JC Player of Year honors in 1977 . . . played against A's 3B Carney Lansford in American Legion . . . grew up as Giants and A's fan . . . brother Steve is in Texas organization . . . father is former Yankee minor league shortstop and 1st time he saw Dave pitch professionally was in clinching game of ALCS at Oakland.

Pitched 4-0 no-hit victory against Boston Red Sox, July 4, 1983.
Named American League Rookie of the Year by Baseball Writers' Association of America, 1981.

YR	CLUB	W-L	ERA	G	GS	CG	Sho	SV	IP	H	R	ER	BB	SO
1977	Asheville	11-3	3.14	17	16	3	0	0	109	98	47	38	53	101
1978	Tulsa-a-b	5-5	3.16	13	13	6	0	0	91	66	40	32	49	127
1979	West Haven-c	4-3	1.96	11	11	3	0	0	69	45	23	15	45	78
	Columbus-d	3-2	2.93	8	6	3	2	0	40	22	13	13	19	44
	YANKEES	0-1	3.71	3	3	0	0	0	17	10	7	7	10	13
1980	Columbus	6-10	4.63	24	23	4	1	0	142	124	79	73	101*	139
1981	Columbus	5-0	1.00	7	7	2	2	0	45	30	8	5	26	50
	YANKEES	8-4	2.06	15	15	2	0	0	105	75	25	24	38	89
1982	Columbus	1-0	2.81	4	4	1	0	0	25.2	22	11	8	12	33
	YANKEES	11-10	3.79	33	27	4	0	1	183.0	155	88	77	108*	163
1983	YANKEES	14-8	3.44	31	31	7	2	0	217.0	194	96	83	67	169
1984	YANKEES-e	5-6	2.34	64	0	0	0	31	96.1	79	29	25	37	90
1985	YANKEES	12-7	2.78	74	0	0	0	29	107.0	96	36	33	45	92
Minor League Totals		**35-23**	**3.17**	**84**	**80**	**22**	**5**	**0**	**521.2**	**407**	**221**	**184**	**305**	**572**
M.L. Totals		**50-36**	**3.09**	**220**	**76**	**13**	**2**	**61**	**725.1**	**609**	**281**	**249**	**305**	**616**

Selected by Texas Rangers' organization in 1st round (ninth player selected) of free-agent draft, January 11, 1977.
a-On disabled list, July 31 to September 2, 1978.
b-Traded with pitchers Mike Griffin and Paul Mirabella and outfielders Juan Beniquez and Greg Jemison to New York Yankees for pitchers Sparky Lyle, Larry McCall and Dave Rajsich, catcher Mike Heath, shortstop Domingo Ramos and cash, November 10, 1978.
c-On disabled list, May 21 to June 28, 1979.
d-On disabled list, June 28 to July 20, and August 2 to August 23, 1979.
e-On disabled list, June 17 to July 2, 1984 with cut left index finger.

DIVISION SERIES RECORD

YR	CLUB, Opp.	W-L	ERA	G	GS	CG	Sho	SV	IP	H	R	ER	BB	SO
1981	N.Y. vs Mil.	2-0	1.00	2	1	0	0	0	9.0	8	1	1	3	13

CHAMPIONSHIP SERIES RECORD

YR	CLUB, Opp.	W-L	ERA	G	GS	CG	Sho	SV	IP	H	R	ER	BB	SO
1981	N.Y. vs Oak.	1-0	0.00	1	1	0	0	0	6.0	4	0	0	2	4

WORLD SERIES RECORD

YR	CLUB Opp.	W-L	ERA	G	GS	CG	Sho	SV	IP	H	R	ER	BB	SO
1981	N.Y. vs L.A.	0-0	13.50	1	1	0	0	0	2.0	5	3	3	2	1

	1985							**CAREER**				
ERA	W-L-S	G	IP	H	ER	Club	ERA	W-L-S	G	IP	H	ER
2.00	1-0-3	6	9.0	6	2	**Baltimore**	2.64	4-4-6	17	64.2	55	19
0.77	2-1-2	8	11.2	11	1	**Boston**	2.35	7-4-6	22	69.0	45	18
0.00	2-0-2	6	8.2	3	0	**California**	2.73	4-2-3	18	59.1	40	18
3.18	1-0-3	7	11.1	10	4	**Chicago**	2.32	4-1-7	17	50.1	37	13
1.35	0-0-5	6	6.2	6	1	**Cleveland**	3.22	3-3-7	19	58.2	49	21
15.43	0-1-0	2	2.1	5	4	**Detroit**	4.30	3-3-2	12	58.2	55	28
2.00	1-1-3	6	9.0	8	2	**Kansas City**	2.66	4-4-6	16	67.2	58	20
3.75	2-1-2	7	12.0	11	5	**Milwaukee**	3.67	4-4-5	19	68.2	65	28
0.00	1-0-2	3	6.1	4	0	**Minnesota**	2.57	3-4-3	16	66.2	53	19
3.09	0-2-0	7	11.2	13	4	**Oakland**	3.95	2-4-3	17	43.1	52	19
2.45	0-0-2	4	3.2	3	1	**Seattle**	4.19	2-2-5	14	34.1	32	16
2.08	2-1-2	5	8.2	7	2	**Texas**	3.93	6-2-3	17	57.2	52	25
10.50	0-0-3	7	6.0	9	8	**Toronto**	4.69	4-1-5	17	40.1	42	21
2.78	12-7-29	74	107.0	96	33	**Total**	3.09	50-36-61	122	725.0	609	249
2.24	9-1-17	38	56.1	48	14	**Home**						
3.38	3-6-12	36	50.2	48	19	**Road**						

—		**Low Hit**	0—7/4/83 vs. Boston	
4—3 times		**K-High**	11—9/11/81 vs. Boston	
5—		**Win Streak**	5—2 times	

S = SAVES

ROBERTSON, ANDRE LEVETT "Andre" (SS) #18

5-10, 162. Born 10/2/57 in Orange, TX, where he resides. Age 28, turns 29 October 2. BR. TR. Married: Lanier Hebert, 12/8/84. College: University of Texas.

MAJOR LEAGUE SERVICE: 3 years and 44 days.

CONTRACT STATUS: Signed 1-year contract for 1986.

1985 SEASON: Showed a good stick despite playing irregularly ... began 1985 by being placed on 21-day DL 3/24 with torn cartilage in left knee ... was assigned to Columbus for rehabilitation May 20 ... went 11/28 .393 BA in 9 games during rehab ... recalled from Rehab May 29 ... hit HR in first start 5/30 vs. California and again in following game 5/31 vs. Seattle ... homers in back to back games 1st in career ... went 7/15 .467 BA in 1st 6 games ... played in only 5 games in June ... hit in 8 of 12 games in July going 11/33 .333 BA ... made 1st ML start @ third base, July 9 vs. KC ... had 3rd career 2 RBI game, 9/4 vs. Seattle ... went 3-for-4 6/1 vs. Seattle, 5th time in career, 1st since 8/16/83 ... played 2 games @ 2nd; 33 @ 3rd and 14 @ SS.

CAREER: 1984—Began the season at Columbus, making a comeback from August '83's car accident ... recalled from Columbus on April 16, and was regular shortstop until being optioned back to Columbus June 15 ... was recalled to NY on September 9 ... 1983—Anchored the Yankee infield with his outstanding defense at shortstop ... hit in 10 straight games from June 8 to 18th, raising his BA from .210 to .266 ... was involved in serious car accident on August 18 in which he suffered a broken neck, forcing him to miss the remainder of season ... 1982— began season at Columbus ... called up to Yankees, May 13 ... hit first ML HR at Oakland, May 16 off Steve McCatty ... optioned to Columbus July 8 and recalled to Yankees August 20 ... played outstanding defense, and showed potential and improvement at the plate ... 1981—named to International League All-Star team as shortstop ... called up to Yankees September 2, when Bucky Dent was disabled with torn hand ligament that required surgery ... singled his first ML at-bat vs Mike Jones at KC, September 3 ... played defensively 1981 ALCS and WS ... 1980— with Yankee organization, progressed from A ball to AA, and finally to AAA in just his second pro season ... 1979—began in Toronto Blue Jays organization.

PERSONAL/MISCELLANEOUS: Grew up in Orange, TX where he attended West Orange High ... played baseball, football, basketball, and track ... was All-State twice and All-American once in baseball ... played Little League, Babe Ruth and American Legion baseball in Orange ... spent three years at University of Texas in Austin, where he teamed with Jerry Don Gleaton and played against Tim Lollar at Arkansas ... was San Francisco Giant fan as youngster, particularly Willie Mays.

Led International League shortstops in fielding percentage with .971, in putouts with 210 and in assists with 362 in 1981.

YR	Club	AVG	G	AB	R	H	2B	3B	HR	RBI	BB	SO	SB
1979	Dunedin	.216	70	264	35	57	24	3	3	28	26	50	2
	Syracuse-a	.000	1	4	0	0	0	0	0	0	0	0	0
1980	Ft. Lauderdale	.249	63	233	30	58	7	4	0	22	17	41	10
	Nashville	.261	13	46	7	12	2	1	1	11	3	3	0
	Columbus	.251	68	215	22	54	7	3	3	19	7	29	2
1981	Columbus	.259	123	402	55	104	13	6	9	49	13	70	4
	YANKEES	.263	10	19	1	5	1	0	0	0	0	3	1
1982	Columbus	.203	57	202	28	41	7	3	3	26	18	40	1
	YANKEES	.220	44	118	16	26	5	0	2	9	8	19	0
1983	YANKEES-b	.248	98	322	37	80	16	3	1	22	8	54	2
1984	Columbus	.239	69	226	30	54	8	1	6	19	8	42	1
	YANKEES	.214	52	140	10	30	5	1	0	6	4	20	0
1985	Columbus	.393	9	28	3	11	1	0	0	1	1	3	0
	YANKEES-c	.328	50	125	16	41	5	0	2	17	6	24	1
Minor League Totals		**.241**	**473**	**1620**	**210**	**391**	**69**	**21**	**25**	**175**	**93**	**278**	**20**
M.L. Totals		**.251**	**254**	**724**	**80**	**182**	**32**	**4**	**5**	**54**	**26**	**120**	**4**

GWRBI: 1982-1, 1983-1, 1984-1, 1985-0. Total-3.

Selected by Toronto Blue Jay's organization in 4th round of free-agent draft, June 5, 1979.
a-Sold to New York Yankees, December 10, 1979.
b-On disabled list from August 18 thru remainder of season with broken neck.
c-On disabled list with cartilage tear in left knee from March 24 to May 29; including rehabilitation assignment to Columbus, May 20 to May 29.

DIVISION SERIES RECORD

YR	Club, Opp.	AVG	G	AB	R	H	2B	3B	HR	RBI	BB	SO	SB
1981	N.Y. vs Mil.					(Eligible, did not play)							

CHAMPIONSHIP SERIES RECORD

YR Club, Opp.	AVG	G	AB	R	H	2B	3B	HR	RBI	BB	SO	SB
1981 N.Y. vs Oak.	.000	1	1	0	0	0	0	0	0	0	0	0

WORLD SERIES RECORD

YR Club, Opp.	AVG	G	AB	R	H	2B	3B	HR	RBI	BB	SO	SB
1981 N.Y. vs L.A.	.000	1	0	0	0	0	0	0	0	0	0	0

1985 vs. OPPONENTS

Club	AB	H	HR	RBI	AVG
Baltimore	12	3	0	0	.250
Boston	8	4	0	1	.500
Cleveland	14	3	0	2	.214
Detroit	9	1	0	1	.111
Milwaukee	11	5	0	2	.455
Toronto	10	1	0	0	.100
California	7	2	1	2	.286
Chicago	10	4	0	1	.400
Kansas City	9	4	0	1	.444
Minnesota	6	4	0	1	.667
Oakland	7	1	0	0	.143
Seattle	13	7	1	4	.538
Texas	9	2	0	2	.222
1st Half	29	13	2	6	.448
2nd Half	96	28	0	11	.292
vs. LHP	101	32	1	14	.317
vs. RHP	24	9	1	3	.375
Home	70	28	2	11	.400
Away	55	13	0	6	.236

ROBERTSON'S BESTS

Season

AVG.	.328–1985
H	80–1983
HR	2–1982, 1985
RBI	22–1983
SB	2–1983
Hit Strk	10 games–1983

Game

H	3–5 times
HR	1–5 times
RBI	2–3 times
SB	1–4 times

ROENICKE, GARY STEVEN (OF-DH) #11

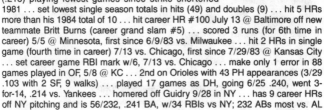

6-3, 200. Born 12/5/54 in Covina, Cal. Age 31, turns 32 December 5. Resides in Covina, Cal. BR. TR. Married: Debra Lynn Britton 10/8/78. Children: Jarett Steven (6) and Joshua James (4).

MAJOR LEAGUE SERVICE: 7 years, 164 days.

CONTRACT STATUS: Signed 3-year contract with Orioles, January 24, 1984 . . . contract extends thru 1986 season.

1985 SEASON: Hit for lowest professional average (.218) playing fewest games since strike shortened 1981 . . . set lowest single season totals in hits (49) and doubles (9) . . . hit 5 HRs more than his 1984 total of 10 . . . hit career HR #100 July 13 @ Baltimore off new teammate Britt Burns (career grand slam #5) . . . scored 3 runs (for 6th time in career) 5/5 @ Minnesota, first since 6/9/83 vs. Milwaukee . . . hit 2 HRs in single game (fourth time in career) 7/13 vs. Chicago, first since 7/29/83 @ Kansas City . . . set career game RBI mark w/6, 7/13 vs. Chicago . . . make only 1 error in 88 games played in OF, 5/8 @ KC . . . 2nd on Orioles with 43 PH appearances (3/29 .103 with 2 SF, 9 walks) . . . played 17 games as DH, going 6/25 .240, went 3-for-14, .214 vs. Yankees . . . homered off Guidry 9/28 in NY . . . has 9 career HRs off NY pitching and is 56/232, .241 BA, w/34 RBIs vs NY; 232 ABs most vs. AL opponent.

CAREER: 1984—Platooned in leftfield mostly with John Lowenstein, but also shared the position with three other Orioles . . . saw action in all three outfield positions, and was third among A.L. outfielders in fielding with a .995 mark . . . hit an eighth inning grand slam in Yankee Stadium on June 17, his fourth career grand slam, and all four were hit on the road . . . was hit by four pitches, second most on the Orioles in 1984 . . . 1983—second busiest pinch hitter in AL behind Chicago's Jerry Hairston . . . batted .211 as a pinch hitter (8/38), and finished third on Orioles with 19 homers and was fourth with 64 RBI . . . reached base 9 times in 10 plate appearances in the ALCS vs. Chicago . . . hit 2-run homer off Floyd Bannister in game #2 . . . 1982—set career highs in batting (.270) and RBI (74) and finished second on team in slugging (.499) . . . of his 106 hits, 47 went for extra bases (44%) . . . hit in career high 16 straight games from Aug. 7-27, also an Oriole team best . . . 1981—batted .328 in first half of season, but only .191 after strike . . . was batting .293 on Sept. 26, before a 1-21 slide in last 14 games brought average down to .269 . . . 1980—hit .341 from May 28 through Aug. 28, despite missing 30 games with a fractured wrist from June 9 thru July 15 . . . hit just .103 in last 30 games . . . underwent surgery that fall for removal of loose bone fragments from right elbow . . . 1979—tied for second on Orioles with a career high 25 homers . . . had 7 straight hits over 2 games, June 2 and 4 . . . hit into a triple play vs. Oakland on May 7, and two days later got Baltimore's only hit off Oakland's Mike Norris . . . was hit in the face by a pitch from White Sox Lerrin LaGrow on April 7, the second

ROENICKE (continued)

game of the season, and 25 stitches were required to close the wound. Returned to action 8 days later using a helmet face guard which he would later discard before the start of the '81 season ... 1978—appeared in only 17 games in 1st six weeks of season and was optioned to Rochester in May ... rejoined Baltimore in Sept. after hitting .366 in last 34 games with the Red Wings.

PERSONAL/MISCELLANEOUS: As an outfielder Gary has a career fielding percentage of .989, making only 16 errors in 1481 total chances ... Gary's brother Ron, 2 years younger, plays for the Padres ... Gary has attended both Cal Poly in Pomona and UCLA in the offseasons ... hobbies include water skiing, fishing, hunting and golf.

Led American League outfielders in fielding with 1.000 percentage in 1980.
Led American Association in being hit by pitch with 13 in 1977.
Led Eastern League outfielders with 22 assists in 1975.
Tied for Eastern League lead in being hit by pitch with 12 in 1975.
Led Florida State League in being hit by pitch with 11 in 1974.
Tied for Florida State League lead in double plays by third basemen with 32 in 1974.
Led New York-Penn League third basemen with 71 putouts and in fielding with .937 percentage in 1973.
Named Eastern League Most Valuable Player, 1975.

YR	Club	AVG	G	AB	R	H	2B	3B	HR	RBI	BB	SO	SB
1973	Jamestown	.298	68	255	48	76	17	6	3	40	37	38	3
1974	West Palm Beach	.277	131	470	68	130	24	0	14	82*	63	61	22
	Quebec City	.333	1	3	0	1	0	0	0	0	0	0	0
1975	Quebec City	.285	131	466	67	133	23	0	14	74*	58	73	6
1976	Denver	.290	77	252	56	73	11	5	12	44	41	39	4
	MONTREAL	.222	29	90	9	20	3	1	2	5	4	18	0
1977	Denver-a	.321	124	448	87	144	31	4	11	72	46	45	12
1978	BALTIMORE	.259	27	58	5	15	3	0	3	15	8	3	0
	Rochester	.307	98	329	49	101	15	1	13	64	34	50	3
1979	BALTIMORE	.261	133	376	60	98	16	1	25	64	61	74	1
1980	BALTIMORE-b	.239	118	297	40	71	13	0	10	28	41	49	2
1981	BALTIMORE	.269	85	219	31	59	16	0	3	20	23	29	1
1982	BALTIMORE	.270	137	393	58	106	25	1	21	74	70	73	6
1983	BALTIMORE	.260	115	323	45	84	13	0	19	64	30	35	2
1984	BALTIMORE	.224	121	326	36	73	19	1	10	44	58	43	1
1985	BALTIMORE-c	.218	113	225	36	49	9	0	15	43	44	36	2
Minor League Totals		**.296**	**630**	**2223**	**375**	**658**	**121**	**16**	**67**	**376**	**279**	**306**	**50**
A.L. Totals		**.250**	**849**	**2217**	**311**	**555**	**114**	**3**	**106**	**352**	**327**	**339**	**15**
M.L. Totals		**.249**	**878**	**2307**	**328**	**575**	**117**	**4**	**108**	**357**	**339**	**360**	**15**

GWRBI: 1979-11, 1980-4, 1981-2, 1982-3, 1983-6, 1984-4, 1985-5. Total-35.

Selected by Montreal Expos' organization in 1st round (eighth player selected) of free agent draft, June 5, 1973.
a-Traded with pitchers Joe Kerrigan and Don Stanhouse to Baltimore Orioles for pitchers Rudy May, Randy Miller and Bryn Smith, December 7, 1977.
b-On disabled list, June 10 to July 15, 1980 with fractured wrist.
c-Traded to New York Yankees with a player to be named later for pitcher Rich Bordi and infielder Rex Hudler, December 11, 1985.

CHAMPIONSHIP SERIES RECORD

Tied Championship Series record for most consecutive games, one or more runs batted in, total Series (4).
Tied American League Championship Series record for most bases on balls, four-game Series (5), 1983.

YR	Club, Opp.	AVG	G	AB	R	H	2B	3B	HR	RBI	BB	SO	SB
1979	Bal. vs Cal.	.200	2	5	1	1	0	0	0	1	0	0	0
1983	Bal. vs Chi.	.750	3	4	4	3	1	0	1	4	5	0	0
L.C.S. Totals		**.444**	**5**	**9**	**5**	**4**	**1**	**0**	**1**	**5**	**5**	**0**	**0**

WORLD SERIES RECORD

YR	Club, Opp.	AVG	G	AB	R	H	2B	3B	HR	RBI	BB	SO	SB
1979	Bal. vs Pit.	.125	6	16	1	2	1	0	0	0	0	6	0
1983	Bal. vs Phi.	.000	3	7	0	0	0	0	0	0	0	2	0
W.S. Totals		**.087**	**9**	**23**	**1**	**2**	**1**	**0**	**0**	**0**	**0**	**8**	**0**

Yankee lefthanded pitchers won 68 games in 1980, establishing a major league record ... Tommy John led the way with 22, Ron Guidry had 17, Rudy May 15, Tom Underwood 13, and Tim Lollar 1.

1985 vs. OPPONENTS

Club	AB	H	HR	RBI	AVG
Baltimore	—	—	—	—	—
Boston	22	6	1	5	.273
Cleveland	20	2	1	4	.100
Detroit	16	3	1	3	.188
Milwaukee	13	4	2	3	.308
Toronto	14	2	2	3	.143
California	10	2	1	2	.200
Chicago	25	6	4	9	.240
Kansas City	13	5	2	3	.385
Minnesota	10	1	0	1	.100
Oakland	21	7	0	4	.333
Seattle	15	3	0	2	.200
Texas	15	2	0	1	.133
1st Half	124	28	8	24	.226
2nd Half	101	21	7	19	.208
vs. LHP	172	36	12	35	.209
vs. RHP	53	13	3	8	.245
Home	116	29	9	26	.250
Away	109	20	6	17	.183

ROENICKE'S BESTS

Season	
AVG.	.270–1982
H	106–1982
HR	25–1979
RBI	74–1982
SB	6–1982
Hit Strk	7 games–1983

Game	
H	4–4 times
HR	2–4 times
RBI	6–vs. Chi. 7-13-85
SB	1–15 times

SCURRY, RODNEY GRANT "Rod" (LHP)   #28

6-2, 195. Born 3/17/56 in Sacramento, CA. Resides in Reno, NV. Age 30, turned 30 March 17. BL. TL. Single.

MAJOR LEAGUE SERVICE: 6 years, 32 days.

CONTRACT STATUS: Signed through 1986 season.

1985 SEASON: The lefthander's contract was purchased from Pittsburgh for an undisclosed amount of cash, September 13 ... made 5 relief appearances while a Yankee, going 1-0 with 1 save, 2.84 ERA ... in his 12.2 IP in NY, K'd 17, walked 10 (4 walk came September 25 vs. Detroit) ... his Yankee save came Sept. 29 (2nd game) vs. Baltimore, while his win came October 4 @ Toronto, pitching 3.1 innings, allowing 1 run on 2 hits, 2 walks, 4 Ks ... before coming to N.Y., was 0-1 with 2 saves, 3.21 ERA at Pittsburgh—30 games, all relief ... had .236 batting average against with Pirates ... only loss with Pirates came in final outing, September 1 @ Cincinnati ... saves came June 1 vs. Atlanta and August 22 vs. Cincy.

CAREER: 1984—Made two relief appearances before going on DL on April 7 when he entered a drug rehabilitation program ... was reactivated on May 13 and returned to action the same day @ Atlanta, striking out the only batter he faced ... appeared in 27 games before returning to the DL on Aug. 5 with a tender left elbow ... Rod appeared in 14 games after coming off the DL on Aug. 27, notching two wins and two saves. In those 14 games he allowed only two earned runs (15.1 IP) for a 1.17 ERA ... opposing batters compiled a mere .175 average vs. Scurry ... underwent arthroscopic surgery on both knees on October 1 to remove loose fragments from both knees ... 1983—started the year strong, picking up two wins and a save in first three appearances ... struggled most of the season, his 5.56 ERA the highest in his major league career ... 1982—was third in the NL in appearances ... his 1.74 ERA was lowest of any major league pitcher with 20 + appearances ... set a Pirate team record for appearances by a lefthander ... 1981—after being used mainly in relief in 1980, Rod earned his first major league win as a starter, on April 19 @ Houston ... 1980—enjoyed a good minor league career as a starter, but was moved to full-time relief when he joined the major league club in 1980 ... rookie season was hampered after suffering a groin pull during the second half of the season ... 1979—finished second on Portland staff in starts and strikeouts and was third in appearances and innings pitched.

PERSONAL/MISCELLANEOUS: Grew up in Auburn, CA, but later moved to Sparks, NV ... was AAA Player of The Year in baseball as a senior at Proctor High School, in Reno, NV ... enjoys playing golf.

Pitched seven-inning, 2-0 no-hit victory against Richmond, July 25, 1977.
Led New York-Pennsylvania League in hit batsmen with 7 in 1974.

YR	CLUB	W-L	ERA	G	GS	CG	Sho	SV	IP	H	R	ER	BB	SO
1974	Niagara Falls	5-6	3.44	14	14	3	0	0	89	55	36	34	74	102
1975	Salem	9-12	3.68	26	26*	5	0	0	150	128	79	61	118	143
1976	Shreveport	8-8	3.87	24	24	1	0	0	123	120	71	53	83	83
1977	Shreveport	3-11	2.87	18	18	6	1	0	113	97	54	36	48	111
	Columbus	3-2	4.58	8	8	1	1	0	37	30	31	19	32	39
1978	Columbus-a	3-3	5.71	16	11	1	0	0	63	69	44	40	43	57
	Shreveport	1-4	4.71	5	5	1	0	0	29	27	19	15	24	38
1979	Portland-b	5-5	4.13	35	15	1	0	0	122	121	64	56	72	94
1980	PITTSBURGH	0-2	2.13	20	0	0	0	0	38	23	12	9	17	28

SCURRY (continued)

Year	Team	W-L	ERA	G				SV	IP	H	R	ER	BB	SO
1981	PITTSBURGH	4-5	3.77	27	7	0	0	7	74	74	33	31	40	65
1982	PITTSBURGH	4-5	1.74	76	0	0	0	14	103.2	79	26	20	64	95
1983	PITTSBURGH	4-9	5.56	61	0	0	0	7	68.0	63	45	42	53	67
1984	PITTSBURGH-c	5-6	2.53	43	0	0	0	4	46.1	28	14	13	22	48
1985	PITTSBURGH-d	0-1	3.21	30	0	0	0	2	47.2	42	22	17	28	43
	YANKEES	1-0	2.84	5	0	0	0	1	12.2	5	4	4	10	17
1985	Totals	1-1	3.13	35	0	0	0	3	60.1	47	26	21	38	60
Minor League Totals		37-51	3.89	146	121	19	2	0	726	647	398	314	494	667
N.L. Totals		17-28	3.15	257	7	0	0	34	377.2	309	152	132	224	346
M.L. Totals		18-28	3.14	262	7	0	0	35	390.1	314	156	136	234	363

Selected by Pittsburgh Pirates' organization in 1st round (11th player selected) of free-agent draft, June 5, 1974.
a-On disabled list, June 12 to July 11, 1978.
b-On disabled list, August 4 to August 14, 1979.
c-On disabled list, April 7 to May 13 and August 5 to August 27, 1984.
d-Sold to New York Yankees, September 15, 1985.

1985								CAREER					
ERA	W-L-S	G	IP	H	ER	Club	ERA	W-L-S	G	IP	H	ER	
0.00	0-0-1	1	3.0	0	0	**Baltimore**	0.00	0-0-1	1	3.0	0	0	
—	—	—	—	—	—	**Boston**	—	—	—	—	—	—	
—	—	—	—	—	—	**California**	—	—	—	—	—	—	
—	—	—	—	—	—	**Chicago**	—	—	—	—	—	—	
—	—	—	—	—	—	**Cleveland**	—	—	—	—	—	—	
6.23	0-0-0	2	4.1	2	3	**Detroit**	6.23	0-0-0	2	4.1	2	3	
—	—	—	—	—	—	**Kansas City**	—	—	—	—	—	—	
—	—	—	—	—	—	**Milwaukee**	—	—	—	—	—	—	
—	—	—	—	—	—	**Minnesota**	—	—	—	—	—	—	
—	—	—	—	—	—	**Oakland**	—	—	—	—	—	—	
—	—	—	—	—	—	**Seattle**	—	—	—	—	—	—	
—	—	—	—	—	—	**Texas**	—	—	—	—	—	—	
1.69	1-0-0	2	5.1	3	1	**Toronto**	1.69	1-0-0	2	5.1	3	1	
2.84	1-0-1	5	12.2	5	4	**Total**	2.84	1-0-1	5	12.2	5	4	
1.29	0-0-1	3	7.0	1	1	**Home**	—	—	—	—	—	—	
4.76	1-0-0	2	5.2	4	3	**Road**	—	—	—	—	—	—	

5—9/25/85 vs. Det.	**Low Hit**	—
1—	**K-High**	7—2 times
	Win Streak	3—1982

S = SAVE

SHIRLEY, ROBERT CHARLES "Bob" (LHP) #29

6-0, 180. Born 6/25/54 in Cushing, OK. Age 31, turns 32 June 25. BR. TL. Resides in Tulsa, OK. Married: Frances Fitzgerald, 10/5/74. Children: Charles (6), Clinton (4), and Clayton (3). College: University of Oklahoma.

MAJOR LEAGUE SERVICE: 9 years.

CONTRACT STATUS: Signed 3-year contract (with option for 4th) on December 15, 1982 ... contract extends thru 1985 season ('86 with option).

1985 SEASON: Had an effective season in middle relief role and as spot starter ... recorded second straight .500 season ... appeared in most games since 1980 with San Diego ... 2.64 ERA best posted as professional ... was 0-1 with 0 saves when asked to make first start, June 10 vs. Toronto, coming up a winner, allowing 1 run in 6.1 IP ... won next start also, June 16 vs. Detroit, spinning 4-hit complete game ... made three more starts prior to All-Star game, going 0-1 ... started just three games after All-Star break, losing @ Cleveland July 30 (2nd game); a no-decision vs. Toronto, September 14; and losing 1-0 to Milwaukee, October 2—another 4-hit CG ... both 4-hitters were career low-hit games ... first save came September 4 vs. Seattle—first save since August 29, 1981 ... second save came September 10 @ Milwaukee ... was 3-2, 0 saves, 3.54 ERA at All-Star break ... then 2-3, 2 saves, 1.93 ERA post ASB ... K:W ratio of 2.1:1 ... was 3-2, 2.27 ERA in relief, 2-3, 3.15 ERA as starter ... 0-4, 1 save, 3.92 ERA on road, 5-1, 1 save, 1.86 ERA at home ... has lifetime Yankee Stadium record of 11-4, 2.35 ERA (53 ER, 203.1 IP, 49 walks, 99 Ks) ... overall, .251 batting average against in '85, .226 in N.Y.

CAREER: Versatile and consistent performer, has split time between starting and relieving in big leagues ... in his rookie season with San Diego, 1977, posted career highs with 12 wins, 25 starts, 214 IP and 146 strikeouts ... made ML debut, beating Cincinnati 12-4 with all runs against him unearned, pitching 8⅔ innings allowing only 4 hits, striking out 11 ... April 23, '77 he retired 1st 25 batters in a game at Houston in registering 4-2 victory ... in '76, split time between Hawaii and Amarillo, both were championship teams ... in 1983, recorded 1st Yankee and AL win with 8-hit shutout at Yankee Stadium vs Royals on April 27 ... in 1984 he appeared in 41 games, 3rd on the Yankee staff ... he has a career record of 11-4 in Yankee Stadium.

PERSONAL/MISCELLANEOUS: Grew up in Oklahoma City, OK ... attended Putnam City (OK) High School ... had a fine collegiate career at University of Oklahoma, was an All-American in 1975, and a teammate of George Frazier ... enjoys golf, restoring antiques, and Bill Murray movies.

YR	CLUB	W-L	ERA	G	GS	CG	Sho	SV	IP	H	R	ER	BB	SO
1976	Amarillo	9-5	3.31	16	16	6	0	0	111	113	55	41	39	90
	Hawaii	5-5	5.22	13	13	4	0	0	81	91	62	47	24	47
1977	SAN DIEGO	12-18	3.70	39	25	1	0	0	214	215	107	88	100	146
1978	SAN DIEGO	8-11	3.69	50	20	2	0	5	166	164	75	68	61	102
1979	SAN DIEGO	8-16	3.38	49	25	4	1	0	205	196	89	77	59	117
1980	SAN DIEGO-a	11-12	3.55	59	12	3	0	7	137	143	58	54	54	67
1981	ST. LOUIS-b	6-4	4.10	28	11	1	0	1	79	78	42	36	34	36
1982	CINCINNATI-c	8-13	3.60	41	20	1	0	0	152.2	138	74	61	73	89
1983	YANKEES	5-8	5.08	25	17	1	1	0	108.0	122	71	61	36	53
1984	YANKEES	3-3	3.38	41	7	1	0	0	114.1	119	47	43	38	48
1985	YANKEES	5-5	2.64	48	8	2	0	2	109.0	103	34	32	26	55
Minor League Totals		14-10	4.13	29	29	10	0	0	192	204	117	88	63	137
N.Y.Y. Totals		13-16	3.69	114	32	4	1	2	331.1	344	152	136	100	156
N.L. Totals		53-74	3.62	266	123	12	1	13	953.2	934	445	384	381	557
M.L. Totals		66-90	3.64	380	155	16	2	15	1285.0	1278	597	520	481	713

Selected by Los Angeles Dodgers' organization in 38th round of free-agent draft, June 6, 1972.
Selected by San Francisco Giants' organization in 5th round of free-agent draft, June 4, 1975.
Selected by San Diego Padres' organization in secondary phase of free-agent draft, January 7, 1976.
a-Traded with pitcher Rollie Fingers, catcher-first baseman Gene Tenace and a player to be named later to St. Louis Cardinals for catchers Terry Kennedy and Steve Swisher, pitchers John Littlefield, Al Olmstead, John Urrea and Kim Seaman and infielder Mike Phillips, December 8, 1980; St. Louis organization acquired catcher Bob Geren to complete deal, December 10, 1980.
b-Traded to Cincinnati Reds for pitchers Jose Brito and Jeff Lahti, April 1, 1982.
c-Granted free-agency, November 10, 1982; signed with New York Yankees, December 15, 1982.

		1985						CAREER				
ERA	W-L-S	G	IP	H	ER	Club	ERA	W-L-S	G	IP	H	ER
0.00	0-0-0	1	1.2	2	0	Baltimore	2.75	1-1-0	5	19.2	17	6
1.74	0-0-0	7	10.1	9	2	Boston	2.93	1-1-0	13	27.2	27	9
3.00	1-0-0	4	9.0	9	3	California	3.57	1-0-0	11	22.2	21	9
3.38	0-1-0	5	8.0	10	3	Chicago	3.13	1-1-0	12	37.1	34	13
2.13	0-1-0	4	12.2	3	3	Cleveland	4.45	0-3-0	9	30.1	30	15
2.35	1-1-0	3	15.1	9	4	Detroit	2.19	2-1-0	9	37.0	30	9
13.50	0-0-0	2	0.2	2	1	Kansas City	5.92	1-2-1	6	24.1	32	16
2.87	0-1-0	6	15.2	16	5	Milwaukee	3.18	1-1-0	12	39.2	42	14
4.91	0-0-0	2	3.2	6	2	Minnesota	6.17	0-1-0	4	11.2	22	8
1.54	1-1-0	5	11.2	8	2	Oakland	4.24	1-2-0	10	23.1	20	11
0.00	0-0-0	2	0.2	1	0	Seattle	3.63	1-2-0	6	17.1	18	7
3.24	1-0-0	3	8.1	8	3	Texas	5.14	1-0-0	7	14.0	18	8
3.18	1-0-0	4	11.1	15	4	Toronto	3.62	2-1-0	10	27.1	33	11
2.64	5-5-0	48	109.0	103	32	**Total**	3.69	13-16-1	114	331.1	344	136
1.86	5-1-0	22	67.2	56	14	**Home**						
3.92	0-4-0	26	41.1	47	18	**Road**						

4—2 times	Low Hit
5—6/16/84 vs. DET.	K-High
2—2 times	Win Streak

S = SHUTOUTS

SOPER, MICHAEL DAVIS "Mike" (SS)   #55

6-1, 165. Born 5/23/65 in Miami, FL. Age 20, turns 21 May 23. Resides in Miami, FL. BR. TR.

CONTRACT STATUS: Signed 1-year contract for 1986 season.

1985 SEASON: Very solid year from Mike both on the field and at the plate ... finished eighth in the Eastern League (AA) in batting (.296) while leading Glens Falls in hits (142) ... appearing in 131 games at SS, Mike finished with a steady .945 fielding percentage.

CAREER: 1983—led the Gulf Coast League in hit by pitch (7) and led Gulf Coast shortstops in games (53) ... 1984—led Midwest League shortstops in games with (128) ... was signed by Walt Widmayer.

SOPER (continued)

PERSONAL/MISCELLANEOUS: Graduated from Palmetto H.S. in Miami, FL, where he was named MVP and earned All-Star honors.

Led Midwest League shortstops in games with 128, putouts with 189 and assists with 350 in 1984.

Led Gulf Coast League in hit by pitch with 7 and led shortstops in games with 53 in 1983.

YR	Club	AVG	G	AB	R	H	2B	3B	HR	RBI	BB	SO	SB
1983	Sarasota	.276	53	199	22	55	11	0	0	26	16	28	2
1984	Appleton	.236	128	444	47	105	18	2	1	48	16	60	3
1985	Glens Falls-a	.296	132	480	50	142	16	0	4	49	26	51	5
Minor League Totals		**.269**	**313**	**1123**	**119**	**302**	**45**	**2**	**5**	**123**	**58**	**139**	**10**

Selected by Chicago White Sox' organization in 4th round of free agent draft, June, 1983.
a-Traded to New York Yankees with pitcher Britt Burns, outfielder Glen Braxton and two players to be named later for catcher Ron Hassey and pitcher Joe Cowley, December 12, 1985.

SOSA, MIGUEL OLEA (IF)   #56

5-10, 165. Born 5/15/60 in La Romana, DR. Age 25, turns 26 May 15. Resides in La Romana, DR. BR. TR.

CONTRACT STATUS: Signed 1-year contract for 1986 season.

1985 SEASON: Played entire year at Richmond, International League ... was the teams regular second baseman playing 100 games at that position while appearing in 12 games at third ... finished second on the club in homers with 14 ... hit three HR against Pawtucket May 9th.

CAREER: A power hitting infielder ... led the Richmond club in Homers (15), playing in only 53 games ... was second, just one behind, in Greenville with 11 HRs in the same year ... In 1983 he led the Southern League with 93 RBI ... hit 2 grand slams ... played both second and short ... In 1982 at Durham, he finished third in the league in total bases (247), fourth in homers (25) and fifth in hits (146), and was named Carolina League All-Star shortstop ... was named to the South Atlantic League All-Star team while with Anderson in 1980.

PERSONAL/MISCELLANEOUS: Graduated from Mercedes Lauka Giar (La Romana) High School in 1978 ... was signed by Pedro Gonzalez, the man he credits for helping his career the most.

Led Carolina League shortstops in assists with 354 and double plays with 83 in 1982.

Led South Atlantic League shortstops in assists with 397 and double plays with 78 in 1980.

Led Gulf Coast League shortstops in errors with 22 in 1979.

YR	Club	AVG	G	AB	R	H	2B	3B	HR	RBI	BB	SO	SB
1969	Bradenton	.281	44	171	25	48	8	2	5	26	11	22	7
1980	Anderson	.268	125	511	81	137	23	3	18	92	34	84	27
	Durham	.348	5	23	5	8	3	0	1	5	1	4	0
1981	Durham	.276	118	479	63	132	22	4	17	70	8	93	18
1982	Durham	.288	132	507	77	146	18	4	25	69	37	101	35
1983	Savannah	.245	125	490	54	120	16	0	17	93*	21	94	26
	Richmond	.333	2	9	2	3	1	0	0	2	0	2	0
1984	Greenville	.294	53	187	30	55	6	1	11	31	4	28	7
	Richmond	.295	64	258	34	76	11	0	15	41	7	50	3
1985	Richmond-a	.192	119	433	49	83	13	2	14	49	13	75	7
Minor League Totals		**.263**	**787**	**3068**	**420**	**808**	**121**	**16**	**123**	**478**	**136**	**553**	**130**

Signed as free agent by Atlanta Braves' organization, December 8, 1978.
a-Traded to New York Yankees for outfielder Billy Sample, December 6, 1985.

TEWKSBURY, ROBERT A. "Bob" (RHP)   #39

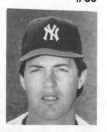

6-4, 180. Born 11/30/60 in Concord, NH. Resides in Penacook, NH. Age 25, turns 26 November 30. BR. TR. College: St. Leo (FL).

CONTRACT STATUS: Signed 1-year contract for 1986 season.

1985 SEASON: After 17 games with Albany, going 6-5, 3.54 ERA, he was moved to Columbus where he posted a 3-0 mark, 1.02 ERA in six starts ... Had .248 batting average against at Albany, just .174 batting average against at Columbus ... Has good control on fastball and sinker.

CAREER: 1984—led the Nashville Sounds in victories (11) and Complete Games (6) . . . 1983—split his pitching time between Nashville and Ft. Lauderdale recording impressive numbers with each . . . 1982—led the Florida State League in ERA (1.88), Wins (15), Shutouts (5) and Complete Games (13) . . . was named Right Handed Pitcher on Florida State League's 1982 All-Star team . . . was New York Yankees Minor League Pitcher of the Year . . . 1981—was the top fielding pitcher in the New York Penn League (1.000), while leading the Oneonta club in Wins (7) and Strikeouts (62).

PERSONAL/MISCELLANEOUS: Bob was signed by Jack Gillis.

Led New York-Pennsylvania League pitchers in fielding with 1.000 percentage in 1981.

YR	CLUB	W-L	ERA	G	GS	CG	Sho	SV	IP	H	R	ER	BB	SO
1981	Oneonta	7-3	3.40	14	14	6	1	0	90	85	43	34	37	62
1982	Ft. Lauderdale	*15-4	1.88*	24	23	13†	5*	1	182.1	146	46	38	47	92
1983	Nashville	5-1	2.82	7	7	3	0	0	51.0	49	20	16	10	15
	Ft. Lauderdale-a	2-0	0.00	2	2	1	0	0	16.0	6	1	0	1	5
1984	Nashville-b	11-9	2.83	26	26	6	0	0	172.0	185	69	54	42	78
1985	Albany	6-5	3.54	17	17	4	2	0	106.2	101	48	42	19	63
	Columbus	3-0	1.02	6	6	1	1	0	44.0	27	5	5	5	21
Minor League Totals		**49-22**	**2.57**	**96**	**95**	**34**	**9**	**1**	**662.0**	**599**	**232**	**189**	**161**	**336**

Selected by New York Yankees' organization in 19th round of free-agent draft, June 8, 1981.
a-On disabled list, April 8 to June 7, 1983.
b-On disabled list, April 9 to April 27, 1984.

WHITSON, EDDIE LEE "Ed" "Whit" (RHP) #38

6-3, 195. Born 5/19/55 at Johnson City, TN. Age 30, turns 31 May 19. BR. TR. Resides in Columbus, OH. Married: Kathleen Ann Mulholand, 11/24/79. Child: Jennifer (4).

MAJOR LEAGUE SERVICE: 7 years and 159 days.

CONTRACT STATUS: Signed 5-year contract on December 27, 1984 . . . contract extends thru 1989 season.

1985 SEASON: First year in pinstripes plagued by inconsistency . . . opened season losing first three decisions (4 games) . . . recorded first win May 1 @ Texas . . . lost next three decisions (6 starts) before turning corner . . . through June 6: 1-6, 6.23 ERA, 11 starts, 47.2 IP, 76 hits, 41 runs-33 earned, 9 HRs, 15 walks, 21 Ks . . . pitched exceptionally well his next 6 starts, beginning with June 11 outing vs. Toronto (threw 9.1 innings, allowing 1 run on 6 hits, 1 walk, 7 Ks) . . . notched 5th career shutout in next start, June 19 @ Baltimore . . . continued roll by winning 3 of next 4 starts, culminating with July 12, 6-0 shutout over Texas . . . over his 6 starts, June 11 to July 12: 4-0, 1.14 ERA, 47.1 IP, 33 hits, 6 runs-earned, 1 HR 7 walks, 21 Ks . . . made 13 starts post All-Star game, going 5-2, 6.64 ERA, 63.2 IP, 94 hits, 52 runs-47 earned, 9 HRs, 19 walks, 44 Ks . . . K'd season high 7, 3 times: June 11 vs. Tor.; Sept. 5 vs. Oak.; & Sept. 10 @ Milw. . . . allowed 2 HRs in game twice: April 16 vs. Chicago; August 25 @ Seattle . . . Yanks went 19-11 in games he started , 10-3 after the break . . . 9.1 innings performance vs. Tor., June 11 was longest by starter . . . 6-6, 5.48 ERA on road; 4-2, 4.08 ERA @ Yankee Stadium . . . 2-4, 5.74 ERA during day; 8-4, 4.44 ERA @ night . . . had .309 batting average against—highest on club, allowing better than 1.2 hits per inning.

CAREER: 1984—set personal highs with his 14 wins and 103 strikeouts . . . pitch in two post-season games, against the Cubs for a win in the NLCS and against the Tigers in the World Series with a no-decision . . . developed his palm ball pitch, necessitated by a cut finger on his pitching hand during the 1983 season . . . 1983—suffered injury plagued season . . . had muscle pull late in spring training and then in late April injured his left knee, requiring arthroscopic surgery . . . struggled then won his final 3 decisions of '83, giving indications of a strong '84 . . . 1982—used mainly in relief by Indians in his only American League season . . . 1981—was N.L.'s pitcher of the month in August . . . 1980—had his best season for the Giants, winning 11 with 3.10 ERA and being named to N.L. All-Star team . . . 1977—originally made it to big leagues with Pirates, defeating Montreal in his first big league start on September 17.

PERSONAL/MISCELLANEOUS: Graduated from Unicoi County High (Erwin, TN) in 1974 where he played baseball, basketball and football . . . Was 2nd team All-State in baseball and all-conference in baseball and basketball . . . also played Babe Ruth and Little League as youngster . . . one of nine children . . . enjoys hunting, fishing, and Willie Nelson music.

YR	CLUB	W-L	ERA	G	GS	CG	Sho	SV	IP	H	R	ER	BB	SO
1974	Bradenton	1-4	4.30	8	8	1	0	0	44	45	28	21	15	25
1975	Charleston, WV	8-15*	5.07	24	24	5	1	0	142	140	96*	80*	99	120
1976	Salem	†15-9	2.53	26	26	16*	2	0	203*	168	75	57	65	186*

WHITSON (continued)

YR	Club	W-L	ERA	G	GS	CG	Sho	SV	IP	H	R	ER	BB	SO
1977	Columbus	8-13	3.34	26	26	9	0	0	175	175	74	65	68	120
	PITTSBURGH	1-0	3.38	5	2	0	0	0	16	11	6	6	9	10
1978	Columbus	2-2	3.71	7	7	1	0	0	51	56	25	21	10	55
	PITTSBURGH	5-6	3.28	43	0	0	0	0	74	66	31	27	37	64
1979	PITTSBURGH-a	2-3	4.34	19	7	0	0	1	57.2	53	36	28	36	31
	SAN FRANCISCO	5-8	3.96	18	17	2	0	0	100.1	98	47	44	39	62
	1979 Totals	7-11	4.10	37	24	2	0	1	158.0	151	83	72	75	93
1980	SAN FRANCISCO	11-13	3.10	34	34	6	2	0	212.0	222	88	73	56	90
1981	SAN FRANCISCO-b	6-9	4.02	22	22	2	1	0	123.0	130	61	55	47	65
1982	CLEVELAND-c	4-2	3.26	40	9	1	1	2	108.0	91	43	39	58	61
1983	SAN DIEGO-d	5-7	4.30	31	21	2	0	1	144.1	143	73	69	50	81
	Las Vegas	1-0	6.75	3	3	0	0	0	12.0	15	9	9	5	11
1984	SAN DIEGO-e	14-8	3.24	31	31	1	0	0	189.0	181	72	68	42	103
1985	YANKEES	10-8	4.88	30	30	2	2	0	158.2	201	100	86	43	89
Minor League Totals		35-43	3.63	94	84	32	3	0	627	599	307	253	262	517
A.L. Totals		14-10	4.22	70	39	3	3	2	266.2	292	143	125	101	150
N.L. Totals		49-54	3.63	203	134	13	3	6	916.1	904	414	370	316	506
M.L. Totals		63-64	3.72	273	173	16	6	8	1183.0	1196	557	495	417	656

Selected by Pittsburgh Pirates' organization in 6th round of free-agent draft, June 5, 1974.

a-Traded with pitchers Fred Breining and Al Holland to San Francisco Giants for infielders Bill Madlock and Lenny Randle and pitcher Dave Roberts, June 28, 1979.

b-Traded to Cleveland Indians for second baseman Duane Kuiper, November 16, 1981.

c-Traded to San Diego Padres for pitcher Juan Eichelberger and first baseman-outfielder Broderick Perkins, November 18, 1982.

d-On disabled list, requiring arthroscopic surgery on April 19, from April 18 to May 28, 1983; included rehabilitation assignment to Las Vegas, May 10 to May 28, 1983.

e-Granted free agency, November 5, 1984; signed with New York Yankees, December 27, 1984.

CHAMPIONSHIP SERIES RECORD

YR	CLUB, Opp.	W-L	ERA	G	GS	CG	Sho	SV	IP	H	R	ER	BB	SO
1984	S.D. vs Chi.	1-0	1.13	1	1	0	0	0	8.0	5	1	1	2	6

WORLD SERIES RECORD

YR	CLUB, Opp.	W-L	ERA	G	GS	CG	Sho	SV	IP	H	R	ER	BB	SO
1984	S.D. vs Det.	0-0	40.5	1	1	0	0	0	0.2	5	3	3	0	0

ALL-STAR GAME RECORD

YR	CLUB, Site	W-L	ERA	G	GS	CG	Sho	SV	IP	H	R	ER	BB	SO
1980	N.L., L.A.						(Selected, did not play)							

	1985					Club		**CAREER**				
ERA	W-L-S	G	IP	H	ER		ERA	W-L-S	G	IP	H	ER
.60	2-0-1	2	15.0	10	1	Baltimore	0.48	2-0-1	4	18.2	12	1
11.12	0-1-0	2	5.2	16	7	Boston	3.00	2-1-1	6	27.0	33	9
6.14	0-1-0	3	14.2	15	10	California	8.82	0-1-0	6	16.1	20	16
5.11	1-1-0	4	24.2	35	14	Chicago	6.30	1-1-0	6	20.0	38	14
2.92	1-1-0	2	12.1	13	4	Cleveland	2.92	1-1-0	2	12.1	13	4
—	—	—	—	—	—	Detroit	0.00	0-0-0	1	2.0	0	0
5.06	0-1-0	1	5.1	8	3	Kansas City	6.23	0-2-0	4	13.0	20	9
7.71	1-1-0	2	11.2	21	10	Milwaukee	3.74	2-1-0	6	33.2	37	14
14.40	0-1-0	4	10.0	29	16	Minnesota	8.20	0-1-0	7	18.2	35	17
4.91	1-0-0	2	11.0	14	6	Oakland	4.15	1-0-0	6	21.2	18	10
6.10	1-0-0	2	10.1	12	7	Seattle	5.14	2-0-0	5	14.0	16	8
.64	2-0-1	2	14.0	9	1	Texas	1.50	2-0-1	4	18.0	14	3
2.63	1-0-0	4	24.0	19	9	Toronto	4.30	1-0-0	9	29.1	25	14
4.88	10-8-2	30	158.2	201	86	**Total**	4.22	14-10-3	70	266.1	292	125
4.08	4-2-1	12	68.1	83	31	**Home**						
5.48	6-6-1	18	90.1	118	55	**Road**						

4—7/12/85 vs. Tex.	**Low Hit**	3—6/15/83 vs. Cin.
7—3 times	**K-High**	10—9/18/84 vs. Mon.
5—	**Win Streak**	5—3 times

S = SHUTOUTS

WINFIELD, DAVID MARK "Dave" (OF) #31

6-6, 220. Born 10/3/51 in St. Paul, MN. Age 34, turns 35 October 3. Resides in Teaneck, NJ. BR. TR. Single. College: Graduated University of Minnesota.

MAJOR LEAGUE SERVICE: 12 years and 105 days.

CONTRACT STATUS: Signed 10-year contract on December 15, 1980 ... contract extends thru 1990 season.

1985 SEASON: Recorded yet another outstanding year at the plate, with the glove, and on the basepaths ... top 10 in American League: 19 GWRBI, 2nd; 114

RBI, 3rd; 66 extra-base hits, T7th; 105 runs, 9th; 298 total bases, 10th ... scored 1000th career run, July 26th @ Texas ... recorded 100 + RBIs (114) for 4th straight year—first Yankee since Yogi Berra (1953–'56) ... first Yankee to score 100 + runs in consecutive seasons since Mickey Mantle (1960–'61) ... first Yankee to record 100 + runs and RBIs since Joe DiMaggio (1941–'42) ... hit 2 HRs in single game twice: June 7 @ Milwaukee and August 8 (first game) vs. Cleveland—now accomplished 14 times in his career ... matched personal single game RBI mark driving in 6, August 8 (first game) vs. Clev.—previously set June 10, 1978 with San Diego vs. Cubs ... also had three 4-RBI games ... lost 17 spring training days, March 17 through April 2, with an infected left elbow, which required a six day hospital stay ... began '85 regular season struggling at the plate, hitting .257 through April, and dropping to a season low .234, May 18 ... at this point began a season high 13-game hitting streak, lasting through June 1, raising BA 23 pct. points (also had 10-game hitting streak, July 9-22) ... went 36-for-105, .343 BA in June, driving average up to .289 ... BA peaked at .300, July 22 ... July 23 to August 18 went 18-for-96, .188 BA, with overall average dropping to .280 ... BA hovered ± .280 through September ... ended season going 1-for last-21 ... 96 strikeouts matched career high set in 1974 ... 19 stolen bases were most since 1980 ... had only 5 HRs through June 6 ... hit HRs in back-to-back games on 3 occasions: July 29–30 (1st game); August 19–20; September 8–9 ... stole home September 7 vs. Oakland ... appeared as DH for fourth time in career, July 14 vs. Texas—first appearance since '82 (also DH'd July 29 @ Clev.) ... made only PH appearance June 12 vs. Toronto ... had 52 multiple-hit games: 38/2 hit; 11/3 hit; & 3/4 hit ... won 4th straight A.L. Gold Glove, sixth overall ... appeared in 9th consecutive All-Star Game.

CAREER: 1984—Finished second in A.L. Batting Championship, to Don Mattingly, with a career high .340 ... 4th with 193 hits and .393 OB%; 6th with 106 runs; ... had his longest hitting streak, 20 games, of career, 8/17 to 9/8 ... he had three 5-hit games in June equaling Ty Cobb's mark of 5-hit games in a month ... won his 4th straight Silver Bat Award ... named to UPI & Sporting News All-Star teams. 1983—led Yankees at plate in games played, at bats, runs scored, hits, triples, homers, RBI, GWRBI and walks ... finished 2nd in AL with 21 GWRBI, 3rd with 116 RBI, 5th with 307 total bases, tied 5th with 32 homers, 8 triples, 7th with .513 slugging percentage and tied 8th with 99 runs scored ... named to 7th consecutive All-Star team and contributed 3 hits in American League's win ... selected as AL player of the week the 1st two weeks of August ... on August 4 at Toronto he fatally beaned a seagull during between innings warm-ups and was charged by Toronto Police with cruelty to animals, charges that were dropped the next day ... named to UPI and Sporting News AL All-Star teams ... won second consecutive American League Gold Glove for outfielders ... 1982—finished 2nd in AL with .560 slugging percentage and 3rd with 37 HR ... also led Yankees with 106 RBI ... 37 HR was his personal season career high ... Joe DiMaggio was only Yankee right handed batter to hit more HR in season (46 HR in '37 and 39 in '48) ... was 9th player to hit 30 or more HR in season in both leagues (D. Allen, B. Bonds, J. Burroughs, F. Howard, F. Robinson, R. Smith, D. Stuart and J. Thompson) ... was named AL player of month for September (.294, 11 HR, 22 RBI, .661 slugging pct.) ... 1981—his 1st season for Yankees, led team in games, at bats, hits, total bases, doubles, RBI, GWRBI and sacrifice flies ... hit 1st HR as Yankee April 29 at Detroit off Jack Morris ... hit 1st Yankee Stadium HR May 23 off Rick Waits ... made 1st appearance in post season competition ... named to 1981 UPI AL All-Star team ... played 8 seasons with San Diego and holds many Padre batting and outfield defense records ... in 1979 finished 3rd in NL MVP voting behind co-winners Willie Stargell and Keith Hernandez ... also voted by players to TSN NL All-Star team and named to both AP and UPI NL All-Star teams ... hit safely in his 1st 6 major league games ... went to majors off the campus of University of Minnesota in 1973 ... never played in minors.

PERSONAL/MISCELLANEOUS: At University of Minnesota was 13-1 on mound in his senior year, while batting over .400 in outfield ... was Gophers team captain and named 1st team All-American ... was MVP in 1973 College World Series ... also played for Minnesota in basketball ... was drafted in 3 different sports; Padres in baseball, Minnesota in football, and Utah (ABA) and Atlanta (NBA) in basketball ... David M. Winfield Foundation has received much acclaim for its work with youth groups and contributions to community ... set up college scholarships program in his native St. Paul/Minneapolis area, and was named 1979 winner of YMCA Brian Piccolo Award for Humanitarian services.

  Led National League in total bases with 333 and intentional bases on balls received with 24 in 1979.
  Won American League Gold Glove as outfielder, 1982, 1983, 1984.
  Won National League Gold Glove as outfielder, 1979, 1980.
  Won American League Silver Bat as outfielder, 1981 through 1984.
  Selected by Atlanta Hawks in 5th round of 1973 NBA draft.
  Selected by Utah Stars in 6th round of 1973 ABA draft.
  Selected by Minnesota Vikings in 17th round of 1973 NFL draft.
  Led National League outfielders in assists with 15 in 1976.
  Tied for National League lead among outfielders with 12 errors in 1974.

WINFIELD (continued)

YR Club	AVG	G	AB	R	H	2B	3B	HR	RBI	BB	SO	SB
1973 SAN DIEGO	.277	56	141	9	39	4	1	3	12	12	19	0
1974 SAN DIEGO	.265	145	498	57	132	18	4	20	75	40	96	9
1975 SAN DIEGO	.267	143	509	74	136	20	2	15	76	69	82	23
1976 SAN DIEGO	.283	137	492	81	139	26	4	13	69	65	78	26
1977 SAN DIEGO	.275	157	615	104	169	29	7	25	92	58	75	16
1978 SAN DIEGO	.308	158	587	88	181	30	5	24	97	55	82	21
1979 SAN DIEGO	.308	159	597	97	184	27	10	34	118*	85	71	15
1980 SAN DIEGO-a	.276	162	558	89	154	25	6	20	87	79	83	23
1981 YANKEES	.294	105	388	52	114	25	1	13	68	43	41	11
1982 YANKEES-b	.280	140	539	84	151	24	8	37	106	45	64	5
1983 YANKEES	.283	152	598	99	169	26	8	32	116	58	77	15
1984 YANKEES-c	.340	141	567	106	193	34	4	19	100	53	71	6
1985 YANKEES	.275	155	633	105	174	34	6	26	114	52	96	19
N.Y.Y. Totals	.294	693	2725	446	801	143	27	127	504	251	349	56
N.L. Totals	.284	1117	3997	599	1134	179	39	154	626	463	586	133
M.L. Totals	.288	1810	6722	1045	1935	322	66	281	1130	714	934	189

GWRBI: 1980-10; 1981-9; 1982-15; 1983-21; 1984-13; 1985-19. Total-87.

Selected by Baltimore Orioles' organization in 40th round of free-agent draft, June 5, 1969.
Selected by San Diego Padres' organization in 1st round (fourth player selected) of free-agent draft, June 5, 1973.
a-Granted free-agency, October 22, 1980; signed by New York Yankees, December 15, 1980.
b-On disabled list, May 20 to June 4, 1982.
c-On disabled list, April 16 to May 1, 1984.

DIVISION SERIES RECORD

YR Club, Opp.	AVG	G	AB	R	H	2B	3B	HR	RBI	BB	SO	SB
1981 N.Y. vs Mil.	.350	5	20	2	7	3	0	0	0	1	5	0

CHAMPIONSHIP SERIES RECORD

YR Club, Opp.	AVG	G	AB	R	H	2B	3B	HR	RBI	BB	SO	SB
1981 N.Y. vs Oak.	.154	3	13	2	2	1	0	0	2	2	2	1

WORLD SERIES RECORD

YR Club, Opp.	AVG	G	AB	R	H	2B	3B	HR	RBI	BB	SO	SB
1981 N.Y. vs L.A.	.045	6	22	0	1	0	0	0	1	5	4	1

ALL-STAR GAME RECORD

Tied All-Star Game record for most at bats, game (5), July 17, 1979.

YR Club, Site	AVG	G	AB	R	H	2B	3B	HR	RBI	BB	SO	SB
1977 N.L., N.Y. (AL)	1.000	1	2	0	2	1	0	0	2	0	0	0
1978 N.L., S.D.	.500	1	2	1	1	0	0	0	0	0	0	0
1979 N.L., Sea.	.200	1	5	1	1	1	0	0	1	0	1	0
1980 N.L., L.A.	.000	1	2	0	0	0	0	0	1	0	0	0
1981 A.L., Cle.	.000	1	4	0	0	0	0	0	0	1	0	0
1982 A.L., Mont.	.500	1	2	0	1	0	0	0	0	0	0	0
1983 A.L., Chi. (AL)	1.000	1	3	2	3	1	0	0	2	0	0	0
1984 A.L., S.F.	.250	1	4	0	1	1	0	0	0	0	0	0
1985 A.L., Min.	.333	1	3	0	1	0	0	0	0	0	0	1
A.S.G. Totals	.370	9	27	4	10	4	0	0	6	1	1	1

1985 vs. OPPONENTS

Club	AB	H	HR	RBI	AVG
Baltimore	53	19	3	15	.358
Boston	53	18	2	13	.340
Cleveland	48	12	4	14	.250
Detroit	50	14	0	7	.280
Milwaukee	57	14	4	7	.246
Toronto	48	14	0	6	.292
California	49	9	1	6	.184
Chicago	48	8	2	5	.167
Kansas City	48	12	0	7	.250
Minnesota	47	13	3	10	.277
Oakland	46	16	2	8	.348
Seattle	47	15	3	12	.319
Texas	39	10	2	4	.256
1st Half	330	98	12	53	.297
2nd Half	303	76	14	61	.251
vs. LHP	215	54	10	36	.251
vs. RHP	418	120	16	78	.287
Home	298	85	15	61	.285
Away	335	89	11	53	.266

WINFIELD'S BESTS

Season

AVG.	.340–1984
H	193–1984
HR	37–1982
RBI	118–1979
SB	26–1976
Hit Strk	20 games–1984

Game

H	5–5 times
HR	2–14 times
RBI	6–2 times
SB	3–at S.F. 9-5-76 (2nd game)

WYNEGAR, HAROLD DELANO, JR. "Butch" (C) #27

6-1, 192. Born 3/14/56 in York, PA. Age 30, turned 30 March 14. Resides in Longwood, FL. BS. TR. Married: Gretchen Oas, December 2, 1977. Children: Lindsay (7), Del (5), and Cale (1).

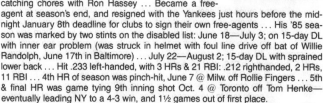

MAJOR LEAGUE SERVICE: 10 years.

CONTRACT STATUS: Signed 3-year contract (with option for 4th) on January 8, 1986 ... contract extends thru 1988 season ('89 with option).

1985 SEASON: The 10-year veteran shared the catching chores with Ron Hassey ... Became a free-agent at season's end, and resigned with the Yankees just hours before the midnight January 8th deadline for clubs to sign their own free-agents ... His '85 season was marked by two stints on the disabled list: June 18—July 3; on 15-day DL with inner ear problem (was struck in helmet with foul line drive off bat of Willie Randolph, June 17th in Baltimore) ... July 22—August 2; 15-day DL with sprained lower back ... Hit .233 left-handed, with 3 HRs & 21 RBI: .212 righthanded, 2 HRs, 11 RBI ... 4th HR of season was pinch-hit, June 7 @ Milw. off Rollie Fingers ... 5th & final HR was game tying 9th inning shot Oct. 4 @ Toronto off Tom Henke—eventually leading NY to a 4-3 win, and 1½ games out of first place.

CAREER: 1984—Was the Yankees regular catcher, appearing in most games since 1980 with Minnesota ... had third highest fielding pct. for catchers with 100 + games at .993. 1983—was Yankees' regular catcher ... batting average never fell below .290 all season ... on May 10 suffered ruptured blood vessel in left arm on tag play at plate and missed half month on DL ... caught Dave Righetti's July 4th no-hitter ... was hampered by sore foot in September ... 1982—his trade to Yankees (May 12) coincided with Rick Cerone's broken thumb (May 11), but trade had been worked out with Minnesota in advance of Cerone's injury ... was Yankees #1 catcher with Cerone on disabled list ... split catching duties with Cerone upon Rick's return on July 15 until Butch was disabled on July 25 with a viral infection ... 1981—missed 1st month and one-half season because of bone chip that was found in throwing elbow and required surgery to remove ... was All-Star selection each of his 1st 4 seasons as professional ... 1976 became, to that point, the youngest player (20 years, 121 days) to appear in major league All-Star game ... hit 1st homerun off Catfish Hunter ... coming into 1985 has thrown out 33% (324 of 989) of runners trying to steal on him ... also coming into 1985 has .262 (668-2546) batting average left-handed and .257 (292-1134) average batting right-handed.

PERSONAL/MISCELLANEOUS: Played third base until moved to catcher his junior year at Red Lion High in York, PA ... was 4-year letterman in baseball ... also lettered in football, basketball and wrestling.

In 1976 named American League Rookie of the Year by The Sporting News.
Led American League catchers in double plays with 13 in 1980.
Led American League catchers in errors with 16 in 1976.
Led California League catchers in fielding percentage with .989, in putouts with 734 and assists with 99 in 1975.
Led Appalachian League catchers in fielding percentage with .987 and double plays with 9 in 1974.

YR Club	AVG	G	AB	R	H	2B	3B	HR	RBI	BB	SO	SB
1974 Elizabethton	.346*	60	191	32	66	10	0	8	51	43	16	0
1975 Reno	.314	139†	468	106	147	18	6	19	112*	142*	55	1
1976 MINNESOTA	.260	149	534	58	139	21	2	10	69	79	63	0
1977 MINNESOTA	.261	144	532	76	139	22	3	10	79	68	61	2
1978 MINNESOTA	.229	135	454	36	104	22	1	4	45	47	42	1
1979 MINNESOTA	.270	149	504	74	136	20	0	7	57	74	36	2
1980 MINNESOTA	.255	146	486	61	124	18	3	5	57	63	36	3
1981 MINNESOTA-a	.147	47	150	11	37	5	0	0	10	17	9	0
1982 MINNESOTA-b	.209	24	86	9	18	4	0	1	8	10	12	0
YANKEES-c	.293	63	191	27	56	8	1	3	20	40	21	0
1982 Totals	.267	87	277	36	74	12	1	4	28	50	33	0
1983 YANKEES-d	.296	94	301	40	89	18	2	6	42	52	29	1
1984 YANKEES	.267	129	442	48	118	13	1	6	45	65	35	1
1985 YANKEES-e	.223	102	309	27	69	15	0	5	32	64	43	0
Minor League Totals	**.323**	**199**	**659**	**138**	**213**	**28**	**6**	**27**	**163**	**185**	**71**	**1**
N.Y.Y. Totals	**.267**	**388**	**1243**	**142**	**332**	**54**	**4**	**20**	**139**	**221**	**128**	**2**
M.L. Totals	**.258**	**1282**	**3989**	**467**	**1029**	**166**	**13**	**57**	**464**	**579**	**387**	**10**

GWRBI: 1980-4; 1981-0; 1982-2; 1983-3; 1984-5; 1985-3. Total-17.

Selected by Minnesota Twins' organization in 2nd round of free-agent draft, June 5, 1974.
a-On disabled list, April 6 to May 16, 1981 for operation to remove bone chip from right elbow; on supplemental disabled list, August 16 to September 11, 1981 with sore right shoulder.
b-Traded with pitcher Roger Erickson to New York Yankees for infielder Larry Milbourne and pitchers Pete Filson and John Pacella, May 12, 1982.

WYNEGAR (continued)

c-On disabled list, July 27 to September 1, 1982 with viral infection.
d-On disabled list, May 11 to May 27 with bruised left arm.
e-Placed on disabled list, June 18 through July 3 with inner ear problem and from July 22 through August 2 with sprained lower back.

ALL-STAR GAME RECORD

YR	Club, Site	AVG	G	AB	R	H	2B	3B	HR	RBI	BB	SO	SB
1976	A.L., Phil.	.000	1	0	0	0	0	0	0	0	1	0	0
1977	A.L., N.Y. (AL)	.500	1	2	1	1	0	0	0	0	0	0	0
A.S.G. Totals		**.500**	**2**	**2**	**1**	**1**	**0**	**0**	**0**	**0**	**1**	**0**	**0**

1985 vs. OPPONENTS

Club	AB	H	HR	RBI	AVG
Baltimore	11	3	0	0	.273
Boston	40	11	0	7	.275
Cleveland	20	5	0	1	.250
Detroit	15	1	0	0	.067
Milwaukee	19	4	1	3	.211
Toronto	24	5	1	2	.208
California	25	8	0	3	.320
Chicago	25	6	1	4	.240
Kansas City	29	3	1	2	.103
Minnesota	21	4	1	6	.190
Oakland	32	7	0	0	.219
Seattle	24	4	0	2	.167
Texas	24	8	0	2	.333
1st Half	206	48	4	23	.233
2nd Half	103	21	1	9	.204
vs. LHP	137	29	2	11	.212
vs. RHP	172	40	3	21	.233
Home	158	31	2	13	.196
Away	151	38	3	19	.252

WYNEGAR'S BESTS

Season

AVG.	.296–1983
H	139–1976, 77
HR	10–1976, 77
RBI	79–1977
SB	3–1980
Hit Strk	16 games–1984

Game

H	4–5 times
HR	2–@ Chicago 9-22-76
RBI	4–2 times
SB	1–10 times

NEW YORK YANKEES TRAINERS

GENE J. MONAHAN
New York Yankees

5-11, 178; born October 24, 1944, Rolla, MO; B.S. in Physical Education from Indiana University (1969); Certified member of NATA; member of PBATS, serving as chairman of grants and scholarship committee; 24 years of service in professional baseball. Started in 1963 at Ft. Lauderdale. Entering his 14th year at the helm of the Yankee training duties.

STEPHEN D. DONOHUE
New York Yankees

5-9, 170; born May 29, 1956, Bronxville, NY; B.S. in Physical Education from the University of Louisville; Certified member of NATA; Certified member of NY state EMT. First season as Yankees' assistant trainer; has been member of Yankees' organization since 1979 working at West Haven (1979), Nashville (1980-81) and Columbus (1982-85). Also assistant trainer New York Jets 1974-78, Assistant trainer of U of Louisville's NCAA Champion basketball team in 1980.

BEHIND THE SCENES ... NICK PRIORE, who was Pete Sheehy's assistant in the Yankees clubhouse for more than 20 seasons, is joined this year by BOB FLEMING ... LOU CUCUZZA is in his 11th year running the visitors clubhouse at the stadium ... JIMMY ESPOSITO, chief of the Yankee grounds crew, began his role in 1960 after 14 seasons with the Brooklyn and Los Angeles Dodgers ... DR. JOHN J. BONAMO enters his 7th year as the Yankees team physician. He is an orthopedic surgeon affiliated with Staten Island and NYU Hospitals, is a graduate of Boston College and New York Medical College ... DOM SCALA, the Yankees bullpen catcher, is in his 9th season in that capacity. He is a graduate of St. John's University and played in the Oakland organization ... MARK BATCHKO is in his 2nd season as batting practice pitcher. Mark charts the Yankee defense, and is in charge of the Yankees' baseball computer statistics ... MIKE BARNETT is in his 5th year coordinating the Yankees' video tape operations.

THE MINOR LEAGUE DEPARTMENT

Vice President, Baseball Administration—Woody Woodward
Director of Player Development—Bobby Hofman
Assistant Player Development Director—Peter Jameson
Assistant Scouting Director—Roy Krasik
Computer Statistics Director—Mark Batchko
Video Coordination Director—Mike Barnett

1986 YANKEE MINOR LEAGUE CLUBS

Classification	City	League	Manager	Coaches
AAA	Columbus, OH	International	Barry Foote	Dave LaRoche
AA	Albany-Colonie, NY	NY Eastern	Jim Saul	John Kennedy Bill Monbouquette
A	Ft. Lauderdale, FL	Florida State	Bucky Dent	Jerry McNertney Hoyt Wilhelm
A	Oneonta, NY	New York-Penn	Buck Showalter	Jack Gillis Russ Meyer
R	Sarasota, FL	Gulf Coast	Fred Ferreira	Brian Butterfield Carlos Lezcano Carlos Tosca

1985 YANKEES MINOR LEAGUE STANDINGS

Club	League	Class	Won-Lost	Pct.	Finish	GA/GB
Columbus	International	AAA	75-64	.540	Third	−3½
Albany-Colonie	NY Eastern	AA	82-57	.590	First	+7
Ft. Lauderdale	Florida State	A	77-63	.550	Fourth	+1½
Oneonta	New York-Penn	A	55-23	.705	First	+8
Sarasota	Gulf Coast	R	43-18	.705	First	+3½

Columbus Clippers tied for third in the regular season; defeated Syracuse 3 games to 1 in semi-finals; lost to Tidewater 3 games to 1 in finals.

Albany-Colonie won the regular season title with a 1st place finish; lost to Vermont 3 games to 1 in the semi-finals.

Ft. Lauderdale finished 4th in the league; defeated Osceola 2 games to 1 in semi-finals; lost to Ft. Myers 3 games to 1 in the finals.

Oneonta won regular season championship with 1st place finish; defeated Geneva in one game semi-final; defeated Auburn 2 games to none to win League Championship.

Sarasota, following a rained out championship game, was declared league champions based on overall winning percentage.

LEAGUE ALL STAR TEAMS

INTERNATIONAL LEAGUE—Juan Bonilla (2B), Dan Pasqua (OF, Most Valuable Player, Rookie-of-the-Year).

EASTERN LEAGUE—Orestes Destrade (DH), Brad Arnsberg (RHP), Barry Foote (Manager of the Year).

FLORIDA STATE LEAGUE—Jay Buhner (CF), Darren Reed (RF).

NEW YORK-PENN LEAGUE—Scott Shaw (3B), Chris Lombardozzi (IF), Dody Rather (RHP), Mike Christopher (RHP), Buck Showalter (Manager-of-the-Year).

GULF COAST LEAGUE—Rob Lambert (2B), Fred Carter (OF), Ted Higgins (OF), Carlos Tosca (Manager).

STATISTICAL LEADERS

INTERNATIONAL LEAGUE—Dan Pasqua led the league in slugging percentage (.599), Juan Bonilla led the league in hitting (.330), Clay Christiansen tied for the league lead in hit batsmen (8), Jim Deshaies led the league in balks (4).

EASTERN LEAGUE—Tony Russell led the league in sacrifice hits (22), Orestes Destrade led the league in striking out (129), Brad Arnsberg led the league with a .875 winning percentage, ERA with a 1.59, and tied for the league lead with 14 wins, Doug Drabek led the league with 153 strikeouts and 192.2 innings pitched, Randle Graham led the league in saves (17).

FLORIDA STATE LEAGUE—Darren Reed led the league in slugging percentage (.477), Jay Buhner led the league in game winning RBI (15), Roberto Kelly led the league in triples (13), Steve George led the league in complete games (12) and shutouts (5).

NEW YORK-PENN LEAGUE—Troy Evers led the league in ERA (1.18) winning percentage (.909) and tied for the league lead in wins (10).

GULF COAST LEAGUE—Robert Lambert led the league in batting average (.350), runs (51), hits (79), stolen bases (34), caught stealing he tied for the lead with 12 and led the league in total bases (92), Darren Mandel led the league in doubles (16) and slugging percentage (.500), Ted Higgins led the league in RBI (36), and Fred Carter tied for the league lead in grounded into double plays (7).

1986 SCOUTING DIRECTORY

Major League Scouts

Hank Bauer
Al Cuccinello
Bob Lemon
Eddie Lopat

Charlie Silvera
Mickey Vernon
Stan Williams

Free Agent Scouts

Bill Livesey—National Crosschecker
Fred Ferreira—Latin American Supervisor
& Special Assignment
Jack Gillis—East Coast Crosschecker
Don Lindeberg—West Coast Crosschecker
Luis Arroyo—Puerto Rico
Joe DiCarlo—New York, New Jersey, Delaware
Orrin Freeman—Southern California, New Mexico
Jack Gillis—Mississippi, Alabama
Ray Goodman—Virginia, West Virginia, Maryland, Washington, DC
Dick Groch—Michigan, Indiana, Ohio
Jim Gruzdis—North Carolina, South Carolina
Don Lindeberg—Southern California, New Mexico, Arizona
Russ Meyer—Northern Illinois
Jim Naples—Upstate New York
Ramon Naranjo—Dominican Republic
Dick Newberg—Connecticut, Rhode Island
Greg Orr—Northern California, Nevada
Meade Palmer—Pennsylvania
Roberto Rivera—Puerto Rico
Joe Robison—Designated Texas areas, Louisiana
Lou Saban—North Carolina
Brian Sabean—Florida, Georgia
Stan Saleski—Texas, Oklahoma
Rudy Santin—Miami Area
Tommy Thompson—Kentucky, Tennessee
Dick Tidrow—Iowa, Missouri, Southern Illinois
Jeff Zimmerman—Washington, Oregon

1985 YANKEES ORGANIZATION OF THE YEAR

The New York Yankees won the Baseball Organization of the Year Award for 1985 as bestowed by the Topps Chewing Gum Company. This is the fifth time the Yankees have received the trophy since its inception in 1966. The club also won in 1968, 1973, 1980 and 1982.

The trophy, presented at the Winter Meetings, is awarded annually to a major league team based upon the players in its organization who receive Topps Awards during the past season. A specific number of points are given for each award.

The Yankees had two Minor League Player of the Year Awards, four Minor League Player of the Month Awards, four players who made the Topps Minor League All-Star Team and one Topps Major League Rookie All-Star.

Dan Pasqua and Rob Lambert received Player of the Year Awards in their respective leagues.

Minor League Player of the Month Awards went to Jay Buhner, Brad Arnsberg, Dody Rather and Ted Higgins.

Members of the Yankee Organization who were named to the Topps Minor League All-Star team are Juan Bonilla, Dan Pasqua, Brad Arnsberg, and Rob Lambert.

In addition, Brian Fisher was named to the Topps Major League Rookie All-Star team.

ELSTON HOWARD PLAYER OF THE WEEK

	Player of the Week	Pitcher of the Week
4/12-4/18	Dan Pasqua (COL)	Kelly Faulk (COL)
4/19-4/25	Jay Buhner (FTL)	Jeff Pries (FTL)
5/3-5/9	Dan Pasqua (COL)	Clay Christiansen (COL)
5/10-5/16	Keith Hughes (ALB)	Jim Deshaies (COL)
5/17-5/23	Tony Russell (ALB)	Ozzie Canseco (FTL)
5/31-6/6	Juan Bonilla (COL)	Brad Arnsberg (ALB)
6/7-6/13	Tom Barrett (COL)	Mark Silva (COL)
6/14-6/20	Mitch Lyden (FTL)	Bill Fulton (FTL)
6/28-7/4	Dan Pasqua (COL)	Bill Fulton (FTL)/Dody Rather (ONEO)
7/5-7/11	Mo Ching (FTL)	Troy Evers (ONEO)
7/12-7/18	Scott Shaw (ONEO)	Ozzie Canseco (SARA)
7/19-7/25	Orestes Destrade (ALB)	Dody Rather (ONEO)
8/1-8/8	Rob Lambert (SARA)	ONEONTA PITCHING STAFF
8/9-8/15	Doug Carpenter (ALB)	Mike Christopher (ONEO)
8/16-8/22	Orestes Destrade (ALB)	Scott Patterson (COL)
8/30-9/5	Mitch Lyden (FTL)	Troy Evers (ONEO)

JACK BUTTERFIELD PLAYER OF THE MONTH

	Player of the Month	Pitcher of the Month
April	Jay Buhner (FTL)	Brad Arnsberg (ALB)
May	Dan Pasqua (COL)	Scott Nielsen (ALB)
June	Darren Reed (FTL)	Brad Arnsberg (ALB)
July	Ted Higgins (SAR)	Dody Rather (ONEO)
August	Mark Blaser (FTL)	Troy Evers (ONEO)

1985 PLAYER OF THE YEAR: Dan Pasqua, Columbus Clippers
1985 PITCHER OF THE YEAR: Brad Arnsberg, Albany-Colonie Yankees

PREVIOUS YANKEE PLAYER/PITCHER
OF THE YEAR AWARDS

PLAYER OF THE YEAR

1984	Scott Bradley—Columbus—C—OF	
1983	Brian Dayett—Columbus—LF	
1982	Matt Winters—Greensboro/Nashville—RHP	
1981	Don Mattingly—Columbus—OF/1B	
1980	Steve Balboni—Nashville—1B	

PITCHER OF THE YEAR

Jim Deshaies—Columbus—LHP	
Jose Rijo—Ft. Laud./Nash.—RHP	
Bob Tewksbury—FtL	RHP
Pete Filson—FtL/Nash	LHP
Gene Nelson—Ft. Lauderdale	RHP

NEW YORK YANKEES
NUMBER ONE DRAFT CHOICES—JUNE

Year	Round/Pick	Name	Pos	School	w/NYY
1965	1/19	Bill Burbach	rhp	Dickeyville, Wisc.	69-71
1966	1/10	Jim Lyttle	of	Florida State Univ.	69-71
1967	1/1	Ron Blomberg	1b	Atlanta, GA	69, 71-77
1968	1/4	Thurman Munson	c	Kent State Univ.	69-79
1969	1/11	Charlie Spikes	of	Bogalusa, LA	72
1970	1/12	Dave Cheadle	lhp	Asheville, NC	—
1971	1/19	Terry Whitfield	of	Blythe, CA	74-76
1972	1/14	Scott McGregor	lhp	El Segundo, CA	—
1973	1/13	Doug Heinold		Victoria, TX	—
1974	1/12	Dennis Sherrill	ss	Miami, FL	78, 80
1975	1/19	James McDonald	1b	Los Angeles, CA	—
1976	1/16	Pat Tabler	of	Cincinnati, OH	—
1977	1/23	Steve Taylor	rhp	Univ. of Delaware	—
1978	1/18-a	Rex Hudler	ss	Fresno, CA	84-85
	1/24-b	Matt Winters	of	Williamsville, NY	—
	1/26	Brian Ryder	rhp	Shrewsbury, MA	—
1979	2/25-c	Todd Demeter	inf	Oklahoma City, OK	—
1980	3/22-d	Billy Cannon	ss	Baton Rouge, LA	—
1981	2/26-e	John Elway	of	Stanford Univ.	—
1982	2/8-f	Tim Birtsas	lhp	Michigan State Univ.	—
	2/22	Bo Jackson	ss	Bessemer, AL	—
1983	4/13-g	Mitch Lyden	c	Beaverton, OR	—
1984	1/22-h	Jeff Pries	rhp	U.C.L.A.	—
1985	1/27-i	Rick Balabon	rhp	Berwyn, PA	—

a-Choice from Chicago (AL) as compensation for signing Ron Blomberg as a free agent.
b-Choice from Boston as compensation for signing Mike Torrez as a free agent.
c-First round choice awarded to Los Angeles as compensation for signing Tommy John as a free agent; Los Angeles chose, rhp, Steve Perry from the University of Michigan.
d-First round choice awarded to Montreal as compensation for signing Rudy May as a free agent; Montreal chose Terry Francona, of, from the University of Arizona. Second round choice awarded to Boston as compensation for signing Bob Watson as a free agent; Boston chose Mike Brown, rhp, from Clemson University. Third round choice of Billy Cannon was voided by Commissioner Kuhn. Fourth round choice was Stephen Madden, of, from New Hartford, NY.
e-First round choice awarded to San Diego as compensation for signing Dave Winfield as a free agent; San Diego chose Frank Castro, c, from University of Miami (FL). In third round with 12th pick, Yankees chose Scott Bradley, c, from University of North Carolina; Yankees were awarded pick as compensation from Atlanta for signing Gaylord Perry as a free agent.
f-First round choice awarded to Cincinnati as compensation for signing Dave Collins as a free agent; Cincinnati chose Scott Jones, lhp, from Hinsdale, IL. In second round Yankees chose Tim Birtsas with choice from California as compensation for signing Reggie Jackson as a free agent.
g-First round choice awarded to Chicago (AL) as compensation for signing Steve Kemp as a free agent; Chicago chose Joel Davis, rhp, from Jacksonville, FL. Second round choice awarded to Cincinnati as compensation for signing Bob Shirley as a free agent; Cincinnati chose Joseph Oliver, c, from Orlando, FL. Third round choice awarded to California as compensation for signing Don Baylor as a free agent; California chose Wally Joyner, 1b, from Brigham Young University.
h-In second round, Yankees chose Keith Miller, of, from Oral Roberts University with 12th pick from San Diego as compensation for signing Rich Gossage as a free agent.
i-First round choice awarded to San Diego as compensation for signing Ed Whitson as free agent; San Diego chose Joey Cora, ss, from Vanderbilt University. Between 1st & 2nd rounds Yankees chose Rick Balabon as special compensation for losing Tim Belcher in 1984 major league compensation draft.

YANKEE TRIPLE-A MINOR LEAGUE CLUBS—Newark (1932-49), Kansas City (1938-54), Denver (1955-58), Richmond (1956-64), Toledo (1965-66), Syracuse (1967-77), Tacoma (1978), and Columbus (1979-present)

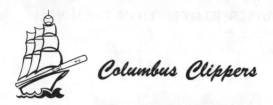

Columbus Clippers

1985 COLUMBUS CLIPPERS
International League

Manager: Stump Merrill (replaced Doug Holmquist, May 7)
Record: 75-64 (finished 4th in regular season; defeated Syracuse, 3 games to 1 in semi-finals; lost to Tidewater, 3 games to 1 in finals.)
All-Stars: Dan Pasqua (OF, Rookie of Year, Most Valuable Player), Juan Bonilla (2B).
League Leaders: Juan Bonilla (.330 Avg.), Dan Pasqua (.599 slugging per.)

MOST USED LINEUP
(Most games at each position)

1B	Dan Briggs	98
2B	Rex Hudler	82
3B	Butch Hobson	82
SS	Keith Smith	114
OF	Vic Mata	103
OF	Dan Pasqua	76
OF	Henry Cotto	75
C	Juan Espino	73
St	Jim Deshaies	21
Rel	Curt Brown	47

FINAL STATISTICS

BATTING	AVG	G	AB	R	H	2B	3B	HR	RBI	BB	SO	SB
Barrett, T.	.260	55	169	27	44	11	1	1	11	17	18	14
Bonilla, J.	.330*	102	388	60	128	22	0	1	52	36	26	9
Bradley, S.	.301	43	163	17	49	10	0	4	27	8	12	2
Briggs, D.	.268	132	403	51	108	27	4	7	60	42	64	1
Cotto. H.	.257	75	272	38	70	16	2	7	36	19	60	10
Dalena, P.	.305	114	357	34	109	21	4	9	65	25	32	1
Espino, J.	.250	74	224	30	56	11	0	3	20	22	36	0
Gray, L.	.253	71	146	16	37	2	0	1	18	11	23	0
Hawkins, J.	.250	22	28	3	7	0	0	0	5	0	5	0
Heath, K.	.257	121	377	83	97	21	4	18	53	101	68	8
Hobson, B.	.236	107	347	44	82	9	1	12	56	47	64	0
Hudler, R.	.250	106	380	62	95	13	4	3	18	17	51	29
Hughes, J.	.296	18	54	7	16	4	0	3	8	2	11	0
Johnson, B.	.000	2	5	0	0	0	0	0	0	0	2	0
Knight, T.	.169	27	71	10	12	2	1	1	10	16	16	2
Lindsey, B.	.211	27	71	10	15	5	0	1	9	14	12	0
Mata, V.	.261	104	375	39	98	14	2	3	27	27	58	2
O'Berry, M.	.228	18	57	7	13	2	0	1	7	5	6	0
Pasqua, D.	.321	78	287	52	92	16	5	18	69	48	62	5
Robertson, A.	.393	9	28	3	11	1	0	0	1	1	3	0
Smith, K.	.241	123	307	40	74	9	1	4	21	39	67	10
Winters, M.	.308	45	130	19	40	14	1	3	19	26	20	2

PITCHING	W-L	ERA	G	GS	CG	SHO	SV	IP	H	R	ER	BB	SO
Armstrong, M.	2-2	6.64	31	3	0	0	2	40.2	49	31	30	26	40
Bradley, B.	1-7	4.83	11	8	0	0	0	54.0	68	35	29	15	11
Briggs, D.	0-0	0.00	2	0	0	0	0	6.0	5	1	0	2	7
Brown, C.	8-3	4.88	47	2	0	0	2	86.2	110	57	47	28	40
Bystrom, M.	2-0	1.88	4	4	0	0	0	24.0	13	7	5	9	16
Christiansen, C.	10-6	3.66	28	18	3	2	1	137.2	128	66	56	59	67
Cooper, D.	7-3	2.37	33	4	0	0	10	68.1	61	23	18	21	59
Dalena, P.	0-0	12.00	2	0	0	0	0	3.0	5	5	4	3	1
Deshaies, J.	8-6	4.31	21	21	3	0	0	131.2	124	67	63	59	106
Faulk, K.	4-7	5.42	18	16	1	0	0	84.2	90	57	51	48	40
Fisher, B.	0-0	2.38	7	0	0	0	0	11.1	8	4	3	7	12
Lindsey, B.	0-0	9.00	1	0	0	0	0	1.0	1	1	1	1	0
Patterson, S.	5-2	3.35	21	0	0	0	3	37.2	30	16	14	12	26
Pulido, A.	11-8	3.39	31	20	4	1	1	146.0	154	66	55	34	67
Rasmussen, D.	0-3	3.80	7	7	1	0	0	45.0	41	24	19	25	43
Scott, K.	4-5	3.99	21	12	3	0	0	94.2	97	47	42	26	32
Silva, M.	6-5	3.90	43	0	0	0	9	60.0	48	31	26	48	31
Tewksbury, B.	3-0	1.02	6	6	1	1	0	44.0	27	5	5	5	21
Underwood, T.	1-2	6.64	19	2	0	0	2	20.1	18	21	15	16	11
Williams, A.	3-5	4.40	26	16	0	0	0	106.1	115	62	52	52	38

*Led League

DID YOU KNOW ... Four Yankee pitchers hit grand slam home runs ... Red Ruffing in 1933, Spud Chandler in 1940, Don Larsen in 1956, and Mel Stottlemyre in 1965.

1985 ALBANY-COLONIE YANKEES
Eastern League

Manager: Barry Foote
Record: 82-57 (won regular season title with 1st place finish; lost to Vermont, 3 games to 1 in semi-finals).
All-Stars: Orestes Destrade (DH), Brad Arnsberg (RHP), Barry Foote (Manager of the Year).
League Leaders: Tony Russell, (22 SH), Orestes Destrade (129 SO), Brad Arnsberg (1.59 ERA, 14 W, .875 W-L %), Doug Drabek (153 SO, 192.2 IP), Randy Graham (17 SV).

MOST USED LINEUP
(Most games at each position)

1B	Orestes Destrade	134
2B	Ron Chapman	99
3B	Jim Riggs	71
SS	Dickie Scott	92
OF	Tony Russell	122
OF	Keith Hughes	104
OF	Doug Carpenter	66
C	Phil Lombardi	65
St	Doug Drabek	26
Rel	Randy Graham	46

FINAL STATISTICS

BATTING	AVG	G	AB	R	H	2B	3B	HR	RBI	BB	SO	SB
Arnsberg, B.	.000	21	1	0	0	0	0	0	0	0	0	0
Barrett, T.	.262	57	233	40	61	8	3	1	18	25	19	23
Blaser, M.	.190	57	184	15	35	5	1	2	21	20	29	3
Bradley, S.	.125	6	24	2	3	1	0	0	2	2	1	0
Byron, T.	.000	27	1	0	0	0	0	0	0	0	0	0
Carpenter, D.	.305	71	203	27	62	11	6	1	26	18	38	10
Carroll, C.	.273	12	44	5	12	1	2	0	1	1	5	0
Cathcart, G.	.244	20	45	4	11	2	0	0	5	6	10	1
Chapman, R.	.237	107	363	74	86	10	6	4	29	78	32	21
Destrade, O.	.253	136	471	82	119	24	5	23	72	86	129*	9
Fennell, M.	.175	16	40	5	7	2	1	2	5	5	13	0
Gallegos, M.	.231	9	26	5	6	0	0	0	1	6	5	4
Hawkins, J.	.138	13	29	4	4	0	0	0	2	3	6	1
Hughes, J.	.286	9	14	3	4	0	0	0	1	4	3	0
Hughes, K.	.269	104	361	53	97	22	5	10	54	51	73	4
Knight, T.	.225	26	80	13	18	5	0	0	9	16	11	1
Landestoy, R.	.232	55	181	18	42	3	3	1	13	10	14	4
Lindsey, B.	.282	69	227	30	64	16	0	6	41	31	23	2
Lombardi, P.	.256	76	250	44	64	13	2	5	32	39	29	5
Mackay, J.	.207	22	58	3	12	3	2	1	9	4	15	0
Peruso, J.	.135	13	37	4	5	1	0	1	4	5	12	1
Riggs, J.	.234	121	415	51	97	19	2	7	60	57	50	2
Russell, T.	.246	123	415	64	102	16	8	6	36	42	96	15
Scott, R.	.214	97	299	30	64	15	4	4	34	27	73	6
Seoane, M.	.196	32	102	9	20	2	0	0	7	9	10	3
Smith, P.	.211	10	38	5	8	1	0	0	3	2	1	1
Winkler, B.	.197	73	249	27	49	7	2	9	41	26	81	7
Winters, M.	.277	14	47	7	13	2	0	2	6	8	10	0

PITCHING	W-L	ERA	G	GS	CG	SHO	SV	IP	H	R	ER	BB	SO
Arnsberg, B.	*14-2	1.59*	20	20	9	2	0	141.1	105	34	25	35	82
Bradley, B.	1-6	5.30	25	5	1	0	3	56.0	69	42	33	26	24
Byron, T.	10-7	3.33	27	25	5	0	0	165.0	158	83	61	79	89
Cloninger, D.	1-3	5.35	13	6	0	0	0	38.2	48	26	23	23	16
Drabek, D.	13-7	2.99	26	26	9	2	0	192.2*	153	71	64	55	153*
Easley, L.	5-3	3.18	29	5	0	0	0	85.0	85	40	30	38	58
Faulk, K.	3-0	3.09	6	5	0	0	0	35.0	32	12	12	14	24
Ferguson, M.	5-3	3.19	17	9	0	0	0	62.0	63	30	22	29	36
Frey, S.	4-7	3.82	40	0	0	0	3	61.1	53	30	26	25	54
Graham, R.	4-4	3.54	46	0	0	0	17*	56.0	60	26	22	7	46
Hickey, K.	1-0	2.92	11	0	0	0	1	12.1	11	5	4	7	11
Hughes, D.	0-0	22.50	1	0	0	0	0	2.0	4	5	5	5	1
Nielsen, S.	6-1	2.95	11	11	3	1	0	73.1	60	26	24	14	31
Patterson, S.	7-2	1.55	27	0	0	0	3	46.1	32	12	8	17	35
Scott, K.	1-3	4.81	8	8	1	0	0	33.2	39	20	18	12	19
Tewksbury, B.	6-5	3.54	17	17	4	2	0	106.2	101	48	42	19	63
Torres, R.	0-1	9.00	1	1	0	0	0	4.0	5	5	4	2	4
Underwood, T.	0-0	9.64	4	0	0	0	0	4.2	13	8	5	4	3
Wever, S.	0-0	4.91	5	0	0	0	1	11.0	12	6	6	10	5
Wex, G.	1-3	8.10	9	1	0	0	1	20.0	26	24	18	19	13

*League Leader

Fort Lauderdale Yankees

1985 FT. LAUDERDALE YANKEES
Florida State League

Manager: Bucky Dent
Record: 77-63 (finished 1st in Southern Division; defeated Osceola, 2 games to 1 in semi-finals; lost to Ft. Myers, 3 games to 1 in finals).
All-Stars: Jay Buhner (CF), Darren Reed (RF).
League Leaders: Roberto Kelly (13 3B), Jay Buhner (15 GWRBI), Darren Reed (.477 Slugging %), Steve George (5 SHO, 12 CG).

MOST USED LINEUP
(Most games at each position)

1B	Mauricio Ching	66
2B	Rich Mattocks	58
3B	Mark Blaser	35
SS	Carlos Martinez	91
OF	Jay Buhner	113
OF	Roberto Kelly	113
OF	Darren Reed	96
C	Mitch Lyden	101
St	Steve George	24
Rel	Bob Devlin	32

FINAL STATISTICS

BATTING	AVG	G	AB	R	H	2B	3B	HR	RBI	BB	SO	SB
Bernaldo, R.	.200	16	25	4	5	1	0	0	2	6	2	0
Blaser, M.	.291	53	175	24	51	13	0	3	30	26	28	0
Buhner, J.	.296	117	409	65	121	18	10	11	76	65	76	6
Carpenter, D.	.232	40	99	18	23	5	0	1	14	24	20	4
Cathcart, G.	.250	76	256	35	64	8	3	0	24	31	44	7
Ching, M.	.300	90	293	38	88	28	3	4	54	47	66	9
Englehart, B.	.272	38	114	14	31	8	1	1	19	25	23	0
Gilles, T.	.200	2	5	1	1	0	0	0	2	2	0	0
Gonzalez, F.	.204	48	137	13	28	1	1	3	13	20	34	0
Heeney, J.	.094	14	32	4	3	0	0	0	2	9	4	1
Henderson, R.	.167	3	6	5	1	0	1	0	3	5	2	1
Johnson, B.	.222	13	45	7	10	2	0	0	0	9	10	0
Kelly, R.	.247	114	417	86	103	4	13	3	38	58	70	49
Lane, P.	.172	11	29	3	5	1	0	0	3	6	6	1
Lawhon, D.	.000	6	4	0	0	0	0	0	0	0	1	0
Lyden, M.	.255	116	400	43	102	21	1	10	58	27	93	1
Mackey, J.	.239	48	138	23	33	4	2	3	17	19	31	1
Martinez, C.	.248	93	311	39	77	15	7	6	44	14	65	8
Mattocks, R.	.261	66	207	44	54	3	2	0	20	42	36	38
Maynard, J.	.286	22	70	13	20	4	0	0	8	14	9	2
Murcer, B.	.083	4	12	3	1	0	0	0	1	3	3	0
Perdomo, F.	.245	90	273	37	67	10	2	2	25	23	53	16
Peruso, S.	.175	15	40	3	7	1	0	0	1	6	5	1
Reed, D.	.317	100	369	63	117	21	4	10	61	36	56	13
Rivera, J.	.223	35	112	12	25	5	3	0	11	15	28	0
Santiago, N.	.200	32	90	10	18	1	0	1	6	8	9	0
Seoane, M.	.275	63	182	22	50	2	2	0	6	11	21	10
Winkler, B.	.264	40	121	20	32	7	1	4	23	18	35	3
Woleslagel, T.	.173	25	81	3	14	4	0	0	4	3	14	1

PITCHING	W-L	ERA	G	GS	CG	SHO	SV	IP	H	R	ER	BB	SO
Beahan, S.	0-0	0.00	3	0	0	0	0	6.1	5	0	0	5	4
Blum, B.	2-1	5.50	4	3	1	0	0	18.0	22	13	11	5	7
Canseco, O.	5-4	3.61	11	11	1	0	0	57.1	42	33	23	42	37
Chastain, D.	3-2	2.12	22	0	0	0	3	34.0	20	11	8	12	35
Cloninger, D.	4-4	3.70	19	6	1	1	0	58.1	62	28	24	21	18
Dersin, E.	4-3	4.05	8	8	0	0	0	46.2	52	28	21	24	29
Devlin, B.	3-5	4.19	32	0	0	0	4	38.2	34	21	18	23	45
Dougherty, P.	0-0	9.00	4	0	0	0	0	8.0	14	8	8	3	8
Easley, L.	1-1	0.95	17	0	0	0	4	19.0	19	6	2	6	16
Frey, S.	1-1	1.21	19	0	0	0	7	22.1	11	4	3	12	15
Fulton, B.	11-2	1.61	15	15	9	1	0	112.0	91	31	20	30	71
George, S.	13-7	1.75	24	24	12	5	0	164.2	120	48	32	76	141
Guercio, M.	2-2	3.09	22	0	0	0	4	43.2	26	19	15	27	41
Harrison, M.	1-0	2.15	22	0	0	0	0	37.2	27	11	9	14	23
Leiter, A.	1-6	6.48	17	17	1	0	0	82.0	87	70	59	57	44
Pries, J.	11-7	3.83	22	22	4	0	0	131.2	117	66	56	49	50
Raftice, R.	0-2	4.58	11	0	0	0	0	17.2	18	11	9	11	11
Rather, D.	2-3	3.47	6	6	1	0	0	36.1	21	17	14	20	35
Rodriguez, Y.	6-5	3.09	30	9	1	0	0	96.0	100	41	33	35	48
Torres, R.	6-6	4.68	17	17	1	1	0	92.1	103	56	48	36	107
Trudeau, K.	0-0	0.00	1	0	0	0	0	2.0	0	0	0	1	1
Underwood, T.	0-1	1.35	5	2	0	0	0	13.1	14	5	2	4	12
Yeager, C.	1-1	1.60	20	0	0	0	3	33.2	22	6	6	14	32

ONEONTA

1985 ONEONTA YANKEES
1985 New York Penn League Champions

Manager: Buck Showalter
Record: 55-23 (finished 1st in Northern Division; defeated Geneva, 1 game to none in semi-finals; defeated Auburn 2 games to none for league championship).
All-Stars: Scott Shaw (3B), Chris Lombardozzi (Utility), Dody Rather (RHP), Mike Christopher (RHP), Buck Showalter (Manager of the Year).
League Leaders: Troy Evers (1.18 ERA, .909 W-L%)

MOST USED LINEUP
(Most games at each position)

1B	Bob Sepanek	60
2B	Chris Lombardozzi	62
3B	Scott Shaw	43
SS	Shane Turner	61
OF	Matt Mainini	67
OF	Corey Viltz	48
OF	Harvey Lee	42
C	Tod Marston	33
St	Evers/Balabon	12
Rel	Bob Davidson	29

FINAL STATISTICS

BATTING	AVG	G	AB	R	H	2B	3B	HR	RBI	BB	SO	SB
Azocar, O.	.000	15	0	1	0	0	0	0	0	0	0	0
Bernaldo, R.	.000	1	1	0	0	0	0	0	0	0	0	0
Calvert, A.	.312	22	77	12	24	2	0	3	14	7	22	1
Ezold, T.	.216	31	88	8	19	5	0	0	12	9	28	1
Gilles, T.	.220	40	118	16	26	6	2	1	19	14	28	2
Green, R.	.260	39	150	24	39	9	3	3	26	23	47	3
Higgins, T.	1.000	1	1	1	1	0	0	1	1	0	0	0
Iavarone, G.	.315	28	54	9	17	1	0	2	9	18	17	1
Lambert, R.	.000	1	0	1	0	0	0	0	0	2	0	2
Lashua, R.	.000	4	4	0	0	0	0	0	0	1	1	0
Lee, H.	.249	52	169	35	42	7	1	3	22	25	41	16
Lombardozzi, C.	.246	66	207	33	51	9	2	2	25	57	55	11
Mass, J.	.286	67	234	37	67	7	2	1	23	51	42	16
Mainini, M.	.260	70	196	30	51	7	1	3	23	52	46	4
Marston, T.	.202	36	109	16	22	2	2	2	15	15	28	3
Meyer, G.	.182	6	11	2	2	1	0	0	0	0	3	0
Pliecones, J.	.221	46	145	17	32	2	1	0	16	11	17	5
Sepanek, B.	.275	63	211	34	58	13	5	5	43	23	37	5
Shaw, S.	.293	72	276	40	81	8	6	4	37	23	54	5
Stanko, E.	.162	27	37	11	6	1	0	0	3	13	14	0
Turner, S.	.246	64	228	35	56	7	3	0	26	35	44	12
Viltz, C.	.246	61	224	39	55	11	1	0	25	38	65	23

PITCHING	W-L	ERA	G	GS	CG	SHO	SV	IP	H	R	ER	BB	SO
Azocar, O.	0-2	4.86	14	2	0	0	0	16.2	21	16	9	9	13
Balabon, R.	5-2	1.74	12	12	3	2	0	72.1	50	16	14	39	68
Carroll, C.	1-0	0.37	12	0	0	0	3	24.1	13	4	1	10	21
Christopher, M.	8-1	1.46	15	9	2	2	0	80.1	58	21	13	22	84
Davidson, R.	1-2	2.50	29	0	0	0	5	36.0	28	14	10	13	44
Dougherty, P.	6-2	1.96	13	11	2	1	0	73.1	53	24	16	30	62
Evers, T.	10-1	1.18*	14	12	4	1	0	99.1	69	21	13	25	85
Ezold, T.	0-0	3.00	1	0	0	0	0	3.0	2	2	1	2	2
Gay, S.	0-1	1.80	2	0	0	0	1	5.0	3	1	1	1	6
Leiter, A.	3-2	2.37	6	6	2	0	0	38.0	27	14	10	25	34
O'Connor, G.	0-0	9.00	2	0	0	0	0	6.0	5	6	6	3	5
Patterson, K.	2-2	4.84	6	6	0	0	0	22.1	23	14	12	14	21
Rather, D.	8-0	0.31	8	8	4	2	0	58.0	22	5	2	16	88
Tirado, A.	2-3	1.99	22	1	0	0	3	45.1	20	15	10	15	68
Torres, P.	1-2	4.50	3	3	0	0	0	16.0	17	10	8	10	13
Trudeau, K.	8-3	1.64	16	8	3	2	1	71.1	42	22	13	24	75
Yeager, C.	0-0	0.00	1	0	0	0	0	1.0	0	0	0	0	2

*Tied for League Lead

DID YOU KNOW ... that the New York Americans (name changed to Yankees a couple of years later) scored 10 runs in the first inning against the St. Louis Browns on May 13, 1911 before the first out was made?

Sarasota

1985 SARASOTA YANKEES
1985 Gulf Coast League Champions

Manager: Carlos Tosca
Record: 43-18 (finished first in regular season in Southern Division; championship playoff was rained out and Yankees declared champions based on overall winning percentage).
All-Stars: Rob Lambert (2B), Fred Carter (OF), Ted Higgins (OF), Carlos Tosca (Manager).
League Leaders: Rob Lambert (.350 BA, 51 R, 92 TB, 79 H, 34 SB, T1 12 CS), Ted Higgins (36 RBI), Darren Mandel (16 2B, .500 Slugging %), Dick Sisler (7 W), Scott Cantrell (2 SHO).

MOST USED LINEUP
(Most games at each position)

1B	David Banks	43
2B	Rob Lambert	57
3B	Dino Johnson	33
SS	Neder Horta	52
OF	Ted Higgins	51
OF	Neal Cargile	41
OF	Fred Carter	39
C	Darren Mandel	33
St	Scott Cantrell	13
Rel	Mike McClear	20

FINAL STATISTICS

BATTING	AVG	G	AB	R	H	2B	3B	HR	RBI	BB	SO	SB
Banks, D.	.228	43	145	15	33	7	1	0	21	24	24	2
Bettencourt, B.	.143	2	7	2	1	0	0	0	1	1	0	0
Calvert, A.	.316	36	136	19	43	8	3	0	26	15	28	4
Canseco, O.	.179	20	39	2	7	0	1	1	5	2	18	0
Cargile, N.	.280	48	118	17	33	3	2	1	20	14	29	9
Carter, F.	.284	57	215	28	61	13	1	0	29	11	45	9
Cuadrado, R.	.120	14	25	3	3	1	0	0	1	1	5	0
Didder, R.	.167	18	30	6	5	0	0	0	4	3	11	2
Gibson, B.	.250	2	8	1	2	0	0	0	1	0	3	1
Gonzalez, A.	.196	33	107	9	21	1	1	0	7	9	25	1
Guzman, H.	.244	15	45	4	11	1	0	0	5	1	5	7
Hauradou, Y.	.309	45	139	19	43	5	0	0	16	14	16	5
Hernandez, B.	.250	41	108	18	27	6	2	2	14	19	30	5
Higgins, T.	.306	55	196	38	60	7	6	0	36	30	14	9
Horta, N.	.245	53	147	42	36	3	0	0	23	46	33	9
Horton, D.	.050	19	20	8	1	0	0	0	0	4	7	4
Johnson, D.	.287	41	143	31	41	7	2	1	16	18	27	4
Kupfner, B.	.000	3	6	0	0	0	0	0	0	2	3	0
Lambert, R.	.350	59	226	51	79	9	2	0	21	29	32	34
Lawhon, D.	.000	7	7	0	0	0	0	0	0	0	4	0
Mandel, D.	.317	55	180	33	57	16	4	3	31	29	23	4
Martinez, R.	.190	16	21	1	4	1	0	0	1	1	4	0
Rivas, J.	.500	2	2	0	1	0	0	0	1	0	0	0

PITCHING	W-L	ERA	G	GS	CG	SHO	SV	IP	H	R	ER	BB	SO
Azocar, O..	4-0	1.45	5	4	2	1	0	37.1	30	8	6	14	36
Bauza, C.	1-2	4.30	4	4	0	0	0	23.0	27	14	11	7	20
Blum, B.	6-0	1.38	8	8	3	0	0	58.2	36	16	9	23	62
Canseco, O.	3-2	1.57	9	7	1	0	0	51.2	43	19	9	11	39
Cantrell, S.	5-4	3.08	13	13	3	2	0	84.2	93	37	29	11	48
Carreno, A.	0-0	4.50	1	0	0	0	0	2.0	1	1	1	1	1
Carroll, C.	2-0	2.10	11	0	0	0	4	25.2	18	8	6	11	33
Clark, D.	4-1	3.31	8	6	0	0	0	35.1	34	17	13	13	31
Hellman, J.	4-0	0.87	7	6	2	1	0	41.1	21	9	4	15	44
Lawhon, D.	0-0	0.00	5	0	0	0	1	8.0	4	3	0	4	5
McClear, M.	6-3	1.40	20	0	0	0	2	38.2	25	9	6	12	46
Reker, T.	1-2	2.73	10	4	1	0	0	29.2	37	15	9	2	17
Rodriguez, G.	0-1	4.03	13	1	0	0	2	22.1	26	15	10	10	14
Shane, J.	0-1	5.40	11	0	0	0	1	16.2	19	15	10	16	9
Sisler, D.	7-2	3.63	13	9	1	0	0	62.0	67	37	25	19	41
Starling, J.	0-0	6.00	2	0	0	0	0	3.0	2	3	2	6	2

DID YOU KNOW ... that from July 30, 1935 to September 15, 1947, Yankee Red Ruffing was the starting pitcher in 241 games without pitching once in relief?

1985 MINOR LEAGUE
MANAGERS AND COACHES

BUTTERFIELD, Brian J.
Coach

HEIGHT: 6-0 **BATS:** S **BORN:** March 9, 1959, Bangor, ME
WEIGHT: 190 **THROWS:** R **RESIDES:** Brewer, ME

Graduated from Florida Southern College with a B.S. in Physical Education in 1980. Signed as a free agent by the Yankees in June, 1979. Coached at Eckerd College (1980-81) and Florida Southern (1979). Named Most Valuable Player of Ft. Lauderdale squad—1981. Son of the late Jack Butterfield, who was Yankees' Vice President of Player Development and Scouting.

POSITIONS PLAYED: IF

YR	CLUB	AVG	G	AB	R	H	2B	3B	HR	RBI	BB	SO	SB
79	Oneonta	.218	58	179	25	39	1	1	0	13	24	27	8
80	Ft. Lauderdale	.125	8	16	3	2	1	1	1	2	4	2	0
80	Greensboro	.227	72	185	29	42	5	0	0	13	30	24	7
81	Ft. Lauderdale	.286	94	259	31	74	7	2	0	27	28	28	3
82	Columbus	.417	13	36	4	15	1	0	0	2	3	1	0
82	Ft. Lauderdale	.259	70	247	42	64	10	1	1	29	48	32	7
82	Nashville	.133	11	30	3	4	0	0	0	3	2	4	0
83	Miami	.238	71	240	34	57	9	1	0	24	45	30	5

COACHING CAREER (All in Yankee Organization)

1984	Roving Infield Instructor, Minor Leagues, Yankees
1985	Coach, Ft. Lauderdale, Florida State League
1986	Coach, Sarasota, Gulf Coast League

DENT, Russell E. (Bucky)
Manager

HEIGHT: 5-11 **BATS:** R **BORN:** Nov. 25, 1951, Savannah, GA
WEIGHT: 180 **THROWS:** R **RESIDES:** Wyckoff, NJ

Drafted by the White Sox in the 1st round of the secondary phase of the 1970 June draft, Bucky played in the 1st major league game he ever saw in 1973. After 4 years in Chicago, he was acquired by the Yankees just prior to the start of the 1977 Championship season. In 1978, Dent won the East Division playoff game for the Yankees at Boston with a dramatic three-run homer off Mike Torrez, erasing a 2-run Red Sox lead. He went on to lead the Yankees in their 6-game World Series victory over the Dodgers, hitting .417 while earning the Most Valuable Player award for the Series. Bucky was traded to the Texas Rangers in August, 1982 and played there through 1983. In 1984, he had a short stint with the Columbus Clippers, before joining the Kansas City Royals for their stretch drive en route to the A.L. West title. Bucky will return to manage Ft. Lauderdale in 1986.

POSITIONS PLAYED: IF

YR	CLUB	AVG	G	AB	R	H	2B	3B	HR	RBI	BB	SO	SB
70	Sarasota	.351	22	77	18	27	2	1	0	13	22	6	2
	Appleton	.258	39	163	23	42	4	2	3	12	20	21	3
71	Appleton	.231	83	294	34	68	16	0	1	29	28	40	0
72	Knoxville	.296	125	453	58	134	10	6	6	56	53	56	6
72	Iowa	.295	95	356	58	105	10	3	3	38	32	43	1
	Chicago (AL)	.248	40	117	17	29	2	0	0	10	10	18	2
74	Chicago (AL)	.274	154	496	55	136	15	3	5	45	28	48	3
75	Chicago (AL)	.264	157	602	52	159	29	4	3	58	36	48	2
76	Chicago (AL)	.246	158	562	44	138	18	4	2	52	43	45	3
77	Yankees	.247	158	477	54	118	18	4	8	49	39	28	1
78	Yankees	.243	123	379	40	92	11	1	5	40	23	24	3
79	Yankees	.230	141	431	47	99	14	2	2	32	37	30	0
80	Yankees	.262	141	489	57	128	26	2	5	52	48	37	0
81	Yankees	.238	73	227	20	54	11	0	7	27	19	17	0
82	Yankees	.169	59	160	11	27	1	1	0	9	8	11	0
	Texas	.219	46	146	16	32	9	0	1	14	13	10	0
83	Texas	.237	131	417	36	99	15	2	2	34	23	31	3
84	Columbus	.250	17	60	4	15	1	0	1	5	1	6	0
	Kansas City	.333	11	9	2	3	0	0	0	1	1	2	0

CHAMPIONSHIP SERIES RECORD

YR	CLUB, Opp.	AVG	G	AB	R	H	2B	3B	HR	RBI	BB	SO	SB
77	N.Y. vs K.C.	.214	5	14	1	3	1	0	0	2	1	0	0
78	N.Y. vs K.C.	.200	4	15	0	3	0	0	0	4	0	0	0
80	N.Y. vs K.C.	.182	3	11	0	2	0	0	0	0	0	1	0
81	N.Y. vs Oak.					(Injured, did not play)							
L.C.S. Totals		**.200**	**12**	**40**	**1**	**8**	**1**	**0**	**0**	**6**	**1**	**1**	**0**

WORLD SERIES RECORD

YR	CLUB, Opp.	AVG	G	AB	R	H	2B	3B	HR	RBI	BB	SO	SB
77	N.Y. vs L.A.	.263	6	19	0	5	0	0	0	2	1	1	0
78	N.Y. vs L.A.	.417	6	24	3	10	1	0	0	7	1	2	0
81	N.Y. vs L.A.					(Injured, did not play)							
Totals		**.349**	**12**	**43**	**3**	**15**	**1**	**0**	**0**	**9**	**2**	**3**	**0**

ALL-STAR GAME RECORD

YR	CLUB, Site	AVG	G	AB	R	H	2B	3B	HR	RBI	BB	SO	SB
75	A.L., Mil.	.000	1	1	0	0	0	0	0	0	0	1	0
80	A.L., L.A.	.500	1	2	0	1	0	0	0	0	0	1	0
81	A.L., Cleve.	1.000	1	2	0	2	1	0	0	0	0	0	0

RECORD AS MANAGER

YR	CLUB	LG	W	L	PCT	FINISH
1985	Ft. Lauderdale	FSL	77	63	.550	(1st in Southern Division)

POST SEASON PLAY

YR	CLUB	LG	W	L	PCT	RESULTS
1985	Ft. Lauderdale	FSL	3	4	.429	(Def. Osceola 2g to 1; Lost to Ft. Myers, 3g to 1 in LCS)

FOOTE, Barry Clinton (Barry)
Manager

HEIGHT: 6-3 **BATS:** R **BORN:** Feb. 16, 1952, Smithfield, NC
WEIGHT: 220 **THROWS:** R **RESIDES:** Raleigh, NC

Drafted in 1st round by Montreal in June, 1970. Named National League Rookie of the Year in 1974; also led NL catchers in assists with 83 in 1974. Had 8 RBI game vs St. Louis in 1980, while playing for Phillies. Homered in 1st at bat as Yankee ... hit 5 HR in his 1st 7 games as Yankee. Skippered Ft. Lauderdale to FSL championship in 1984, his rookie year in managing. Named FSL Manager of the Year, 1984. Named Eastern League Manager of the Year, 1985. Barry will manage the Columbus Clippers in 1986.

POSITIONS PLAYED:

YR	CLUB	AVG	G	AB	R	H	2B	3B	HR	RBI	BB	SO	SB
70	Bradenton	.226	48	143	26	38	7	0	3	29	24	22	0
71	W. Palm Beach	.230	115	366	45	84	14	5	8	42	30	87	6
72	Quebec City	.253	124	427	62	108	23	0	16	75	51	78	5
73	Peninsula	.262	137	465	63	122	22	2	19	65	40	84	2
	Montreal	.667	6	6	0	4	0	1	0	1	0	0	0
74	Montreal	.262	125	420	44	110	23	4	11	60	35	74	2
75	Montreal	.194	118	387	25	75	16	1	7	30	17	48	0
76	Montreal	.234	105	350	32	82	12	2	7	27	17	32	2
77	Montreal	.245	15	49	4	12	3	1	2	8	4	10	0
	Philadelphia	.219	18	32	3	7	1	0	1	3	3	6	0
78	Philadelphia	.158	39	57	4	9	0	0	1	4	1	11	0
79	Chicago (NL)	.254	132	429	47	109	26	0	16	56	34	49	5
80	Chicago (NL)	.238	63	202	16	48	13	1	6	28	13	18	1
81	Chicago (NL)	.000	9	22	0	0	0	0	0	1	3	7	0
	Yankees	.208	40	125	12	26	4	0	6	10	8	21	0
82	Columbus	.385	7	26	1	10	2	0	1	5	1	7	0
	Yankees	.146	17	48	4	7	5	0	0	2	1	11	0

DIVISION SERIES RECORD

YR	CLUB, OPP.	AVG	G	AB	R	H	2B	3B	HR	RBI	BB	SO	SB
81	N.Y. vs Milw.	.000	1	0	0	0	0	0	0	0	0	0	0

CHAMPIONSHIP SERIES RECORD

YR	CLUB, OPP.	AVG	G	AB	R	H	2B	3B	HR	RBI	BB	SO	SB
77	Phi. vs L.A.	(Eligible, did not play)											
78	Phi. vs L.A.	.000	1	1	0	0	0	0	0	0	0	1	0
81	N.Y. vs L.A.	1.000	2	1	0	1	0	0	0	0	0	0	0
L.C.S. Totals		**.500**	**3**	**2**	**0**	**1**	**0**	**0**	**0**	**0**	**0**	**1**	**0**

WORLD SERIES RECORD

YR	CLUB, OPP.	AVG	G	AB	R	H	2B	3B	HR	RBI	BB	SO	SB
81	N.Y. vs L.A.	.000	1	1	0	0	0	0	0	0	0	1	0

MANAGERIAL/COACHING CAREER

1984	Manager, Ft. Lauderdale, Florida State League
1985	Manager, Albany-Colonie, Eastern League

RECORD AS MANAGER

YR	CLUB	LG	W	L	PCT	FINISH
1984	Ft. Lauderdale	FSL	74	68	.521	(4th in 1st half; 1st in 2nd half; Won LCS)
1985	Albany	EAS	82	57	.590	(1st in regular season)
CAREER TOTALS (2 years)			**156**	**125**	**.555**	

POST SEASON PLAY

YR	CLUB	LG	W	L	PCT	RESULTS
1984	Ft. Lauderdale	FSL	5	3	.625	(Def. Ft. Myers 2g to 1; Def. Tampa 3g to 2 for LCS)
1985	Albany	EAS	1	3	.250	(Lost to Vermont 3g to 1, in semifinals)

GILLIS, Jack
Coach

HEIGHT: 5-8   **BORN:** Oct. 28, 1949, Worcester, MA
WEIGHT: 175   **RESIDES:** Worcester, MA

Did not play pro baseball, but built strong reputation as college coach at two Florida schools—Eckerd and St. Leo. Joined Yankees organization in 1980 as coach at Oneonta. Managed Sarasota Yankees in 1984. Returns to coach at Oneonta in 1986. Jack also scouts high school and college talent for the Yankees in the off-season.

(NO PROFESSIONAL PLAYING EXPERIENCE)

MANAGERIAL/COACHING CAREER (Joined Yankees Organization in 1980)

1971-77	Head coach, Eckerd College, St. Petersburg, Fla.
1978-79	Head coach, Saint Leo College, Saint Leo, Fla.
1980-82	Coach, Oneonta, New York-Penn League
1983	Coach, Ft. Lauderdale Yankees, Florida State League.
1984	Manager, Sarasota Yankees, Gulf Coast League.
1985	Coach, Oneonta, New York-Penn League.
1986	Coach, Oneonta, New York-Penn League.

RECORD AS MANAGER

YR	CLUB	LG	W	L	PCT	FINISH
1984	Sarasota	GCL	28	35	.444	(4th in Southern Division)

KENNEDY, John Edward
Coach

HEIGHT: 6-0   **BATS:** R   **BORN:** May 29, 1941, Chicago, IL
WEIGHT: 185   **THROWS:** R   **RESIDES:** Peabody, MA

Originally signed with the Washington Senators in 1961. Traded to the Los Angeles Dodgers with pitcher Claude Osteen and cash for outfielder Frank Howard, infielder Ken McMullen and pitchers Phil Ortega and Pete Richert, 12/4/64; first baseman Dick Nen was transferred to Senators, 12/15/64, to complete deal. Traded to New York Yankees for pitcher Jack Cullen, outfielder John Miller and $25,000, 4/3/67. Sold to Seattle Pilots, 11/13/68. Purchased by Boston Red Sox, 6/26/70. Retired after 1974 season. Managed in the Red Sox' system from 1975-77. Managed Jersey City (Oakland) in 1978, where Rickey Henderson played for John. Moved to the Yankees as a coach at Winter Haven in '79. Scouted in the New England area for the Yankees from 1980-85. John returns to coaching in 1986 for the Albany-Colonie Yankees.

POSITIONS PLAYED: 2B, SS, 3B.

YR	CLUB	AVG	G	AB	R	H	2B	3B	HR	RBI	BB	SO	SB
61	Pensacola	.254	115	418	69	106	10	6	3	46	70	75	5
62	Raleigh	.302	139	523	78	158	23	10	6	72	71	99	9
	Washington	.262	14	42	6	11	0	1	1	2	2	7	0
63	York	.289	30	121	20	35	7	1	6	17	13	21	3
	Hawaii	.290	67	231	32	67	12	4	2	28	18	47	1
	Washington	.177	36	62	3	11	1	1	0	4	6	22	2
64	Washington-a	.230	148	482	55	111	16	4	7	35	28	119	3
65	Los Angeles	.171	104	105	12	18	3	0	1	5	8	33	1
66	Los Angeles-b	.201	125	274	15	55	9	2	3	24	10	64	1
67	New York (A)	.196	78	179	22	35	4	0	1	17	17	35	2
68	Syra-Col.-c	.268	140	471	65	126	21	5	8	57	57	113	2
69	Seattle	.234	61	128	18	30	3	1	4	14	14	25	4
70	Milwaukee	.255	25	55	8	14	2	0	2	6	5	9	0
	Portland-d	.246	31	118	19	29	7	3	2	17	9	21	2
	Boston	.256	43	129	15	33	7	1	4	17	6	14	0
71	Boston	.276	74	272	41	75	12	5	5	22	14	42	1
72	Boston	.245	71	212	22	52	11	1	2	22	18	40	0
73	Boston	.181	67	155	17	28	9	1	1	16	12	45	0
74	Pawtucket	.215	57	158	16	34	4	1	4	13	14	46	0
	Boston	.133	10	15	3	2	0	0	1	1	1	6	0
N.L. Totals		**.193**	**229**	**379**	**27**	**73**	**12**	**2**	**4**	**29**	**18**	**97**	**2**
A.L. Totals		**.232**	**627**	**1731**	**210**	**402**	**65**	**15**	**28**	**156**	**123**	**364**	**12**
M.L. Totals		**.225**	**956**	**2110**	**237**	**475**	**77**	**17**	**32**	**185**	**141**	**461**	**14**

MANAGERIAL/COACHING CAREER (Joined Yankees Organization in 1980)

1975	Manager, Winston-Salem, Carolina League
1976-77	Manager, Bristol, Eastern League
1978	Manager, Jersey City, Eastern League
1979	Coach, Winter Haven, Eastern League
1986	Coach, Albany-Colonie, Eastern League

RECORD AS MANAGER

YR	CLUB	LG	W	L	PCT	FINISH
1975	Winston-Salem	WCL	81	62	.566	(10½ GB, 2nd place)
1976	Bristol	EAS	74	60	.552	(3½ GB, 2nd place)
1977	Bristol	EAS	72	67	.518	(14½ GB, 4th place)
1978	Jersey City	EAS	54	83	.394	(27 GB, 6th place)
CAREER TOTALS (4 years)			**281**	**272**	**.508**	

LaROCHE, David Eugene (Dave)
Pitching Coach

HEIGHT: 6-2 **BATS:** L **BORN:** May 14, 1948, Colorado Springs, CO
WEIGHT: 195 **THROWS:** L **RESIDES:** Ft. Scott, KS

Signed as free agent with California Angels organization in 1967. Originally an out-fielder, converted to pitcher in 1968. Named Indians' Man of the Year in 1975, tying club record for saves with 17. Set club record the following year with 21 saves. Came up with "trick" pitch, dubbed "La Lob," which stymied hitters and amused fans due to its unorthodox nature. Pitching coach for Ft. Lauderdale in 1984, and served in the same capacity for Albany-Colonie in 1985. Dave will move to Columbus with manager Barry Foote in 1986.

YR	CLUB	W-L	ERA	G	GS	CG	Sho	SV	IP	H	R	ER	BB	SO
1968	Quad Cities	5-7	2.36	33	5	0	0	—	84	76	33	22	29	80
1969	San Jose	2-1	3.68	11	0	0	0	1	21	21	11	9	8	19
	El Paso	6-3	2.94	33	0	0	0	8	49	43	16	16	25	46
1970	Hawaii	6-0	1.24	22	1	0	0	5	58	31	11	8	19	67
	CALIFORNIA	4-1	3.42	38	0	0	0	4	50	41	20	19	21	44
1971	CALIFORNIA	5-1	2.50	56	0	0	0	9	72	55	21	20	27	63
1972	MINNESOTA	5-7	2.84	62	0	0	0	10	951	72	33	30	39	79
1973	CHICAGO (NL)-c	4-1	5.83	45	0	0	0	4	54	55	37	35	29	34
1974	Wichita	1-3	5.12	6	6	1	0	0	32	37	19	18	7	17
	CHICAGO (NL)-d	5-6	4.79	49	4	0	0	5	92	106	54	49	47	49
1975	CLEVELAND	5-3	2.20	61	0	0	0	17	82	61	26	20	57	94
1976	CLEVELAND	1-4	2.25	61	0	0	0	21	96	57	25	24	49	104
1977	CLEVELAND-e	2-2	5.30	18	0	0	0	4	19	16	13	11	7	18
	CALIFORNIA	6-5	3.10	46	0	0	0	13	81	64	31	28	37	61
1977	Totals	8-7	3.51	59	0	0	0	17	100	79	44	39	44	79
1978	CALIFORNIA	10-9	2.81	59	0	0	0	25	96	73	35	30	48	70
1979	CALIFORNIA	7-11	5.57	53	1	0	0	10	86	107	54	53	32	69
1980	CALIFORNIA-f	3-5	4.08	52	9	1	0	4	128	122	62	56	39	69
1981	YANKEES-gh	4-1	2.49	26	1	0	0	4	47	38	16	13	16	24
1982	Columbus	3-1	3.77	17	0	0	0	4	31	27	17	13	14	20
	YANKEES-i	4-2	3.42	25	0	0	0	0	50	54	19	19	11	31
1983	Columbus	1-1	5.40	7	0	0	0	2	8.1	11	5	5	7	8
	YANKEES	0-0	18.00	1	0	0	0	0	1.0	2	2	2	0	0
N.Y.Y. Totals		**8-3**	**3.12**	**52**	**1**	**0**	**0**	**0**	**98.0**	**94**	**37**	**34**	**27**	**55**
A.L. Totals		**56-51**	**3.26**	**553**	**11**	**1**	**0**	**117**	**903.0**	**761**	**357**	**327**	**385**	**736**
N.L. Totals		**9-7**	**5.18**	**94**	**4**	**0**	**0**	**9**	**146**	**158**	**91**	**84**	**76**	**83**
M.L. Totals		**65-58**	**3.53**	**647**	**15**	**1**	**0**	**126**	**1049**	**919**	**448**	**411**	**461**	**819**

Signed as free agent by California Angels' organization, March 9, 1967.
a-Traded to Minnesota Twins for shortstop Leo Cardenas, November 30, 1972.
b-Traded to Chicago Cubs for pitchers Bill Hands, George (Joe) Decker and Bob Maneely, November 30, 1972.
c-On disabled list, March 25 to April 17, 1973.
d-Traded with outfielder Brock Davis to Cleveland Indians for pitcher Milt Wilcox, February 28, 1975.
e-Traded with pitcher Dave Schuler to California Angels for first baseman-outfielder Bruce Bochte, pitcher Sid Monge, and cash, May 11, 1977.
f-Released by California Angels, April 1, 1981.
g-Signed as free agent by New York Yankees, April 16, 1981.
h-Granted free agency, November 13, 1981.
i-Released, October 20, 1982.

DIVISION SERIES RECORD

YR	CLUB, Opp.	W-L	ERA	G	GS	CG	Sho	SV	IP	H	R	ER	BB	SO
1981	N.Y. vs Mil.						(Eligible, did not pitch)							

CHAMPIONSHIP SERIES RECORD

YR	CLUB, Opp.	W-L	ERA	G	GS	CG	Sho	SV	IP	H	R	ER	BB	SO
1979	CAL. vs Bal.	0-0	6.75	1	0	0	0	0	1.1	2	1	1	1	1
1981	N.Y. vs Oak.						(Eligible, did not pitch)							

WORLD SERIES RECORD

YR	CLUB, Opp.	W-L	ERA	G	GS	CG	Sho	SV	IP	H	R	ER	BB	SO
1981	N.Y. vs L.A.	0-0	0.00	1	0	0	0	0	1.0	0	0	0	0	2

ALL-STAR GAME RECORD

YR	CLUB, Site	W-L	ERA	G	GS	CG	Sho	SV	IP	H	R	ER	BB	SO
1976	A.L., Phi.						(Selected, did not play)							
1977	N.L., N.Y. (AL)	0-0	0.00	1	0	0	0	0	1.0	1	0	0	1	0

COACHING CAREER

1984	Pitching Coach, Ft. Lauderdale, Florida State League
1985	Pitching Coach, Albany-Colonie, Eastern League
1986	Pitching Coach, Columbus, International League

DID YOU KNOW ... After Babe Ruth, uniform number 3 was worn by George Selkirk, Allie Clark, Joe Medwick (in spring training), Bud Methany, and Cliff Mapes, until it was retired.

LEZCANO, Carlos
Coach

HEIGHT: 6-1   **BATS:** R   **BORN:** September 30, 1955, Arecibo, Puerto Rico
WEIGHT: 185   **THROWS:** R   **RESIDES:** Ft. Lauderdale, FL

SIGNED BY: Chicago Cubs

HOW OBTAINED: Signed by the Cubs as a free agent, 5/23/77. Signed as a 6-year free agent with Oakland, 1/14/84. Released, 5/19/84. Signed as a free agent with Detroit, 6/8/84. Released, 7/11/84. Worked as an outfield and hitting instructor for Oneonta Yankees, 1985. Carlos will coach at Sarasota in 1986.

YR	CLUB	AVG	G	AB	R	H	2B	3B	HR	RBI	BB	SO	SB
77	Midland	.231	71	225	27	52	8	1	6	22	20	68	4
78	Midland	(Injured, did not appear)											
79	Midland	.326	124	457	94	149	28	9	11	82	50	86	23
80	CHICAGO (N)	.205	42	88	15	18	4	1	3	12	11	29	1
	Wichita	.232	77	293	46	68	9	7	19	56	28	62	10
81	CHICAGO (N)	.071	7	14	1	1	0	0	0	2	0	4	0
	Iowa	.217	57	175	15	38	2	4	2	18	22	41	7
82	Midland	.278	125	453	70	126	16	8	13	64	47	108	10
83	Midland	.290	71	255	44	74	18	3	12	42	29	71	8
	Des Moines	.186	32	118	13	22	4	1	4	13	9	39	1
84	Tacoma	.219	25	73	8	16	3	1	1	8	8	19	1
	Birmingham	.222	22	72	13	16	4	0	1	12	13	14	1
M.L. Totals		**.186**	**49**	**102**	**16**	**19**	**4**	**1**	**3**	**14**	**11**	**33**	**1**

COACHING CAREER

1985	Coach, Oneonta, New York-Penn League
1986	Coach, Sarasota, Gulf Coast League

McNERTNEY, Gerald Edward (Jerry)
Coach

HEIGHT: 6-1   **BATS:** R   **BORN:** August 7, 1936, Boone, IA
WEIGHT: 195   **THROWS:** R   **RESIDES:** Gilbert, IA

Attended Iowa State University. His first 11 seasons in pro baseball were spent in White Sox organization after signing with them in 1958. Began career as first baseman-outfielder, but switched to catching in 1961. Caught four years in Chicago (1964-66-67-68), then went to Seattle Pilots in 1969 expansion draft. Wound up playing career with Cardinals and Pirates in NL in 1971-72-73. Joined Yankees as coach at West Haven in 1978 and has been coaching at Columbus since 1979. Best year as batter was 1960, when he hit .341 and drove in 125 runs for Idaho Falls in Pioneer League. Tied for Nebraska State League lead in doubles in 1958 with 16. Jerry moves to Ft. Lauderdale in 1986.

POSITIONS PLAYED: 1958 (1B-56); 1959 Duluth-Superior (OF-38, 1B-29), Lincoln (1B-OF); 1960 (1B-130); 1962 (C-96); 1963 (C-83); 1964 (C-69); 1965 (C-15); 1966 (C-37); 1967 (C-52); 1968 (C-64); 1969 (C-122); 1970 (C-94, 1B-13); 1971 (C-36); 1972 (C-10); 1973 Tucson (C-9), Pittsburgh (C-9).

YR	CLUB	AVG	G	AB	R	H	2B	3B	HR	RBI	BB	SO	SB
58	Holdrege	.328	63	256	41	84	16	5	1	51	24	18	3
59	Dul.-Superior	.230	90	335	38	77	14	3	2	33	54	38	1
	Lincoln	.289	14	45	7	13	2	0	0	3	7	17	1
60	Idaho Falls	.341	130	516	109	176	32	10	13	125	52	47	2
61	Charleston	.273	134	498	64	136	21	3	6	79	53	76	9
62	Indianapolis	.267	101	344	43	92	14	5	8	51	30	53	0
63	Indianapolis	.224	93	290	20	65	6	2	6	34	23	45	2
64	Chicago	.215	73	186	16	40	5	0	3	23	19	24	0
65	Indianapolis	.292	15	48	6	14	4	0	2	11	0	7	0
66	Chicago	.220	44	49	3	13	0	0	0	1	7	6	1
67	Chicago	.228	56	123	8	28	6	0	3	13	6	14	0
68	Chicago	.219	74	169	18	37	4	1	3	18	18	29	0
69	Seattle	.241	128	410	39	99	18	1	8	55	29	63	1
70	Milwaukee	.243	111	296	27	72	11	1	6	22	22	33	1
71	St. Louis	.289	56	128	15	37	4	2	4	22	12	14	0
72	St. Louis	.208	39	48	3	10	3	1	0	9	6	16	0
73	Tucson	.344	10	32	2	11	2	1	0	4	2	4	0
	Pittsburgh	.250	9	4	0	1	0	0	0	0	0	0	0

COACHING CAREER (Joined Yankees Organization in 1978)

1978	Coach, West Haven, Eastern League
1979-84	Coach, Columbus, International League
1984	Coach, New York Yankees, American League
1985	Coach, Columbus, International League
1986	Coach, Ft. Lauderdale, Florida State League

MEYER, Russell Charles (Russ)
Pitching Coach

HEIGHT: 6-1   **BATS:** S   **BORN:** Oct. 25, 1923, Peru, IL
WEIGHT: 195   **THROWS:** R   **RESIDES:** Peru, IL

Began professional baseball career in 1942. Led 1946 Southern Association pitchers with 48 appearances. Made major league debut in 1946 with the Cubs and played in the

MEYER (continued)

majors through 1959. Was a member of the 1950 NL champion Philadelphia Phillies. He has been a coach at Illinois Valley Community College since 1980 and joined the Yankees organization in 1981. "Monk's" staff had a combined ERA of 1.87 at Oneonta in 1985.

YR	CLUB	W-L	ERA	G	GS	CG	Sho	SV	IP	H	R	ER	BB	SO
42	Superior	7-8	4.21	32	—	—	0	—	184	193	—	—	67	75
43	Superior					(In Military Service)								
44	Nashville	9-12	5.30	38	—	—	0	—	146	187	106	86	70	66
45	Nashville	11-13	4.43	34	—	—	0	—	183	203	108	90	62	114
46	Nashville	13-8	3.53	48	—	—	0	—	191	190	101	75	91	139
	Chicago	0-0	3.18	4	1	0	0	—	17	21	7	6	10	10
47	Chicago	3-2	3.40	23	2	1	0	0	45	43	17	17	14	22
48	Chicago	10-10	3.65	29	26	8	3	0	165	157	75	67	77	89
49	Philadelphia	17-8	3.08	37	28	14	2	1	213	199	84	73	70	78
50	Philadelphia	9-11	5.29	32	25	3	0	1	160	193	108	94	67	74
51	Philadelphia	8-9	3.48	28	24	7	2	0	168	172	69	65	55	65
52	Philadelphia	13-14	3.14	37	32	14	0	1	232	235	99	81	65	92
53	Brooklyn	15-5	4.57	34	32	10	2	0	191	201	109	97	63	106
54	Brooklyn	11-6	4.00	36	28	6	2	0	180	193	89	80	49	70
55	Brooklyn	6-2	5.42	18	11	2	1	0	73	86	46	44	31	26
56	Chic/Cinn	1-6	6.21	21	9	0	0	0	58	72	41	40	26	29
57	Seattle	1-3	4.68	10	7	0	0	—	42	54	22	22	11	10
	Boston	0-0	5.40	2	1	0	0	—	5	10	5	3	3	1
58						(Did not play)								
59	St. Paul	5-5	2.80	13	11	6	0	—	90	85	34	28	18	38
	Kansas City	1-0	4.50	18	0	0	0	1	24	24	12	12	11	10

COACHING CAREER (Joined Yankees Organization in 1981)

1980-82	Coach, Illinois Valley Community College
1981	Minor league pitching instructor and evaluator, New York Yankees organization
1982	Pitching coach, Bradenton Yankees, Gulf Coast League
1983-86	Pitching coach, Oneonta Yankees, NY-Penn League

MONBOUQUETTE, William Charles (Bill)
Pitching Coach

HEIGHT: 5-11   **BATS:** R   **BORN:** Aug. 11, 1936, Medford, MA
WEIGHT: 200   **THROWS:** R   **RESIDES:** New Boston, NH

Set an American League record with 17 strikeouts in a night game, May 12, 1961, a mark later broken in 1974 by Nolan Ryan. Pitched a no-hitter against the Chicago White Sox on August 1, 1962. Named to the American League All-Star team in 1960-62-63. In 1963, Bill won 20 games for the Red Sox. Scouted for Yankees 1969-74. After scouting and doing instructional work for the Yankees in 1984, Monbo became the pitching coach in 1984. Lauderdale in 1985. Bill worked the last two months of '85 as the Yankees major league pitching coach. Monbo will guide the Albany-Colonie hurlers in 1986.

YR	CLUB	W-L	ERA	G	GS	CG	Sho	SV	IP	H	R	ER	BB	SO
55	Corning	0-0	13.50	1	1	0			2	6	4	3	2	0
	Bluefield	2-4	3.06	10	7	3			46	46	23	16	21	30
56	Corning	15-7	2.45	27	22	16			184	171	67	50	65	177
57	Albany	1-1	5.57	6	3	1			21	27	20	13	10	13
	Greensboro	11-6	3.77	26	23	11			172	167	84	72	73	137
58	Minneapolis	8-9	3.16	22	19	9			134	107	52	46	45	94
	Boston (AL)	3-4	3.33	10	8	3	0	0	54	52	25	20	20	30
59	Boston (AL)	7-7	4.20	34	17	4	0	0	152	165	86	70	33	87
60	Boston (AL)	14-11	3.64	35	30	12	3	0	215	217	91	87	68	134
61	Boston (AL)	14-14	3.39	32	32	12	1	0	236	233	106	89	100	161
62	Boston (AL)	15-13	3.33	35	35	11	4	0	235	227	100	87	65	153
63	Boston (AL)	20-10	3.81	37	36	13	1	0	267	258	119	113	32	174
64	Boston (AL)	13-14	4.04	36	35	7	5	1	234	258	114	105	40	120
65	Boston (AL)	10-18	3.69	35	35	10	2	0	229	239	114	94	40	110
66	Detroit (AL)	7-8	4.72	30	14	2	1	1	103	120	60	54	22	61
67	Detroit-N.Y. (AL)	6-5	2.33	35	10	2	1	0	135	123	39	35	17	55
68	New York (AL)	5-7	4.45	17	11	2	0	1	89	92	47	44	13	32
	San Francisco (NL)	0-1	3.75	7	0	0	0	0	12	11	9	5	2	5
M.L. Totals		**114-112**	**3.68**	**343**	**283**	**78**			**1961**	**1995**	**910**	**803**	**462**	**1122**

ALL STAR RECORD

YR	LEAGUE, SITE	W-L	ERA	G	GS	CG	Sho	SV	IP	H	R	ER	BB	SO
1960 Amer., NY (AL)		0-1	18.00	1	0	0	0	0	2	5	4	4	0	2
1962 Amer., Washington					(Selected; did not play)									
1963 Amer., Cleveland					(Selected; did not play)									
A.S.G. Totals		0-1	18.00	1	0	0	0	0	2	5	4	4	0	2

MANAGERIAL/COACHING CAREER (Rejoined Yankees in 1984)

1969	Manager, Johnson City, Appalachian League (Yankees)
1976	Manager, Wausau, Midwest League (Mets)
1977-81	Coach, Mets Minor League Pitching Instructor
1982-83	Pitching Coach, New York Mets, National League
1984	Pitching Coach, Yankees Instructional League team
1985	Pitching Coach, Ft. Lauderdale, Florida State League
1985	Pitching Coach, New York Yankees, American League
1986	Pitching Coach, Albany-Colonie, Eastern League

RECORD AS MANAGER

YR	CLUB	LG	W	L	PCT	FINISH
1969	Johnson City	APP	37	31	.544	(1st)
1976	Wausau	MW	56	83	.403	(4th in 1st half; 5th in 2nd half)
CAREER TOTALS (2 years)			**93**	**114**	**.449**	

SAUL, James, Allen (Jim)
Manager

HEIGHT: 6-3　**BATS:** R　**BORN:** Nov. 24, 1939, Bristol VA
WEIGHT: 210　**THROWS:** L　**RESIDES:** Bristol, VA

Jim returns to the managing ranks in '86, at the helm of the Albany-Colonie Yankees.

POSITIONS PLAYED: Catcher

YR	CLUB	AVG	G	AB	R	H	2B	3B	HR	RBI	BB	SO	SB
59	Daytona Beach	.183	37	109	7	20	5	0	0	10	19	31	1
59	Wytheville	.316	29	76	22	24	6	0	1	22	27	11	0
59	Tulsa	.217	9	23	2	5	1	1	0				
60	Keokuk	.232	107	315	48	73	19	5	13	52	65	98	2
61	Lancaster	.321	32	84	18	27	5	1	3	18	16	19	0
61	Charleston-Col.	.269	50	130	12	35	4	0	2	5	10	18	0
62	Atlanta†	.186	34	86	6	16	3	0	0	6	11	23	0
62	Tulsa	.398	31	93	14	37	9	1	2	19	18	19	0
63	Portland-San D.	.251	140	451	59	113	19	3	12	52	50	80	0
64	Jacksonville‡	.257	18	35	2	9	1	0	0	4	5	9	0
64	San Diego	.249	61	189	22	47	7	2	4	18	23	44	0
65	San Diego	.219	100	237	22	52	5	0	3	20	40	32	0
66	Hawaii§	.241	73	174	16	42	5	0	5	21	14	32	0
67	Tacoma	.303	13	33	5	10	1	0	1	7	6	9	0
67	Dallas-Ft. W.	.254	84	228	21	58	8	0	4	32	33	41	1
68	Portland	.207	56	145	11	30	3	0	2	16	27	24	0
69	Hawaii	.216	35	74	9	16	3	0	2	18	10	14	0
70	Haw. Tacoma	.222	48	90	11	20	1	0	2	5	28	31	0
70	San Antonio	.091	5	11	1	1	0	0	0	0	2	3	0
71	San Antonio	.190	13	21	4	4	1	0	0	3	6	6	0
71	Quincy	.286	6	7	0	2	1	0	0	3	3	2	0
72	Wichita	.280	32	50	4	14	3	0	1	7	4	10	0

MANAGERIAL COACHING CAREER

1973-74	Manager, Salinas, California League
1975-76	Coach, Chicago Cubs, National League
1977-78	Manager, Midland, Texas League
1979	Coach, Oakland A's, American League
1980	Manager, El Paso, Texas League
1981	Manager, Holyoke, Eastern League
1982	Manager, Portland, Pacific Coast League
1983-84	Coach, Nashville, Southern League
1985	Coach, Albany—Colonie, Eastern League
1986	Manager, Albany-Colonie, Eastern League

RECORD AS MANAGER

YR	CLUB	LG	W	L	PCT	FINISH
1973	Salinas	Cal.	77	61	.558	(2nd, 4th)
1974	Salinas	Cal.	78	62	.557	(2nd, 3rd)
1977	Midland	Tex	70	60	.538	(2nd)
1978	Midland	Tex.	70	65	.519	(3rd)
1980	El Paso	Tex	50	86	.368	(4th)
1981	Holyoke	Eas	68	70	.493	(2nd, 4th)
1982	Portland	PCL	65	79	.451	(5th)
CAREER TOTALS (7 years)			**478**	**483**	**.497**	

SHOWALTER, William Nathaniel III (Buck)
Manager

HEIGHT: 5-10　**BATS:** L　**BORN:** May 23, 1957, DeFuniak Springs, FL
WEIGHT: 185　**THROWS:** L　**RESIDES:** Century, FL

Graduated from Central (FL) H.S. in 1975. Attended Chipola J.C. in Marianna, FL and graduated from Mississippi State University in 1979. Named All-American at Chipola and Mississippi State. Led Southern League in hits and finished second in batting in 1980. Named to 1980 Southern League All-Star team. Led Southern League in hits with 152 in 1982. Coached Ft. Lauderdale in 1984. Buck earned NY-Penn League "Manager of the Year" laurels in his inaugural campaign of 1985. The O-Yanks set a league record of 55 wins under Showalter's guidance. He'll return to Oneonta in his 2nd managerial season.

POSITIONS PLAYED: 1977 (OF-55); 1978 (OF-115); 1979 (OF-32); 1980 (OF-31); 1981 Nashville (OF-33, 1B-19), Columbus (OF-12); 1982 (1B-120, OF-2); 1983 Columbus (1B-16), Nashville (1B-15, OF-15).

YR	CLUB	AVG	G	AB	R	H	2B	3B	HR	RBI	BB	SO	SB
77	Ft. Lauderdale	.362	56	196	32	71	8	1	1	25	36	13	4
78	West Haven	.289	123	429	52	124	13	2	3	46	55	34	19
79	West Haven	.279	129	469	71	131	7	3	6	51	36	30	8
80	Nashville	.324	142	550	84	178	19	3	1	82	53	23	6

SHOWALTER (continued)

81	Nashville	.264	90	307	46	81	17	6	0	38	46	16	3
	Columbus	.189	14	37	6	7	1	0	1	3	3	0	0
82	Nashville	.294	132	517	66	152	29	3	3	46	61	42	2
83	Columbus	.238	18	63	9	15	3	0	1	8	7	3	1
	Nashville	.276	89	297	35	82	13	4	1	37	39	22	1

MANAGERIAL/COACHING CAREER

1984	Coach, Ft. Lauderdale, Florida State League
1985	Manager, Oneonta, New York-Penn League
1986	Manager, Oneonta, New York-Penn League

RECORD AS MANAGER

YR	CLUB	LG	W	L	PCT	FINISH
85	Oneonta	NYP	55	23	.705	1st in Northern Division

POST SEASON PLAY

YR	CLUB	LG	W	L	PCT	RESULTS
85	Oneonta	NYP	3	0	1.000	Defeated Geneva in 1 game semifinal. Beat Auburn 2g to 1 to win championship.

TOSCA, Carlos
Coach

HEIGHT: 5-7 **BORN:** September 29, 1953, Pinar Del Rio, Cuba
WEIGHT: 150 **RESIDES:** Temple Terrace, FL

Joined Yankees organization as coach in 1978. Made debut as manager at Bradenton in Gulf Coast League in 1980. Managed Greensboro Hornets to 1st half division title in 1984. Carlos managed Sarasota to the Gulf Coast League Championship in 1985. Earned GCL Manager of the Year honors in '85. He will serve as a coach at Sarasota in 1986.

MANAGERIAL/COACHING CAREER

1978-79	Coach, Oneonta, New York-Penn League
1980-82	Manager, Bradenton Yankees, Gulf Coast League
1983-84	Manager, Greensboro Hornets, South Atlantic League
1985	Manager, Sarasota, Gulf Coast League
1986	Coach, Sarasota, Gulf Coast League

RECORD AS MANAGER

YR	CLUB	LG	W	L	PCT	FINISH
1980	Bradenton Yankees	GCL	27	35	.435	(7th)
1981	Bradenton Yankees	GCL	30	29	.508	(7th)
1982	Bradenton Yankees	GCL	42	21	.667	(1st)
1983	Greensboro Hornets	SAL	73	71	.507	(3rd)
1984	Greensboro Hornets	SAL	75	69	.521	(1st in 1st half; 4th in 2nd half; lost to Asheville 2 g to 1 in playoffs)
1985	Sarasota Yankees	GCL	43	18	.705	1st in Southern Division
CAREER TOTALS (6 years)			290	243	.544	

POST SEASON PLAY

YR	CLUB	LG	W	L	PCT	RESULTS
1984	Greensboro	SAL	1	2	.333	(Lost to Asheville 2 g to 1 in semi-finals)

WILHELM, James Hoyt (Hoyt)
Pitching Coach

HEIGHT: 6-0 **BATS:** R **BORN:** July 23, 1926, Huntersville, NC
WEIGHT: 185 **THROWS:** R **RESIDES:** Sarasota, FL

Began pro career in 1942 for independent Mooresville, N.C., club, near hometown of Huntersville. Moved into Giants farm system in 1948 at Knoxville and reached big leagues in 1952. Remained in majors for next 21 years, retiring in 1972 at age 46—as baseball's all-time premier relief pitcher. Holds following major league career records—most games pitched (1,070), most games in relief (1,018), most innings in relief (1,870), most games finished (651), most wins in relief (124). Used as starter in middle of his career (1958-60) and hurled no-hitter for Orioles against Yankees in 1958. Also holds distinction of hitting homer in first major league at-bat (April 23, 1952). Participated in 1954 World Series with Giants and named to NL All-Star team in 1953 and 1970; named to AL All-Star team in 1959-61-62. Elected to Baseball Hall of Fame in January, 1985.

NO-HIT GAME: Baltimore vs. Yankees, 1-0, September 20, 1958 (at Baltimore).

YR	CLUB	W-L	ERA	G	GS	CG	Sho	SV	IP	H	R	ER	BB	SO
42	Mooresville	10-3	4.25	23	—	—	—	—	108	105	58	51	28	56
43	Mooresville					(Did not play)								
44	Mooresville					(Did not play)								
45	Mooresville					(Did not play)								
46	Mooresville	21-8	2.47	34	—	22	2	—	233	221	102	64	50	185
47	Mooresville	20-7	3.38	31	—	25	3	—	250	243	124	94	92	198
48	Jacksonville	0-0	8.18	6	—	—	2	—	11	18	11	10	9	5
	Knoxville	13-9	3.62	24	—	16	—	—	189	194	104	76	62	104
49	Jacksonville	17-12	2.66	33	—	18	1	—	223	198	96	66	92	126
50	Minneapolis	15-11	4.95	35	25	10	1	—	180	190	109	99	64	99
51	Minneapolis	11-14	3.94	40	29	12	1	—	210	219	107	92	82	148

YR	CLUB	W-L	ERA	G	GS	CG	Sho	SV	IP	H	R	ER	BB	SO
52	New York (NL)	15-3	2.43	71	0	0	—	11	159	127	60	43	57	108
53	New York (NL)	7-8	3.04	68	0	0	—	15	145	127	61	49	77	71
54	New York (NL)	12-4	2.11	57	0	0	—	7	111	77	32	26	52	64
55	New York (NL)	4-1	3.93	59	0	0	—	0	103	104	53	45	40	71
56	New York (NL)	4-9	3.84	64	0	0	—	8	89	97	45	38	43	71
57	St. Louis	1-4	4.25	40	0	0	—	11	55	52	28	26	21	29
	Cleveland	1-0	2.25	2	0	0	—	1	4	2	1	1	1	0
58	Cleve/Balt	3-10	2.34	39	10	4	1	5	131	95	41	34	45	92
59	Baltimore	15-11	2.19	32	27	13	3	0	226	178	64	55	77	139
60	Baltimore	11-8	3.31	41	11	3	1	7	147	125	69	54	39	107
61	Baltimore	9-7	2.29	51	1	0	—	18	110	89	35	28	41	87
62	Baltimore	7-10	1.94	52	0	0	—	15	93	64	28	20	34	90
63	Chicago	5-8	2.65	55	3	0	—	21	136	106	47	40	30	111
64	Chicago	12-9	1.99	73	0	0	—	27	131	94	35	29	30	95
65	Chicago	7-7	1.81	66	0	0	—	20	144	88	34	29	32	106
66	Chicago	5-2	1.67	46	0	0	—	6	81	50	21	15	17	61
67	Chicago	8-3	1.31	49	0	0	—	12	89	58	21	13	34	76
68	Chicago	4-4	1.72	72	0	0	—	12	94	69	20	18	24	72
69	California	5-7	2.45	44	0	0	—	10	66	45	21	18	18	53
	Atlanta	2-0	0.75	8	0	0	—	4	12	5	1	1	4	14
70	Atl/Chi	6-5	3.40	53	0	0	—	13	82	73	33	31	42	68
71	Spokane	2-3	3.89	8	0	0	—	1	37	39	16	16	9	24
	Atlanta/LA	0-1	2.70	12	0	0	—	3	20	12	7	6	5	16
72	Los Angeles	0-1	4.68	16	0	0	—	1	25	20	16	13	15	9

MANAGERIAL/COACHING CAREER (Joined Yankees Organization in 1976)

1973	Manager, Greenwich, Western Carolinas League (Braves)
1974	Manager, Kingsport, Appalachian League (Braves)
1975	Minor league pitching coach, Atlanta Braves organization
1976-80	Minor league pitching coach, New York Yankees organization
1981	Pitching coach, Bradenton Yankees, Gulf Coast League
1982-84	Pitching coach, Nashville, Southern League
1985	Pitching coach, Sarasota, Gulf Coast League
1986	Pitching Coach, Ft. Lauderdale, Florida State League

RECORD AS MANAGER

YR	CLUB	LG	W	L	PCT	FINISH
1973	Greenwood	WCL	61	66	.480	(4th)
1974	Kingsport	Appy	31	39	.443	(4th in Div.)
	CAREER TOTALS (2 years)		92	105	.467	

POST SEASON PLAY
None

YANKEES MINOR LEAGUE SYSTEM PLAYERS

ARNSBERG, Bradley Jeff (Brad)

HEIGHT: 6-4 **BATS:** R **BORN:** Aug. 20, 1963, Seattle, WA
WEIGHT: 205 **THROWS:** R **RESIDES:** Medford, OR

SIGNED BY: Gary Hughes
HOW OBTAINED: Yankees 1st round draft choice in the secondary phase of the June, 1983 free agent draft.

Brad attended Merced Community College where he received his associate degree in June of 1983. Selected by Cleveland Indians organization in 18th round of June, 1981 free agent draft. Selected by St. Louis Cardinals organization in 1st round of secondary phase in January, 1982 free agent draft. Selected by Baltimore Orioles organization in 1st round of secondary phase in June, 1982 free agent draft. Selected by California Angels organization in 1st round of secondary phase in January, 1983 free agent draft. Tied for South Atlantic League lead in shutouts (4) and complete games (10), 1984. Led Eastern League in winning pct. (.842) and ERA (1.59) and tied for lead in wins (14), 1985. Named Eastern League All-Star RHP. Named to Topps AA All-Star team. Voted Yankees 1985 Minor League Pitcher of the Year.

YR	CLUB	W-L	ERA	G	GS	CG	Sho	SV	IP	H	R	ER	BB	SO
84	Greensboro	12-5	2.95	23	23	10	4	0	158.2	121	61	52	59	112
85	Albany	14-2	1.59	20	20	9	2	0	141.1	105	34	25	35	82

AZOCAR, Oscar

HEIGHT: 6-1 **BATS:** L **BORN:** Feb. 21, 1965, Caracas, Venezuela
WEIGHT: 170 **THROWS:** L **RESIDES:** Caracas, Venezuela

SIGNED BY: Fred Ferreira
HOW OBTAINED: Signed as a free agent on November 22, 1983.

YR	CLUB	W-L	ERA	G	GS	CG	Sho	SV	IP	H	R	ER	BB	SO
84	Sarasota	4-1	1.28	11	10	2	0	0	56.1	37	12	8	17	60
85	Sarasota	4-0	1.45	5	4	2	1	0	37.1	30	8	6	14	36
	Oneonta	0-2	4.86	14	2	0	0	0	16.2	21	16	9	9	13

BALABON, Anthony Richard (Rick)

HEIGHT: 6-2   **BATS:** R   **BORN:** April 26, 1967, Philadelphia, PA
WEIGHT: 175   **THROWS:** R   **RESIDES:** Wayne, PA
SIGNED BY: Meade Palmer
HOW OBTAINED: Selected by Yankees as a special pick following the 1st round (#28 overall in draft) in June 1985 free agent draft. Draft pick had been awarded Yankees as compensation for loss of Tim Belcher to Oakland in re-entry compensation pool.

Graduated from Conestoga H.S. in Berwyn, PA.

YR	CLUB	W-L	ERA	G	GS	CG	Sho	SV	IP	H	R	ER	BB	SO
85	Oneonta	5-2	1.74	12	12	3	2	0	72.1	50	16	14	39	68

BANKS, David Michael

HEIGHT: 6-1   **BATS:** L   **BORN:** April 3, 1963, Portsmouth, VA
WEIGHT: 190   **THROWS:** L   **RESIDES:** Leesburg, GA
SIGNED BY: Tommy Thompson
HOW OBTAINED: Yankees' 25th round pick in regular phase of June '85 free agent draft.

Received a B.S. in Computer Science from Troy State (Alabama).

POSITIONS PLAYED: 1B-43.

YR	CLUB	AVG	G	AB	R	H	2B	3B	HR	RBI	BB	SO	SB
85	Sarasota	.228	43	145	15	33	7	1	0	21	24	24	2

BARRETT, Thomas Loren (Tom)

HEIGHT: 5-9   **BATS:** S   **BORN:** April 2, 1960, San Fernando, CA
WEIGHT: 157   **THROWS:** R   **RESIDES:** Las Vegas, NV
SIGNED BY: Don Lindeberg
HOW OBTAINED: Yankees' 26th selection in the June, 1982 draft.

1983 led Florida State league with a .327 average. Selected as the Florida State League's All-Star 3B. Finished 2nd in the league with 55 stolen bases despite missing final month of season with injury. Brother of Red Sox infielder Marty Barrett. Attended University of Arizona.

POSITIONS PLAYED: 1982 (2B-61); 1983 (2B-32, 3B-84); 1984 Nashville (2B-132), Columbus (3B-2); 1985 Albany (2B-18, 3B-18, OF-2), Columbus (3B-28, OF-9, 2B-7, SS-1).

YR	CLUB	AVG	G	AB	R	H	2B	3B	HR	RBI	BB	SO	SB
82	Paintsville	.364	61	231	59	84	5	2	0	21	42	17	20
83	Ft. Lauderdale	.327	103	397	80	130	21	1	0	32	46	16	55
84	Nashville	.308	135	510	82	157	22	6	0	44	86	41	53
	Columbus	.381	5	21	3	8	1	0	0	0	2	3	0
85	Albany	.262	57	233	40	61	8	3	1	18	25	19	23
	Columbus	.260	55	169	27	44	11	1	1	11	17	18	14

BERNALDO, Richard C. (Rick)

HEIGHT: 5-10   **BATS:** R   **BORN:** August 7, 1962, Tampa, FL
WEIGHT: 170   **THROWS:** R   **RESIDES:** Tampa, FL
SIGNED BY: Brian Sabean
HOW OBTAINED: Signed as a free agent on March 8, 1985.

Graduated from University of Tampa.

POSITIONS PLAYED: Ft. Lauderdale (2B-10), Oneonta (3B-1).

YR	CLUB	AVG	G	AB	R	H	2B	3B	HR	RBI	BB	SO	SB
85	Ft. Lauderdale	.200	16	25	4	5	1	0	0	2	6	2	0
	Oneonta	.000	1	1	0	0	0	0	0	0	0	0	0

BLASER, Mark Allen (Mark)

HEIGHT: 5-10   **BATS:** R   **BORN:** Oct. 19, 1960, Sacramento, CA
WEIGHT: 181   **THROWS:** R   **RESIDES:** Sacramento, CA
SIGNED BY: Gary Hughes
HOW OBTAINED: Yankees' fourth pick in 1981 January draft.

Graduated from La Sierra H.S. in Carmichael, Cal. in 1979 where he was MVP in baseball and football. Attended Butte College in Chico, Cal.

POSITIONS PLAYED: 1981 Paintsville (3B-2), Bradenton (C-17); 1982 Greensboro (C-11, 3B-12, OF-25); 1983 Greensboro (3B-22, OF-27); 1984 Ft. Lauderdale (2B-4, 3B-76), Nashville (3B-42, OF-1); 1985 Ft. Lauderdale (3B-35, 1B-21), Albany (3B-36, 2B-6, 1B-1).

YR	CLUB	AVG	G	AB	R	H	2B	3B	HR	RBI	BB	SO	SB
81	Paintsville	.327	17	52	10	17	1	0	1	8	9	6	0
	Bradenton	.284	21	67	11	19	2	1	1	8	5	9	3
82	Greensboro	.314	80	239	42	75	15	1	5	33	35	33	1
83	Nashville	.294	17	51	9	15	4	1	3	6	5	15	1
	Greensboro	.289	76	242	44	70	14	1	7	48	24	44	4
84	Ft. Lauderdale	.242	81	273	36	66	12	3	8	44	27	47	7
	Nashville	.275	45	149	21	41	5	0	5	25	8	19	0

		AVG	G	AB	R	H	2B	3B	HR	RBI	BB	SO	SB
85	Ft. Lauderdale	.291	53	175	24	51	13	0	3	30	26	28	0
	Albany	.190	57	184	15	35	5	1	2	21	20	29	3

BLUM, Brent Allen

HEIGHT: 6-4 **BATS:** L **BORN:** September, 16, 1962
WEIGHT: 205 **THROWS:** L **RESIDES:** Bellevue, WA

SIGNED BY: Charlie Silvera
HOW OBTAINED: Yankees 16th round pick in regular phase of June 1985 free agent draft.

Attended East Washington University. Named Howe News Bureau 1985 "Star of Stars"—Gulf Coast League.

YR	CLUB	W-L	ERA	G	GS	CG	Sho	SV	IP	H	R	ER	BB	SO
85	Ft. Lauderdale	2-1	5.50	4	3	1	0	0	18.0	22	13	11	5	7
	Sarasota	6-0	1.38	8	8	3	0	0	58.2	36	16	9	23	62

BRAXTON, Glen Dell

HEIGHT: 6-0 **BATS:** L **BORN:** April 17, 1967, Idabel, OK
WEIGHT: 210 **THROWS:** L **RESIDES:** Idabel, OK

SIGNED BY: Ken Stauffer (White Sox)
HOW OBTAINED: White Sox 3rd pick in regular phase of June 1985 free agent draft. Traded to Yankees along with Britt Burns and Mike Soper from White Sox in exchange for Joe Cowley and Ron Hassey, December 12, 1985.

POSITIONS PLAYED: OF-54.

YR	CLUB	AVG	G	AB	R	H	2B	3B	HR	RBI	BB	SO	SB
85	Sarasota W. Sox	.255	56	204	35	52	2	4	0	21	19	49	11

BRITO, Ysaias (Casanova)

HEIGHT: 6-1 **BATS:** R **BORN:** August 2, 1967
WEIGHT: 160 **THROWS:** R **RESIDES:** San Cristobal, Dominican Republic

SIGNED BY: Fred Ferreira
HOW OBTAINED: Signed as a free agent on April 14, 1985 after attending Yankee Academy in San Cristobal, Dominican Republic.

1986 will be first professional season.

BROW, Steve Dennis (Dennis)

HEIGHT: 6-3 **BATS:** R **BORN:** March 25, 1966, St. Croix, Virgin Islands
WEIGHT: 205 **THROWS:** R **RESIDES:** St. Croix, Virgin Islands

SIGNED BY: Fred Ferreira
HOW OBTAINED: Signed as a free agent on December 16, 1985.
POSITIONS PLAYED: 1B-OF.

1986 will be first professional season.

BUHNER, Jay Campbell

HEIGHT: 6-3 **BATS:** R **BORN:** August 13, 1964
WEIGHT: 205 **THROWS:** R **RESIDES:** Houston, TX

SIGNED BY: Pittsburgh Pirates
HOW OBTAINED: Selected by Pittsburgh in the 2nd round of the secondary phase of the January '84 free agent draft. Acquired by Yankees along with Dale Berra and Alfonso Pulido for Steve Kemp & Tim Foli. Led New York-Penn League in RBI's (58), 1984. Named to NY-Penn League All-Star team (OF), 1984. Named "Star of Stars" in Florida State League All-Star game, 1985. Led FSL in GWRBI (15), 1985. Named to FSL All-Star team (OF), 1985.

POSITIONS PLAYED: 1984 (OF-64); 1985 (OF-113).

YR	CLUB	AVG	G	AB	R	H	2B	3B	HR	RBI	BB	SO	SB
84	Watertown	.323	65	229	43	74	16	3	9	58	42	58	3
85	Ft. Lauderdale	.296	117	409	65	121	18	10	11	76	65	76	6

BYRON, Timothy Anthony (Tim)

HEIGHT: 6-2 **BATS:** R **BORN:** June 3, 1960, Newark, NJ
WEIGHT: 205 **THROWS:** R **RESIDES:** Florham Park, NJ

SIGNED BY: Al Cuccinello
HOW OBTAINED: Yankees' 19th selection in the June, 1982 free agent draft.

Graduated from Our Lady of the Valley H.S. in 1978 and was named All-State in Baseball. He received his B.S. degree from Seton Hall University in 1982, while there he was named to all NJ college team all 4 years.

Led Eastern League pitchers in double plays (6), 1985.

YR	CLUB	W-L	ERA	G	GS	CG	Sho	SV	IP	H	R	ER	BB	SO
82	Oneonta	3-5	4.80	12	11	0	0	0	57.2	53	38	31	34	37

BYRON (continued)

83	Greensboro	2-4	4.59	10	6	2	0	0	49.0	49	28	25	23	34
	Oneonta	1-2	5.29	8	5	0	0	0	32.1	40	22	19	18	24
84	Ft. Lauderdale	11-4	3.50	37	13	3	1	0	126.0	106	58	49	68	81
85	Albany	10-7	3.33	27	25	5	0	0	165.0	158	83	61	79	89

CALVERT, Arthur Lee (Art)

HEIGHT: 6-1 **BATS:** R **BORN:** Oct. 11, 1983
WEIGHT: 200 **THROWS:** R **RESIDES:** San Diego, CA

SIGNED BY: Orin Freeman
HOW OBTAINED: Selected by Yankees in 8th round of June '84 free agent draft.

Art received a B.A. in International & Intercultural Studies from U.S. International University in 1985.

POSITIONS PLAYED: Sarasota (OF-25), Oneonta (OF-22).

YR	CLUB	AVG	G	AB	R	H	2B	3B	HR	RBI	BB	SO	SB
85	Sarasota	.316	36	136	19	43	8	3	0	26	15	28	4
	Oneonta	.312	22	77	12	24	2	0	3	14	7	22	1

CANSECO, Osvaldo Capas (Ozzie)

HEIGHT: 6-2 **BATS:** R **BORN:** July 2, 1964, Havana, Cuba
WEIGHT: 185 **THROWS:** R **RESIDES:** Miami, FL

SIGNED BY: Fred Ferreira
HOW OBTAINED: Yankees' 2nd round pick in the January, 1983 free agent draft.

Attended Miami Dade South J.C. Brother of Oakland outfielder Jose Canseco.

POSITIONS PLAYED: 1985 Sarasota (OF-1).

PITCHING RECORD:

YR	CLUB	W-L	ERA	G	GS	CG	Sho	SV	IP	H	R	ER	BB	SO
83	Greensboro	3-6	5.05	27	13	1	1	0	87.1	98	62	49	49	59
84	Oneonta	1-6	3.53	14	4	1	1	0	43.1	44	29	17	21	40
	Greensboro	1-1	4.86	6	2	0	0	0	16.2	19	13	9	22	9
85	Sarasota	3-2	1.57	9	7	1	0	0	51.2	43	19	9	11	39
	Ft. Lauderdale	5-4	3.61	11	11	1	0	0	57.1	42	33	23	42	37

BATTING RECORD:

YR	CLUB	AVG	G	AB	R	H	2B	3B	HR	RBI	BB	SO
85	Sarasota	.179	20	39	2	7	0	1	1	5	2	18

CANTRELL, Scott Jay

HEIGHT: 6-3 **BATS:** R **BORN:** October 15, 1963, Daytona Beach, FL
WEIGHT: 195 **THROWS:** R **RESIDES:** Daytona Beach, FL

SIGNED BY: NY Yankees
HOW OBTAINED: Yankees' 31st round pick in regular phase of June 1985 free agent draft.

Attended University of Toledo.

YR	CLUB	W-L	ERA	G	GS	CG	Sho	SV	IP	H	R	ER	BB	SO
85	Sarasota	5-4	3.08	13	13	3	2	0	84.2	93	37	29	11	48

CARGILE, Richard Neal (Neal)

HEIGHT: 6-3 **BATS:** R **BORN:** July 25, 1963, Robersonville, NC
WEIGHT: 185 **THROWS:** R **RESIDES:** Robersonville, NC

SIGNED BY: Jim Gruzdis
HOW OBTAINED: Yankees' 12th round pick in regular phase of June 1985 free agent draft.

Attended Gardner-Webb College, Boiling Springs, NC.

POSITIONS PLAYED: OF-41.

YR	CLUB	AVG	G	AB	R	H	2B	3B	HR	RBI	BB	SO	SB
85	Sarasota	.280	48	118	17	33	3	2	1	20	14	29	9

CARPENTER, Douglas Paul (Doug)

HEIGHT: 5-11 **BATS:** R **BORN:** Feb. 9, 1962, Olean, NY
WEIGHT: 175 **THROWS:** R **RESIDES:** Lake Worth, FL

SIGNED BY: Fred Ferreira
HOW OBTAINED: Yankees' 29th selection in the June, 1983 free agent draft.

Attended Palm Beach Junior College and Florida International University.

POSITIONS PLAYED: 1983 Greensboro (OF-14), Oneonta (OF-6); 1984 (OF-115, SS-1); 1985 Ft. Lauderdale (OF-38), Albany (OF-66).

YR	CLUB	AVG	G	AB	R	H	2B	3B	HR	RBI	BB	SO	SB
83	Greensboro	.143	24	35	10	5	3	1	0	4	7	18	1
	Oneonta	.250	7	8	4	2	1	0	1	3	8	3	1
84	Greensboro	.211	122	365	58	77	17	3	7	44	72	90	27
85	Ft. Lauderdale	.232	40	99	18	23	5	0	1	14	24	20	4
	Albany	.305	71	203	27	62	11	6	1	26	18	38	10

CARRENO, Amalio Rafael

HEIGHT: 6-0   **BATS:** R   **BORN:** April 11, 1964, Venezuela
WEIGHT: 170   **THROWS:** R   **RESIDES:** Esparta, Venezuela

SIGNED BY: Fred Ferreira
HOW OBTAINED: Signed as a free agent November 22, 1983.

YR	CLUB	W-L	ERA	G	GS	CG	Sho	SV	IP	H	R	ER	BB	SO
84	Sarasota	1-6	4.91	9	7	1	0	0	33.0	37	28	18	26	31
85	Sarasota	0-0	4.50	1	0	0	0	0	2	1	1	1	1	1

CARROLL, Christopher (Chris)

HEIGHT: 6-3   **BATS:** R   **BORN:** May 21, 1963
WEIGHT: 205   **THROWS:** R   **RESIDES:** Goodlettsville, TN

SIGNED BY: Bill Livesey
HOW OBTAINED: Yankees' 27th round pick in regular phase of June 1985 free agent draft. Attended University of Kentucky.

YR	CLUB	W-L	ERA	G	GS	CG	Sho	SV	IP	H	R	ER	BB	SO
85	Oneonta	1-0	0.37	12	0	0	0	3	24.1	13	4	1	10	21
	Sarasota	2-0	2.10	11	0	0	0	4	25.2	18	8	6	11	33

CARROLL, Carson W.

HEIGHT: 6-1   **BATS:** R   **BORN:** September 23, 1959, Glendale, CA
WEIGHT: 170   **THROWS:** R   **RESIDES:** Sunland, CA

SIGNED BY: Jess Flores and Buck Borning (Twins)
HOW OBTAINED: Purchased from Miami Marlins on August 19, 1985.

Graduated from University of California (Irvine) in 1981. Drafted by Twins on 17th round, June 1981. Named Florida State League All-Star second baseman, 1985.

POSITIONS PLAYED: 1981 (2B-64); 1982 (2B-81, 3B-13, 1B-5, OF-2); 1983 Wis. Rapids (2B-46, 3B-2), Orlando (2B-38, 3B-15, OF-5, 1B-3, SS-1); 1984 (2B-123, 1B-12); 1985 Albany (2B-7, 3B-3, SS-1, OF-1), Miami (2B-120, SS-2, OF-2, 3B-1).

YR	CLUB	AVG	G	AB	R	H	2B	3B	HR	RBI	BB	SO	SB
81	Elizabethton	.253	64	221	33	56	12	2	2	27	39	23	10
82	Visalia	.233	102	339	51	79	4	3	3	39	41	71	21
83	Wis. Rapids	.270	48	178	28	48	6	3	1	19	25	29	24
	Orlando	.202	63	168	15	34	5	0	1	16	13	35	9
84	Visalia	.286	134	482	67	138	15	9	4	64	68	90	35
85	Albany	.273	12	44	5	12	1	2	0	1	1	5	0
	Miami	.273	126	454	63	124	12	5	1	56	54	65	45

CARTER, Frederick Jerome (Fred)

HEIGHT: 6-3   **BATS:** R   **BORN:** Aug. 23, 1964, Oklahoma City, OK
WEIGHT: 205   **THROWS:** R   **RESIDES:** Oklahoma City, OK

SIGNED BY: NY Yankees
HOW OBTAINED: Selected by Yankees in 7th round of the secondary phase of the June '84 free agent draft.

Named to Gulf Coast League All-Star team (OF), 1985. Brother of Indians OF Joe Carter.

POSITIONS PLAYED: (OF-39), (1B-14).

YR	CLUB	AVG	G	AB	R	H	2B	3B	HR	RBI	BB	SO	SB
85	Sarasota	.284	57	215	28	61	13	1	0	29	11	45	9

CATHCART, Gary John

HEIGHT: 6-2   **BATS:** L   **BORN:** Dec. 23, 1962
WEIGHT: 170   **THROWS:** L   **RESIDES:** New Bedford, MA

SIGNED BY: Jack Gillis
HOW OBTAINED: Selected by Yankees in 33rd round of the June '84 free agent draft.

POSITIONS PLAYED: 1984 (OF-74); 1985 Ft. Lauderdale (OF-33, 1B-32), Albany (OF-19).

YR	CLUB	AVG	G	AB	R	H	2B	3B	HR	RBI	BB	SO	SB
84	Oneonta	.238	74	286	37	68	9	1	3	26	38	49	5
85	Ft. Lauderdale	.250	76	256	35	64	8	3	0	24	31	44	7
	Albany	.244	20	45	4	11	2	0	0	5	6	10	1

CHAPMAN, Ronald (Ronnie, Chap)

HEIGHT: 5-10   **BATS:** S   **BORN:** Jan. 14, 1961, Greenville, NC
WEIGHT: 170   **THROWS:** R   **RESIDES:** Greenville, NC

SIGNED BY: Tim Wilem (Toronto Blue Jays)
HOW OBTAINED: Signed as a free agent on 4-4-84.

POSITIONS PLAYED: 1982 (2B-63); 1983 (2B-34, 3B-19); 1984 (2B-78, SS-2, 3B-1, OF-1); 1985 (2B-99, SS-2).

YR	CLUB	AVG	G	AB	R	H	2B	3B	HR	RBI	BB	SO	SB
82	Medicine Hat	.275	63	247	57	68	10	3	4	35	50	50	26
83	Florence	.261	99	253	51	66	4	4	1	23	55	33	17
84	Ft. Lauderdale	.260	97	281	56	73	9	3	0	19	45	19	31
85	Albany	.237	107	363	74	86	10	6	4	29	78	32	21

CHASTAIN, Dennis Eugene (Chaz)

HEIGHT: 6-0   **BATS:** R   **BORN:** Feb. 19, 1963, Los Alamos, NM
WEIGHT: 180   **THROWS:** L   **RESIDES:** Auburndale, FL

SIGNED BY: Gust Poulos
HOW OBTAINED: Selected by the Yankees in the 12th round of the June '84 free agent draft.

YR	CLUB	W-L	ERA	G	GS	CG	Sho	SV	IP	H	R	ER	BB	SO
84	Oneonta	4-4	4.70	15	13	1	0	0	67.0	75	41	35	30	45
85	Ft. Lauderdale	3-2	2.12	22	0	0	0	3	34.0	20	11	8	12	35

CHING, Mauricio Rogello (Mo)

HEIGHT: 6-2   **BATS:** L   **BORN:** July 11, 1963
WEIGHT: 195   **THROWS:** L   **RESIDES:** Cristobal, Panama

SIGNED BY: Fred Ferreira
HOW OBTAINED: Signed as free agent on November 16, 1981.

Named to South Atlantic League All-Star team (DH), 1984. Named to play in Florida State League All-Star game (DH), 1985.

POSITIONS PLAYED: 1982 Greensboro (1B-8, OF-10); Paintsville (1B-31); 1983 (1B-74); 1984 (1B-54); 1985 (1B-66).

YR	CLUB	AVG	G	AB	R	H	2B	3B	HR	RBI	BB	SO	SB
82	Greensboro	.206	35	102	14	21	4	0	4	16	17	35	0
	Paintsville	.271	65	240	33	65	18	0	6	43	36	62	0
83	Greensboro	.269	118	402	61	108	20	1	11	59	84	123	9
84	Greensboro	.298	110	325	52	97	17	3	14	62	67	93	7
85	Ft. Lauderdale	.300	90	293	38	88	28	3	4	54	47	66	9

CHRISTIANSEN, Clay C.

HEIGHT: 6-4   **BATS:** R   **BORN:** June 28, 1958, Wichita, KS
WEIGHT: 220   **THROWS:** R   **RESIDES:** Columbus, KS

SIGNED BY: Russ Sehon
HOW OBTAINED: Yankees' 15th round pick in regular phase of June 1980 free agent draft.

Attended University of Kansas in Lawrence, KS. Tied for Southern League lead in wins (16) in 1982. Also tied for Southern League lead in fielding pct. (1.000) among pitchers in '82. Led International League in wild pitches (16), 1983.

YR	CLUB	W-L	ERA	G	GS	CG	Sho	SV	IP	H	R	ER	BB	SO
80	Oneonta	4-3	2.54	15	13	5	2	0	92	89	43	26	24	62
81	Ft. Lauderdale	16-7	2.28	26	25	14	2	0	178	158	59	45	46	98
82	Nashville	† 16-8	3.07	29	29	13	2	0	214.1	214	102	73	80	157
83	Columbus	8-9	5.44	32	19	1	0	0	160.1	196*	118	97	81	92
84	Columbus	6-3	3.10	22	13	4	0	2	107.1	109	44	37	39	56
	YANKEES	2-4	6.05	24	1	0	0	2	38.2	50	28	26	12	27
85	Columbus	10-6	3.66	28	18	3	2	1	137.2	128	66	56	59	67
Minor Lg. Totals		60-36	3.38	152	117	40	8	3	889.2	894	432	334	329	532
M.L. Totals		2-4	6.05	24	1	0	0	2	38.2	50	28	26	12	27

CHRISTOPHER, Michael Wayne (Mike)

HEIGHT: 6-5   **BATS:** R   **BORN:** November 3, 1963, Petersburg, VA
WEIGHT: 195   **THROWS:** R   **RESIDES:** Church Rd, VA

SIGNED BY: Jim Gruzdis
HOW OBTAINED: Yankees' 7th round pick in regular phase of June 1985 free agent draft.

Attended E. Carolina University. Named to 1985 New York-Penn League All-Star team.

YR	CLUB	W-L	ERA	G	GS	CG	Sho	SV	IP	H	R	ER	BB	SO
85	Oneonta	8-1	1.46	15	9	2	2	0	80.1	58	21	13	22	84

CLARK, David Eugene

HEIGHT: 6-3   **BATS:** L   **BORN:** September 11, 1964, Oakland, CA
WEIGHT: 170   **THROWS:** L   **RESIDES:** Berkeley, CA

SIGNED BY: Greg Orr
HOW OBTAINED: Yankees' 1st round pick in regular phase of January 1985 free agent draft.

Attended Laney Junior College, Oakland, CA.

YR	CLUB	W-L	ERA	G	GS	CG	Sho	SV	IP	H	R	ER	BB	SO
85	Sarasota	4-1	3.31	8	6	0	0	0	35.1	34	17	13	13	31

CLONINGER, Darin Trent

HEIGHT: 5-10   **BATS:** R   **BORN:** Oct. 1, 1962
WEIGHT: 190   **THROWS:** R   **RESIDES:** Iron Station, NC

SIGNED BY: San Diego organization
HOW OBTAINED: Selected by the Padres in 11th round of the June '83 free agent draft. Acquired from San Diego as the player to be named later along with Dennis Rasmussen for Graig Nettles, 4-26-84.

YR	CLUB	W-L	ERA	G	GS	CG	Sho	SV	IP	H	R	ER	BB	SO
83	Spokane	0-3	3.54	5	4	1	0	0	28.0	24	15	11	13	32
84	Ft. Lauderdale	4-9	2.85	29	17	0	0	2	129.1	120	57	41	66	67
	Miami	0-2	2.53	3	2	0	0	1	10.2	7	4	3	9	5
85	Ft. Lauderdale	4-4	3.70	19	6	1	1	0	58.1	62	28	24	21	18
	Albany	1-3	5.35	13	6	0	0	0	38.2	48	26	23	23	16

CUADRADO, Roberto

HEIGHT: 6-1   **BATS:** S   **BORN:** May 16, 1966
WEIGHT: 197   **THROWS:** R   **RESIDES:** Carolina, Puerto Rico

SIGNED BY: Fred Ferreira
HOW OBTAINED: Signed as a free agent Nov. 3 1984.

POSITIONS PLAYED: (C-9).

YR	CLUB	AVG	G	AB	R	H	2B	3B	HR	RBI	BB	SO	SB
85	Sarasota	.120	14	25	3	3	1	0	0	1	1	5	0

DALENA, Peter Martin (Pete)

HEIGHT: 5-11   **BATS:** L   **BORN:** June 26, 1960, Fresno, CA
WEIGHT: 200   **THROWS:** R   **RESIDES:** Fresno, CA

SIGNED BY: Gary Hughes
HOW OBTAINED: Yankees' 27th selection in the June, 1982 free agent draft.

Graduated from San Joaquin Memorial H.S. in 1978 and attended Cal State Fresno.

POSITIONS PLAYED: 1982 (1B-62); 1983 Nashville (1B-88), Ft. Lauderdale (1B-20), 1984 Nashville (1B-125), Columbus (1B-4); 1985 (1B-51, 3B-1).

YR	CLUB	AVG	G	AB	R	H	2B	3B	HR	RBI	BB	SO	SB
82	Greensboro	.285	71	281	27	80	15	0	10	43	24	49	0
83	Nashville	.322	89	335	52	108	23	4	13	59	29	36	0
	Ft. Lauderdale	.314	49	169	16	53	9	2	2	28	17	16	0
84	Nashville	.297	125	488	60	145	28	0	14	83	49	48	4
	Columbus	.111	10	27	1	3	0	0	0	0	3	8	0
85	Columbus	.305	114	357	34	109	21	4	9	65	25	32	1

DAVIDSON, Robert Banks (Bob)

HEIGHT: 6-0   **BATS:** R   **BORN:** Jan. 6, 1963
WEIGHT: 185   **THROWS:** R   **RESIDES:** Greensboro, NC

SIGNED BY: Jim Gruzdis
HOW OBTAINED: Selected by the Yankees in the 24th round of the June '84 free agent draft.

YR	CLUB	W-L	ERA	G	GS	CG	Sho	SV	IP	H	R	ER	BB	SO
84	Oneonta	2-5	3.45	24	0	0	0	10	28.2	27	18	11	11	26
85	Oneonta	1-2	2.50	29	0	0	0	5	36.0	28	14	10	13	44

DERSIN, Eric Lynn

HEIGHT: 6-1   **BATS:** R   **BORN:** January 6, 1964, Cumberland, MD
WEIGHT: 195   **THROWS:** R   **RESIDES:** Ft. Ashby, WV

SIGNED BY: Joe Branzell (Rangers)
HOW OBTAINED: Acquired as player to be named later from Texas to complete trade of Billy Sample in exchange for Toby Harrah on July 14, 1985.

Named to 1984 Northwest League All-Star team after finishing second in league in wins (10). Starting pitcher for Northern Division in 1985 Florida State League All-Star game.

YR	CLUB	W-L	ERA	G	GS	CG	Sho	SV	IP	H	R	ER	BB	SO
82	Sar. Rangers	1-1	9.39	6	0	0	0	0	8.0	11	9	8	4	5

DERSIN (continued)

83	Sar. Rangers	1-2	2.75	7	4	0	0	0	20.0	19	9	6	7	21
84	Burlington	1-2	7.32	5	4	0	0	0	20.0	34	27	16	8	14
	Tri-Cities	10-1	2.58	14	13	2	0	0	91.0	80	37	26	35	80
85	Ft. Lauderdale	4-3	4.05	8	8	0	0	0	46.2	52	28	21	24	29
	Daytona Beach	5-5	2.50	17	17	5	0	0	108.0	101	37	30	45	80

DIDDER, Rayborne Patrick (Ray)

HEIGHT: 5-11 **BATS:** R **BORN:** April 13, 1967, Aruba
WEIGHT: 175 **THROWS:** R **RESIDES:** San Nicolaus, Aruba
SIGNED BY: Fred Ferreira
HOW OBTAINED: Signed as free agent on April 15, 1985.

Played for Santiago Club in Dominican Summer League, 1985.

POSITIONS PLAYED: 2B-11.

YR	CLUB	AVG	G	AB	R	H	2B	3B	HR	RBI	BB	SO	SB
85	Sarasota	.167	18	30	6	5	0	0	0	4	3	11	2

DOYLE, Timothy Jude (Tim)

HEIGHT: 6-0 **BATS:** R **BORN:** July 13, 1967, Springfield, MA
WEIGHT: 185 **THROWS:** L **RESIDES:** Springfield, MA
SIGNED BY: John Kennedy
HOW OBTAINED: Signed as a free agent on August 20, 1985.

YR	CLUB	W-L	ERA	G	GS	CG	Sho	SV	IP	H	R	ER	BB	SO

1986 will be first professional season.

EASLEY, Kenneth Logan (Logan)

HEIGHT: 6-1 **BATS:** R **BORN:** Nov. 4, 1961, Salt Lake City, UT
WEIGHT: 185 **THROWS:** R **RESIDES:** Salt Lake City, UT
SIGNED BY: Jerry Zimmerman
HOW OBTAINED: Yankees' 20th round pick in the June, 1980 free agent draft.

Graduate of Twin Falls (ID) H.S. in 1979. Attended College of South Idaho in Twin Falls. 1983 led South Atlantic league in Shutouts with 4.

YR	CLUB	W-L	ERA	G	GS	CG	Sho	SV	IP	H	R	ER	BB	SO
81	Paintsville	2-2	3.91	22	1	0	0	2	53	60	36	23	24	26
82	Paintsville	7-4	2.56	13	12	4	1	0	84.1	77	31	24	28	59
83	Greensboro	14-8	4.04	29	22	7	4	1	158.1	157	82	71	62	116
84	Ft. Lauderdale	5-7	3.85	32	19	1	0	1	131.0	150	76	56	44	57
85	Ft. Lauderdale	1-1	0.95	17	0	0	0	4	19	19	6	2	6	16
	Albany	5-3	3.18	29	5	0	0	0	85	85	40	30	38	58

ENGLEHART, William Fred (Bill)

HEIGHT: 6-0 **BATS:** L **BORN:** Sept. 23, 1962, Philadelphia, PA
WEIGHT: 230 **THROWS:** L **RESIDES:** Cheltenham, PA
SIGNED BY: Meade Palmer
HOW OBTAINED: Signed as a free agent on June 23, 1983.

Attended Montgomery County College in Blue Bell, PA.

POSITIONS PLAYED: 1983 (1B-49); 1984 (1B-70); 1985 (1B-28).

YR	CLUB	AVG	G	AB	R	H	2B	3B	HR	RBI	BB	SO	SB
83	Oneonta	.258	57	163	18	42	9	1	4	19	32	37	2
84	Greensboro	.282	100	326	53	92	11	1	11	55	61	50	3
85	Ft. Lauderdale	.272	38	114	14	31	8	1	1	19	25	23	0

EVERS, Troy Mark

HEIGHT: 6-4 **BATS:** R **BORN:** February 4, 1964, Kaukauna, WI
WEIGHT: 205 **THROWS:** R **RESIDES:** Appleton, WI
SIGNED BY: Dick Tidrow
HOW OBTAINED: Yankees 2nd round pick in regular phase of June 1985 free agent draft.

Attended Iowa State University.

Pitched a no-hitter in semifinal playoff game vs. Geneva Cubs, 9/3/85.

YR	CLUB	W-L	ERA	G	GS	CG	Sho	SV	IP	H	R	ER	BB	SO
85	Oneonta	10-1	1.18	14	12	4	1	0	99.1	69	21	13	25	85

EZOLD, Todd Wayne

HEIGHT: 6-1 **BATS:** R **BORN:** May 6, 1963, Springfield, MA
WEIGHT: 190 **THROWS:** R **RESIDES:** Springfield, MA
SIGNED BY: John Kennedy
HOW OBTAINED: Yankees 18th round pick in regular phase of June '85 free agent draft.

Attended University of Massachusetts.

POSITIONS PLAYED: C-30

YR	CLUB	AVG	G	AB	R	H	2B	3B	HR	RBI	BB	SO	SB
85	Oneonta	.216	31	88	8	19	5	0	0	12	9	28	1

FAULK, Mitchell Kelly (Kelly)

HEIGHT: 6-3 **BATS:** R **BORN:** April 23, 1959, Crowley, LA
WEIGHT: 205 **THROWS:** R **RESIDES:** Crowley, LA

SIGNED BY: Doug Gassaway (Phillies)
HOW OBTAINED: Phillies' 1st choice in secondary phase of June, 1979 free agent draft. Acquired from Philadelphia along with Jim Rasmussen in exchange for pitcher Dave Wehrmeister.

Attended Wharton Junior College. Selected by the Atlanta Braves organization in 1st round of January, 1979 free agent draft.

YR	CLUB	W-L	ERA	G	GS	CG	Sho	SV	IP	H	R	ER	BB	SO
79	Bend	8-4	3.18	14	14	5	0	0	102	100	52	36	35	70
80	Peninsula	1-3	2.30	31	0	0	0	13	43	47	12	11	19	31
	Reading	4-1	4.95	29	0	0	0	8	40	45	27	22	19	24
81	Okla. City	0-0	5.63	4	0	0	0	2	8	10	6	5	4	5
	Reading	10-4	3.84	48	0	0	0	10	82	65	40	35	34	48
82	Okla. City	1-4	4.43	14	3	0	0	1	41	50	22	20	17	14
	Reading	3-9	2.63	40	0	0	0	11	65	46	22	19	15	52
83	Portland	1-1	4.30	10	0	0	0	1	14.2	18	9	7	6	5
	Nashville	0-0	4.50	4	0	0	0	0	8.0	3	4	4	7	2
84	Nashville	1-0	2.08	9	2	0	0	1	26.0	19	8	6	13	11
	Columbus	11-1	2.82	19	17	2	0	0	118.0	93	38	37	48	51
85	Albany	3-0	3.09	6	5	0	0	0	35	32	12	12	14	24
	Columbus	4-7	5.42	18	16	1	0	0	84.2	90	57	51	48	40

FERNANDEZ, Reynaldo Martin

HEIGHT: 5-11 **BATS:** L **BORN:** July 31, 1965
WEIGHT: 175 **THROWS:** L **RESIDES:** Panama City, Panama

SIGNED BY: Fred Ferreira
HOW OBTAINED: Signed as a free agent April 4, 1985.

Played on Santiago Club in Dominican Summer League, 1985.

POSITIONS PLAYED: 1B

YR	CLUB	AVG	G	AB	R	H	2B	3B	HR	RBI	BB	SO	SB
		1986 will be first professional season											

FIGUEROA, Fernando

HEIGHT: 6-1 **BATS:** L **BORN:** October 19, 1964, Caguas, Puerto Rico
WEIGHT: 170 **THROWS:** L **RESIDES:** Caguas, Puerto Rico

SIGNED BY: Fred Ferreira
HOW OBTAINED: Signed as a free agent September 9, 1985.

YR	CLUB	W-L	ERA	G	GS	CG	Sho	SV	IP	H	R	ER	BB	SO
		1986 will be first professional season											

FRANKLIN, Glen Kirk

HEIGHT: 5-11 **BATS:** L **BORN:** March 6, 1958, St. Louis, MO
WEIGHT: 175 **THROWS:** R **RESIDES:** St. Louis, MO

SIGNED BY: Billy Adair (Expos)
HOW OBTAINED: Montreal Expos 9th round pick in regular phase of June 1978 free agent draft. Traded to Cincinnati Reds for Ernie Gause, 4/8/82. Signed as a 6-yr. minor league free agent with Cleveland, 1/15/85. Released by Cleveland, 3/28/85. Played for Cordoba Cafeteros of Mexican League in 1985. Signed as a free agent by Yankees, 8/31/85.

Attended Chipola J.C., Marianna, FL.

POSITIONS PLAYED: 1978 Jamestown (SS-35), W. Palm Beach (SS-23 2B-9, 3B-5); 1979 (SS-88, 3B-3); 1980 (OF-38, 3B-24, SS-11, 2B-1); 1981 Memphis (2B-48, 3B-26, OF-9), Oklahoma City (2B-26, OF-5); 1982 (3B-39, 2B-13, SS-13); 1983 Waterbury (2B-8, 3B-7, SS-7), Indianapolis (2B-34, 3B-26, SS-1); 1984 (3B-35, 2B-27, SS-24, OF-5).

YR	CLUB	AVG	G	AB	R	H	2B	3B	HR	RBI	BB	SO	SB
78	Jamestown	.354	38	144	31	51	12	3	2	21	33	19	8
	W. Palm Beach	.250	24	56	5	14	2	0	0	5	17	8	9
79	W. Palm Beach	.289	120	447	66	129	12	3	5	52	54	46	24
80	Memphis	.277	124	426	61	118	27	4	8	52	42	55	20
81	Memphis	.253	88	324	56	82	12	2	12	43	34	46	32
	Oklahoma City	.250	34	96	14	24	5	2	0	10	9	11	6
82	Waterbury	.293	109	259	38	76	10	1	3	31	25	29	13
83	Waterbury	.278	26	79	10	22	3	0	0	4	6	4	5
	Indianapolis	.322	72	208	33	67	8	5	5	29	25	34	4
84	Vermont	.302	102	324	49	98	9	5	5	43	42	26	17
85	Cordoba	.335	68	218	41	73	10	2	5	37	43	36	33

FREY, Steven Francis (Steve)

HEIGHT: 5-9   **BATS:** R   **BORN:** July 29, 1963, Meadowbrook, PA
WEIGHT: 170   **THROWS:** L   **RESIDES:** Southampton, PA

SIGNED BY: Meade Palmer
HOW OBTAINED: Yankees' 12th selection in the June, 1983 free agent draft.

Attended Bucks Community College in Newtown, PA.

YR	CLUB	W-L	ERA	G	GS	CG	Sho	SV	IP	H	R	ER	BB	SO
83	Oneonta	4-6	2.74	28	1	0	0	9	72.1	47	27	22	35	86
84	Ft. Lauderdale	4-2	2.09	47	0	0	0	4	64.2	46	26	15	34	66
85	Ft. Lauderdale	1-1	1.21	19	0	0	0	7	22.1	11	4	3	12	15
	Albany	4-7	3.82	40	0	0	0	3	61.1	53	30	26	25	54

GAY, Scott Douglas

HEIGHT: 6-1   **BATS:** R   **BORN:** March 24, 1964, Nashua, NH
WEIGHT: 170   **THROWS:** R   **RESIDES:** Milford, NH

SIGNED BY: Jim Gruzdis
HOW OBTAINED: Yankees' 4th round pick in regular phase of June '85 free agent draft.

Attended Western Carolina University (North Carolina).

YR	CLUB	W-L	ERA	G	GS	CG	Sho	SV	IP	H	R	ER	BB	SO
85	Oneonta	0-1	1.80	2	0	0	0	1	5.0	3	1	1	1	6

GEREN, Robert Peter

HEIGHT: 6-3   **BATS:** R   **BORN:** September 22, 1961, San Diego, CA
WEIGHT: 205   **THROWS:** R   **RESIDES:** San Diego, CA

SIGNED BY: Bob Fontaine (Padres)
HOW OBTAINED: Graduated from Claremont (San Diego) H.S. in 1979. Selected by San Diego Padres organization in 1st round of regular phase of free agent draft, June, 1979.

Acquired by the St. Louis Cardinals December 8, 1980, from the San Diego Padres along with pitchers Rollie Fingers & Bob Shirley and catcher Gene Tenace in exchange for catchers Terry Kennedy, Steve Swisher, infielder Mike Phillips and pitchers Al Olmsted, John Urrea, Kim Seaman and John Littlefield. Led 1982 Florida State League catchers in games (96) & assists (72). Tied for 3rd in 1983 Midwest League home runs with 24. Led 1983 Midwest League catchers in total chances (939), putouts (826) and assists (102). Signed as a 6-year minor league free agent by the Yankees on 11/7/85.

POSITIONS PLAYED: 1979 (C-37, 1B-4); 1980 Reno (C-18), Walla Walla (C-47, 1B-3); 1981 (C-51); 1982 (C-96, 1B-1, OF-1); 1983 (C-104, 1B-1); 1984 Arkansas (C-79, 1B-3), Louisville (C-13); 1985 Louisville (C-5), Arkansas (C-77, 1B-21).

YR	CLUB	AVG	G	AB	R	H	2B	3B	HR	RBI	BB	SO	SB
79	Walla Walla	.220	54	151	19	26	5	0	0	16	32	39	0
80	Reno	.287	48	157	24	25	7	1	4	23	24	41	1
	Walla Walla	.254	51	177	19	45	8	1	2	28	24	33	1
81	St. Petersburg	.222	64	167	15	37	9	1	0	13	13	32	0
82	St. Petersburg	.244	110	352	38	86	24	1	1	45	29	68	3
83	Springfield	.265	124	434	67	115	21	3	24	73	40	127	0
84	Arkansas	.247	86	292	39	72	12	0	15	40	34	69	1
	Louisville	.175	15	40	3	7	1	0	0	3	5	8	0
85	Louisville	.357	5	14	2	5	2	0	1	3	0	1	0
	Arkansas	.225	103	315	38	71	18	1	5	40	31	74	3

GILLES, Thomas Bradford

HEIGHT: 6-1   **BATS:** R   **BORN:** July 2, 1962
WEIGHT: 185   **THROWS:** R   **RESIDES:** Kickapoo, IL

SIGNED BY: New York Yankees
HOW OBTAINED: Selected by Yankees in the 47th round of the June '84 free agent draft.

POSITIONS PLAYED: 1984 (1B-34, 3B-7); 1985 Oneonta (1B-26, 3B-11, OF-1), Ft. Lauderdale (3B-2, 1B-1).

YR	CLUB	AVG	G	AB	R	H	2B	3B	HR	RBI	BB	SO	SB
84	Sarasota	.241	42	145	14	35	4	2	2	13	10	16	4
85	Oneonta	.220	40	118	16	26	6	2	1	19	14	28	2
	Ft. Lauderdale	.200	2	5	1	1	0	0	0	2	2	0	0

GIRON, Ysidro

HEIGHT: 6-2   **BATS:** R   **BORN:** May 15, 1964
WEIGHT: 195   **THROWS:** R   **RESIDES:** Santo Domingo, Dominican Republic

SIGNED BY: Fred Ferreira
HOW OBTAINED: Signed as a free agent by Detroit Tigers for 1983 season. Released by Tigers 9/30/83. Signed by the Yankees on 10/1/85.

POSITIONS PLAYED: 1983 (1B-6).

YR	CLUB		AVG	G	AB	R	H	2B	3B	HR	RBI	BB	SO	SB
83	Bristol		.000	6	7	0	0	0	0	0	0	1	3	0

YR	CLUB		W-L	ERA	G	GS	CG	Sho	SV	IP		H	R	ER	BB	SO

Giron has been converted to pitcher.

GONZALEZ, Andres Heredia

HEIGHT: 6-1   **BATS:** R   **BORN:** Jan. 1, 1966, Dominican Republic
WEIGHT: 170   **THROWS:** R   **RESIDES:** Santo Domingo, Dominican Republic

SIGNED BY: Fred Ferreira
HOW OBTAINED: Signed as a free agent April 15, 1983.

POSITIONS PLAYED: 1983 (Did not play) C; 1984 (C-19); 1985 (C-28).

YR	CLUB		AVG	G	AB	R	H	2B	3B	HR	RBI	BB	SO	SB
84	Sarasota		.115	26	78	12	9	1	2	1	3	3	30	5
85	Sarasota		.196	33	107	9	21	1	1	0	7	9	25	1

GONZALEZ, Fredi Jesus (Fredi)

HEIGHT: 5-11   **BATS:** R   **BORN:** Jan. 28, 1964, Havana, Cuba
WEIGHT: 204   **THROWS:** R   **RESIDES:** Miami, FL

SIGNED BY: Fred Ferreira
HOW OBTAINED: Yankees' 16th selection in the June, 1982 free agent draft.

Graduated from Miami Southridge H.S. in 1982.

POSITIONS PLAYED: 1982 (C-40); 1983 (1B-1, C-52); 1984 (C-76, 1B-5); 1985 (C-37, 1B-6).

YR	CLUB		AVG	G	AB	R	H	2B	3B	HR	RBI	BB	SO	SB
82	Bradenton		.240	40	129	17	31	4	0	2	16	16	32	0
83	Greensboro		.192	56	151	25	29	6	0	6	23	37	62	2
84	Greensboro		.196	85	250	21	49	11	0	3	33	27	72	4
85	Ft. Lauderdale		.204	48	137	13	28	1	1	3	13	20	34	0

GRAHAM, Randall Lewis (Randy)

HEIGHT: 6-0   **BATS:** R   **BORN:** May 21, 1961, Sebastopol, CA
WEIGHT: 195   **THROWS:** R   **RESIDES:** Sebastapol, CA

SIGNED BY: Gary Hughes
HOW OBTAINED: Signed as a free agent on June 15, 1982.

Attended Fresno State University where he was an All-American. Tied for Southern League lead in saves (17), 1984. Led Eastern League in saves (17), 1985.

YR	CLUB		W-L	ERA	G	GS	CG	Sho	SV	IP		H	R	ER	BB	SO
82	Oneonta		6-0	3.06	22	0	0	0	8	35.1		33	13	12	15	34
83	Greensboro		6-11	4.90	30	10	2	0	0	97.1		125	63	53	18	51
84	Ft. Lauderdale		2-1	1.96	12	0	0	0	5	18.1		16	4	4	2	15
	Nashville		3-7	2.16	41	0	0	0	17	66.2		64	29	16	18	38
85	Albany		4-4	3.54	46	0	0	0	17	56		60	26	22	7	46

GREEN, Robert Joseph (Bob)

HEIGHT: 6-1   **BATS:** R   **BORN:** May 20, 1963
WEIGHT: 180   **THROWS:** R   **RESIDES:** Arvada, CO

SIGNED BY: Brian Sabean
HOW OBTAINED: Yankees 5th round pick in the regular phase of the June 1985 free agent draft.

POSITIONS PLAYED: OF-35.

YR	CLUB		AVG	G	AB	R	H	2B	3B	HR	RBI	BB	SO	SB
85	Oneonta		.260	39	150	24	39	9	3	3	26	23	47	3

GUERCIO, Maurice Mario

HEIGHT: 6-4   **BATS:** R   **BORN:** Sept. 1, 1964, Rome, Italy
WEIGHT: 180   **THROWS:** R   **RESIDES:** Brooklyn, NY

SIGNED BY: Joe DiCarlo
HOW OBTAINED: Signed by Yankees out of tryout camp, July 8, 1984.

YR	CLUB		W-L	ERA	G	GS	CG	Sho	SV	IP		H	R	ER	BB	SO
84	Sarasota		1-3	4.96	9	0	0	0	3	16.1		17	14	9	10	24
85	Ft. Lauderdale		2-2	3.09	22	0	0	0	4	43.2		26	19	15	27	41

GUZMAN, Hector Rafael (Rafael)

HEIGHT: 6-0   **BATS:** R   **BORN:** Nov. 18, 1964
WEIGHT: 175   **THROWS:** R   **RESIDES:** Vega Alta, Puerto Rico

SIGNED BY: Fred Ferreira
HOW OBTAINED: Signed as a free agent on March 9, 1985.

GUZMAN (continued)

POSITIONS PLAYED: OF-12.

YR	CLUB	AVG	G	AB	R	H	2B	3B	HR	RBI	BB	SO	SB
85	Sarasota	.244	15	45	4	11	1	0	0	5	1	5	7

GUZMAN, Jose Antonio

HEIGHT: 6-4 **BATS:** R **BORN:** Sept. 5, 1967, San Cristobal, DR
WEIGHT: 175 **THROWS:** R **RESIDES:** San Cristobal, Dominican Republic

SIGNED BY: Fred Ferreira
HOW OBTAINED: Signed as free agent on September 19, 1985.

Attended Yankee Academy in San Cristobal, Dominican Republic.

POSITIONS PLAYED: OF.

YR	CLUB	AVG	G	AB	R	H	2B	3B	HR	RBI	BB	SO	SB

1986 will be first professional season.

HARRISON, Matthew Creevey

HEIGHT: 6-3 **BATS:** L **BORN:** Dec. 31, 1962
WEIGHT: 195 **THROWS:** L **RESIDES:** Glen Falls, NY

SIGNED BY: Joe DiCarlo
HOW OBTAINED: Selected by Yankees in 9th round of June '84 free agent draft.

YR	CLUB	W-L	ERA	G	GS	CG	Sho	SV	IP	H	R	ER	BB	SO
84	Oneonta	4-6	3.05	16	14	1	1	0	91.1	83	45	31	31	62
85	Ft. Lauderdale	1-0	2.15	22	0	0	0	6	37.2	27	11	9	14	23

HAURADOU, Yanko

HEIGHT: 5-11 **BATS:** R **BORN:** July 31, 1965
WEIGHT: 175 **THROWS:** R **RESIDES:** Panama City, Panama

SIGNED BY: Fred Ferreira
HOW OBTAINED: Signed as a free agent, 4/24/85.

POSITIONS PLAYED: 3B-30, SS-10, OF-1.

YR	CLUB	AVG	G	AB	R	H	2B	3B	HR	RBI	BB	SO	SB
85	Sarasota	.309	45	139	19	43	5	0	0	16	14	16	5

HAWKINS, Johnny Battiste

HEIGHT: 5-8 **BATS:** S **BORN:** Oct. 25, 1960, Mobile, AL
WEIGHT: 180 **THROWS:** R **RESIDES:** Pensacola, FL

SIGNED BY: Gust Poulos
HOW OBTAINED: Selected by Yankees in the 5th round of Jan. '81 free agent draft.

POSITIONS PLAYED: 1981 (C-34); 1982 Oneonta (C-39), Ft. Lauderdale (C-2); 1983 Greensboro (C-24), Ft. Lauderdale (C-31); 1984 Nashville (C-70, 3B-1), Ft. Lauderdale (C-9, 3B-1); 1985 Columbus (C-20), Albany (C-12).

YR	CLUB	AVG	G	AB	R	H	2B	3B	HR	RBI	BB	SO	SB
81	Paintsville	.351	36	114	24	40	5	0	3	18	11	13	0
82	Ft. Lauderdale	.000	2	4	1	0	0	0	0	0	1	0	0
	Oneonta	.248	42	137	19	34	3	0	2	21	18	28	1
83	Greensboro	.185	33	92	12	17	1	0	1	10	14	15	3
	Ft. Lauderdale	.221	41	104	17	23	2	0	0	15	10	12	3
84	Nashville	.226	71	217	21	49	7	2	0	18	30	24	1
	Ft. Lauderdale	.340	19	53	4	18	3	0	0	3	1	3	0
85	Columbus	.250	22	28	3	7	0	0	0	5	0	5	0
	Albany	.138	13	29	4	4	0	0	0	2	3	6	1

HELLMAN, Jeff Bernardus

HEIGHT: 6-1 **BATS:** R **BORN:** February 2, 1963, Cincinnati, OH
WEIGHT: 180 **THROWS:** R **RESIDES:** Cincinnati, OH

SIGNED BY: Hop Cassady
HOW OBTAINED: Signed as a free agent, 7/10/85.

Attended University of Kentucky.

YR	CLUB	W-L	ERA	G	GS	CG	Sho	SV	IP	H	R	ER	BB	SO
85	Sarasota	4-0	0.87	7	6	2	1	0	41.1	21	9	4	15	44

HERNANDEZ, Leonardo Jesus (Leo)

HEIGHT: 5-11 **BATS:** R **BORN:** November 6, 1959, Estado Miranda, Venezuela
WEIGHT: 195 **THROWS:** R **RESIDES:** Estado Miranda, Venezuela

SIGNED BY: Reggie Otero (Dodgers)

HOW OBTAINED: Signed as a free agent by the Los Angeles Dodgers organization on 1/18/78. Tied for Texas League lead in GWRBI (12) in 1981. Acquired by Baltimore Orioles in exchange for catcher Jose Morales on 4/28/82. Acquired by Yankees with outfielder Gary Roenicke in exchange for pitcher Rich Bordi & infielder Rex Hudler on 12/11/86.

POSITIONS PLAYED: 1978 (3B-112), 1979 Clinton (3B-29), Lodi (3B-61), San Antonio (3B-33); 1980 San Antonio (3B-33), Vero Beach (3B-46, OF-15, 1B-3); 1981 (3B-128); 1982 San Antonio (3B-18, 1B-2), Charlotte (3B-47, 1B-12, OF-3, 2B-2), Rochester (3B-45, OF-3, 1B-1), Baltimore (PH-2); 1983 Baltimore (3B-64), Rochester (3B-41, OF-12, 1B-1); 1984 Rochester (OF-112, 3B-15, 1B-10); 1985 Baltimore (1B-1, OF-1), Rochester (OF-81, 3B-34, 1B-4).

YR	CLUB	AVG	G	AB	R	H	2B	3B	HR	RBI	BB	SO	SB
78	Clinton	.277	122	444	65	123	21	4	17	73	19	66	5
79	Clinton	.336	29	113	24	38	8	1	2	23	6	12	3
	Lodi	.319	61	257	48	82	12	2	8	52	15	20	4
	San Antonio	.250	36	128	19	32	7	0	2	11	8	15	0
80	San Antonio	.243	41	136	27	33	9	2	2	26	11	12	1
	Vero Beach	.309	82	307	53	95	13	3	10	46	30	37	10
81	San Antonio	.298	131	497	90	148	34	3	25	91	33	74	8
82	San Antonio	.320	19	75	8	24	4	1	3	14	3	3	0
	Charlotte	.289	68	270	46	78	18	2	20	61	7	40	13
	Rochester	.317	53	202	29	64	10	3	11	43	13	28	7
	Baltimore	.000	2	2	0	0	0	0	0	0	0	2	0
83	Baltimore	.246	64	203	21	50	6	1	6	26	12	19	1
	Rochester	.343	57	201	24	69	13	2	8	25	8	22	0
84	Rochester	.275	136	512	66	141	25	4	21	83	21	73	3
85	Baltimore	.048	12	21	0	1	0	0	0	0	0	4	0
	Rochester	.269	124	475	59	128	31	2	17	69	22	52	1

HERNANDEZ, William Valentin

HEIGHT: 5-10   **BATS:** R   **BORN:** September 17, 1966
WEIGHT: 165   **THROWS:** R   **RESIDES:** San Francisco deMacoris, Dominican Republic

SIGNED BY: Fred Ferreira
HOW OBTAINED: Signed as a free agent on 3/3/85.

Attended Yankee Academy in San Cristobal, Dominican Republic and was first player signed by Yankees out of the school.

POSITIONS PLAYED: OF-33.

YR	CLUB	AVG	G	AB	R	H	2B	3B	HR	RBI	BB	SO	SB
85	Sarasota	.250	41	108	18	27	6	2	2	14	19	30	5

HIGGINS, Theodore Lee II (Ted)

HEIGHT: 5-10   **BATS:** L   **BORN:** June 13, 1963, Los Angeles, CA
WEIGHT: 170   **THROWS:** L   **RESIDES:** Saugus, CA

SIGNED BY: Gregg Orr
HOW OBTAINED: Yankees 23rd round pick in regular phase of June 1985 free agent draft.

Attended the University of Nevada @ Reno where he set the single season HR mark (19) in 1985. Led Gulf Coast League in RBI's (36), 1985. Named to Gulf Coast League All-Star team (OF), 1985.

YR	CLUB	AVG	G	AB	R	H	2B	3B	HR	RBI	BB	SO	SB
85	Oneonta	1.000	1	1	1	1	0	0	1	1	0	0	0
	Sarasota	.306	55	196	38	60	7	6	0	36	30	14	9

HORTON, Darryl W.

HEIGHT: 6-2   **BATS:** R   **BORN:** October 10, 1963, Detroit, MI
WEIGHT: 195   **THROWS:** R   **RESIDES:** Detroit, MI

SIGNED BY: Brian Sabean
HOW OBTAINED: Signed as a free agent by Detroit Tigers organization, 1985. Released during spring training, 1985. Signed by Yankees as a free agent, 6/20/85.

Son of former Tigers and Mariners outfielder Willie Horton, currently the batting coach for the Chicago White Sox.

POSITIONS PLAYED: OF-6.

YR	CLUB	AVG	G	AB	R	H	2B	3B	HR	RBI	BB	SO	SB
85	Sarasota	.050	19	20	8	1	0	0	0	0	4	7	4

HUGHES, Darrell Ray

HEIGHT: 5-11   **BATS:** R   **BORN:** Jan. 23, 1963
WEIGHT: 165   **THROWS:** R   **RESIDES:** Radcliff, KY

SIGNED BY: Front Office
HOW OBTAINED: Signed as free agent on 8/14/85.

HUGHES (continued)

POSITIONS PLAYED: OF-1, 2B-1, 3B-1.

YR	CLUB	AVG	G	AB	R	H	2B	3B	HR	RBI	BB	SO	SB
85	Albany	.286	9	14	3	4	0	0	0	1	4	3	0

HUGHES, Keith Wills

HEIGHT: 6-3　　**BATS:** L　　**BORN:** Sept. 12, 1963
WEIGHT: 210　　**THROWS:** L　　**RESIDES:** Paoli, PA

SIGNED BY: Philadelphia Phillies Organization
HOW OBTAINED: Acquired, with Marty Bystrom, from Philadelphia for Shane Rawley, 6/30/84.

POSITIONS PLAYED: 1982 (OF-51); 1983 (OF-44, 1B-12); 1984 Reading (OF-58), Nashville (OF-14); 1985 Columbus (OF-18), Albany (OF-104).

Named to South Atlantic League All-Star team (DH), 1983.

YR	CLUB	AVG	G	AB	R	H	2B	3B	HR	RBI	BB	SO	SB
82	Bend	.257	55	179	29	46	10	2	3	26	30	42	2
83	Spartanburg	.329	131	484	80	159	31	4	15	90	67	83	16
84	Reading	.261	70	230	35	60	7	5	2	20	31	43	1
	Nashville	.180	21	50	6	9	0	0	0	5	10	14	0
85	Columbus	.296	18	54	7	16	4	0	3	8	2	11	0
	Albany	.269	104	361	53	97	22	5	10	54	51	73	4

IAVARONE, Gregory Speedy (Greg)

HEIGHT: 6-0　　**BATS:** R　　**BORN:** September 2, 1963, Oak Park, IL
WEIGHT: 185　　**THROWS:** R　　**RESIDES:** Wood Dale, IL

SIGNED BY: Joe Begani
HOW OBTAINED: Yankees 14th round pick in the regular phase of the June 1985 free agent draft.

Attended University of Illinois.

POSITIONS PLAYED: C-27.

YR	CLUB	AVG	G	AB	R	H	2B	3B	HR	RBI	BB	SO	SB
85	Oneonta	.315	28	54	9	17	1	0	2	9	18	17	1

IMPAGLIAZZO, Joseph Michael (Pags)

HEIGHT: 6-0　　**BATS:** R　　**BORN:** April 30, 1960, Providence, RI
WEIGHT: 175　　**THROWS:** R　　**RESIDES:** Johnston, RI

SIGNED BY: Skip Paine (Expos)
HOW OBTAINED: Signed as a free agent by Montreal Expos organization, 6/17/83. Named Pioneer League Rolaids Relief Pitcher of the Year as he led league in saves (12), 1983. Also named to All-Star team. Acquired from Expos in exchange for outfielder Dallas Williams, 10/18/85.

Received a Bachelor of Arts Degree from Yale University, 1983. Played both baseball & football at Yale.

YR	CLUB	W-L	ERA	G	GS	CG	Sho	SV	IP	H	R	ER	BB	SO
83	Calgary	6-1	1.83	28	0	0	0	12	39	22	10	8	23	62
84	Gastonia	3-8	4.69	42	0	0	0	12	71	62	38	37	50	87
	W. Palm Beach	1-2	1.32	11	0	0	0	3	14	8	3	2	10	13
85	W. Palm Beach	3-3	2.56	37	0	0	0	3	59.2	57	27	17	30	45

JOHNSON, Dino Columbus

HEIGHT: 5-9　　**BATS:** R　　**BORN:** Dec. 6, 1963, Sacramento, CA
WEIGHT: 170　　**THROWS:** R　　**RESIDES:** Sacramento, CA

SIGNED BY: Greg Orr
HOW OBTAINED: Yankees 6th round pick in the regular phase of the January 1985 free agent draft.

Attended Sacramento City College.

POSITIONS PLAYED: 3B-33.

YR	CLUB	AVG	G	AB	R	H	2B	3B	HR	RBI	BB	SO	SB
85	Sarasota	.287	41	143	31	41	7	2	1	16	18	27	4

KELLY, Roberto Conrado (Roberto)

HEIGHT: 6-2　　**BATS:** R　　**BORN:** Oct. 1, 1964, Panama
WEIGHT: 180　　**THROWS:** R　　**RESIDES:** Panama

SIGNED BY: Fred Ferreira
HOW OBTAINED: Signed as a free agent by Yankees on February 21, 1982.

Attended Jose Dolores Moscote College in Panama. Led Florida State League in triples (13), 1985.

POSITIONS PLAYED: 1982 (SS-28, OF-1); 1983 Greensboro (SS-2, OF-16), Oneonta
(3B-3, OF-39); 1984 (OF-100, 1B-2); 1985 (OF-113).

YR	CLUB	AVG	G	AB	R	H	2B	3B	HR	RBI	BB	SO	SB
82	Bradenton	.198	31	86	13	17	1	1	1	18	10	18	3
83	Greensboro	.265	20	49	6	13	0	0	0	3	3	5	3
	Oneonta	.216	48	167	17	36	1	2	2	17	12	20	12
84	Greensboro	.238	111	361	68	86	13	2	1	26	57	49	42
85	Ft. Lauderdale	.247	114	417	86	103	4	13	3	38	58	70	49

LABOY, Jose Enrique

HEIGHT: 6-2   **BATS:** R   **BORN:** Feb. 9, 1966
WEIGHT: 170   **THROWS:** R   **RESIDES:** Yabucoa, Puerto Rico

SIGNED BY: Fred Ferreira
HOW OBTAINED: Signed as a free agent on October 29, 1983.

POSITIONS PLAYED: 1984 (3B-40, SS-4).

YR	CLUB	AVG	G	AB	R	H	2B	3B	HR	RBI	BB	SO	SB
84	Sarasota	.262	51	191	15	50	6	2	0	18	9	40	4
85		Injured—did not play											

LAMBERT, Robert Alan (Rob)

HEIGHT: 5-10   **BATS:** R   **BORN:** April 19, 1963
WEIGHT: 180   **THROWS:** R   **RESIDES:** Danville, CA

SIGNED BY: Orrin Freeman
HOW OBTAINED: Yankees 20th round pick in the regular phase of the June 1985 free
agent draft.

Led Gulf Coast in batting (.350), runs (51), hits (79), total bases (92) and stolen bases
(34), 1985. Named Topps Minor League Player-of-the-Year in Gulf Coast League, 1985.
Named Gulf Coast League Most Valuable Player & All-Star second baseman, 1985. Attended Cal Poly-San Luis Obispo.

POSITIONS PLAYED: 2B-57.

YR	CLUB	AVG	G	AB	R	H	2B	3B	HR	RBI	BB	SO	SB
85	Sarasota	.350	59	226	51	79	9	2	0	21	29	32	34

LAWHON, Geral Duane (Duane)

HEIGHT: 6-0   **BATS:** R   **BORN:** May 14, 1964, Beaumont, TX
WEIGHT: 180   **THROWS:** R   **RESIDES:** Vidor, TX

SIGNED BY: Fred Ferreira
HOW OBTAINED: Signed as a free agent, 6/11/85.

Attended Alvin Community College, Alvin, TX.

POSITIONS PLAYED: Ft. Lauderdale (C-4), Sarasota (P-5, C-2).

YR	CLUB	W-L	ERA	G	GS	CG	Sho	SV	IP	H	R	ER	BB	SO
85	Sarasota	0.0	0.00	5	0	0	0	1	8.0	4	3	0	4	5

YR	CLUB	AVG	G	AB	R	H	2B	3B	HR	RBI	BB	SO	SB
85	Ft. Lauderdale	.000	6	4	0	0	0	0	0	0	0	1	0
	Sarasota	.000	7	7	0	0	0	0	0	0	0	4	0

LEE, Harvey Dewey Jr.

HEIGHT: 6-1   **BATS:** R   **BORN:** Jan. 24, 1964, Ft. Pierce, FL
WEIGHT: 180   **THROWS:** R   **RESIDES:** Ft. Pierce, FL

SIGNED BY: Fred Ferreira
HOW OBTAINED: Signed as a free agent, Aug. 21, 1984.

POSITIONS PLAYED: OF-42.

YR	CLUB	AVG	G	AB	R	H	2B	3B	HR	RBI	BB	SO	SB
85	Oneonta	.249	52	169	35	42	7	1	3	22	25	41	16

LEITER, Alois Terry (Al)

HEIGHT: 6-2   **BATS:** L   **BORN:** Oct. 23, 1965, Toms River, NJ
WEIGHT: 200   **THROWS:** L   **RESIDES:** Pine Beach, NJ

SIGNED BY: Joe DiCarlo
HOW OBTAINED: Selected by the Yankees in the 2nd round of the June '84 free agent
draft.

YR	CLUB	W-L	ERA	G	GS	CG	Sho	SV	IP	H	R	ER	BB	SO
84	Oneonta	3-2	3.63	10	10	0	0	0	57.0	52	32	23	26	48
85	Ft. Lauderdale	1-6	6.48	17	17	1	0	0	82.0	87	70	59	57	44
	Oneonta	3-2	2.37	6	6	2	0	0	38.0	27	14	10	25	34

LEWIS, Donald

HEIGHT: 6-2   **BATS:** R   **BORN:** July 19, 1965
WEIGHT: 175   **THROWS:** R   **RESIDES:** San Francisco, CA

SIGNED BY: NY Yankees
HOW OBTAINED: Selected by the Yankees in the 3rd round of the secondary phase of the Jan. '84 free agent draft.

YR	CLUB	W-L	ERA	G	GS	CG	Sho	SV	IP	H	R	ER	BB	SO
84	Sarasota	0-1	0.00	1	0	0	0	0	3.0	3	2	0	1	2
85				Did not play										

LEYRITZ, James Joseph (Jim)

HEIGHT: 6-0   **BATS:** S   **BORN:** December 27, 1963, Lakewood, OH
WEIGHT: 190   **THROWS:** R   **RESIDES:** Cincinnati, OH

SIGNED BY: Bill Livesey
HOW OBTAINED: Signed as free agent, 8/24/85.

Attended Middle Georgia Junior College. Attended University of Kentucky.

POSITIONS PLAYED: 3B, C.

YR	CLUB	AVG	G	AB	R	H	2B	3B	HR	RBI	BB	SO	SB
		1986 will be first professional season.											

LINDSEY, William Donald (Bill)

HEIGHT: 6-3   **BATS:** R   **BORN:** April 12, 1960, Staten Island, NY
WEIGHT: 195   **THROWS:** R   **RESIDES:** Boca Raton, FL

SIGNED BY: Fred Ferreira
HOW OBTAINED: Signed as free agent by Yankees on April 27, 1981.

Graduated from Hollywood Hills H.S. in 1978 where he played baseball and basketball. Attended Ft. Lauderdale (Fla.) College.

POSITIONS PLAYED: 1981 (1B-25); 1982 (C-59, 1B-30); 1983 Columbus (C-1), Nashville (C-3), Ft. Lauderdale (1B-3, C-57); 1984 Ft. Lauderdale (C-35), Nashville (C-11, 1B-1), Columbus (C-8); 1985 Columbus (C-25), Albany (C-54, 1B-5, OF-2).

YR	CLUB	AVG	G	AB	R	H	2B	3B	HR	RBI	BB	SO	SB
81	Paintsville	.296	51	162	28	48	8	1	8	28	11	28	0
82	Greensboro	.271	102	336	55	91	20	0	5	47	49	39	4
83	Columbus	.000	1	4	1	0	0	0	0	0	0	0	0
	Nashville	.273	3	11	1	3	0	0	0	0	1	1	0
	Ft. Lauderdale	.242	82	260	33	63	12	0	6	33	20	35	2
84	Ft. Lauderdale	.307	35	101	8	31	4	1	0	12	14	11	1
	Nashville	.189	13	37	3	7	1	1	0	4	6	3	0
	Columbus	.136	8	22	2	3	0	1	1	0	1	1	0
85	Columbus	.211	27	71	10	15	5	0	1	9	14	12	0
	Albany	.282	69	227	30	64	16	0	6	41	31	23	2

LOMBARDOZZI, Christopher (Chris)

HEIGHT: 6-1   **BATS:** L   **BORN:** January 29, 1965, Malden, MA
WEIGHT: 185   **THROWS:** R   **RESIDES:** Manlius, NY

SIGNED BY: Vince Capece
HOW OBTAINED: Yankees 9th round pick in regular phase of June 1985 free agent draft.

Attended University of Florida. Named to 1985 New York-Penn League All-Star team (utility). Brother of Minnesota Twins second baseman Steve Lombardozzi.

POSITIONS PLAYED: 2B-62.

YR	CLUB	AVG	G	AB	R	H	2B	3B	HR	RBI	BB	SO	SB
85	Oneonta	.246	66	207	33	51	9	2	2	25	57	55	11

MAAS, Jason Gregory

HEIGHT: 6-2   **BATS:** L   **BORN:** March 17, 1963
WEIGHT: 190   **THROWS:** R   **RESIDES:** Castro Valley, CA

SIGNED BY: Orrin Freeman
HOW OBTAINED: Yankees 10th round pick in regular phase of June 1985 free agent draft.

Attended Cal Poly-San Luis Obispo, where he was named All-American in 1984 and Academic All-American in 1985.

POSITIONS PLAYED: OF-32, 3B-23, 2B-1.

YR	CLUB	AVG	G	AB	R	H	2B	3B	HR	RBI	BB	SO	SB
85	Oneonta	.286	67	234	37	67	7	2	1	23	51	42	16

MACKAY, Joey Dean (Joey)

HEIGHT: 6-0   **BATS:** R   **BORN:** Jan. 6, 1964, Harbor City, CA
WEIGHT: 185   **THROWS:** R   **RESIDES:** Anaheim, CA

SIGNED BY: Don Lindeberg
HOW OBTAINED: Yankees' 9th selection in the June, 1982 draft.

Graduated from Villa Park H.S. in 1982.

POSITIONS PLAYED: 1982 (OF-42); 1983 (OF-125); 1984 Greensboro (OF-69, 38-3), Ft. Lauderdale (OF-18); 1985 Albany (OF-19), Ft. Lauderdale (OF-25).

YR	CLUB	AVG	G	AB	R	H	2B	3B	HR	RBI	BB	SO	SB
82	Bradenton	.219	42	146	24	32	5	2	3	16	21	26	8
83	Greensboro	.250	128	420	61	105	25	4	5	57	42	105	8
84	Greensboro	.210	84	248	27	52	9	1	1	25	32	38	8
	Ft. Lauderdale	.167	23	72	9	12	4	0	2	8	9	15	2
85	Albany	.207	22	58	3	12	3	2	1	9	4	15	0
	Ft. Lauderdale	.239	48	138	23	33	4	2	3	17	19	31	1

MAININI, Matthew Kimball (Matt)

HEIGHT: 5-11 **BATS:** L **BORN:** August 11, 1962, Quincy, MA
WEIGHT: 170 **THROWS:** L **RESIDES:** Rockland, MA

SIGNED BY: Brian Sabean
HOW OBTAINED: Yankees' 15th round pick in regular phase of June 1985 free agent draft.

Attended University of Southern Florida.

POSITIONS PLAYED: OF-67.

YR	CLUB	AVG	G	AB	R	H	2B	3B	HR	RBI	BB	SO	SB
85	Oneonta	.260	70	196	30	51	7	1	3	23	52	46	4

MANDEL, Darren Troy

HEIGHT: 5-11 **BATS:** R **BORN:** August 27, 1963, Brooklyn, NY
WEIGHT: 200 **THROWS:** R **RESIDES:** West Palm Beach, FL

SIGNED BY: Fred Ferreira
HOW OBTAINED: Selected by Yankees in the 21st round of the June 1984 free agent draft.

Led Gulf Coast League in doubles (16) and slugging pct. (.500), 1985.

POSITIONS PLAYED: 1984 (1B-24); 1985 (C-33, 1B-8).

YR	CLUB	AVG	G	AB	R	H	2B	3B	HR	RBI	BB	SO	SB
84	Oneonta	.239	69	222	40	53	5	0	13	40	55	58	0
85	Sarasota	.317	55	180	33	57	16	4	3	31	29	23	4

MANERING, Mark Allen

HEIGHT: 6-0 **BATS:** L **BORN:** June 20, 1963
WEIGHT: 175 **THROWS:** L **RESIDES:** LaPorte, IN

SIGNED BY: Dick Groch

HOW OBTAINED: Yankees 1st selection in secondary phase of January 1986 free agent draft. Attended Miami of Ohio in Oxford, OH.

POSITION: 1B

YR	CLUB	AVG	G	AB	R	H	2B	3B	HR	RBI	BB	SO	SB
	1986 will be first professional season.												

MANON, Ramon

HEIGHT: 6-0 **BATS:** R **BORN:** January 20, 1968
WEIGHT: 150 **THROWS:** R **RESIDES:** Villa Mella, Dominican Republic

SIGNED BY: Fred Ferreira
HOW OBTAINED: Attended Yankee Academy in San Cristobal, Dominican Republic. Signed as a free agent, 7/5/85.

YR	CLUB	W-L	ERA	G	GS	CG	Sho	SV	IP	H	R	ER	BB	SO
	1986 will be first professional season.													

MARSTON, Tod R.

HEIGHT: 6-0 **BATS:** R **BORN:** Nov. 3, 1962
WEIGHT: 185 **THROWS:** R **RESIDES:** Fair Oaks, CA

SIGNED BY: Gregg Orr
HOW OBTAINED: Selected by Yankees in the 31st round of the June 1984 free agent draft.

POSITIONS PLAYED: 1984 Pocatello (C-9), Sarasota (C-4); 1985 Albany (C-33).

YR	CLUB	AVG	G	AB	R	H	2B	3B	HR	RBI	BB	SO	SB
84	Sarasota	.250	4	12	1	3	0	0	0	1	2	2	0
	Pocatello	.260	57	177	40	46	8	5	2	15	33	42	0
85	Oneonta	.202	36	109	16	22	2	2	2	15	15	28	3

MARTINEZ, Carlos Alberto

HEIGHT: 6-5   **BATS:** R   **BORN:** August 11, 1965, La Guaira, Venezuela
WEIGHT: 175   **THROWS:** R   **RESIDES:** La Guaira, Venezuela

SIGNED BY: Fred Ferreira
HOW OBTAINED: Signed as a free agent, Nov. 17, 1983.

Named to Florida State League All-Star team (SS), 1985.

POSITIONS PLAYED: 1984 (SS-31); 1985 (SS-91).

YR	CLUB	AVG	G	AB	R	H	2B	3B	HR	RBI	BB	SO	SB
84	Sarasota	.154	31	91	9	14	1	1	0	4	6	15	3
85	Ft. Lauderdale	.248	93	311	39	77	15	7	6	44	14	65	8

MARTINEZ, Ricardo

HEIGHT: 5-11   **BATS:** R   **BORN:** June 3, 1965
WEIGHT: 155   **THROWS:** R   **RESIDES:** Santo Domingo, Dominican Republic

SIGNED BY: Fred Ferreira
HOW OBTAINED: Signed with Yankees as a free agent, 3/3/85.

POSITIONS PLAYED: SS-16.

YR	CLUB	AVG	G	AB	R	H	2B	3B	HR	RBI	BB	SO	SB
85	Sarasota	.190	16	21	1	4	1	0	0	1	1	4	0

MAYNARD, Chris

HEIGHT: 6-0   **BATS:** R   **BORN:** Sept. 29, 1962
WEIGHT: 175   **THROWS:** R   **RESIDES:** Fairfield, OH

SIGNED BY: Yankees Organization
HOW OBTAINED: Signed as a free agent, July 1, 1984.

POSITIONS PLAYED: 1984 (SS-53); 1985 (SS-19, 2B-1, 3B-1).

YR	CLUB	AVG	G	AB	R	H	2B	3B	HR	RBI	BB	SO	SB
84	Oneonta	.274	53	197	21	54	2	1	0	15	9	37	8
85	Ft. Lauderdale	.286	22	70	13	20	4	0	0	8	14	9	2

McCLEAR, Michael James

HEIGHT: 6-1   **BATS:** S   **BORN:** March 30, 1963, Royal Oak, MI
WEIGHT: 190   **THROWS:** R   **RESIDES:** Troy, MI

SIGNED BY: Dick Groch
HOW OBTAINED: Signed by Yankees as a free agent, June 19, 1984.

YR	CLUB	W-L	ERA	G	GS	CG	Sho	SV	IP	H	R	ER	BB	SO
84	Sarasota	3-2	2.35	11	10	2	1	0	65.0	49	22	17	19	43
85	Sarasota	6-3	1.40	20	0	0	0	2	38.2	25	9	6	12	46

McNEALY, Derwin Antonio

HEIGHT: 6-2   **BATS:** L   **BORN:** April 25, 1960, Los Angeles, CA
WEIGHT: 165   **THROWS:** L   **RESIDES:** Los Angeles, CA

SIGNED BY: Don Lindeberg
HOW OBTAINED: Yankees 21st round pick in regular phase of June 1985 free agent draft. Traded to Toronto organization in exchange for pitcher Don Cooper, 3/13/84. Led Southern League outfielders in games (144) and total chances (384) in 1984. Signed with the Yankees organization as a 6-year minor league free agent, 11/24/85.

POSITIONS PLAYED: 1979 (OF-17); 1980 (OF-62); 1981 (OF-67); 1982 (OF-114); 1983 (OF-126); 1984 (OF-144); 1985 (OF-134).

YR	CLUB	AVG	G	AB	R	H	2B	3B	HR	RBI	BB	SO	SB
79	Paintsville	.263	32	76	12	20	5	0	2	13	7	22	1
80	Brad Yankees	.260	62	200	31	52	7	1	0	14	30	51	13
81	Oneonta	.273	68	187	35	51	6	3	5	27	27	43	18
82	Ft. Lauderdale	.261	121	322	61	84	12	4	0	16	20	60	20
83	Nashville	.242	127	421	75	102	11	6	3	37	48	76	39
84	Knoxville	.230	144	540	63	124	12	4	2	51	52	91	31
85	Syracuse	.265	135	472	49	125	13	6	1	42	36	74	22

MEULENS, Hensley Filemon

HEIGHT: 6-3   **BATS:** R   **BORN:** June 23, 1967, Curacao.
WEIGHT: 190   **THROWS:** R   **RESIDES:** Curacao, Netherlands Antilles

SIGNED BY: Fred Ferreira
HOW OBTAINED: Signed with Yankees as a free agent, 10/31/85.

POSITIONS PLAYED: 3B.

YR	CLUB	AVG	G	AB	R	H	2B	3B	HR	RBI	BB	SO	SB

1986 will be his first professional season.

MORALES, Edgar

HEIGHT: 6-0 **BATS:** R **BORN:** October 14, 1966, New York, NY
WEIGHT: 180 **THROWS:** R **RESIDES:** Carolina, Puerto Rico

SIGNED BY: Fred Ferreira
HOW OBTAINED: Signed by Yankees as a free agent, 9/9/85.

YR	CLUB	W-L	ERA	G	GS	CG	Sho	SV	IP	H	R	ER	BB	SO
			1986 will be first professional season.											

MORALES, Roberto Cabrera

HEIGHT: 5-11 **BATS:** R **BORN:** September 7, 1963
WEIGHT: 150 **THROWS:** R **RESIDES:** Ponce, Puerto Rico

SIGNED BY: Fred Ferreira
HOW OBTAINED: Signed by Yankees as a free agent, 8/27/85.

YR	CLUB	W-L	ERA	G	GS	CG	Sho	SV	IP	H	R	ER	BB	SO
			1986 will be first professional season.											

NIELSEN, Jeffrey Scott (Scott)

HEIGHT: 6-1 **BATS:** R **BORN:** Dec. 18, 1958, Salt Lake City, UT
WEIGHT: 190 **THROWS:** R **RESIDES:** Salt Lake City, UT

SIGNED BY: Jeff Malinoff (Seattle)
HOW OBTAINED: Selected by Mariners in the 6th round of the June '83 free agent draft. Acquired by Yankees from Seattle with Eric Parent for Larry Milbourne, 2/14/84.

YR	CLUB	W-L	ERA	G	GS	CG	Sho	SV	IP	H	R	ER	BB	SO
83	Chattanooga	2-4	6.39	13	9	1	0	0	63.1	81	49	45	27	24
	Bellingham	2-0	2.08	2	2	0	0	0	13.0	11	4	3	2	13
84	Columbus	5-4	3.97	11	10	1	0	0	56.2	59	27	25	23	21
	Nashville	6-3	2.44	10	10	2	0	0	73.2	55	34	20	15	27
	Ft. Lauderdale	2-1	1.08	4	3	1	0	0	16.2	16	8	2	5	7
85	Albany	6-1	2.95	11	11	4	1	0	73.1	60	26	24	14	31

PATTERSON, Kenneth Brian (Ken)

HEIGHT: 6-4 **BATS:** L **BORN:** July 8, 1964, Costa Mesa, CA
WEIGHT: 210 **THROWS:** L **RESIDES:** McGregor, TX

SIGNED BY: Stan Saleski
HOW OBTAINED: Yankees 3rd round pick in regular phase of June 1985 free agent draft.

Attended Baylor University, Waco, TX.

YR	CLUB	W-L	ERA	G	GS	CG	Sho	SV	IP	H	R	ER	BB	SO
85	Oneonta	2-2	4.84	6	6	0	0	0	22.1	23	14	12	14	21

PERDOMO, Felix E. (Felix)

HEIGHT: 5-9 **BATS:** R **BORN:** Sept. 11, 1963, Bani, Dominican Republic
WEIGHT: 153 **THROWS:** R **RESIDES:** Peravia, Dominican Republic

SIGNED BY: Nino Escalara (Mets)
HOW OBTAINED: Signed as a free agent by the Mets on September 3, 1980. Acquired from the Mets on April 27, 1983 along with Steve Ray in exchange for Tucker Ashford.

Cousin of Red Sox SS Julio Valdez.

POSITIONS PLAYED: 1981 (2B-37, SS-18); 1982 (2B-111, SS-8); 1983 Greensboro (2B-80, SS-30), Columbia (2B-15); 1984 Greensboro (3B-28, SS-17, 2B-6), Ft. Lauderdale (2B-40, SS-32); 1985 (2B-44, SS-34, 3B-11).

YR	CLUB	AVG	G	AB	R	H	2B	3B	HR	RBI	BB	SO	SB
81	Kingsport	.310	56	213	40	66	17	1	5	29	9	37	6
82	Shelby	.260	121	465	69	121	21	6	8	61	31	79	22
83	Greensboro	.253	112	383	54	97	17	5	9	60	29	111	10
	Columbia	.255	15	55	9	14	1	1	0	9	3	12	4
84	Ft. Lauderdale	.236	72	225	19	53	7	1	2	24	15	47	4
	Greensboro	.263	53	160	18	42	5	1	0	24	19	32	6
85	Ft. Lauderdale	.245	90	273	37	67	10	2	2	25	23	53	16

PLEICONES, Johnnie Mack, Jr.

HEIGHT: 5-10 **BATS:** R **BORN:** June 1, 1963, Orlando FL
WEIGHT: 150 **THROWS:** R **RESIDES:** Orlando, FL

SIGNED BY: Brian Sabean
HOW OBTAINED: Yankees' 19th round pick in regular phase of June 1985 free agent draft.

Graduated from Florida Southern College in 1985.

POSITIONS PLAYED: SS-24, 2B-17, 3B-6.

YR	CLUB	AVG	G	AB	R	H	2B	3B	HR	RBI	BB	SO	SB
85	Oneonta	.221	46	145	17	32	2	1	0	16	11	17	5

PRIES, Jeffrey John

HEIGHT: 6-5 **BATS:** R **BORN:** Jan. 5, 1963, Alameda, CA
WEIGHT: 200 **THROWS:** R **RESIDES:** Newport Beach, CA
SIGNED BY: Don Lindeberg
HOW OBTAINED: Selected by Yankees in the 1st round of the June '84 free agent draft.

YR	CLUB	W-L	ERA	G	GS	CG	Sho	SV	IP	H	R	ER	BB	SO
84	Oneonta	3-4	2.48	11	11	0	0	0	65.1	50	26	18	27	41
85	Ft. Lauderdale	11-7	3.83	22	22	4	0	0	131.2	117	66	56	49	50

PULIDO, Alfonso

HEIGHT: 5-11 **BATS:** L **BORN:** January 23, 1957, Vera Cruz, Mexico
WEIGHT: 170 **THROWS:** L **RESIDES:** Mexico City, MX
SIGNED BY:
HOW OBTAINED: Signed first professional contract with Arandas of Mexican Center League in 1977 after borrowing a glove and spikes and trying out in street clothes. Sold to Pittsburgh Pirates, 7/22/83. Traded to Yankees with infielder Dale Berra and outfielder Jay Buhner for outfielder Steve Kemp and infielder Tim Foli and cash, 12/20/84.

Tied for Mexican League lead in wins (17) in 1983 and was member of All-Star team. Named the Pacific Coast League's lefthanded pitcher of the year in 1984. Led the PCL in innings pitched (216.0), complete games (16), and shutouts (4) in 1984.

YR	CLUB	W-L	ERA	G	GS	CG	Sho	SV	IP	H	R	ER	BB	SO
77	Arandas	6-6	4.36	14	14†	9	1	0	64	85	59	40	31	31
78	Matamoros	10-3	2.11	18	16*	10	3†	2	111	103	39	26	16	81
	Cordoba	2-0	0.75	5	1	1	0	0	12	5	1	1	2	10
79	Cordoba	3-2	4.21	20	5	1	1	0	47	50	22	22	19	23
80	Reynosa	12-10	3.22	33	20	11	3	1	179	201	76	64	52	88
81	Mexico City	5-6	3.07	31	17	7	2	0	126	121	46	43	25	46
82	Mexico City	8-8	2.41	43	1	1	1	2	93.1	94	34	25	31	50
83	Mexico City-a	† 17-3	2.02	29	23	15	6	2	187.1	170	46	42	31	83
	PITTSBURGH	0-0	9.00	1	1	0	0	0	2.0	4	3	2	1	1
84	Hawaii	18-6	2.54	28	28	16*	4	0	216.0*	190	73	61	46	123
	PITTSBURGH-b	0-0	9.00	1	0	0	0	0	2.0	3	2	2	1	2
85	Columbus	11-8	3.39	31	20	4	1	1	146.0	154	66	55	34	67
Minor Lg. Totals		92-52	2.89	252	145	75	22	8	1181.2	1173	462	379	287	602
M.L. Totals		0-0	9.00	2	1	0	0	0	4.0	7	5	4	2	3

RAMON, Julio Cesar

HEIGHT: 6-0 **BATS:** R **BORN:** July 2, 1966, San Cristobal, D.R.
WEIGHT: 170 **THROWS:** R **RESIDES:** San Cristobal, Dominican Republic
SIGNED BY: Fred Ferreira
HOW OBTAINED: Attended Yankee Academy and signed as free agent, 4/14/85. Played for Santiago Club in Dominican Summer League, 1985.

POSITIONS PLAYED: C, OF.

YR	CLUB	AVG	G	AB	R	H	2B	3B	HR	RBI	BB	SO	SB
		1986 will be first professional season.											

REED, Darren Douglas

HEIGHT: 6-1 **BATS:** R **BORN:** Oct. 16, 1965, Ventura, CA
WEIGHT: 190 **THROWS:** R **RESIDES:** Ventura, CA
SIGNED BY: Orrin Freeman
HOW OBTAINED: Selected by Yankees in the 3rd round of the Secondary Phase of the June '84 free agent draft.

Named to Florida State League All-Star team (OF), 1985. Led FSL in slugging pct. (.477), 1985.

POSITIONS PLAYED: 1984 (OF-36, C-1); 1985 (OF-96).

YR	CLUB	AVG	G	AB	R	H	2B	3B	HR	RBI	BB	SO	SB
84	Oneonta	.230	40	113	17	26	7	0	2	9	10	19	2
85	Ft. Lauderdale	.317	100	369	63	117	21	4	10	61	36	56	13

REKER, Timothy Walter (Tim)

HEIGHT: 6-4 **BATS:** L **BORN:** June 2, 1962, Miami, FL
WEIGHT: 210 **THROWS:** L **RESIDES:** Miami, FL
SIGNED BY: Fred Ferreira
HOW OBTAINED: Yankees' 27th round pick in regular phase of June 1985 free agent draft.

Attended Florida International University.

YR	CLUB	W-L	ERA	G	GS	CG	Sho	SV	IP	H	R	ER	BB	SO
85	Sarasota	1-2	2.73	10	4	1	0	0	29.2	37	15	9	2	17

REYNOLDS, Leonardo Alfredo (Papito)

HEIGHT: 6-1   **BATS:** R   **BORN:** Dec. 23, 1959, San Pedro de Macoris, D.R.
WEIGHT: 175   **THROWS:** R   **RESIDES:** Newark, NJ

SIGNED BY: Francisco Acevedo (Phillies)
HOW OBTAINED: Signed by Philadelphia organization as a free agent, 4/29/80. Released, 5/10/83. Signed by Yankees after annual tryout at Yankee Stadium, 9/10/85.

POSITIONS PLAYED: 1980 (SS-53); 1981 (SS-85); 1982 (SS-38); 1983 (SS-12).

YR	CLUB	AVG	G	AB	R	H	2B	3B	HR	RBI	BB	SO	SB
80	Bend	.254	56	213	29	54	8	2	4	29	8	58	13
81	Spartanburg	.215	90	317	25	68	14	0	3	33	14	66	8
82	Peninsula	.293	40	133	11	39	6	1	2	22	1	23	5
83	Peninsula	.234	13	47	3	11	0	0	1	7	1	13	1

RIGGS, James Ray (Jim)

HEIGHT: 6-1   **BATS:** L   **BORN:** Nov. 4, 1960, Monroe, MI
WEIGHT: 180   **THROWS:** R   **RESIDES:** Monroe, MI

SIGNED BY: Stan Sanders
HOW OBTAINED: Yankees' 4th selection in the June, 1982 draft.

Graduated from Monroe H.S. in 1980 and attended Eastern Michigan University. Named to the 1982 New York-Penn League All-Star team as a utility infielder. Named to play in Eastern League All-Star game (3B), 1985.

POSITIONS PLAYED: 1982 (3B-69); 1983 (1B-1, 2B-1, 3B-120); 1984 (3B-55, OF-1); 1985 (3B-71).

YR	CLUB	AVG	G	AB	R	H	2B	3B	HR	RBI	BB	SO	SB
82	Oneonta	.309	72	272	45	84	16	2	6	44	35	32	9
83	Greensboro	.262	133	481	77	126	23	4	13	95	68	53	5
84	Ft. Lauderdale	.270	111	337	38	91	21	2	10	58	41	33	1
85	Albany	.234	121	415	51	97	19	2	7	60	57	50	2

RIVAS, Manuel Ricardo (Manny)

HEIGHT: 5-11   **BATS:** R   **BORN:** Oct. 11, 1966, Coral Gables, FL
WEIGHT: 180   **THROWS:** R   **RESIDES:** Miami, FL

SIGNED BY: Fred Ferreira
HOW OBTAINED: Selected by Yankees in the 32nd round of the June '84 free agent draft.

POSITIONS PLAYED: 1984 (C-5, 2B-1).

YR	CLUB	AVG	G	AB	R	H	2B	3B	HR	RBI	BB	SO	SB
84	Sarasota	.158	8	19	0	3	0	0	0	1	0	5	2
85					(Did not play)								

ROBINSON, Elmer Warren Jr. (Robbie)

HEIGHT: 6-6   **BATS:** R   **BORN:** Nov. 26, 1966, La Grange, IL
WEIGHT: 215   **THROWS:** R   **RESIDES:** La Grange, IL

SIGNED BY: Joe Begani
HOW OBTAINED: Selected by Yankees in the 11th round of the June '84 free agent draft.

Plays on Iowa State basketball team.

YR	CLUB	W-L	ERA	G	GS	CG	Sho	SV	IP	H	R	ER	BB	SO
84	Sarasota	0-0	3.00	1	0	0	0	0	3.0	3	1	1	5	0
85						(Did not play)								

RODRIGUEZ, Gabriel Alcangel

HEIGHT: 6-0   **BATS:** R   **BORN:** December 29, 1967
WEIGHT: 170   **THROWS:** R   **RESIDES:** Dorado, Puerto Rico

SIGNED BY: Fred Ferreira
HOW OBTAINED: Signed by the Yankees as a free agent, 12/29/84.

YR	CLUB	W-L	ERA	G	GS	CG	Sho	SV	IP	H	R	ER	BB	SO
85	Sarasota	0-1	4.03	13	1	0	0	2	22.1	26	15	10	10	14

RODRIGUEZ, Yonis Rafael

HEIGHT: 6-1   **BATS:** R   **BORN:** Oct. 31, 1961
WEIGHT: 165   **THROWS:** R   **RESIDES:** Dominican Republic

SIGNED BY: Philadelphia Phillies Organization
HOW OBTAINED: Signed as a free agent, March 21, 1984.

YR	CLUB	W-L	ERA	G	GS	CG	Sho	SV	IP	H	R	ER	BB	SO
80	Helena	4-2	2.12	13	2	2	0	4	51.0	47	19	12	19	47
81	Spartanburg	0-1	7.56	11	1	0	0	1	25.0	34	21	21	6	19
	Bend	4-3	4.17	13	11	1	0	0	69.0	68	39	32	35	40
82	Spartanburg	8-5	4.33	24	17	1	0	0	112.1	120	73	54	50	77

RODRIGUEZ (continued)

83	Peninsula	1-2	7.98	6	6	0	0	0	29.0	44	29	26	15	19
	Spartanburg	7-5	3.89	21	12	6	1	1	106.0	116	60	46	31	65
84	Greensboro	7-7	2.98	27	12	4	1	4	108.2	109	50	36	46	46
85	Ft. Lauderdale	6-5	3.09	30	9	1	0	0	96.0	100	41	33	35	48

RUSSELL, Anthony Silas (Tony)

HEIGHT: 5-11 **BATS:** R **BORN:** Aug. 8, 1961, Cincinnati, OH
WEIGHT: 165 **THROWS:** R **RESIDES:** Athens, GA

SIGNED BY: Gust Poulos
HOW OBTAINED: Yankees' 3rd selection in the January, 1982 draft.

Graduated from Windsor Forest H.S. in 1979 and attended Middle Georgia J.C. Led Eastern League in sacrifice hits (22), 1985.

POSITIONS PLAYED: 1982 Bradenton (OF-26), Oneonta (OF-27); 1983 (OF-114); 1984 (OF-126); 1985 (OF-122).

YR	CLUB	AVG	G	AB	R	H	2B	3B	HR	RBI	BB	SO	SB
82	Bradenton	.327	29	110	19	36	7	1	0	10	14	15	7
	Oneonta	.281	30	121	15	34	5	2	2	15	12	22	20
83	Greensboro	.285	129	471	97	134	18	7	4	56	97	103	43
84	Ft. Lauderdale	.229	131	420	74	96	8	7	2	29	72	84	32
85	Albany	.246	123	415	64	102	16	8	6	36	42	96	15

SANTIAGO, Norman Bruce (Norm)

HEIGHT: 6-0 **BATS:** R **BORN:** May 13, 1963, Los Angeles, CA
WEIGHT: 185 **THROWS:** R **RESIDES:** Baldwin Park, CA

SIGNED BY: Duane Shaffer (White Sox)
HOW OBTAINED: Chicago White Sox 4th round pick in regular phase of January 1984 free agent draft. Named to 1985 Gulf Coast League All-Star team (3B).

Acquired by Yankees on 2/13/85 as player to be named later in trade of infielder Roy Smalley to White Sox on 7/18/84 in exchange for pitchers Kevin Hickey & Doug Drabek.

POSITIONS PLAYED: 1984 (3B-23, 2B-17, SS-8); 1985 (3B-24).

YR	CLUB	AVG	G	AB	R	H	2B	3B	HR	RBI	BB	SO	SB
84	Sar. White Sox	.315	53	203	30	64	10	3	2	32	13	18	4
85	Ft. Lauderdale	.200	32	90	10	18	1	0	1	6	8	9	0

SCOTT, Richard Edward (Dick)

HEIGHT: 6-1 **BATS:** R **BORN:** July 19, 1962, Ellsworth, ME
WEIGHT: 172 **THROWS:** R **RESIDES:** Ellsworth, ME

SIGNED BY: John Kennedy
HOW OBTAINED: Yankees' 17th pick in 1981 June draft.

Graduated from Ellsworth (Maine) H.S. in 1981 where he played baseball, basketball and soccer. 1983 named to the Florida State League All-Star team.

POSITIONS PLAYED: 1981 (SS-47); 1982 Columbus (SS-5), Ft. Lauderdale (SS-89); 1983 Columbus (SS-1), Ft. Lauderdale (2B-1), (SS-119); 1984 Ft. Lauderdale (SS-111), Nashville (3B-18); 1985 (SS-92, 1B-2, OF-2).

YR	CLUB	AVG	G	AB	R	H	2B	3B	HR	RBI	BB	SO	SB
81	Bradenton	.235	48	132	11	31	5	2	0	15	21	33	5
82	Columbus	.500	5	10	2	5	0	0	1	1	1	2	0
	Ft. Lauderdale	.187	90	235	26	44	6	2	3	24	37	56	4
83	Columbus	.000	1	2	0	0	0	0	0	0	0	1	0
	Ft. Lauderdale	.217	120	345	40	75	11	2	4	32	44	93	7
84	Nashville	.222	18	63	4	14	1	1	0	4	8	12	3
	Ft. Lauderdale	.245	111	351	43	86	20	1	6	37	37	70	6
85	Albany	.214	97	299	30	64	15	4	4	34	27	73	6

SCOTT, Thomas Kelly (Kelly)

HEIGHT: 5-10 **BATS:** R **BORN:** Oct. 4, 1959, Sanford, FL
WEIGHT: 165 **THROWS:** R **RESIDES:** Key West, FL

SIGNED BY: Gust Poulos
HOW OBTAINED: Signed as a free agent on June 30, 1980.

Tied for 1981 South Atlantic League lead with 16 wins and was tied for second with 10 complete games. Threw no-hitter in SAL the same year. 1983 tied for Southern League lead in shutouts with 3. Received his degree in Business Administration from Valdosta (GA) State College in 1983.

YR	CLUB	W-L	ERA	G	GS	CG	Sho	SV	IP	H	R	ER	BB	SO
80	Bradenton	0-0	0.00	1	1	0	0	0	2	3	1	0	0	4
	Oneonta	4-4	2.70	15	1	0	0	0	40	30	15	12	12	34
81	Greensboro	16-6	2.98	24	22	10	2	1	169	136	69	56	51	130
82	Nashville	0-2	7.50	6	6	0	0	0	30.0	38	28	25	13	20
	Ft. Lauderdale	10-3	2.61	16	16	8	0	0	117.1	115	44	34	21	54
83	Nashville	14-7	2.92	26	26	12	3	0	188.0	189	74	61	48	113

84	Columbus	8-9	3.99	25	21	5	2	0	119.2	123	70	53	42	46
85	Columbus	4-5	3.99	21	12	3	0	0	94.2	97	47	42	26	32
	Albany	1-3	4.81	8	8	1	0	0	33.2	39	20	18	12	19

SEOANE, Mitch

HEIGHT: 5-9   **BATS:** R   **BORN:** Feb. 9, 1961, Tampa, FL
WEIGHT: 160   **THROWS:** R   **RESIDES:** Tampa, FL

SIGNED BY: Carlos Tosca
HOW OBTAINED: Signed as a free agent on August 2, 1983.

Graduate of Tampa Catholic H.S. and attended University of Miami. Participated in Miami's championship season of 1982.

POSITIONS PLAYED: 1983 (2B-27); 1984 Greensboro (SS-72, 3B-19, 2B-6), Ft. Lauderdale (3B-8, 2B-4); 1985 Albany (SS-30, 2B-1, 3B-1), Ft. Lauderdale (2B-40, 3B-20, SS-2, OF-1).

YR	CLUB	AVG	G	AB	R	H	2B	3B	HR	RBI	BB	SO	SB
83	Greensboro	.228	27	92	13	21	3	1	0	8	5	19	3
84	Ft. Lauderdale	.333	17	42	4	14	2	0	0	7	5	4	5
	Greensboro	.246	97	342	43	84	1	1	0	21	36	36	23
85	Albany	.196	32	102	9	20	2	0	0	7	9	10	3
	Ft. Lauderdale	.275	63	182	22	50	2	2	0	6	11	21	10

SEPANEK, Robert, Jr. (Rob)

HEIGHT: 6-3   **BATS:** L   **BORN:** March 31, 1963, Ypsilanti, MI
WEIGHT: 195   **THROWS:** L   **RESIDES:** Ypsilanti, MI

SIGNED BY: Tony Stiel (Atlanta)
HOW OBTAINED: Atlanta Braves 6th pick in regular phase of June 1984 free agent draft. Released, Spring 1985. Signed by Yankees as free agent, 5/14/85.

Attended Eastern Michigan University, Ypsilanti, MI.

POSITIONS PLAYED: 1984 (1B-45); 1985 (1B-60).

YR	CLUB	AVG	G	AB	R	H	2B	3B	HR	RBI	BB	SO	SB
84	Anderson	.219	52	128	21	28	6	2	3	21	34	30	1
85	Oneonta	.275	63	211	34	58	13	5	5	43	23	37	5

SHANE, Jon Earl

HEIGHT: 6-0   **BATS:** R   **BORN:** June 19, 1964, Milwaukee, WI
WEIGHT: 180   **THROWS:** R   **RESIDES:** Hortonville, WI

SIGNED BY: Joe Begani
HOW OBTAINED: Yankees' 17th round pick in regular phase of June 1985 free agent draft.

Attended University of Wisconsin-Stevens Point.

YR	CLUB	W-L	ERA	G	GS	CG	Sho	SV	IP	H	R	ER	BB	SO
85	Sarasota	0-1	5.40	11	0	0	0	1	16.2	19	15	10	16	9

SHAW, Scott Keith

HEIGHT: 6-0   **BATS:** R   **BORN:** Dec. 24, 1963, Phillipsburg, NJ
WEIGHT: 185   **THROWS:** R   **RESIDES:** High Bridge, NJ

SIGNED BY: Brian Sabean
HOW OBTAINED: Yankees' 11th round pick in regular phase of June 1985 free agent draft.

Attended Eckerd College, St. Petersburg, FL. Tied for NY-Penn League lead in triples (6), 1985. Named to 1985 New York-Penn League All-Star team (3B).

POSITIONS PLAYED: 3B-43

YR	CLUB	AVG	G	AB	R	H	2B	3B	HR	RBI	BB	SO	SB
85	Oneonta	.293	72	276	40	81	8	6	4	37	23	54	5

SILVA, Mark Ronald (Mark)

HEIGHT: 6-3   **BATS:** R   **BORN:** Sept. 17, 1958, Santa Maria, CA
WEIGHT: 195   **THROWS:** R   **RESIDES:** Santa Maria, CA

SIGNED BY: Don Lindeberg
HOW OBTAINED: Yankees' 25th pick in 1981 June draft.

Graduated from St. Joseph H.S. in 1977, where he was twice named All-League in baseball and football. Attended California Poly State University in San Luis Obispo, Cal. 1982, tied for South Atlantic League lead in wins (14).

YR	CLUB	W-L	ERA	G	GS	CG	Sho	SV	IP	H	R	ER	BB	SO
81	Paintsville	6-4	3.00	13	11	4	3	0	81	59	37	27	38	77
	Ft. Lauderdale	1-0	0.00	1	0	0	0	0	0	0	0	0	0	0
82	Greensboro	14-7	2.92	30	27	12	0	0	184.2	161	87	60	82	140
83	Nashville	5-1	3.11	37	3	2	1	6	81.0	74	41	28	37	53
	Ft. Lauderdale	0-1	2.63	8	1	0	0	3	13.2	14	6	4	7	12

SILVA (continued)

		W-L	ERA	G	GS	CG	Sho	SV	IP	H	R	ER	BB	SO
84	Columbus	3-3	2.67	42	0	0	0	14	67.1	51	22	20	42	59
	Nashville	2-1	6.38	10	0	0	0	1	18.1	20	14	13	13	7
85	Columbus	6-5	3.90	43	0	0	0	9	60.0	48	31	26	48	31

SISLER, Richard Allan, Jr. (Ric)

HEIGHT: 6-4   **BATS:** L   **BORN:** May 12, 1963, Nashville, TN
WEIGHT: 215   **THROWS:** R   **RESIDES:** Nashville, TN

SIGNED BY: Sammy Ellis
HOW OBTAINED: Yankees' 32nd round pick in regular phase of June 1985 free agent draft.

Attended University of Tennessee-Martin. Tied for Gulf Coast League lead in wins (7), and home runs allowed (4), 1985.

YR	CLUB	W-L	ERA	G	GS	CG	Sho	SV	IP	H	R	ER	BB	SO
85	Sarasota	7-2	3.63	13	9	1	0	0	62.0	67	37	25	19	41

SMITH, Patrick Keith (Keith)

HEIGHT: 6-1   **BATS:** S   **BORN:** Oct. 20, 1961, Los Angeles, CA
WEIGHT: 185   **THROWS:** R   **RESIDES:** Canyon Country, CA

SIGNED BY: Don Lindeberg
HOW OBTAINED: Yankees' 15th round pick in regular phase of June 1979 free agent draft.

Led 1980 NY-Penn League shortstops in fielding pct. (.932) and led NY-Penn League in sacrifice hits (9) the same year. Named to Southern League All-Star team (SS), 1984. Led Southern League in sacrifice hits (17), 1984. Led Southern League shortstops in games (138), assists (440), errors (46) and double plays (97), 1984.

POSITIONS PLAYED: 1979 (SS-56); 1980 Greensboro (SS-20), Oneonta (SS-64); 1981 Oneonta (SS-19), Greenboro (SS-28); 1982 Ft. Lauderdale (SS-56, 2B-33, 3B-9, 1B-2, OF-1), Nashville (SS-4); 1983 (SS-137, 2B-4); 1984 New York (SS-2), Nashville (SS-138); 1985 New York (SS-3), Columbus (SS-114, 2B-3, 3B-1).

YR	CLUB	AVG	G	AB	R	H	2B	3B	HR	RBI	BB	SO	SB
79	Oneonta	.244	56	119	19	29	0	0	0	9	33	30	9
80	Greensboro	.190	21	63	10	12	3	0	0	1	5	17	4
	Oneonta	.244	65	193	32	47	2	0	0	11	25	46	10
81	Oneonta	.200	19	50	8	10	1	0	0	3	14	11	4
	Greensboro	.200	33	60	14	12	0	0	0	4	12	14	7
82	Ft. Lauderdale	.219	94	178	26	39	8	0	0	11	31	31	6
	Nashville	.000	4	12	0	0	0	0	0	0	2	6	0
83	Nashville	.258	141	426	78	110	8	4	8	38	92	103	22
84	Nashville	.273	138	460	80	128	15	1	3	42	105	85	21
	YANKEES	.000	2	4	0	0	0	0	0	0	0	2	0
85	Columbus	.241	123	307	40	74	9	1	4	21	39	66	10
	YANKEES	.000	4	0	1	0	0	0	0	0	0	0	0
Minor Lg. Totals		.247	694	1868	307	461	46	6	15	140	358	409	93
M.L. Totals		.000	6	4	1	0	0	0	0	0	0	2	0

SMITH, Philander Earl (Phil)

HEIGHT: 5-9   **BATS:** R   **BORN:** Oct. 27, 1959, Birmingham, AL
WEIGHT: 165   **THROWS:** R   **RESIDES:** Tehachapi, CA

SIGNED BY: Reggie Waller (Astros)
HOW OBTAINED: Houston Astros 13th round pick in regular phase of June 1981 free agent draft. Released, 3/31/83. Signed as free agent by San Jose Bees (Independent), 3/31/85. Yankees purchased contract from San Jose Bees, 8/21/85.

Attended Lewis-Clark State College.

POSITIONS PLAYED: 1981 Daytona Beach (2B-11), Sarasota (2B-30); 1982 (2B-110, OF-4); 1985 Albany (2B-6, OF-1), San Jose (2B-113, SS-9).

YR	CLUB	AVG	G	AB	R	H	2B	3B	HR	RBI	BB	SO	SB
81	Daytona Beach	.368	17	68	14	25	4	1	1	9	4	5	7
	Sarasota Astros	.396	38	144	18	57	3	3	0	9	9	10	22
82	Daytona Beach	.251	122	387	59	97	5	4	0	29	41	35	20
83						(Did not play)							
84						(Did not play)							
85	Albany	.211	10	38	5	8	1	0	0	3	2	1	1
	San Jose	.318	121	444	76	141	12	2	2	44	60	48	30

STANKO, Edward John (Ed)

HEIGHT: 5-11   **BATS:** L   **BORN:** July 21, 1965, Brooklyn, NY
WEIGHT: 175   **THROWS:** L   **RESIDES:** Brooklyn, NY

SIGNED BY: Ray Goodman
HOW OBTAINED: Yankees 13th round pick in regular phase of June 1985 free agent draft.

Attended William & Mary College, Williamsburg, VA.

POSITIONS PLAYED: OF-5, 1B-3.

YR	CLUB	AVG	G	AB	R	H	2B	3B	HR	RBI	BB	SO	SB
85	Oneonta	.162	27	37	11	6	1	0	0	3	13	14	0

STEGMAN, David William (Dave)

HEIGHT: 5-11 **BATS:** R **BORN:** Jan. 30, 1954, Inglewood, CA
WEIGHT: 185 **THROWS:** R **RESIDES:** Lompoc, CA

SIGNED BY: Tigers
HOW OBTAINED: Detroit Tigers 1st pick in secondary phase of June 1976 free agent draft. Previously drafted by Twins ('72), Red Sox ('75), Braves (Jan. '76), but did not sign. Traded to San Diego Padres for pitcher Dennis Kinney, 12/12/80. Traded by San Diego to New York Yankees, 4/30/81, completing deal in which New York traded pitcher Byron Ballard for a player to be named later, 4/6/81. Granted free agency, 10/22/82; signed by Chicago White Sox, 1/26/83. Granted free agency, 10/15/84; signed by Toronto, 2/6/85. Granted free agency, 10/15/85; signed by Yankees as 6-yr. minor league free agent, 1/14/86.

Tied for American Association lead in games (135), led outfielders in fielding pct. (.990), 1978. Led American Association outfielders in putouts (322), 1979. Led American Association in base on balls (100), and was named to A.A. All-Star team, 1983.

Earned a B.S. in Engineering & Math from the University of Arizona.

POSITIONS PLAYED: 1976 (OF-61); 1977 Montgomery (OF-67), Evansville (OF-45); 1978 Evansville (OF-134, C-1), Detroit (OF-8); 1979 Evansville (OF-133), Detroit (OF-12); 1980 Evansville (OF-15), Detroit (OF-57); 1981 (OF-82); 1982 Columbus (OF-109, 3B-6), New York (PR-2); 1983 Denver (OF-111), Chicago (OF-29); 1984 Chicago (OF-46), Denver (OF-30); 1985 (OF-81).

YR	CLUB	AVG	G	AB	R	H	2B	3B	HR	RBI	BB	SO	SB
76	Montgomery	.266	61	188	31	50	8	0	0	20	33	24	15
77	Montgomery	.345	67	226	55	78	19	5	11	59	62	33	16
	Evansville	.222	50	153	25	34	12	0	6	18	26	46	4
78	Evansville	.264	135	462	95	122	30	1	14	67	87	85	17
	DETROIT	.286	8	14	3	4	2	0	1	3	1	2	0
79	Evansville	.302	133	506	95	153	33	2	11	60	81	83	17
	DETROIT	.194	12	31	6	6	0	0	3	5	2	3	1
80	Evansville	.203	18	59	11	12	2	1	1	6	11	13	2
	DETROIT	.177	65	130	12	23	5	0	2	9	14	23	1
81	Columbus	.291	90	227	42	66	15	1	6	24	35	38	3
82	Columbus	.272	115	383	71	104	18	2	10	53	66	41	11
	NEW YORK	.000	2	0	0	0	0	0	0	0	0	0	0
83	Denver	.334	111	395	94	132	30	6	7	54	100	55	4
	CHICAGO	.170	29	53	5	9	2	0	0	4	10	9	0
84	CHICAGO	.261	55	92	13	24	1	2	2	11	4	18	3
	Denver	.286	34	105	17	30	10	1	2	9	30	24	7
85	Syracuse	.319	89	257	36	82	15	4	10	45	40	35	1

TIRADO, Aristarco (Aris)

HEIGHT: 5-8 **BATS:** R **BORN:** March 31, 1963, Manati, Puerto Rico
WEIGHT: 160 **THROWS:** R **RESIDES:** Vega Baja, Puerto Rico

SIGNED BY: Joe McIlvaine
HOW OBTAINED: Signed as a free agent by New York Mets for 1981 season. Released, 9/82. Signed as a free agent by Yankees, 3/9/85.

YR	CLUB	W-L	ERA	G	GS	CG	Sho	SV	IP	H	R	ER	BB	SO
84	Kingsport	1-8	5.70	13	13	1	0	0	71.0	76	61	45	48	41
82	Kingsport	0-5	7.52	13	2	0	0	0	32.1	51	39	27	13	28
83						(Did not play)								
84						(Did not play)								
85	Oneonta	2-3	1.99	22	1	0	0	3	45.1	20	15	10	15	68

TORRES (Rodriquez), Herick Ricardo (Ricky)

HEIGHT: 6-2 **BATS:** R **BORN:** Dec. 31, 1963, Cidra, PR
WEIGHT: 195 **THROWS:** R **RESIDES:** Cidra, PR

SIGNED BY: Fred Ferrira
HOW OBTAINED: Signed as a free agent, Feb. 23, 1984

YR	CLUB	W-L	ERA	G	GS	CG	Sho	SV	IP	H	R	ER	BB	SO
84	Greensboro	8-4	3.69	20	19	3	0	0	117.0	97	59	48	49	110
85	Albany	0-1	9.00	1	1	0	0	0	4.0	5	5	4	2	4
	Ft. Lauderdale	6-6	4.68	17	17	1	1	0	92.1	103	56	48	36	107
	Oneonta	1-2	4.50	3	3	0	0	0	16.0	17	10	8	10	13

TRUDEAU, Kevin Thomas

HEIGHT: 6-2 **BATS:** R **BORN:** Oct. 12, 1963
WEIGHT: 180 **THROWS:** R **RESIDES:** Livermore, CA

SIGNED BY: Dick Wilson
HOW OBTAINED: Selected by Yankees in the 6th round of the Jan., 1984 free agent draft.

TRUDEAU (continued)

YR	CLUB	W-L	ERA	G	GS	CG	Sho	SV	IP	H	R	ER	BB	SO
84	Sarasota	2-1	1.96	10	8	0	0	0	46.0	37	13	10	15	35
85	Oneonta	8-3	1.64	16	8	3	2	1	71.1	42	22	13	24	75

TURNER, Shane Lee

HEIGHT: 5-10 **BATS:** L **BORN:** January 8, 1963, Los Angeles, CA
WEIGHT: 180 **THROWS:** R **RESIDES:** Pomona, CA
SIGNED BY: Don Lindeberg ·
HOW OBTAINED: Yankees 6th round pick in regular phase of June 1985 free agent draft. Led New York-Penn League shorts tops in fielding pct. (.948), 1985.

Attended Cal. State-Fullerton.

POSITIONS PLAYED: SS-61, 2B-1.

YR	CLUB	AVG	G	AB	R	H	2B	3B	HR	RBI	BB	SO	SB
85	Oneonta	.246	64	228	35	56	7	3	0	26	35	44	12

VARGAS, Hector

HEIGHT: 5-11 **BATS:** R **BORN:** June 3, 1966, Arecibo, Puerto Rico
WEIGHT: 155 **THROWS:** R **RESIDES:** Arecibo, Puerto Rico
SIGNED BY: Fred Ferreira
HOW OBTAINED: Signed as a free agent by Yankees, 9/4/85.

POSITIONS PLAYED: SS, 3B.

YR	CLUB	AVG	G	AB	R	H	2B	3B	HR	RBI	BB	SO	SB
	1986 will be first professional season.												

VILTZ, Corey Alan

HEIGHT: 6-1 **BATS:** R **BORN:** March 15, 1966, The Dalles, OR
WEIGHT: 190 **THROWS:** L **RESIDES:** The Dalles, OR
SIGNED BY: Whitey Dehart
HOW OBTAINED: Selected by Yankees in the 5th round of the June, 1984 free agent draft.

POSITIONS PLAYED: 1984 (OF-48)

YR	CLUB	AVG	G	AB	R	H	2B	3B	HR	RBI	BB	SO	SB
84	Sarasota	.168	48	149	14	25	3	0	0	12	35	53	4
85	Oneonta	.246	61	224	39	55	11	1	0	25	38	65	23

WILLIAMS, Bernabe (Bernie)

HEIGHT: 6-2 **BATS:** R **BORN:** September 13, 1968, San Juan, Puerto Rico
WEIGHT: 180 **THROWS:** R **RESIDES:** Vega Atta, Puerto Rico
SIGNED BY: Fred Ferreira
HOW OBTAINED: Signed as a free agent by Yankees, 9/13/85.

POSITIONS PLAYED: OF

YR	CLUB	AVG	G	AB	R	H	2B	3B	HR	RBI	BB	SO	SB
	1986 will be first professional season.												

WINKLER, Bradley M. (Brad)

HEIGHT: 5-11 **BATS:** L **BORN:** June 22, 1960, Richmond, KY
WEIGHT: 185 **THROWS:** R **RESIDES:** Jackson, MS
SIGNED BY: Cedric Tallis
HOW OBTAINED: Signed as a free agent on July 15, 1983.

Graduate of Mississippi State University in 1983 receiving his B.S. degree in Physical Education. Named to South Atlantic League All-Star team (DH), 1984.

POSITIONS PLAYED: 1983 (OF-40); 1984 Greensboro (OF-61), Ft. Lauderdale (OF-49); 1985 Albany (OF-65), Ft. Lauderdale (OF-7).

YR	CLUB	AVG	G	AB	R	H	2B	3B	HR	RBI	BB	SO	SB
83	Oneonta	.252	47	155	17	39	9	2	2	16	21	40	2
84	Ft. Lauderdale	.297	52	165	32	49	11	1	6	18	20	35	3
	Greensboro	.298	71	262	50	78	13	6	13	59	38	79	6
85	Albany	.197	73	249	27	49	7	2	9	41	26	81	7
	Ft. Lauderdale	.264	40	121	20	32	7	1	4	23	18	35	3

YAEGER, Charles Joseph

HEIGHT: 6-0 **BATS:** L **BORN:**
WEIGHT: 210 **THROWS:** L **RESIDES:** Camarillo, CA
SIGNED BY: Yankees organization
HOW OBTAINED: Signed as a free agent.

YR	CLUB	W-L	ERA	G	GS	CG	Sho	SV	IP	H	R	ER	BB	SO
84	Sarasota	5-1	0.58	17	0	0	0	7	46.1	34	5	3	6	34
85	Ft. Lauderdale	1-1	1.60	20	0	0	0	3	33.2	22	6	6	14	32
	Oneonta	0-0	0.00	1	0	0	0	0	1.0	0	0	0	0	2

IN MEMORIAM

MARIS, ROGER EUGENE (OF) #9

6-0, 205. Born on 9/10/34 in Fargo, N.D. Died 12/4/85, age 51. Resided in Gainesville, FL. BL. TR. Married: Patricia Ann Carvell, 10/13/56. Children: Susan (28), Roger Jr. (27), Kevin (25), Randy (24), Richard (22) and Sandra (20).

CAREER: One of the most feared power hitters in baseball in the early 1960's ... a complete ballplayer who was a tremendous defensive rightfielder, possessing a cannon arm ... above average speed enabled him to be a daring base runner who often made heads-up plays on the base paths ... career was frequently interrupted by a succession of injuries ... reached big leagues with Cleveland after four seasons in minors ... broke into majors with a nine-game hitting streak ... first major league home run was an eleventh inning grand slam (4/18/57) ... suffered first of many career injuries in a base path collision he fractured two ribs hindering rookie season ... traded to Kansas City in mid-season 1958 ... posted career highs in games and at-bats in '58 ... in 1959 was leading the American League in hitting before an appendix operation weakened him ... appeared in first of seven All-Star games in '59 ... key man in Yankees-Athletics big 7-player trade in winter of '59 ... once again off to fast start in 1960, had 27 HR's, 69 RBI and .320 avg at midway point of season ... excelled against Boston in '60 hitting .361 ... drove in 100 runs first of three consecutive seasons ... 1961 the season that made Roger the new single-season HR king ... hit 61 HR's but struck out only 67 times for a fine HR-SO ratio ... hit 30 HR's at Yankee Stadium, tying stadium record ... in June hit 15 HR's the most ever hit in that month in ML history ... hit 13 HR's against the White Sox, the most ever hit against one club since ML expanded in 1961 ... hit his 50th HR on Aug. 22, becoming first player ever to hit 50th HR in August ... 61st HR also gave Maris RBI title 142 to 141 over Oriole Jim Gentile ... In 1962 topped Yankees in HR's for second straight season ... posted career high (34) doubles in '62 ... In 1963 a series of injuries limited Roger to only 90 games ... Rebounded for good season in 1964, especially tough on Red Sox again hitting .410 with 5 HR's and 15 RBI ... 1964 fielding average (.996) is highest ever recorded by a Yankee rightfielder ... injuries hit Roger hard in 1965 ... first, a hamstring muscle, and then a fractured hand in May idled him for most of the campaign ... traded in December of 1966 to St. Louis Cardinals ... closed out career with two solid seasons for the Cardinals ... his veteran leadership led Cardinals to World Series appearances in '67 and '68 ... was one of the stars of St. Louis' World Series victory in '67.

PERSONAL/MISCELLANEOUS: A High School standout in football and baseball ... easily distinguishable by his crew cut hairstyle ... served as 1962 Multiple Sclerosis Society volunteer national co-chairman ... appeared with Mickey Mantle in Columbia Pictures' motion picture "Safe at Home" ... also authored (with writer Jim Ogle) "Roger Maris at Bat," the story of his 61 home run season ... ran a Budweiser beer distributorship in Gainesville, Florida since his retirement ... enjoyed Golf and Hunting in his spare time.

CAREER PLAYING RECORD

Established major league records for most home runs, season (61) (162-game season), 1961; combined with Mickey Mantle to break Babe Ruth and Lou Gehrig's 1927 home run total of 115 in 1961. (112 in 154 decisions); longest doubleheader with no chances offered (24 innings), August 6, 1961.

Tied major league mark for most home runs, six consecutive games (7), August 11-12-13-13-15-16, 1961

Established American League mark for most intentional bases on ball in game (4), 12-inning game, May 22, 1962.

Tied American League standard for most home runs, doubleheader (4), July 25, 1961-hitting two in each game.

Led American League in slugging percentage with .581 in 1960; led in total bases with 366 in 1961.

Named Most Valuable Player in American League, 1960-61.

Named Player of the Year by THE SPORTING NEWS, 1961.

Named "Sportsman of the Year" by SPORTS ILLUSTRATED, 1961.

Named "Man of the Year" by SPORT MAGAZINE, 1961.

Named as Outfielder on THE SPORTING NEWS' All-Star Major League Team, 60-61.

Received American League Gold Glove for outfield play, 1960.

Winner of Hickok Belt as Top Professional Athlete of Year, 1961.

A.P. Professional Athlete of Year, 1961.

"Sultan of Swat" Award winner in 60-61.

Ranks 6th on the all-time Yankee slugging list (.515); 7th on the Yanks all-time HR list (203); and 6th on all-time World Series runs scored list (26).

MARIS (continued)

YR	Club	AVG	G	AB	R	H	2B	3B	HR	RBI	BB	SO	SB
1953	Fargo-M'rhead	.325	114	418	74	136	18	13	9	80	76	62	14
1954	Keokuk	.315	134	502	105	158	26	6	32	111	80	53	25
1955	Tulsa	.233	25	90	9	21	1	0	1	9	15	18	2
	Reading	.289	113	374	74	108	15	3	19	78	77	60	24
1956	Indianapolis	.293	131	433	77	127	20	8	17	75	41	55	7
1957	CLEVELAND	.235	116	358	61	84	9	5	14	51	60	79	8
1958	CLEVELAND-a	.225	51	182	26	41	5	1	9	27	17	33	4
	KANSAS CITY	.247	99	401	61	99	14	3	19	53	28	52	0
	1958 Totals	.240	150	583	87	140	19	4	28	80	45	85	4
1959	KANSAS CITY-b	.273	122	433	69	118	21	7	16	72	58	53	2
1960	YANKEES	.283	136	499	98	141	18	7	39	112*	70	65	2
1961	YANKEES	.269	161	590	132	159	16	4	61*	142*	94	67	0
1962	YANKEES	.256	157	590	92	151	34	1	33	100	87	78	1
1963	YANKEES	.269	90	312	53	84	14	1	23	53	35	40	1
1964	YANKEES	.281	141	513	86	144	12	2	26	71	62	78	3
1965	YANKEES	.239	46	155	22	37	7	0	8	27	29	29	0
1966	YANKEES-c	.233	119	348	37	81	9	2	13	43	36	60	0
1967	ST. LOUIS	.261	125	410	64	107	18	7	9	55	52	61	0
1968	ST. LOUIS	.255	100	310	25	79	18	2	5	45	24	38	0
N.Y.Y. Totals		**.265**	**850**	**3007**	**520**	**797**	**110**	**17**	**203**	**548**	**413**	**417**	**7**
A.L. Totals		**.260**	**1238**	**4381**	**737**	**1139**	**159**	**33**	**261**	**751**	**576**	**634**	**21**
N.L. Totals		**.258**	**225**	**720**	**89**	**186**	**36**	**9**	**14**	**100**	**76**	**99**	**0**
M.L. Totals		**.260**	**1463**	**5101**	**826**	**1325**	**195**	**42**	**275**	**851**	**652**	**733**	**21**

a-Traded to Kansas City Athletics with Pitcher Dick Tomanek and Infielder Preston Ward for Infielder Vic Power and Infielder-Outfielder Woodie Held, June 15, 1958.

b-Traded to New York Yankees with First Baseman Kent Hadley and Shortstop Joe DeMaestri for Pitcher Don Larsen, First Baseman Marv Throneberry and Outfielders Hank Bauer and Norm Siebern, December 11, 1959.

c-Traded to St. Louis Cardinals for Third Baseman Charlie Smith, December 8, 1966.

WORLD SERIES RECORD

Tied World Series records for most consecutive series played (5), 1960-1964 and most putouts, inning, center fielder (3), October 11, 1964, third inning. Homered in first World Series at-bat, October 5, 1960.

YR	Club, Opp.	AVG	G	AB	R	H	2B	3B	HR	RBI	BB	SO	SB
1960	N.Y. vs Pit.	.267	7	30	6	6	1	0	2	2	3	4	0
1961	N.Y. vs Cin.	.105	5	19	4	2	1	0	1	2	4	6	0
1962	N.Y. vs S.F.	.174	7	23	4	4	1	0	1	5	5	2	0
1963	N.Y. vs L.A.	.000	2	5	0	0	0	0	0	0	0	1	0
1964	N.Y. vs StL.	.200	7	30	4	6	0	0	1	1	1	4	0
1967	StL. vs Bos.	.385	7	26	3	10	1	0	1	7	1	3	0
1968	StL. vs Det.	.158	6	19	5	3	1	0	0	1	3	3	0
W.S. Totals		**.217**	**41**	**152**	**26**	**33**	**5**	**0**	**6**	**18**	**18**	**21**	**0**

ALL-STAR GAME RECORD

YR	Club, Site	AVG	G	AB	R	H	2B	3B	HR	RBI	BB	SO	SB
1959	A.L., L.A.-N	.000	1	2	0	0	0	0	0	0	0	1	0
1960	A.L., K.C., N.Y.-A	.000	2	6	0	0	0	0	0	0	0	1	0
1961	A.L., S.F., Bos.	.200	2	5	0	1	0	0	0	0	1	2	0
1962	A.L., Was., Chi.-N	.167	2	6	2	1	1	0	0	2	1	1	0
A.S. Totals		**.105**	**7**	**19**	**2**	**2**	**1**	**0**	**0**	**2**	**2**	**5**	**0**

*Led league

PETE SHEEHY

Like pennants and great ballplayers, Yankee equipment manager Michael Joseph "Pete" Sheehy had been part of the Yankee scene since, as a boy of sixteen, he appeared outside the Yankee players' gate one day in 1927.

He was asked inside to lend a hand in the Yankee clubhouse. He was asked back the next day after that. Before long Pete spent every working day for the next 59 years in the Yankee clubhouse. From that unexpected start not only did the man and the job find each other, but yet another Yankee legend was born.

Before Pete's death last August 13, he witnessed an amazing parade of ballplayers and events: Babe Ruth's 60 home runs, the decline of Lou Gehrig, Joe DiMaggio's 56-game streak, Mickey Mantle's injuries, Don Larsen's perfect game, Roger Maris' 61 home runs, the 'greatest comeback ever' in 1978 and everything in between.

In 1976, the Yankee Stadium clubhouse was officially designated The Pete Sheehy Clubhouse, a singularly appropriate honor for a man who was a unique link with the Yankee past. A quiet, classy guy who was a complete pro at his job, Pete earned the affection and respect of generations of ballplayers. In his own way he represented a special kind of Yankee excellence.

The Yankees will wear black armbands on their uniforms in 1986 in honor of Roger Maris and Pete Sheehy.
